Global Environmental Change and Human Security

Global Environmental Change and Human Security

Edited by Richard A. Matthew, Jon Barnett, Bryan McDonald, and Karen L. O'Brien

The MIT Press
Cambridge, Massachusetts
London, England

© 2010 Massachusetts Institute of Technology

For information about special quantity discounts, please email special_sales@mitpress.mit.edu

This book was set in Sabon on 3B2 by Asco Typesetters, Hong Kong.
Printed and bound in the United States of America.

Library of Congress Cataloging-in-Publication Data

Global environmental change and human security / edited by Richard A. Matthew ... [et al.].
   p. cm.
Includes bibliographical references and index.
ISBN 978-0-262-01340-6 (hardcover : alk. paper)—ISBN 978-0-262-51308-1 (pbk. : alk. paper)
1. Global environmental change—Social aspects. 2. Human beings—Effect of environment on. 3. Security, International—Environmental aspects. I. Matthew, Richard Anthony.
GE149.G553   2010
304.2'5—dc22   2009011078

10 9 8 7 6 5 4 3 2 1

To future generations who will face the challenges of global environmental change and its implications for human security

Contents

Foreword   ix
Geoffrey D. Dabelko
Acknowledgments   xi

I   Introduction   1

1   Global Environmental Change and Human Security: An
     Introduction   3
     Jon Barnett, Richard A. Matthew, and Karen L. O'Brien

II   Global Environmental Change and Human Insecurity   33

2   Human Security, Vulnerability, and Global Environmental
     Change   35
     Mike Brklacich, May Chazan, and Hans-Georg Bohle

3   Global Health and Human Security: Addressing Impacts from
     Globalization and Environmental Change   53
     Bryan McDonald

4   The Vulnerability of Urban Slum Dwellers to Global Environmental
     Change   77
     Laura Little and Chris Cocklin

5   Environmental Change, Disasters, and Vulnerability: The Case of
     Hurricane Katrina and New Orleans   97
     Victoria Basolo

III Global Environmental Change, Conflict, and Cooperation   117

6   Environmental Change, Human Security, and Violent
     Conflict   119
     Jon Barnett and W. Neil Adger

7 Environmental Change and Human Security in Nepal   137
   Richard A. Matthew and Bishnu Raj Upreti

IV Human Security and Sustainable Development   155

8 Global Environmental Change, Equity, and Human Security   157
   Karen L. O'Brien and Robin M. Leichenko

9 Approaches to Enhancing Human Security   177
   Marvin S. Soroos

10 Rethinking the Role of Population in Human Security   193
   Betsy Hartmann

11 Women, Global Environmental Change, and Human
    Security   215
    Heather Goldsworthy

12 Human Security as a Prerequisite for Development   237
    Kwasi Nsiah-Gyabaah

13 Free to Squander? Democracy and Sustainable Development,
    1975–2000   261
    Indra de Soysa, Jennifer Bailey, and Eric Neumayer

14 Environmental Transborder Cooperation in Latin America:
    Challenges to the Westphalia Order   291
    Alexander López

V Conclusion   305

15 Charting the Next Generation of Global Environmental
    Change and Human Security Research   307
    Jon Barnett, Richard A. Matthew, and Karen L. O'Brien

List of Contributors   317
Index   323

Foreword

Geoffrey D. Dabelko

Say "global environmental change" and the first images typically conjured up are melting ice caps and pin-striped UN negotiators struggling to agree on carbon emissions targets and timetables. Many fine books have been (and will be) written about tackling these problems at the global level. The Earth and those of us living on it need such contributions to deepen our understanding and jumpstart real action to address these challenges.

But add "human security" to global environmental change and you evoke very different images—and a very different kind of book, as evidenced by this excellent offering from editors Richard A. Matthew, Jon Barnett, Bryan McDonald, and Karen L. O'Brien. Human security evokes the faces of the world's poor, in rural and urban areas, struggling to earn a living. The name itself places the individual and human well-being at center stage, revealing the insufficiency of a state-based approach to security. The connections among the individual, the state, and the globe must be tackled together as environmental change not only impacts people's lives and options but also puts pressure on emerging political systems in many fragile states and conflict-prone parts of the world. The links between natural resources and poverty lead to us to examine larger questions of human vulnerability, the dynamics of conflict and cooperation, and, ultimately, equity and justice.

Human insecurity, conflict and cooperation, and sustainable development form the backbone of this volume, distinguishing it from most of the environmental security literature of the 1990s, which focused on narrower questions of natural resources and high thresholds of conflict. This book's more inclusive approach makes the ideas of environmental security more relevant to the daily lives of the world's poorest and most vulnerable people. For example, the problem of "vulnerability"—a much-used but often misunderstood term—is made tangible through the case studies in this volume.

The grounded quality of the research in this book does double duty: it advances intellectual inquiry and expands academic debates on these topics, while at the same time offering practical insights to policymakers and practitioners facing inboxes overflowing with problems directly related to global environmental change and human security. Unlike many scholarly works, this books' chapters are both academically rigorous and policy relevant, as the contributors include many who are actively involved in advising governments, international organizations, non-governmental organizations (NGOs), and civil society.

Global Environmental Change and Human Security is a must-read for members of the environment, development, and security communities. No one reader will find all of its arguments utterly persuasive; I certainly did not. The topics remain highly contested and the research points to productive new avenues for investigation. But this diversity of perspective broadens our inquiries, challenges our assumptions, and pushes scholars and practitioners alike to tackle the pressing problems created by global environmental change and human insecurity.

Acknowledgments

As the Global Environmental Change and Human Security (GECHS) program, founded in 1996, matured as a global research network, it became clear that it was developing a distinctive voice in the field of environmental security. From the outset, the focus on human security attracted researchers interested in issues of vulnerability, poverty and justice, and concerned that simple linkages being forged between environmental change and national security might inspire and justify policy behavior that could deepen global inequality and division, securitize the environment, and lose sight of the victims of unsustainable behaviors and practices of displacement and projection. This volume brings together a number of the scholars associated with the GECHS program and representative of its output.

The editors would like to acknowledge Stephen Lonergan, Mike Brklacich, and Dina Giannikopoulos for important contributions made in the early stages of this project. We would also like to thank the external reviewers for their detailed comments on the first draft of this volume and Clay Morgan at the MIT Press for his invaluable advice and great patience and understanding. The editors are also grateful for considerable editorial support, and in particular the services of Pamela Donohoo, provided through the University of California Irvine's Center for Unconventional Security Affairs. We would also like to thank the International Institute for Sustainable Development for its support during the preparation of this volume.

I

Introduction

Global Environmental Change and Human Security: An Introduction

Jon Barnett, Richard A. Matthew, and Karen L. O'Brien

Introduction

Throughout most of human history, the constraints imposed by local environmental conditions and their natural variability were powerful determinants of the security of individuals and societies: animals, droughts, floods, frosts, pathogens, storms, and other environmental perturbations were significant causes of mortality, morbidity, and social disruption. In today's modern societies, technology, trade, industrialization, the use of fossil fuels, occupational specialization, and higher levels of social organization have all weakened the constraints that local environments place on human security. Since the Industrial Revolution and the consolidation of the modern trading nation-state, there have been thousandfold increases in the production of goods and the use of energy, and hundredfold increases in international trade in goods and services. Over the same period, the global population has increased from one billion to over six billion people, and most people now live longer, consume more, and are better educated than in previous generations.

Yet the risks that environmental change poses to human security have not been eliminated. The scale of consumption and pollution in modern, high-energy societies has caused large decreases in primary forest cover; biodiversity losses; depletion of fish stocks; land degradation; water pollution and scarcity; coastal and marine degradation; the contamination of people, plants, and animals by chemicals and radioactive substances; and climate change and sea-level rise. These environmental changes are "global" because they are ubiquitous and because some pollutants such as greenhouse gases and radioactive wastes have global consequences (Turner et al. 1990). They are also "global" inasmuch as their origins lie in the consumption of resources in markets that are often very distant from the sites of resource extraction. For example, the wealthiest 20 percent of the world's population consumes 84 percent of all paper, consumes 45 percent of all meat and fish, and owns 87 percent of the world's vehicles (UNDP 1998); and the United States and the European Union countries emitted 52.4 percent of all CO2 between 1900–1999 (Baumert and Kete 2001). "Global" in this sense does not mean that responsibility for environmental change is shared equally among all people, or that the impacts of these changes are uniformly distributed among all places. Instead, *global* refers to the linkages between environmental changes and social consequences across distant places, groups, and time horizons (UNEP 1997).

Across the world, the prospects for human security are deeply affected by local and global processes of environmental change. The objective of this volume is to examine this complex relationship at different scales, across different issues, and in different places on the planet. Our general argument is that global environmental change poses new and in some cases unprecedented threats to human security. The complex links between processes of environmental change and their outcomes across both space and time add a new dimension to the concept of human security—a dimension that raises important questions about both equity and sustainability. As the chapters in this book demonstrate, global environmental change challenges human security in ways that transcend the North-South binary and the "rich-poor" dichotomy. Environmental change reveals the connections—as well as the frictions—between the security of individuals and communities and the security and sustainability of ecosystems and species, including humanity. The point that is underscored throughout this volume is that global environmental change is inherently a question about the capacity to respond to new challenges and to reconcile the growing disparities that undermine human security.

In this chapter we trace the evolution of recent thinking about the relationship between people, the environment, and security. We introduce the three key themes that are the concern of this book. First, we explain the transition from concerns about security to concerns about human security, which is a move that deepens and broadens both security studies and development studies. Human security intersects with the issue of environmental change to create new sets of issues concerning sustainable development (albeit issues that have been raised earlier to some extent by "Global Ecology" thinkers [Sachs 1993]). We then introduce the literature that links environmental change with human security and violent conflict. Finally, we explain the ways in which global environmental change poses risks to human security, and we discuss the implications of exploring global environmental change with a human security discourse. In this chapter we also present the Global Environmental Change and Human Security (GECHS) project's definition of human security, and we discuss how a human security orientation to environmental change can contribute to initiatives such as the Millennium Development Goals (MDGs).

Security and Human Security

The broad field that is known as environmental security studies emerges from the intersection of two powerful political concerns—for security and for the environment. As both are important policy arenas, so too are both important areas for scholarship. Both, however, are highly contested policy arenas, and both are ambiguous concepts. Thus, the intersection of environment and security gives rise to a number of interpretations of what environmental security means. In this section we discuss the competing meanings of security.

The concept of security in general refers to freedom from the risk of loss or damage to a thing that is important to survival and well-being. It can have both broad and narrow application, and it can apply to a limited set of objects to be secured, or to a deeper array of interconnected elements in a social system. In its shallowest and narrowest form, which is also its most influential and widespread interpretation, security refers to the security of the nation-state from attack from armed forces. It is largely in the name of this most narrow of interpretations of security that the governments of the world spent US$1.339 trillion on their military readiness in 2007—an amount equivalent to 2.5 percent of global GDP, or $202 for every person on the planet (Stålenheim, Perdomo, and Sköns 2008).

However, scholars from within the field of international relations, and, to a lesser extent, foreign policymakers, increasingly recognize that there are a wider range of risks to the sovereign integrity of the state than just that of military invasion. Richard Ullman (1983), for example, has defined a national security threat as anything that can quickly degrade the quality of life of the inhabitants of a state, or that narrows the choices available to people and organizations within the state (Westing 1976; Stewart and Fitzgerald 2000). On the basis of this logic, various other risks to national security—sometimes called "unconventional" security issues—have been identified, including the risk of reduced supply of energy resources (energy security), recessions triggered by intentional or inadvertent changes in global markets (economic security), and drug trafficking (which gives rise to the "war on drugs"). It is in this context of broadening the security agenda that environmental change came to be seen as a security issue (environmental security). Often, however, what is being secured through the identification of these nonmilitary risks is the institutions of the state, including the military and the state itself, who appropriate these concerns to justify their relevance (Campbell 1992; Klein 1997). Broadening security in this way, then, does not necessarily change the object to be secured, which under most interpretations remains the state.

Indeed, because security is a "speech act" that raises the profile of a problem to be of paramount importance to whoever constructs the discourse, broadening the range of security risks without explicitly identifying a referent object that is not the state most often operationalizes state monopolization of responses to meet the new security challenges. This is what is implied in the idea of "securitization": once a risk is labeled a security issue, its status changes from a problem that is able to be dealt with through mainstream institutions to one requiring extraordinary measures (Waever 1995, 55). When the state identifies something as a security issue, it often implies that the state has the option of addressing it in a manner commensurate with the way it would address a war—that is, with extraordinary allocations of resources, and with some lassitude with respect to the normal checks on state behavior. This was the move that the early environmentalists such as Lester Brown (1977) sought to effect by labeling environmental changes as risks to national security, and it is the move that environmentalists now seek to effect by labeling climate change a security issue, which may seemingly allow the state to bypass democratic barriers to action and massively reduce emissions (e.g., Dilley 2000; WGBU 2007). This is a very important aspect of the use of security: it justifies drastic and potentially unaccountable action, and in so doing it may lead to counterproductive outcomes.

The adverse outcomes of securitization are particularly relevant to our concern in this book with environmental change and human security. It has long been argued that early and uncritical interpretations of environmental security led to state monopolization of the issue and continued justification for the need for counterproductive institutions such as armed forces (Deudney 1990; Renner 1991; Dalby 1992; Barnett 2001; Floyd 2007). However, as we argue later, in identifying environmental change as a human security issue, the possibility of counterproductive outcomes arising from state monopolization is minimized.

In part because of the way in which securitization of an issue can lead to a concentration of power in the hands of the state, national security, regardless of the risks to it, does not necessarily translate into enhanced security for people. Indeed, in countries where democracy is absent or deficient, national security may mean very high levels of insecurity for people: if they are perceived to be risks to the state, they may be detained, forcibly removed, assaulted, or killed; if they are not important to the state by virtue of their inability to pay taxes or rents, or because their dissent can in no way challenge the state, they may simply be ignored, and so be deprived of entitlements that others in their country enjoy. Indeed, even in democratic countries the security of some individuals may be sacrificed for the imperative of maintaining national security, as civil libertarians have argued in response to counterterrorism measures such as the USA Patriot Act in the United States in the wake of the September 11 attacks in New York.

Recognition that national security does not necessarily equate to better lives for most people gave rise to the concept of human security, which, as it originated from within international relations, served to critique the effects of national security on human well-being (Booth 1991). The human security perspective also tied in with the growing recognition that the end of the cold war, advances in communication technologies, increasing economic interdependence, and environmental change, among other factors, meant that the meaning and practice of "security" was becoming increasingly elusive (Walker 1987). These changes gave rise to the question: Whose security? This question alone undermines the hegemonic discourse of security as "national security" by opening space to consider alternative meanings and referents of security, as well as alternative strategies for achieving security. Decentralizing security away from states in this way, and focusing on the myriad local, national, global, and "glocal" (Rosenau 1990) interactions that create security and insecurity, invites consideration of the way some people's security occurs at the expense of others (Booth 1991). It also invites consideration of the many processes that can undermine security, including poverty, energy shortages, trade imbalances, environmental changes, and changes in access to food. Security has thus become more pluralized in this way, moving away from states and an emphasis on military force and war, and toward people and the multitudinous risks they must manage. As such, human security has increasingly become a general concept of social science (Shaw 1993).

However, there remains within international relations a continuum of positions on human security. There is resistance from some within the mainstream security community, who consider ideas such as human security to be distractions from the imperative of national security (Walt 1991). There are those, such as MacFarlane and Foong Khong (2006), who argue that human security should be narrowly restricted to threats to a person's physical integrity, which is the dominant concern of the Canadian approach to human security (Axworthy 1997). Others, such as Thomas (2001), see it as being far broader, including the things necessary for meaningful participation in community life. At its broadest point, human security as framed from within international relations is a very different idea—one that is much deeper and broader than that of the mainstream concern for national security against the risk of armed invasion. At this broadest and deepest extent, human security from an international relations perspective becomes indistinguishable from the way it is used within development studies, where human security synthesizes concerns for basic needs, human development, and human rights (Gasper 2005).

This intellectual convergence is not surprising given that, at the same time that critical security studies was using the human referent to critique national security, a parallel development on human security was emerging within development theory and practice. In fact, the concept of human security came to prominence through the 1994 *Human Development Report*, which defined human security as a "concern with human life and dignity" (UNDP 1994, 22), and which adopted a comprehensive approach by identifying economic, food, health, environmental, personal, community, and political components to human security. The orientation is therefore firmly on human beings, and, in this early formulation, on basic needs ("human life") as well as psychosocial elements of being ("dignity"). Through the use of the word *security*, this and later formulations of human security also pointed to the need for the things that are important to human life and dignity to be maintained despite sudden and incremental changes in the social and environmental milieu that determine (and so may undermine) their provision.

There have been a wide range of definitions of human security since the 1994 *Human Development Report*. Notable among these is the international Commission on Human Security's definition of human security as "to protect the vital core of all human lives in ways that enhance human freedoms and human fulfilment," and which encompasses "human rights, good governance, access to education and health care . . . the freedom of future generations to inherit a healthy natural environment" (2003, 4). This definition continues the focus on human dignity ("fulfilment") and builds on Amartya Sen's (1999) groundbreaking work on the importance of freedoms to human development (Sen was a key figure in the commission). Sen argues that development is not so much something that can be done to others, but is instead something that people do *for themselves* given sufficient "economic opportunities, political liberties, social powers, and the enabling conditions of good health, basic education, and the encouragement and cultivation of initiatives" (1999, 4). These opportunities are, in Sen's words, "freedoms," and it is freedom, he argues, that should be both the means (how to attain) as well as the ends (the goal) of development. The idea of a "vital core" in the commission's definition recognizes that there are many different kinds of valued lives within a population, and seeks to avoid the problem of value homogenization that arises when prescribing a universal policy goal such as "increasing income."

A very important and distinctive contribution of human security is that it securitizes (makes a priority of) what individuals themselves see as their paramount concerns, and so pluralizes the meaning of security and opens up space for alternative security practices. It adds to the concept of human development, which is itself a refinement of the crude idea of "welfare" as used in public policy, by referring to stability in the provision of freedom and opportunities, by focusing on immediate concerns such as basic needs and peace, and by directing attention toward the most vulnerable (Gasper and Truong 2005).

So, the concept of human security, and the larger discourse that is associated with it, unites a number of disparate strands of thought that have become increasingly influential in the international policy community. Human security is a powerful "boundary object" in that it facilitates interfaces between diverse and often otherwise disconnected intellectual and policy communities (St. Clair 2004). As Gasper (2005) argues, human security has forged a confluence of various groups within the field of development studies and policy, who now also interface with some sections of the security research and policy communities. It therefore helps to bridge a number of the interests of the UN system (Paris 2001). Further, as environmental change is linked to human security, it also opens up new points of connection between policy communities concerned with foreign affairs, development, and sustainable development and environmental change. This is a very important and distinctive contribution of a human security perspective on environmental change: it brings together and offers the prospect of better understanding leading to more coordinated action among otherwise disparate policy communities. This book seeks to consolidate the interconnections and promote better understanding among these diverse research and policy concerns.

Environmental Change and Violent Conflict

The matrix of problems that require securing against, and referent objects to be secured, gives rise to a number of different meanings of environmental security. In this book we focus on the two most prominent of these: the ways in which environmental change may induce violent conflicts, and the ways in which environmental change undermines human security. There are other, more peripheral subfields of environmental security studies, including the risks human activity poses to ecosystems (sometimes called ecological security), the role of armed forces in environmental management, and the way environmental change poses nonmilitary threats to national security (see Barnett 2001). However, we focus on the conflict dimensions because our primary normative concern is for the security of individuals, and violent conflict is a powerful cause of human insecurity, which may be influenced in some way by environmental change. Further, the majority of the research on environmental security, and most of its policy manifestations, are concerned with the issue of environmentally induced conflicts. We focus on the human security dimension because this is, at least to the editors and most authors of this book, the primary reason for concern about environmental change—that is, because it puts at risk people's basic needs, human rights, and things that they value in order to lead dignified lives. This bottom-line reason for concern is not adequately recognized in research and policy concerning environmental change, security, and development. In this section we introduce the issue of environmental change and violent conflict. In the following section, we discuss environmental change as an issue of human security.

There is a long tradition of concern over the relationship among humans, the environment, and the potential for conflict. Over two hundred years ago, Thomas Malthus (1798) wrote *An Essay on the Principle of Population*, in which he argued "that the power of population is indefinitely greater than the power of the earth to produce subsistence for man." The imbalance between human needs and food availability, Malthus predicted, would lead to famine, disease, and war. Writing 150 years later, Fairfield Osborn (1948, 200–201) reiterated this concern: "When will it be openly recognized that one of the principal causes of the aggressive attitudes of individual nations and of much of the present discord among groups of nations is traceable to diminishing productive lands and to increasing population pressures?" As the scale of global change has increased since Malthus's time, the link between environment change and conflict has gained more attention.

Since the late 1960s, the idea that environmental change is a cause of violent conflict has become increasingly popular in academic and policy circles. However, the relationship between environmental change and conflict has been a major theme of security studies only since 1989 when at least ten articles on the subject were published. The year 1989 was significant in both international security and global environmental politics. It was the year the Berlin Wall fell, creating a "vertigo" in international security studies and policy in which conventional understandings of security were no longer so obviously politically relevant (Ó Tuathail 1996). It was also two years after the publication of the influential World Commission on Environment and Development's report *Our Common Future*, when planning for the landmark 1992 United Nations Conference on Environment and Development (UNCED) in Rio de Janeiro was well under way. This led to a flood of information about climate change, biodiversity loss, deforestation, and land degradation, with much of it channeled into preparatory studies and reports. These initiatives resulted in considerable political and societal attention to issues of environmental change in the early 1990s.

This confluence of moments in global security and environmental politics perhaps explains the sudden swell in writing about environmental security and in particular about environmental causes of violent conflicts (Dalby 1992; Deudney and Matthew 1999; Matthew 2002). The Malthusian perspective, enriched by the Canadian scholar Thomas

Homer-Dixon (1999) and others, became a significant part of this rethinking exercise and quickly attracted government and foundation interest. Flush with new resources, the subfield of environmental conflicts expanded rapidly.

Determining the relative contribution of environmental factors in generating violent conflicts is difficult. Clearly, the insecurities to which environmental stress contributes often have long social and political histories. In places such as Cambodia, Indonesia, Nepal, Pakistan, Liberia, and Rwanda, for example, conflict is grounded in patterns of insecurity based on longstanding political and economic practices of exclusion and exploitation, which reshaped the natural environment (see, e.g., Matthew and Upreti 2007). The new and more virulent forms of environmental degradation characteristic of the twentieth century have arguably aggravated practices of violence and insecurity that have long histories.

Throughout human history social factors have interacted with population growth and environmental change to generate conflict. The statistical work of Paul Collier and Anke Hoeffler (2000), that of Wenche Hauge and Tanja Ellingsen (1998), and the *State Failure Task Force Report: Phase II Findings* (State Failure Task Force 1999), suggests a typical scenario that is highly conflict prone: it includes an economy dependent on a lucrative natural resource (gold or oil rather than water or biodiversity) to which access can be controlled; a fractious ethnic cleavage that the dominant group has been unable to resolve; low education and high infant mortality rates; inadequate dispute resolution mechanisms and corrupt governance institutions; a history of violent conflict; and a diaspora community of angry emigrants and refugees forced to leave and willing to back one side in a civil war. The work of Thomas Homer-Dixon (1999; Homer-Dixon and Blitt 1998) makes a very similar argument but focuses instead on the adverse social effects of scarcity of resources linked in very immediate ways to satisfying basic needs, such as water, cropland, and pasture.

Violent conflict is most likely where a range of motivations converge to persuade sufficiently large numbers of people that a resort to violence is justified, profitable, inevitable, or transformational. The general point for all researchers linking the environment and conflict is that environmental stress of one kind or another will figure in some, but not all, of these motivations, and hence it will be an elusive but at times significant element of the causal network that generates conflict.

Of course, as extensive research on conflict makes clear, the outcome of any cluster of variables is never assured. Why this is the case is explained, at least partially, by those environmental security researchers who study the capacity of communities at all scales to adjust and adapt to many forms of stress, including those related to environmental change. Both the simplified, Malthusian-inspired, scarcity-conflict story and the resource curse story tend to downplay and, in some cases, explicitly deny this capacity (Homer-Dixon 1999). But recent human history identifies few Easter Islands—states confronted with severe environmental stress that have collapsed into violence and subsequently disappeared —and many Rwandas—states confronted with severe environmental stress that have experienced great violence and then begun to recover. In fact, many of the cases used to demonstrate the validity of the scarcity-conflict thesis are not nearly as straightforward as has been suggested. Much recent research has pointed to the environment as a source of cooperation and peace, rather than a source of conflict and war. For example, Wolf et al. (2006) point out that international cooperation around water has a long and successful history, with water serving as a greater pathway to peace than to conflict in international river basins.

There has also emerged an alternative approach to studying environmental conflicts that is firmly grounded in longstanding environment-society studies conducted by geographers, anthropologists, and sociologists that is now sometimes called "political ecology." This work offers detailed, contextualized, and more nuanced insights into environmental problems and violence. The importance of unequal outcomes of social and environmental changes is highlighted in a number of these case studies. For example, inadequate distribution of the returns from resource extraction activities has been a factor in violence in West Kalimantan (Peluso and Harwell 2001) and the Niger Delta (Mochizuki 2004; Watts 2001). In his analysis of land invasions in a district of Chiapas, Bobrow-Swain (2001) shows that declining agricultural production caused by economic and political forces (rather than environmental scarcity), and the unequal distribution of returns from production, was an important factor in land conflicts. Timura (2001) also shows that unequal access to economic and political resources was an important factor in the Zapatista rebellion, the "Guinea Fowl" war in Ghana, and conflict in Para, Brazil. Suliman (1999) compares the different responses of people in the Fur and Boran regions to drought and shows that land rights was an important variable in determining whether drought results in violent or peaceful outcomes, as well as the role of leaders and institutions for resource sharing.

There is a discernable message in these studies that individual and group's perceptions of the distribution of material and social power is important in the generation of violence. For example, groups may respond to a perception that other groups are faring better or may be threatening, and act to get their share, or to defend themselves in ways that make violent outcomes more likely. The role of leaders in generating or mitigating these cycles of antipathy is critical (David 1997). This emphasis on perceptions contrasts with the somewhat more functionalist accounts of the earlier studies that suggest that material changes translate directly into observable social actions.

These studies are contributing to a more nuanced understanding of the connections between environment and violence. In none of them is "environmental scarcity" seen to be a simple causal factor in conflict. Instead, a range of economic, political, and cultural processes that structure both material and institutional forms of power are seen to be more important than scarcity per se. Their insights do not give rise to a generalized model in the manner of Homer-Dixon's results (1999), but may instead be seen as a reflection of the plurality of responses to environmental change and the plurality of ways in which violent conflict arises. One theme that does, however, emerge repeatedly from these studies is that equity, as well as perceptions of equity, do matter when it comes to environmental security.

Clearly the relationships between environmental change and violent conflict are complex, and simple theoretical models and assertions that promise high levels of generalizability are inevitably lightening rods for controversy and critique. What a survey of the literature of the past two decades does make clear is the myriad ways in which various dimensions of this relationship affect the security of individuals and groups. Resource scarcities are more likely to force the poor to migrate into marginal environments or across cultural or political boundaries into spaces where they are unwelcome. During a violent conflict, government or rebel forces may seek to fund their efforts—or enrich themselves—by monopolizing and overexploiting natural resources, with the poor forced into servitude, caught in the crossfire, or left with a toxic legacy. Military activity itself can cause great damage as soldiers set up camps and draw down local resources, plant mines that are left behind along with other munitions, build tunnels and other infrastructure, or seek to expose their adversaries by burning or cutting forest cover. And for years after a violent conflict has formally ended, the poor may find themselves forced to survive in dangerous or impoverished natural environments. All of these examples link the environmental security literature to human security.

Global Environmental Change and Human Security

The expansion of research on environmental security, along with the rise of human security as both a concept and a discourse, has created a wide opening for interrogation of the links between global environmental change and human security. Surprisingly, there has been very little direct attention to this area of research. While there has been some discussion on the relationship between climate change and conflict (Myers 1993; Gleick 1994; Barnett 2001), and on the relationship between biodiversity conservation and violence (Matthew 2002, 2004; Matthew, Halle, and Switzer 2002), there has been little emphasis on the broader implications of global environmental change for human security, including how increased human security can potentially mitigate environmental change. Perhaps more surprising is the absence, until quite recently, of global environmental change on international human security agendas. Priority topics for human security research and policy have traditionally included human rights; HIV/AIDS and health; gender and security; terrorism; armed conflict; armies, paramilitaries, and non-state armed groups; humanitarian intervention; conflict resolution and peacemaking; small arms, light weapons, and landmines; and poverty and people-centered development. Yet, despite growing international concern about climate change, biodiversity loss, and other environmental changes, these issues are only beginning to be recognized as priority areas for human security research.

There are several explanations as to why the relationship between global environmental change and human security has been overlooked or underestimated, and we focus here on two. The first is that global environmental change has been largely framed as an issue of science, with a focus on understanding the large-scale processes of the earth system, and not its outcomes on peoples' needs, rights, and values (O'Brien and Leichenko 2000; O'Brien 2006). The identification of global-scale environmental changes has long been the domain of earth system scientists who focus on the interactions between large-scale geosphere-biosphere systems and the natural and human-induced changes in them. This research has been invaluable in identifying global- and regional-scale environmental changes such as ozone depletion, climate change, and biodiversity loss, and increasingly it is identifying the cascading effects of these macrochanges on smaller biophysical systems and phenomenon such as the coastal zone, water resources, agriculture, and species distribution. The sequence of assessment is along an assumed and often linear chain of causality: from the bench sciences through to the biological and earth sciences, ending with the social sciences (and at that largely with economics); and correspondingly from global to regional and finally to more local scales of assessment (Proctor 1998; Redclift 1998; Taylor and Buttel 1992). The emphasis remains on the higher-order and larger scales of this assessment sequence. There remains very little effort—as may be measured in terms of funding, personnel, or publications—to examine what these changes in turn mean for local social systems and for individuals and communities who will be differentially affected by them (Demeritt 2001; Shackley et al. 1998). Instead, much effort is directed toward resolving the uncertainties in the science of environmental change, arguably at the expense of focusing on the social drivers that are known to generate both environmental change and vulnerability to environmental change.

The second explanation is that there has been a tendency to downplay issues of development, equity, ethics, power relations, and social justice in global change research, prioritizing instead a general, aggregated notion of welfare. Although social drivers of change are well recognized in global environmental change research, analyses have historically tended to focus on the absolute numbers of people and on talks of amorphous and aggregated social categories such as "humanity," "society," "Africa," "small islands," and so on. Consequently, the potential contributions of social sciences to global change research have been undervalued, despite the fact that global environmental change is a social problem as much as it is a natural system phenomenon. Almost all environmental change problems are the by-products of modern development practices and the social disparities they produce. For example, climate change is caused by the emissions of gases from fossil fuel use and land use changes; forests are cleared to meet the demand for paper, timber, and new land for agriculture and grazing; biodiversity is lost through land clearing for agriculture and infrastructure; rivers are dammed and diverted to control flooding, for hydropower and to secure the supply of water to irrigators; coasts and reefs are modified to support human settlements and are then polluted or destroyed by those settlements; fisheries are depleted by more intense applications of more efficient fishing techniques; and land is degraded by unsustainable farming practices.

Global environmental change is thus an inherently social problem, and one that has the potential to undermine human security—namely, the needs, rights, and values of people and communities. Human insecurity from environmental change is a function of many social processes that cause some people to be more sensitive and less able to prepare for and respond to sudden and incremental environmental changes. People who are most dependent on natural resources and ecosystem services for their livelihoods are often the most sensitive to environmental change (Adger 1999, 2003; Blaikie et al. 1994; Bohle, Downing, and Watts 1994). For example, in terms of needs, a change in soil moisture can undermine nutrition in subsistence farming households, a decline in fish abundance can undermine nutrition and income for fishers, and a decline in surface or groundwater quality can undermine maternal and child health in communities without reticulated water supply. Just as important as sensitivity is people's capacity to anticipate, plan for, and adapt to environmental changes. These response strategies are functions of various social factors, including institutions, information, health, education, and access to food and nutrition, money and resources, and social support networks. Underlying many of these determinants of adaptive capacity is the effectiveness of the state. States that consciously or unconsciously, actively (through violence) or passively (through denial of entitlements), discriminate against social groups on the basis of political opposition, class, ethnicity, and/or location create vulnerable groups.

Many of the factors that influence adaptive capacity have been impacted by globalization processes, which in many cases have reduced the capacity of individuals, communities, and institutions to respond to stressors and shocks linked to environmental change (McGrew and Poku 2007; Leichenko and O'Brien 2008). The changing context in which global environmental change is experienced suggests that greater attention should be paid to how human security changes through time, and particularly the dynamics of vulnerability in the context of multiple processes of change. It is, for example, increasingly important to monitor how human security is affected by both financial and environmental shocks, and to assess what this means for the environment (Leichenko and O'Brien 2008).

The dynamic factors that influence sensitivity and adaptive capacity mean that human security from environmental change is by no means equally distributed. There are differences in the human security of people within every scale of analysis: between regions, countries, cities, villages, and households. In many cases the differences can be explained by the dependence on natural resources and ecosystem services, coupled with the degree of social power in relation to economic, political, and cultural processes (Matthew 2005). However, global environmental changes also introduce new threats that potentially influence the security of much wider and diverse groups of people. Sea level rise, a higher frequency or magnitude of storms and extreme weather, the melting of glaciers, the spread of invasive species, and changes in water quality and availability are likely to threaten human security in new and unexpected ways. The impacts of the Chicago and Paris heat waves on elderly citizens in 1995 and 2003, for example, revealed some of the new challenges posed by global environmental change, as well as the importance of addressing the underlying causes of vulnerability (Leichenko and O'Brien 2008).

Against this background, we define human security as something that is achieved when and where individuals and communities have the options necessary to end, mitigate, or adapt to threats to their human, environmental, and social rights; have the capacity and freedom to exercise these options; and actively participate in pursuing these options (GECHS 1999). In other words, human security is a variable condition where people and communities have the capacity to manage stresses to their needs, rights, and values. When people do not have enough options to avoid or to adapt to environmental change such that their needs, rights, and values are likely to be undermined, then they can be said to be environmentally insecure.

This definition gives attention to values and recognizes that human security concerns both needs and rights. The characterization of human security as "variable" highlights the ways in which it varies over space and across time: not all people are equally secure, and people are not equally secure throughout the course of their lifetimes. This points to the need for analysis of the asymmetries and interdependencies in human security strategies such that the security of some can come at the expense of others, and to the possibility that in both ethical and practical terms strategies for human security may ultimately only be successful if they do not generate insecurity elsewhere or for later generations (see Booth 1999). Further, "variable" suggests that human security is not about static lives, but about flourishing lives where people pursue their legitimate aspirations for a good life, pointing to the nature of human security as a *process* toward self-articulated goals.

The GECHS definition of human security also explicitly includes communities, and not just individuals. This is of course implied in other definitions, but explicit mention of communities is nevertheless important, as in many cultures the collective social group is of more value than the individual, and decisions and strategies are determined by the group, in the interests of the group, rather than by individuals. It is somewhat ethnocentric to assume, as Western social science often does, that the individual is the most important element of a society. A focus on "the capacity to manage stresses" builds on the capabilities-and-freedoms approach of Sen (1999), in that it considers people and communities not as passive victims, but as agents of their own human security, whose actions to manage stresses to their needs, rights, and values are most effective given certain freedoms and opportunities. Sen (1999) lists five important freedoms: economic opportunities, political freedoms, social opportunities, transparency guarantees, and protective security. One can add to this list freedom from direct violence, and the equitable allocation of freedoms within and between generations as important additional freedoms that enhance people and communities' capacities to make and maintain their lives in the face of social and environmental changes (Barnett 2008).

The GECHS definition also offers a slightly different articulation of what the UNDP referred to as "human life and dignity" and what the Commission on Human Security referred to as the "vital core." The GECHS definition considers needs, rights, and values as a means to highlight the need for some stability in the provision of the basic needs required to function as an equal member of a society, the fundamental rights to which people are entitled, and the unique things that people and communities value for themselves. In doing so, the definition (like Sen [1999] and the Commission on Human Security) seeks to avoid prescribing in much detail what is good for people and communities. However, it does acknowledge that there are basic needs such as access to nutritious food and clean drinking water, and basic rights such as the freedom from personal injury and forced migration, that are essential to every life.

The GECHS definition of human security is consistent with a larger discourse on human security that includes prioritizing the well-being of people and communities ahead of states; analytical integration of multiple drivers of human security; an insistence on basic human needs, rights, and responsibilities; and a concern for justice. It is also consistent with the idea that human security is what people themselves see as important in that human security in terms of environmental change is about identifying and responding to the outcomes that matter most to those who are exposed to it, which means that researchers and decision makers should listen to the voices of the vulnerable. This is not to say that there are not universal values at risk (such as the right to clean water and food), or that what the vulnerable identify as their priority concerns are necessarily well informed or without guile, but it is to say that their articulations of needs, rights, and values cannot be ignored if responses to environmental change are to be effective.

A human security perspective on environmental change does in effect securitize environmental change inasmuch as it does raise the profile of some risks over others. Yet this is unlikely to lead to the kinds of counterproductive outcomes that come from securitization by the state; indeed it points to a role for the state in mitigating the drivers of environmental change and in facilitating responses to minimize insecurities (Barnett 2001). There is a significant difference, then, between securitization constructed by the state, and securitization constructed by individuals. Securitization to prioritize individual and community needs, rights, and values at risk from environmental change also engages diverse policy communities, including those concerned with development policies, sustainable development policy, human rights, and foreign policy. Thus the meaning of "human security" is not left to the traditional purveyors of security and is instead continually negotiated in ways that are far less likely to justify the strengthening of the state at the expense of human security.

Despite the inclusion of environment as one of the UNDP's (1994) seven components of human security, there has thus far been little interface between this expanded human security community and the global environmental change research and policy community—including those within the UN system. The United Nations has been pushing for more interaction between the global environmental change and human security communities (Matthew 2008), and many of the current and planned initiatives are described by Dodds and Pippard (2005). Although both human security and environmental considerations are central to the

MDGs, there is no explicit recognition of the implications of global environmental change for these goals. For example, efforts and initiatives to eradicate extreme poverty and hunger are likely to be negatively affected by climate change, as many of the people that are most vulnerable to climate variability and change are already poor and hungry. Likewise, efforts to reduce child mortality; combat HIV/AIDS, malaria, and other diseases; and promote gender equality are likely to be affected—and potentially offset—by global environmental change. The one MDG that addresses the environment (goal 7: ensure environmental sustainability) does not consider the challenges posed by environmental change. Consequently, there is substantial potential for global environmental change and human security research to contribute to a wide range of other human security concerns (Matthew and Gaulin 2002).

As many chapters in his book demonstrate, global environmental change poses real risks to human security: it undermines access to basic needs such as productive soils, clean water, and food; it puts at risk enshrined human, civil, and political human rights such as to the means of subsistence, property, and nationality; it can undermine the provision of economic and social opportunities required to foster human security; and in these and other ways it can undermine people's ability to pursue the kinds of lives they value. It may also be an indirect factor in the generation of violent conflicts. Just as human security has a much larger role to play in global environmental change research, global environmental change is of central importance to human security assessment and policy.

Objectives and Structure of This Volume

This volume brings together perspectives and research findings that have emerged from the Global Environmental Change and Human Security Project since its start in 1999. It is intended for scholars and decision makers concerned with the implications of environmental change for people, the implications of environmental change for peace, and the ways in which sustainable development can enhance human security and peace. It aims to consolidate the connections among and the dialogue across these groups.

The book is structured according to the three interweaving themes that emerge from the literature on the interconnections between environmental change and human security. Part II contains four chapters about global environmental change and human insecurity. These chapters explain the ways in which environmental change undermines human security. The chapters offer frameworks for analyzing the connections, discussions of specific risks such as changing exposure to diseases arising form environmental change, discussions of specific places such as urban slum areas, and cases of specific events such as Hurricane Katrina.

Given that environmental change poses risks to human security, as established in part II, the two chapters in part III then go on to examine the interconnections between environmental change, human security, and peace and conflict. They present a framework for analysis, a review of the evidence about the links between environmental change and violent conflict, and a case study.

The seven chapters in part IV of the book are focused on the interconnections between sustainable development and human security. These include frameworks for analyzing the connections between environmental change and development, discussion of crosscutting issues such as gender and population, examination of the interactions between development and environmental security, and a case study from Central America.

Brief Summaries of Chapters

The chapters in part II, "Global Environmental Change and Human Insecurity," are united by a concern for the ways in which environmental change both creates and exacerbates the insecurities experienced by people around the world. From climate change to disease to the growth of slums, the authors show that, although environmental change and disaster have always been a threat, recent environmental changes have created unprecedented global challenges to social stability, health, and material life (O'Brien et al. 2005).

In chapter 2, "Human Security, Vulnerability, and Global Environmental Change," Mike Brklacich, May Chazan, and Hans-Georg Bohle provide a framework for evaluating the ways global environmental change makes some human populations increasingly vulnerable to both personal and society-wide disasters even while it creates new opportunities for others. The authors argue that vulnerability and insecurity are underlying conditions for all human communities; global environmental change is only one external threat; and consideration of exposure to risks needs to be balanced against assessments of the capacity to respond to threats.

In chapter 3, "Global Health and Human Security: Addressing Impacts from Globalization and Environmental Change," Bryan McDonald posits that an increasingly networked world—where infected individuals can cross oceans in a matter of hours and food supplies (one of the primary modes of disease distribution, after humans themselves) are shipped around the globe—has raised the stakes for pandemics and other potentially disastrous disease effects. Global environmental change, McDonald argues, exacerbates the problems of disease. It is, in the framework of Brklacich, Chazan, and Bohle, a further stressor on communities already suffering from an HIV/AIDS epidemic or strained under the toll of chronic and persistent diseases such as waterborne parasites, malaria, or even influenza.

In chapter 4, "The Vulnerability of Urban Slum Dwellers to Global Environmental Change," Laura Little and Chris Cocklin examine the relationships between urbanization and environmental change. As the world nears the end of a period of massive urbanization—a period that began during the second Industrial Revolution of the nineteenth century and that will almost certainly end with the vast majority of humanity living in cities in almost every country in the world—Little and Cocklin focus on the way environmental change will exacerbate the insecurities already experienced by the urban poor, largely because of their restricted access to entitlements necessary for them to adapt—an approach that is informed by the development-oriented understanding of human security discussed earlier in this chapter. Little and Cocklin detail those aspects of slum dwellers' lives that will be most affected by environmental change, from rising transportation and housing costs to the inaccessibility of necessary government services. Solutions for the complex material effects of environmental change on this vulnerable population, the authors assert, will only be found by examining the underlying political and economic barriers that limit the opportunities of slum dwellers to act to improve their lives.

In chapter 5, "Environmental Change, Disasters, and Vulnerability: The Case of Hurricane Katrina and New Orleans," Victoria Basolo historicizes and contextualizes the events of August 2005, asserting that both environmental and urban policy failures made New Orleans and many of its people vulnerable to disaster. Basolo asserts that while human development and in some cases mismanagement of the natural environment set the stage for the Katrina disaster, it was government and individual lack of preparedness that led to the hurricane's destructive results, which so viscerally unmasked the social inequalities of New Orleans. This chapter continues a theme developed in the earlier chapters: that it is not so much exposure to environmental risks that causes disaster, but rather the inherent vulnerabilities arising from social and political and economic processes.

In part III, "Global Environmental Change, Conflict, and Cooperation," two chapters address the relationship between human security, the environment, and violence.

In chapter 6, "Environmental Change, Human Security, and Violent Conflict," Jon Barnett and W. Neil Adger build on the arguments of earlier authors that environmental change negatively impacts human security, and then argue that this human *in*security can under certain circumstances increase the risk of violent conflict. They examine the multiple ways that human insecurity exacerbated by environmental change can create or enhance the conditions for violent conflict, which include by decreasing the opportunity costs to individuals of joining armed groups and by decreasing state capacity to peacefully manage conflict. They argue for detailed analysis of conflict risk factors at the local level and for careful analysis of the role of institutions at various scales in preventing conflict.

In chapter 7, "Environmental Change and Human Security in Nepal," Richard A. Matthew and Bishnu Raj Upreti illustrate the relationship between environmental change and conflict through a case study of Nepal's decade-long civil war. Such a case-based approach offers an alternative to research from peace studies that seeks generalizable findings based on statistical data. Matthew and Upreti argue that environmental stress has been a primary cause of the violent conflict in Nepal, in particular pointing to demographic trends and land pressures. They warn that it is unlikely that the conflict will be resolved without addressing demographic and environmental conditions.

In part IV the chapters on "Human Security and Sustainable Development" apply many of the lessons from research and policy on sustainable development to the more particular problem of human insecurity created and exacerbated by environmental change.

In chapter 8, "Global Environmental Change, Equity, and Human Security," Karen L. O'Brien and Robin M. Leichenko highlight equity issues surrounding both mitigation of and adaptation to global environmental change. They argue that these equity dimensions must be comprehensively addressed if enhanced human security is an objective. Equity-based responses to global environmental change address the many processes and factors that influence vulnerability and adaptive capacity and recognize that environmental change is not simply a North-South issue, but one that cuts across national boundaries and needs to be addressed comprehensively, at different scales and units of analysis.

In chapter 9, "Approaches to Enhancing Human Security," Marvin S. Soroos examines potential responses to global environmental change. By learning from earlier generations' efforts to respond to and manage environmental change, Soroos argues that the best responses will be anticipatory, not reactive. Most important, Soroos emphasizes, societies and states with the capacity to prepare for and confront environmental change must, in the interest of greater stability, aid those societies with less capacity, or risk further threats to stability and security. This issue of common but differentiated responsibility is a principle of the agreements (such as the UN Climate Change Convention) signed at the United Nations Conference on Environment and Development, and it remains highly relevant to environmental security.

In chapter 10, "Rethinking the Role of Population in Human Security," Betsy Hartmann questions the persistent Western belief in a coming Malthusian crisis, where population outstrips global resources. This emphasis on population control and the dangers of overpopulation, Hartmann argues, have misdirected policies and reinforced stereotypes of an explosive and burgeoning Third World population—an imagination of the developing world that critical development scholars have long sought to contest. Transposed on top of concern for environmental change, this demographic pessimism leads to defensive policies that anticipate that, with massive environmental change, overpopulated Third World countries will threaten the security of more affluent regions. Hartmann systematically critiques this assumption and the misguided implications for policy that flow from it.

In chapter 11, "Women, Global Environmental Change, and Human Security," Heather Goldsworthy explores the impact that global environmental change will have on the security of women. Consistent with many approaches to gender and development, Goldsworthy argues that women are uniquely vulnerable to environmental change as well as to policies that attempt to curb that change, from restrictions on use of land to draconian measures to reduce population. Goldsworthy points us to the enormous potential women have been shown to hold in regard to preserving and protecting natural resources, and suggests a gender-based approach to environmental security.

In chapter 12, "Human Security as a Prerequisite for Development," Kwasi Nsiah-Gyabaah outlines the many ways that human security issues interleave with sustainable development issues. He argues that reducing poverty, preventing conflicts, and controlling environmental change are not only fundamental tenets of the human security agenda but are also important precursors to sustainable development. As the ideas of human security have bloomed and spread, Nsiah-Gyabaah emphasizes the importance of strengthened international communication and collaboration to articulate and implement policies that support both human security and sustainable development.

In chapter 13, "Free to Squander? Democracy and Sustainable Development, 1975–2000," Indra de Soysa, Jennifer Bailey, and Eric Neumayer take Nsiah-Gyabaah's relationship between development and human security one step further to specifically examine the relationship of those issues to the emergence of democracy. Asserting that sustainable economic development is not just about growth but instead about how a society uses resources to protect its current and future populations against disaster and deprivation, the authors conclude that higher levels of democracy are related to higher development as democracies tend to invest more in their populations. This in turn reduced vulnerability to environmental change, and so human security is enhanced by democracy.

In chapter 14, "Environmental Transborder Cooperation in Latin America: Challenges to the Westphalia Order," Alexander López investigates how the internationalization of environmental problems—as well as their solutions—has manifested itself in the use and management of two regional resources in Latin America, the Mesoamerican Biological Corridor and the Plata Basin. The state cooperation over management of these resources, López argues, stands as a challenge to the notions of national sovereignty enshrined in the Westphalia order. Environmental concerns that transcend state boundaries, such as the two López examines, have increasingly impressed on state leaders the benefits of state cooperation in resource management. López concludes that state sovereignty and this kind of cooperation actually do not threaten one another but instead strengthen the security of both, as well as reduce the risks that environmental change poses to people who might otherwise be vulnerable to the twin effects of environmental degradation and border disputes.

Finally, in chapter 15, "Charting the Next Generation of Global Environmental Change and Human Security Research," Jon Barnett, Richard A. Matthew, and Karen L. O'Brien lay out future directions of research in the human security implications of environmental change.

The chapters in this book cover diverse topics and present different and sometimes contrasting viewpoints on environmental change and human security. Nevertheless, they raise two important points. First, global environmental change is adding impetus to the realization that traditional understandings of security are limited and are an inadequate basis for making policy: they make it clear that to varying degrees environmental change is a risk to citizens of states, to states themselves, and to peace. Second, they show that global environmental change is raising new and unavoidable questions of equity and sustainability, which already underlie every aspect of human security. The chapters call for enhanced attention to the ways that different societies are organized and function, including their technologies, economies, systems of governance, and material and social cultures, and to the ways these shape the repertoire of habits, skills, and styles that people use to act in the world (Swidler 1986). From this more detailed understanding of social order can arise deeper insights into why some societies consume more and pollute more, and how pathways to social change that result in more secure, equitable, and sustainable societies may be achieved. Finally, the chapters call for a greater focus on the distributional effects of environmental change, and the effects of skewed distributions of goods and services on vulnerability to environmental change. They call for greater integration of the security, development, and sustainable development research and policy communities, which have for too long been too distinct.

References

Adger, W. 1999. Social vulnerability to climate change and extremes in coastal Vietnam. *World Development* 27 (2): 249–269.

Adger, W. 2003. Social capital, collective action, and adaptation to climate change. *Economic Geography* 79 (4): 387–404.

Axworthy, L. 1997. Canada and human security: The need for leadership. *International Journal* 52 (2): 183–196.

Barnett, J. 2001. *The meaning of environmental security*. London: Zed Books.

Barnett, J. 2008. Peace and development: Towards a new synthesis. *Journal of Peace Research*: 45 (1): 75–89.

Baumert, K., and N. Kete. 2001. *United States, developing countries, and climate protection: Leadership or stalemate?* Washington, DC: World Resources Institute.

Blaikie, P., T. Cannon, I. Davies, and B. Wisner. 1994. *At risk: Natural hazards, people's vulnerability, and disasters*. Routledge: London.

Bobrow-Strain, A. 2001. Between a ranch and a hard place: Violence, scarcity, and meaning in Chiapas, Mexico. In *Violent environments*, ed. N. Peluso and M. Watts, 155–185. Ithaca: Cornell University Press.

Bohle, H., T. Downing, and M. Watts. 1994. Climate change and social vulnerability: Toward a sociology and geography of food insecurity. *Global Environmental Change* 4 (1): 37–48.

Booth, K. 1991. Security and emancipation. *Review of International Studies* 17 (4): 313–326.

Booth, K. 1999. Three tyrannies. In *Human rights in global politics*, ed. T. Dunne and N. Wheeler, 31–70. Cambridge, UK: Cambridge University Press.

Brown, L. 1977. Redefining national security. Worldwatch paper no. 14. Washington, DC: Worldwatch Institute.

Campbell, D. 1992. *Writing security: United States foreign policy and the politics of identity*. Manchester: Manchester University Press.

Collier, Paul, and Anke Hoeffler. 2000. *Greed and grievance in civil war*. Washington, DC : World Bank, Development Research Group.

Commission on Human Security. 2003. *Human security now*. New York: Commission on Human Security.

Dalby, S. 1992. Ecopolitical discourse: "Environmental security" and political geography. *Progress in Human Geography* 16 (4): 503–522.

David, S. 1997. Internal war: Causes and cures. *World Politics* 49 (4): 552–576.

Demeritt, D. 2001. The construction of global warming and the politics of science. *Annals of the Association of American Geographers* 91:307–337.

Deudney, D. 1990. The case against linking environmental degradation and national security. *Millennium: Journal of International Studies* 19 (3): 461–476.

Deudney, Daniel, and Richard Matthew, eds. 1999. *Contested grounds: Security and conflict in the new environmental politics*. Albany: SUNY Press.

Dilley, M. 2000. Reducing vulnerability to climate variability in southern Africa: The growing role of climate information. *Climatic Change* 45 (1): 63–73.

Dodds, F., and T. Pippard, eds. 2005. *Human and environmental security: An agenda for change*. London: Earthscan.

Ehrlich, P., and A. Ehrlich. 1991. Population growth and environmental security. *Georgia Review* 45 (2): 223–232.

Floyd, R. 2007. *Typologies of securitisation and desecuritisation: The case of US environmental security 1993–2006.* PhD diss., University of Warwick.

Gasper, D. 2005. Securing humanity: Situating "human security" as concept and discourse. *Journal of Human Development* 6 (2): 221–245.

Gasper D., and T. Truong. 2005. Deepening development ethics: From economism to human development to human security. *The European Journal of Development Research* 17 (3): 372–384.

GECHS. 1999. *Global environmental change and human security: GECHS science plan.* IHDP: Bonn.

Gleick, P. 1994. Ultimate security: How environmental concerns affect global political stability. *Bulletin of the Atomic Scientists* 50:2–55.

Hauge, Wenche, and Tanja Ellingsen. 1998. Beyond environmental scarcity: Causal pathways to conflict. *Journal of Peace Research* 35 (3): 299–317.

Homer-Dixon, T. 1999. *Environment, scarcity, and violence.* Princeton: Princeton University Press.

Homer-Dixon. T., and J. Blitt, eds. 1998. *Ecoviolence.* New York: Rowman & Littlefield.

Klein, B. 1997. Every month is "Security Awareness Month." In *Critical security studies: Concepts and cases*, ed. K. Krause and M. Williams, 359-368. Minneapolis: University of Minnesota Press.

Leichenko, R. M., and K.L. O'Brien. 2008. *Environmental change and globalization: Double exposures.* New York: Oxford University Press.

MacFarlane, S., and Y. Foong Khong. 2006. *Human security and the UN: A critical history.* Bloomington: Indiana University Press.

Malthus T. R. 1798. *An essay on the principle of population.* Oxford World's Classics. Oxford: Oxford University Press, 1999.

Matthew, Richard A. 2002. In defense of environment and security research. *Environmental Change and Security Project Report* 8 (Summer): 109–124.

Matthew, Richard. 2004. Networks of threat and vulnerability: Lessons from environmental security research. *Environmental Change and Security Project Report* 10:36–42.

Matthew, R. 2005. Sustainable livelihoods, environmental security and conflict mitigation: Four cases in South Asia. Poverty, Equity and Rights in Conservation Working Paper Series. Geneva: IUCN. http://www.iucn.org/themes/spg/Files/IUED/Case%20Study%20South%20Asia.pdf (accessed November 15, 2008).

Matthew, R. A. 2008. *Resource scarcity: Responding to the security challenge.* New York: International Peace Institute.

Matthew, R., and T. Gaulin. 2002. The ecology of peace. *Peace Review* 14 (1): 33–39.

Matthew, R., M. Halle, and J. Switzer, eds. 2002. *Conserving the peace: Resources, livelihoods, and security.* Geneva and Winnipeg: IISD Press.

Matthew, R., and B. Upreti. 2007. Environmental stress and demographic change in Nepal: Underlying conditions contributing to a decade of insurgency. *Environmental Change and Security Project Report* 11:29–39.

McGrew, A., and N. K. Poku. 2007. *Globalization, development and human security.* Cambridge, UK: Polity.

Mochizuki, K. 2004. Conflict and people's insecurity: An insight from the experiences of Nigeria. In *Conflict and Human Security: A Search for New Approaches of Peace-Building,* ed. H. Shinoda and H. Jeong, 207–228. Hiroshima: Institute for Peace Science Hiroshima University.

Myers, N. 1993. *Ultimate security: The environmental basis of political stability.* New York: W. W. Norton.

O'Brien, K. 2006. Are we missing the point? Global environmental change as an issue of human security. *Global Environmental Change* 16:1–3.

O'Brien, K., and R. Leichenko. 2000. Double exposure: Assessing the impacts of climate change within the context of economic globalisation. *Global Environmental Change* 10:221–232.

O'Brien, K., J. Barnett, I. De Soysa, R. Matthew, L. Mehta, J. Seager, M. Woodrow, and H. Bohle. 2005. Hurricane Katrina reveals challenges to human security. *AVISO* 14:1–8.

Osborn, F. 1948. *Our plundered planet.* London: Faber and Faber.

Ó Tuathail, G. 1996. *Critical geopolitics.* London: Routledge.

Paris, R. 2001. Human security: Paradigm shift or hot air? *International Security* 26 (2): 87–102.

Peluso, N., and E. Harwell. 2001. Territory, custom, and the cultural politics of ethnic war in West Kalimantan, Indonesia. In *Violent Environments,* ed. N. Peluso and K. Watts, 83–116. Ithaca: Cornell University Press.

Proctor, J. 1998. The meaning of culture in global environmental change: Retheorizing culture in human dimensions research. *Global Environmental Change* 8:227–248.

Redclift, M. 1998. Dances with wolves? Interdisciplinary research on the global environment. *Global Environmental Change* 8:177–182.

Renner, M. 1991. Assessing the military's war on the environment. In *State of the world 1991,* ed. L. Brown, 132–152. New York: W. W. Norton.

Rosenau, J. 1990. *Turbulence in world politics: A theory of change and continuity.* Princeton: Princeton University Press.

Sachs, W., ed. 1993. *Global ecology: A new arena of political conflict.* London: Zed Books.

Sen, A. 1999. *Development as freedom.* New York: Anchor Books.

Shackley, S., P. Young, S. Parkinson, and B. Wynne. 1998. Uncertainty, complexity and concepts of good science in climate change modelling: Are GCMs the best tools? *Climatic Change* 38:159–205.

Shaw, M. 1993. There is no such thing as society: Beyond individualism and statism in international security studies. *Review of International Studies* 19 (2): 159–175.

Stålenheim, P., C. Perdomo, and E. Sköns. 2008. Military expenditure. In *SIPRI Yearbook 2008: Summary*, ed. Stockholm International Peace Research Institute, 10–11. Stockholm: SIPRI.

St. Clair, A. L. 2004. The role of ideas in the United Nations Development Programme. In *Global institutions and development: Framing the world?*, ed. M. Bøås, and D. McNeill. London: Routledge.

State Failure Task Force. 1999. State failure task force report: Phase II findings. In *Environmental Change and Security Project Report* (Summer): 49–72. Washington, DC: The Woodrow Wilson Center.

Stewart, F., and V. Fitzgerald. 2000. *War and underdevelopment: Volume 1. The economic and social consequences of conflict*. Oxford: Oxford University Press.

Suliman, M. 1999. Conflict resolution among the Borana and the Fur: Similar features, different outcomes. In *Environment, politics and violent conflict*, ed. M. Suliman, 286–290. London: Zed Books.

Swidler, A. 1986. Culture in action: Symbols and strategies. *American Sociological Review* 51:273–286.

Taylor, P., and F. Buttel. 1992. How do we know we have global environmental problems? Science and the globalization of environmental discourse. *Geoforum* 23:405–416.

Thomas, C. 2001. Global governance, development, and human security: exploring the links. *Third World Quarterly* 22 (2): 159–175.

Timura, C. 2001. "Environmental conflict" and the social life of environmental security discourse. *Anthropological Quarterly* 74 (3): 104–113.

Turner, B. L., II, et al. 1990. *The earth as transformed by human action: Global and regional changes in the biosphere over the past 300 years*. Cambridge, UK: Cambridge University Press.

Ullman, R. H. 1983. Redefining security. *International Security* 8 (1): 129–153.

UNDP (United Nations Development Program). 1994. *Human development report 1994*. New York: Oxford University Press.

UNDP (United Nations Development Program). 1996. *Human development report 1996*. New York: Oxford University Press.

UNEP (United Nations Environment Program). 1997. *Global state of the environment report*. London: Earthscan.

Waever, O. 1995. Securitization and desecuritization. In *On security*, ed. R. Lipschutz, 46–86. New York: Columbia University Press.

Walker, R. 1987. Culture, discourse and insecurity. In *Towards a just world: Perspectives from social movements*, ed. S. Mendlovitz and R. Walker, 171–190. London: Butterworths.

Walt, S. 1991. The renaissance of security studies. *International Studies Quarterly* 35 (2): 211–239.

Watts, M. 2001. Petro-violence: Community, extraction, and political ecology of a mythic commodity. In *Violent environments*, ed. N. Peluso and M. Watts, 189–212. Ithaca: Cornell University Press.

Westing, A. 1976. *Ecological consequences of the second Indochina war*. Stockholm: Almquist and Wiksell.

WGBU (German Advisory Council on Global Change). 2007. *World in transition: Climate change as a security risk—Summary for policy makers*. Berlin: WBGU.

Wolf, Aaron T., Annika Kramer, Alexander Carius, and Geoffrey D. Dabelko. 2006. Water can be a pathway to peace, not war. *Navigating Peace* 1 (Woodrow Wilson International Center for Scholars): 1–6.

Wisner, Ben. 2001. Capitalism and the shifting spatial and social distribution of hazard and vulnerability. *Australian Journal of Emergency Management* 16:44–50.

II

Global Environmental Change and Human Insecurity

2

Human Security, Vulnerability, and Global Environmental Change

Mike Brklacich, May Chazan, and Hans-Georg Bohle

As communities around the world face rapidly changing conditions, driven in part by global environmental and societal changes, there is an increasing need to understand why these cumulative changes threaten human livelihoods in some cases and create opportunities for others, how communities cope with and in some cases adapt to these cumulative stresses, and how public policy might reduce threats and enhance human security. It is within this complex and dynamic environment that individuals and communities negotiate their lives, their livelihoods, and their overall well-being, and therefore it is crucial that assessments of human vulnerability and security to global environmental change (GEC) go beyond simple attempts to understand individual changes in isolation.

This chapter develops a conceptual framework for understanding human vulnerability to GEC and other stressors. It builds upon the vulnerability-security literature that has to a large degree developed in response to famines, natural hazards, and disasters. The chapter aims to bring together recent scholarship on human security, vulnerability, and global environmental change into a single conceptual framework, noting that its application is beyond the chapter's scope. Overall, the chapter develops a comprehensive conceptual framework for assessing human vulnerability and security by addressing three key questions:

1. What is known about current human vulnerability to environmental stresses, and how does this relate to human security?
2. How would global change, including but not limited to GEC, reshape human vulnerability–environmental stress relationships?
3. How might we best advance our understanding of human vulnerability and security in light of global change?

In responding to these questions, this chapter draws together elements from several existing frameworks to develop a comprehensive human vulnerability-security model that synthesizes and extends recent thinking in the areas of human security, vulnerability, and global environmental change.

Toward a Human Vulnerability-Security Framework

What is known about current human vulnerability to environmental stress, and how does this relate to human security?
Human vulnerability to environmental stress is not a new concept. Some of the earliest work dates back to the 1940s and Gilbert White's pioneering research into human activities in the floodplains of major river systems throughout the United States. White's work forged the foundation for the next four decades of natural hazards research and several studies that eventually resulted in a thorough characterization of hazards (e.g., magnitude of the event, return period frequencies), created a typology of hazards (i.e., natural, quasi-natural, and anthropocentric hazards), and classified responses (e.g., mitigation of the event, spread of risk) (for reviews, see Burton, Kates, and White 1993; Mitchell 1989). Much of this natural hazards research as well as famine research were place-based, and therefore they effectively captured the net impacts of cumulative or multiple stressors, including biophysical and socioeconomic factors, on human well-being. A key consequence however of focusing on outcomes (e.g., incidence of hunger, number of people displaced by extreme weather, etc.) of multiple stressors was that this research provided limited insight into the root causes of these human tragedies.

There have been several notable changes to this initial foundation for vulnerability research over the past fifteen years. One has involved a reorientation of hazards and famine research in order to better understand how coping capacity and external stressors or shocks collectively define a state of human vulnerability (Emel and Peet 1989; Watts and Bohle 1993). This has contributed to a recasting of vulnerability concepts, and there is now overwhelming evidence that vulnerability is a fundamental characteristic of all human systems and that an external stress such as an extreme weather event exposes rather than causes vulnerability (Adger 1999; Mustafa 1998). In addition, the scope of vulnerability research has broadened considerably and emerging stressors such as economic globalization and HIV/AIDS are now considered to be drivers of human vulnerability (Chen and Narasimhan 2003). And finally, it is now recognized that it is no longer sufficient to simply focus

Vulnerability ◄————————► Human security

Figure 2.1
Vulnerability-security continuum

on identifying vulnerabilities but it is also essential to extend the research scope and consider opportunities and strategies to move from a state of human vulnerability to one of human security (Bohle 2001; Twigg and Bhatt 1998; O'Brien and Vogel 2004).

Human security is achieved when and where individuals and communities live with three basic conditions: (1) the options necessary to end, mitigate, or adapt to threats to their human, environmental, and social rights; (2) the capacity and freedom to exercise these options; and (3) the opportunity to actively participate in attaining these options (Lonergan 1999). Human security and vulnerability are intimately linked: *human security* is the capacity to overcome *vulnerability* and to respond positively to environmental change. From this perspective, vulnerability and human security occupy opposite ends of a common continuum (see figure 2.1).

Research on human vulnerability to environmental stress, much of which has taken place in the context of hazards, disasters, famines, and, more recently, climate change, can therefore inform efforts to conceptualize and promote human security amid emerging social and environmental threats.

This conceptualization affords two observations that are consistent with recent theorizing on vulnerability. First, vulnerability is not a residual to any particular environmental event or stressor, but rather it is a preexisting, underlying state. An individual's, a community's, or a nation's underlying level of vulnerability may, however, be unveiled or revealed as a result of certain stressors (O'Brien and Vogel 2004). Second, vulnerability is not the end product of singular events or strategies; people and groups dynamically slide back and forth along the vulnerability-security continuum. Overall, figure 2.1 suggests that vulnerability and security are not static states, but are the result of dynamic processes, and these processes are likely in motion prior to observable effects from any given environmental perturbation.

Much is known about factors that inhibit certain people and groups from achieving security and about what drives vulnerability to environmental stress. Numerous researchers, development practitioners, and decision makers have sought to identify factors that enable and constrain movement along the vulnerability-security continuum in order to determine how best to promote security and reduce vulnerability. Many of these studies have focused on natural phenomena and engineering or technocratic solutions, but more recently social scientists have expanded the scope to consider how coping and adaptive capacity can shape and modify potential for human losses (Brklacich and Bohle 2006; Emel and Peet 1989). A key point is that the capacity of individuals and communities to cope with and if necessary adapt to local through global change is central to understanding human vulnerability. The greater the coping and adaptive capacities, the more likely the individual or the community will be able to move toward a more secure state. Bohle (2001) defines human vulnerability as having a "double structure," or as the interaction between two "sides." The external side of vulnerability, which has been more widely studied, involves exposure to environmental stress and is predominantly structural in nature. It focuses on stressors that are largely beyond the control of a particular community (e.g., global climatic change, economic globalization). The internal side, which has received less attention in human vulnerability research, involves the capacity to cope with insecurity and encompasses factors that enable and constrain human agency (see Bohle 2001 and Brklacich and Bohle 2006 for further discussion of the "double structure" of vulnerability). The internal side focuses on the inner workings of communities and their ability to recognize as well as respond to stressors associated with the external side of vulnerability. Incorporating this "double structure," exposure to stressors and the capacity to cope with insecurity together influence how people and groups negotiate movement along the human vulnerability-security continuum (see figure 2.2). For example, a community with a relatively high level of coping and/or adaptive capacity may be able to withstand and recover from exposure to a relative severe event (e.g., a hurricane) and thereby maintain an advanced level of security. Conversely, for a community that is already in a vulnerable state and with a limited coping capacity, exposure to a relatively modest environmental stress (e.g., a short period of mild drought) may well be pushed into a heightened state of vulnerability.

Figure 2.2 expands Bohle's (2001) internal side of vulnerability to include a range of human responses, from the capacity to cope with stresses in the short term and the capacity to adapt to and recover from changing conditions over the longer term. It also suggests that "expo-

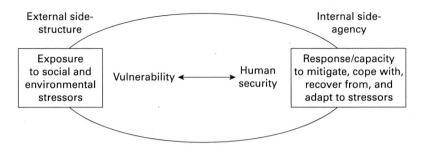

Figure 2.2
Incorporating human vulnerability's "double structure"

sure" and "response" interact with and feed back upon each other, and thereby vulnerability is generated and accumulated over time.

Recently, traditional engineering perspectives and technocratic solutions have been charged with placing a low priority on underlying social factors, being too capital-intensive for those most vulnerable, and not providing sustainable long-term solutions (Mustafa 1998). In addition, the shift toward comprehensive notions of human vulnerability has led social scientists to examine human perceptions of risk and investigate the sociopolitical causality of vulnerability (Brklacich and Bohle 2006). Many researchers are therefore seeking to re-prioritize efforts toward identifying social, political, and economic drivers of vulnerability rather than focusing on technocratic solutions that ultimately reinforce the status quo and thereby deepen human vulnerability to stress.

A number of frameworks have emerged, and the contextual characteristics that appear to shape vulnerability can be broadly clustered into four interrelated groups: (1) control of and access to assets; (2) institutional factors; (3) distribution of rights and resources; (4) ecological and geographical factors (see figure 2.3).

Several existing frameworks and supporting studies characterize the first three of these groups—control of and access to assets, institutional factors, and distribution of rights and resources—as interactively underpinning human vulnerability. Bohle (2001) suggests, for instance, that access to and control of "coping resources," or economic, sociopolitical, infrastructural, ecological, and personal "assets," influence internal coping capacity. Social assets play a particularly important role for the most vulnerable who often control few economic, political, infrastructural, ecological, or personal assets (Bohle 2001). Moreover, Watts and Bohle

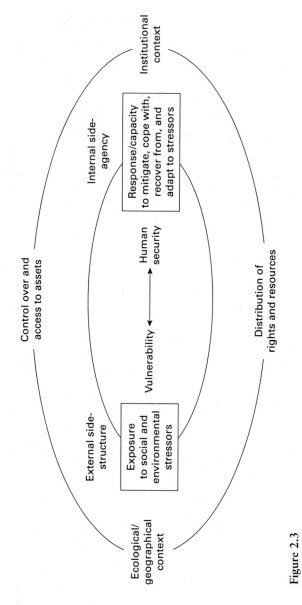

Figure 2.3
Contextualizing vulnerability

(1993) relate external exposure to stress to the distribution of resources, access to institutions and rights, and strength of political voice. This is supported by Mustafa's (1998) research on flood hazards in Pakistan, which demonstrates how human vulnerability can be driven by the combination of powerlessness, poverty, institutional relations, political economy, and entitlements. Adger (1999) builds on these themes and proposes that lack of access to resources, poverty, and marginalization translate into vulnerability through the erosion of the coping capacity and increasing exposure to stress. He distinguishes between individual vulnerability (influenced by access, income diversity, and social status, and operationalized as poverty and resource dependency) and collective vulnerability (influenced by market structures and institutions, and operationalized as inequality and institutional adaptation) (Adger 1999). In addition, Kelly and Adger (2000) demonstrate how socioeconomic and institutional constraints can limit the capacity to respond to climatic stressors. They reveal that human vulnerability is driven by an "architecture of entitlements" and reflects access to resources, the institutional context, and society's level of inequality or maldistribution (Kelly and Adger 2000).

With growing interest in these sociopolitical drivers of vulnerability, social scientists have placed relatively less emphasis on traditionally studied geographical, ecological, and biophysical factors (i.e., the fourth group of drivers, which are depicted in figure 2.3). Yet, these remain central to both level of exposure and the capacity to adaptively respond. What has become increasingly clear however is that ecological and geographical factors are not disconnected from the social fabric and institutional context of societies. Cutter (2001) suggests that the interaction of biophysical and social vulnerability (with feedback loops) creates "place vulnerability": risk and response interact to produce hazard potential which is filtered through the social and geographical contexts of the society (Cutter 2001). As depicted in figure 2.3, then, geographical marginalization and critical ecological living conditions are mediated by societal institutions and distribution of rights, while such conditions also contribute to the maintenance of certain institutions and impact on people's and groups' access to assets.

In summary, vulnerability and human security are dynamic states that preexist particular perturbations in the environment or other external stressors. Given their strong inverse relationship, the growing body of human vulnerability research may provide important insights into the nature, causality, and enhancement of human security. This research suggests four key groups of interrelated drivers: control of and access to assets, institutional factors, distribution of rights and resources, and ecological and geographical conditions. Individually and cumulatively, these factors underpin both sides of vulnerability: exposure to stressors and the human capacity for positive response. As such, they provide the contextual backdrop against which individuals and groups negotiate movement along the vulnerability-security continuum, though specific webs of causality are less well understood and likely vary between places, communities, and individuals.

Changing Threats to Human Security

How would global change, including but not limited to global environmental change, reshape human vulnerability–environmental stress relationships?

While scientists have long studied relationships between localized environmental conditions and human well-being, the cumulative effects of human activities is prompting global-scale environmental degradation (Steffen and Tyson 2001). *Global environmental change* is caused by both changes to the earth's biophysical systems (e.g., climate change and ozone depletion) and the cumulative effects of localized changes taking place globally (e.g., biodiversity declines due to large-scale marshland loss and deforestation). Although some GECs are inherently natural processes, human activities are impacting the magnitude and rate of these changes (Wuebbles and Rosenberg 1998). Table 2.1 outlines six ongoing and human-induced GEC processes (adapted from McMichael and Beaglehole 2000).

The significant changes in the type, frequency, and scale of environmental stressors that have emerged over the past few decades are predicted to continue; however, the mechanisms by which these stressors threaten human security are intricate and have not yet been fully unraveled. Global environmental changes are most often linked with ecological changes and thus human exposure to threats (i.e., the external side of vulnerability as depicted in figure 2.3). Biodiversity loss, for instance, has led to changes in the distribution and seasonality of certain disease-carrying vector species, while climate change is predicted to lead to coastal flooding and inundation of water supplies in some areas (Martens, McMichael and Patz, 2000).

Table 2.1
Global environmental changes

Climate Change
Forecasted changes to global patterns of temperature, precipitation and climate variability due to accumulation of heat-trapping greenhouse gases in the troposphere; associated with industrialization and fossil fuel burning.

Biodiversity Loss
Rapid extinction of plant and animal species due to agricultural intensification, deforestation, land use changes, and desertification; associated with bioinvasion of non-native plant and animal species.

Stratospheric Ozone Depletion
Destruction of stratospheric ozone layer by human-made gases such as chlorofluorocarbons.

Freshwater Declines
Depletion of freshwater aquifers and other freshwater sources due to industrial and agricultural demand, amplified by population growth.

Impairment of Food-Producing Ecosystems
Increasing stress on world's arable lands and pastures (1/3 of previously productive land is damaged by erosion, compaction, salinization, water-logging, and chemicalization); depletion of ocean's fisheries.

Persistent Organic Pollution
Worldwide dissemination of various semi-volatile organic chemicals and heavy metals through the lower atmosphere; bioaccumulate through food chain; for example, PCBs, DDT, mercury.

GEC is most often characterized by relatively long temporal scales as well far-reaching spatial scales. For example, the full effects of human activities on the earth's atmospheric systems are expected to take place over the course of several decades but these longer-term changes can be punctuated by more abrupt weather variations (Steffan et al 2004). The extension of both the spatial and temporal scales of environmental stress suggests that exposures and responses must now be considered at these extended and variable temporal scales as well (Brklacich and Bohle 2006). Furthermore, to equate potential ecological changes with human impacts, as in much early GEC research, is to present a narrow picture that neglects human capacity for adaptation and de-contextualizes vulnerability.

Indeed, the complex social systems that mediate human exposure to threats and underlie the human capacity for response are not static (Brklacich and Bohle 2006). Like GEC, dramatic global economic, political, social, and demographic changes have taken place over the past two decades and are predicted to continue. While societal changes are creating new opportunities for some, they are posing new risks and perpetuating vulnerabilities for many others (Bohle 2001). Alongside GEC, multi-scale societal changes like urbanization and economic globalization are therefore significantly altering threats to human security (see figure 2.4).

Such macro-scale societal transformation is associated with changes to both the inner and middle rings of figure 2.4, or with a changing exposure to stressors, a shifting capacity for response, and an alteration of contextual drivers. Economic globalization, for example, has led to increased inequality (i.e., uneven distribution of resources) and overall impoverishment (i.e., reduced access to assets) for some but also new opportunities for others that will ultimately increase their security (Mittelman 2002; Weisbrot et al. 2002). Global trends toward market liberalization and democratization also means rapidly changing institutions and norms in many parts of the world. Furthermore, it is predicted that by 2025, 61 percent of the world's people will live in large cities (Nicastri, Girardi, and Ippolito 2001). Despite creating new economic, social, and political opportunities, urbanization has led to deteriorating ecological conditions (e.g., slums), increased socioenvironmental risk (e.g., violence), and reduced access to infrastructural assets for many people (Davis 2004). Human security and GEC research must therefore consider simultaneous environmental and societal transformation at multiple spatial and temporal scales, and recognize that socioeconomic transformations can increase vulnerability for some communities while other communities that are able to adapt will be more able to improve security.

Figure 2.4 further demonstrates that environmental and societal changes are not only occurring simultaneously, but are also interactive, convergent, and cumulative. For example, urban residents tend to consume higher per capita fossil fuels than their rural counterparts (Leitmann 2003), and because fossil fuel consumption is the main cause of predicted climate change, urbanization underlies global environmental change. Conversely, biodiversity losses, such as deforestation, are associated with migration to urban centers (Daily and Erlich 1996), and thus global environmental change underlies urbanization. Likewise, links between globalization and global environmental change exist in both directions: globalization drives global environmental change as transnational

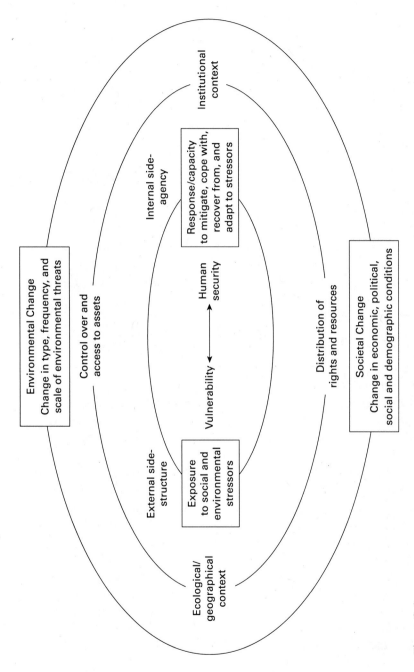

Figure 2.4
Global change and comprehensive security vulnerability

corporations settle in locations with lax environmental standards (McMichael et al. 1999); global environmental change, such as freshwater decline, could motivate further deregulation of trade markets as countries with declining resources seek out new reservoirs.

Cumulatively, social and environmental stressors tend to converge on certain places, ecosystems, social groups, and economic sectors (O'Brien and Leichenko 2000). In addition, as supranational processes increasingly drive environmental and social changes, the locus of control of emerging threats is shifting away from the individuals and groups who are likely to be most exposed. The global-scale, externally driven nature of outer-ring changes is associated with a sense of paralysis at the individual and community levels and with a declining sense of control over social and environmental conditions (Bandura 1995; Williams, Labonte, and O'Brien 2003). While global mitigation campaigns depend on a willingness to take action on global changes distant in both place and time (Wilbanks and Kates 1999), there are now several studies suggesting that those most vulnerable tend to contribute least to environmental change while exerting minimal control over regulatory policies (Mimura et al. 2007). In addition to raising issues of equity, this suggests that global-scale environmental change could reduce local control over environmental and economic assets, and this could impact coping and adaptive capacity.

GEC therefore introduces both new threats and new conceptual challenges to the vulnerability-security picture. Human-induced changes to the earth's systems have altered the temporal and spatial scales of environmental stressors and human responses, and have changed the type, frequency, and magnitude of threats to human security. In addition, these changes are inextricably and interactively linked with ongoing societal transformation. Global economic, social, demographic, and political changes are exposing some people to new socioecological threats, and dynamic social systems are intrinsic to individuals' and groups' capacities to respond to emerging stressors. Nevertheless, research into the additive, interactive, and cumulative effects of multiple stressors remains extremely sparse. Though much empirical research is needed, some of the complex relationships between changing socioenvironmental conditions and differential human security are captured in the interactions between and within the three rings of figure 2.4. Based on existing conceptual frameworks and incorporating current theorizing in human dimensions of GEC research, this comprehensive human vulnerability-security model situates human security within the context of ongoing environmental and societal transformation.

Applications for Research and Intervention

How might we best advance our understanding of human vulnerability and security in light of global change?
The conceptual relationships and methodological challenges highlighted through the development of figure 2.4 are not only theoretically relevant, but can be applied to assessments and intervention strategies as well. However, just as issues of scale are central to understanding the changing nature of threats to human security, vulnerability assessments are also inherently scale-dependent. Supranational processes increasingly drive human security, and yet vulnerabilities to changing socioenvironmental conditions are dynamically and subjectively enacted at the individual, household, and community levels. Furthermore, vulnerability at different scales may be characterized by different causal structures and response options. Local vulnerabilities cannot be summed to give a national estimate, while national estimates may mask differential vulnerabilities subnationally (Clark et al. 2000). The result is a variety of macro and micro approaches to vulnerability assessment.

Vulnerability assessment has most often relied on large-scale, aggregated indicators and indexes preselected from afar by scientists, policymakers, and practitioners (Corburn 2002). Early climatic change research was likewise predominantly large-scale, involving top-down, scenario-based, predictive assessments of climate change impacts. Overall, these macro-level assessments usually involve some combination of aggregating proxy measures of vulnerability, taking outer-ring threats as a starting point (i.e., an outside-in approach to figure 2.4), predicting national and regional exposure, and/ or considering institutional and group response options. While they provide critical data for such interventions as humanitarian resource allocation, processes appearing homogeneous at aggregated scales may be heterogeneous at finer scales (Stephen and Downing 2002). Furthermore, large-scale assessments capture neither the complex experiences nor the uneven distributions of vulnerabilities within heterogeneous communities.

More recently, GEC research has undergone a reorientation toward assessments that take current vulnerabilities (rather than future threat scenarios) as a starting point (Brklacich and Bohle 2006), and researchers have begun examining differential vulnerabilities within nations, communities, and households (e.g., Kelly and Adger 2000). This suggests a growing trend toward micro-level, inside-out approaches: that is, starting from the inside of figure 2.4 to determine present-day and differential levels of vulnerability security for heterogeneous communities, and then attempting to map out the complex webs of causality and interaction within and between the three rings. Such approaches are "precautionary" in that they attempt to reduce current vulnerabilities by enabling individuals and communities to respond to current stressors and, in so doing, aim to simultaneously enhance longer-term security to multiple stressors (Kelly and Adger 2000).

Evidence that localized data adds value to vulnerability assessments contrasts, however, with a relative lack of studies on local areas and conditions (Stephen and Downing 2002). According to Cutter (2001), microlevel vulnerability assessment is constrained by a lack of data availability and appropriate analytical techniques. The trend to downscale is growing in academic circles, but significant gaps remain among academic, policy, and practitioner communities. There is a need to bridge these gaps as well as to develop participatory assessment strategies that involve multiple end-user groups, incorporate scientific and local expertise, recognize the subjective nature of vulnerability, and couple assessment with intervention.

The conceptual relationship among human security, vulnerability, and GEC that is depicted in figure 2.4 may therefore serve to guide future research and intervention strategies. Not discounting the place and contribution of large-scale assessments, the contextual nature of vulnerability supports recent emphasis on downscaled approaches that take current vulnerabilities as their starting point (i.e., microlevel inside-out approaches). These assessments focus subnationally and aim to enable response capacity in the immediate and longer terms by unraveling the complex causal webs that drive differential exposures and responses. While figure 2.4 offers some clues for investigating these intricate webs, further efforts are needed to refine local assessment methodologies and to bridge academic, policy, and practitioner communities.

Closing Remarks

Rapidly changing ecological, social, economic, demographic, and political conditions are altering the nature, magnitude, and frequency of threats facing communities worldwide. Spatially and temporally distant actions drive many of these changes, and social and environmental stressors tend to converge on certain places, sectors, and social groups. Those most vulnerable to global transformation are most often the least able to cope with or adapt to these changes, and there is an urgent need to understand the relationships between human security, vulnerability, and global change in order to improve the immediate and future well-being of individuals and communities.

This chapter provides a framework for conceptualizing the links between global environmental change and human security, as well as for guiding vulnerability assessments. This framework defines vulnerability and human security as dynamic, inversely related processes that predate GEC and other socioenvironmental stresses. It also delineates vulnerability as the interaction between external exposure to threats and internal capacity for response. Furthermore, four broad interrelated groups of sociopolitical and geographical attributes—control of and access to assets, institutional factors, distribution of rights and resources, and ecological and geographical conditions—underlie both exposure and response, and the centrality of these drivers contrasts earlier tendencies to de-contextualize or de-politicize vulnerability.

Exposure, response, and underlying drivers may all be impacted by the multiple and converging stressors resulting from cumulative effects of environmental and societal change. A significant challenge arising from the changing nature of threats to human security is that stressors and responses must now be considered at a variety of spatial and temporal scales. Movement along the continuum from vulnerability to security is most likely influenced by context-specific, local interactions between multi-scale stressors, exposure to threats, capacity for response, and socioenvironmental drivers. This contextual nature of vulnerability supports trends toward micro-level approaches to vulnerability assessment.

References

Adger, N. 1999. Social vulnerability to climate change and extremes in coastal Vietnam. *World Development* 27 (2): 249–269.

Bandura, Albert. 1995. Exercise of personal and collective efficacy in changing societies. In *Self-efficacy in changing societies*, ed. Albert Bandura, 1–68. Cambridge, UK: Cambridge University Press.

Bohle, H-G. 2001. Vulnerability and criticality. *IHDP Newsletter Update* 2: Article 1.

Brklacich, M., and H-G. Bohle. 2006. Assessing human vulnerability to climatic change. In *Earth system science in the Anthropocene: Emerging issues and problems*, ed T. Krafft and E. Ehliers, 51–61. New York: Springer.

Burton, Ian, Robert W. Kates, and Gilbert F. White. 1993. *The environment as hazard*. New York: Guilford.

Chen, L., and V. Narasimhan. 2003. A human security agenda for global health. In *Global health challenges and for human security*, ed. L. Chen, J. Leaning, and V. Narasimhan, 3–12. Cambridge, MA: Global Equity Initiative Asia Center, Harvard University.

Clark, William C., et al. 2000. *Assessing the vulnerability to global environmental risks*. Cambridge, MA: Belfer Center for Science & International Affairs, Harvard University.

Corburn, J. 2002. Environmental justice, local knowledge and risk: The discourse of a community-based cumulative exposure assessment. *Environmental Management* 29 (4): 451–466.

Cutter, S. 2001. A research agenda for vulnerability and environmental hazards. *IHDP Newsletter Update* 2: Article 3.

Daily, G., and P. Ehrlich. 1996. Global change and human susceptibility to disease. *Annual Review of Energy and Environment* 21:125–144.

Davis, M. 2004. *Late Victorian holocausts: El Niño famines and the making of the Third World*. London: Verso.

Emel, J., and R. Peet. 1989. Resources management and natural hazards. In *New models in geography, volume 1*, ed. R. Peet and N. Thrift, 49–76. London: Unwin Hyman.

Kelly, M., and N. Adger. 2000. Theory and practice in assessing vulnerability to climate change and facilitating adaptation. *Climatic Change* 47:325–352.

Leitmann, J. 2003. Urbanization and environmental change: Issues and options for human security. *AVISO*, Issue 11.1.

Lonergan, S. 1999. *Global Environmental Change and Human Security (GECHS) science plan*. IHDP Report No. 11. Bonn, Germany: IHDP.

Martens, P., A. J. McMichael, and J. A. Patz. 2000. Globalisation, environmental change and health. *Global Change and Human Health* 1 (1): 4–8.

McMichael, A., and R. Beaglehole. 2000. The changing global context on public health. *The Lancet* 356:489–499.

McMichael, A., et al. 1999. Globalization and the sustainability of human health: An ecological perspective. *BioScience* 49 (3): 205–209.

Mimura, N., L. Nurse, R. F. McLean, J. Agard, L. Briguglio, P. Lefale, R. Payet, and G. Sem. 2007. Small islands. Climate Change 2007: Impacts, Adaptation and Vulnerability. In *Contribution of Working Group II to the Fourth Assessment Report of the Intergovernmental Panel on Climate Change*, ed. M. L. Parry, O. F. Canziani, J. P. Palutikof, P. J. van der Linden, and C. E. Hanson, 687–716. Cambridge, UK: Cambridge University Press.

Mitchell, J. K. 1989. Hazards research. In *Geography in America*, ed. G. Gaile C. Willmott, 410–424. Columbus, OH: Merrill.

Mittelman, J. 2002. Making globalization work for the have-nots. *International Journal on World Peace* 19 (2): 3–25.

Mustafa, D. 1998. Structural causes of vulnerability to flood hazard in Pakistan. *Economic Geography* 74 (3): 289–305.

Nicastri, E., E. Girardi, and G. Ippolito. 2001. Determinants of emerging and re-emerging infectious diseases. *Journal of Biological Regulators and Homeostatic Agents* 15 (3): 212–217.

O'Brien, K., and R. Leichenko. 2000. Double exposure: Assessing the impacts of climate change within the context of economic globalisation. *Global Environmental Change* 10:221–232.

O'Brien, K., and C. Vogel. 2004. Vulnerability to global environmental change: Rhetoric and reality. *AVISO*, Issue 13.

Steffan, W., et al., eds. 2004. *Global change and the earth systems: A planet under stress*. Berlin: Springer-Verlag.

Stephen, L., and T. Downing. 2002. Getting the scale right: A comparison of analytical methods for vulnerability assessment and household-level targeting. *Disasters* 25:113–135.

Twigg, John, and Mihir R. Bhatt, eds. 1998. *Understanding vulnerability: South Asian perspectives*. London: Intermediate Technology Publications.

Watts, M. J., and H-G. Bohle. 1993. The space of vulnerability and the causal structure of hunger and famine. *Progress in Human Geography* 17:43–67.

Weisbrot, M., D. Baker, E. Kraev, and J. Chen. 2002. The scorecard on globalization 1980–2000: Its consequences for economic and social well-being. *International Journal of Health Services* 32 (2): 229–253.

Wilbanks, T., and R. Kates. 1999. Global change in local places: How scale matters. *Climatic Change* 43: 601–628.

Williams, L., R. Labonte, and M. O'Brien. 2003. Empowering social action through narratives of identity and culture. *Health Promotion International* 18 (1): 33–40.

Wuebbles, D. J., and N. J. Rosenberg. 1998. The natural science of global climate change. In *Human choice andclimate change: An international assessment, Volume 2, Resources and technology*, ed. S. Rayner and E. L. Malone, 1–78. Columbus, OH: Battelle Press.

3

Global Health and Human Security: Addressing Impacts from Globalization and Environmental Change

Bryan McDonald

During the twentieth century, it was hoped that advances in medicine, technology, and public health would significantly reduce, and perhaps even eradicate, health threats to human security. Efforts to improve human health and fight disease have resulted in significant improvements in global health: vaccinations dramatically reduced incidences of polio, the development of antibiotics provided an important tool in treating many bacteriological infections, and a decade-long international effort was successful at eradicating smallpox as a naturally occurring disease (Armelagos 1998). To many in the global health community, it seemed as if humanity stood on the verge of a golden age where science and medicine— along with improvements in sanitation, infrastructure, and technology —would lead to a future where persistent health threats from sources such as infectious disease could be treated and cured.

The dawn of the twenty-first century, however, has seen an increased recognition of the continued threats to human security from global health challenges. In an increasingly globalized and interconnected world, the landscape of health threats that contribute to human insecurity is being reshaped by an array of factors including population growth, increased volume of international trade flows, changing patterns of human habitation, and global environmental change. When seeking to understand the security implications of such changes, it is helpful to expand discussions beyond consideration of the security of states to also include human security issues that impact the safety and livelihoods of individuals. While the origin and impact of the concept of human security has been assessed in detail elsewhere in this volume (see chapter 1), it is worth briefly considering the relevance of the concept to the current discussion of global health.

Human security has been broadly defined as freedom from fear and want, or as protecting and empowering the world's most vulnerable people. The concept of human security was the focus of the United Nations Development Programme's (UNDP) 1994 Human Development Report. The idea of human security was identified as having two main aspects: "It means, first, safety from such chronic threats as hunger, disease and repression. And second, it means protection from sudden and harmful disruptions in the patterns of daily life ... the loss of human security can be a slow, silent process-or an abrupt, loud emergency" (UNDP 1994, 23). UNDP identified seven main categories of threat to human security: economic security, food security, health security, environmental security, personal security, community security, and political security. Additionally, the report identifies four essential characteristics of human security: it is a universal concern, its components are interdependent, it is easier to ensure through early prevention rather than later intervention, and it is people-centered (UNDP 1994). The Global Environmental Change and Human Security (GECHS) project further refines the definition of human security "as something that is achieved when and where individuals and communities have the options necessary to end, mitigate or adapt to threats to their human, environmental and social rights; have the capacity and freedom to exercise these options; and actively participate in pursuing these options" (GECHS 1999). These definitions stress the importance of moving discussions of security beyond the scale of the nation-state, to include issues that impact the daily lives of individuals and communities around the world.

Adopting a human security perspective on global health challenges also recognizes the broad significance of good health and that localized health emergencies can become global situations very rapidly. The Commission on Human Security found that good health is essential to human security "because the very heart of human security is protecting lives" (2003, 96). Interconnections between health and human security have also led to a commonalty of purpose between efforts to improve health and well-being and national security efforts to ensure stable public health in a shared focus on ensuring national security by dramatically improving global public health (National Intelligence Council 2000; Brower and Chalk 2003).

An important characteristic of human security is its emphasis on the importance of preventive measures as opposed to reactive efforts. Many threats to global health can be most effectively addressed through preventive measures. In developing countries, efforts to improve the distribution of cheap, reliable bed nets demonstrate that, despite advances in the treatment of malaria, the most effective interventions are simple ones that reduce the spread of disease among human populations. In developed countries, recognition of the health costs of growing epidemics of obesity and of diseases such as diabetes has prompted a renewed interest in promoting good health during a person's lifespan rather than waiting for the development of a costly and difficult-to-treat health condition. Persistent health threats, such as malnutrition, contribute to multiple sources of human insecurity; improving the health and well-being of individuals is one strategy to address these enduring failures of development. While the increasing speed and scale of transnational interactions has created or amplified many security challenges, in terms of the magnitude of impact of the daily lives of people and communities around the world, threats to global health remain one of the most significant and unrelenting challenges facing humanity in the twenty-first century.

This chapter argues that improving global health is a significant and necessary component of efforts to ensure human security. Following an overview of the links between health and human security, this chapter considers two main dimensions of the relationship between global health and human security. First, it explores how increased global interconnectedness between human populations facilitates the rapid diffusion of infectious diseases and other global health threats. Second, the chapter examines how global environmental changes are accelerating and extending disease vectors and complicating global health challenges. Next, the chapter considers actions necessary to address global health challenges, including the role of actors and institutions at a variety of levels of activities. Finally, it concludes with a discussion of the relevance of human security to developing the programs, policies, and tools necessary to enable individual and communities to take active and meaningful roles in helping define, prioritize, and address global health needs.

Global Health and Human Security

A number of factors—including the October 2001 anthrax incidents in the United States, the 2003 outbreak of severe acute respiratory syndrome (SARS), and the more recent attention to the ongoing danger of pandemic influenza—have raised awareness of the need to address health threats to human security (Garrett 2005; Karesh and Cook 2005;

WHO 2007d). The World Health Organization (WHO) refers to this challenge as improving global public health security or as "the activities required, both proactive and reactive, to minimize vulnerability to acute public health events that endanger the collective health of populations living across geographical regions and international boundaries" (WHO 2007d, xi). This definition highlights the varied, fluid, and transnational nature of threats to global health.

A major source of global health threats to human security comes from infectious diseases. Infectious diseases "are caused by pathogenic micro-organisms, such as bacteria, viruses, parasites or fungi; the diseases can be spread, directly or indirectly, from one person to another" (WHO 2008). Infectious diseases are spread through the transmission of a pathogenic microorganism from an infected host to another organism along four pathways: (1) direct contact with an infected organism; (2) airborne transmission when microorganisms attach to dust particles or when they are contained in aerosols; (3) contact with a contaminated common vehicle, such as food, water, or blood; and (4) by vector-borne spread such as an insect (McNamara 2007).

Infectious diseases are a major global cause of death. As shown in table 3.1, the everyday health and well-being of many people is also impacted by infectious diseases, and each year millions of people succumb to diseases like HIV/AIDS, malaria, and tuberculosis. There are also im-

Table 3.1
Magnitude and impact of HIV/AIDS, malaria, and tuberculosis

Disease	Magnitude and impacts
HIV/AIDS	There are between 30.6 and 36.1 million people living with HIV and between 1.9 and 2.4 million annual deaths from AIDS (United Nations Programme on HIV/AIDS and World Health Organization 2007).
Malaria	Malaria remains a persistent threat to human health. Approximately 40 percent of the world's population, many of whom live in the world's poorest countries, are at risk of malaria. Every year, more than 500 million people become severely ill with malaria (WHO 2007a).
Tuberculosis	In 2005 there were 8.8 million new cases of Tuberculosis (TB), 7.4 million of these cases occurring in sub-Saharan Africa and Asia. In the same year, 1.6 million people died of TB, including 195,000 who were also infected with HIV (WHO 2007b).

portant and significant interactive effects between diseases. For example, though deadly in its own right, tuberculosis (TB) has made the news in recent years due to an increase in rates of infection among individuals with compromised immune systems; attention has also been focused on tuberculosis by a few cases involving globe-spanning travel by individuals with drug-resistant strains of the disease (U.S. Centers for Disease Control 2007). Though disease has always had the ability to destabilize localized populations and economies, the increasing speed and scale of interactions of widely dispersed human populations adds to the potential scope and impact of disease's resulting disorder.

Alongside the increasingly globalized spread of disease, emerging forms of infectious disease are a major challenge to global health (Jones et al. 2008). "Since the 1970s, newly emerging diseases have been identified at an unprecedented rate of one or more per year. There are now 40 diseases that were unknown a decade ago" (WHO 2007d, 6). The 2003 outbreak of severe acute respiratory syndrome provided a real-world example of the rapid pace with which infectious diseases could emerge and spread. "SARS was first reported in Asia in February 2003. Over the next few months, the illness spread to more than two dozen countries in North America, South America, Europe, and Asia before the SARS global outbreak of 2003 was contained" (U.S. Centers for Disease Control 2005). Newly emerging diseases are reminders that the landscape of disease humanity faces is continually evolving.

Infectious diseases contribute to, exacerbate, and sometimes even cause significant and widespread impacts on individuals, communities, and societies. Table 3.2 discusses three historical examples of the widespread and significant impacts of infectious disease on human societies. The impacts of disease are not limited to causing death and illness. A 2003 study by the Institute of Medicine found that "the ability of infectious agents to destabilize populations, economies, and governments is fast becoming a sad fact of life. The prevention and control of infectious diseases are fundamental to individual, national, and global health and security" (Smolinski, Hamburg, and Lederberg 2003). Not only does ill health negatively impact individuals, but it is directly correlated to poverty and other forms of disenfranchisement. The World Health Organization reports that "ongoing ill-health is one of the main reasons why the poor stay poor. Infections lead to poverty, and poverty leads to infections. For every person who died, many more still lived on, but were

Table 3.2
Historical examples of infectious disease impacts

Disease	Impact
Bubonic Plague	An outbreak of bubonic plague that struck Europe between 1346 and 1350 is estimated to have caused mortality in approximately one third of the total population of Europe (McNeill 1998).
Pandemic Influenza	The 1918 Spanish Influenza pandemic sickened approximately 20–40 percent of the global population and is estimated to have killed more than 500,000 in the United States and 20 million people globally (Crosby 1990; U.S. Department of Health and Human Services 2004).
Smallpox	The eradication of smallpox as a naturally occurring disease is often cited as one of the greatest triumphs of medicine in the twentieth century, for good reason. In the century prior to its eradication, smallpox claimed hundreds of millions of lives and by some estimates killed half a billion people (Tucker 2001).

reduced to poverty, their health and their lives affected by frequent bouts of illness" (WHO 2002, 12).

The impact of infectious diseases and ill health is increased by interactive effects from hunger and poor nutrition. For example, beyond the health problems directly caused by lack of proper nutrition, malnutrition "magnifies the effect of every disease, including measles and malaria" (World Hunger Education Service 2006). Negative impacts from threats to health also include weakening the workforce and the economic foundation of a state, undermining confidence in a state's ability to protect and provide for its population, challenging the ability of states to recruit, train, and retain security relevant forces such as military forces (a challenge that is especially acute in areas such as sub-Saharan Africa that are heavily impacted by HIV/AIDS) as well as negatively affecting peoples' social and cultural lives (Brower and Chalk 2003).

In addition to naturally occurring infectious diseases, threats to global health also exist from the intentional use of biological agents for purposes such as warfare, terrorism, or criminal endeavors. Awareness of the possibility of such intentional use of biological agents to cause harm was increased after the events of September 11, 2001, and the Amerithrax anthrax incidents in the fall of 2001. Beginning one week after the September 11 attacks, the Amerithrax incidents occurred between September and November 2001 and involved anthrax spores spread through the mail system in letters containing anthrax spores. These letters sent to media organizations in New York and Florida as well as the offices of two Democratic senators, Tom Daschle of South Dakota and Patrick Leahy of Vermont, resulted in anthrax infections in at least twenty-two individuals, with eleven of these cases presenting as life-threatening inhalation anthrax, and caused the death of five people (Federal Bureau of Investigation 2008). The anthrax attacks were especially catalyzing in terms of the potential impact of attacks using biological agents, and following the incidents, much attention was given to the vulnerability of citizens, livestock, and the food supplies to intentional attacks using biological weapons (Whitby and Rogers 1997; U.S. Centers for Disease Control 2000; 2001a, b; U.S. Food and Drug Administration 2003).

Security threats from the intentional use of biological agents are not new; there is a general sense that advances in technology, coupled with increased mobility, have created the conditions for a new, more elusive threat from biological weapons. The Biological and Toxin Weapons Convention (BTWC), which was opened for signature in April 1972 and entered into force in March 1975, outlawed the development and use of biological weapons and led to the closure of most state-based research in offensive biological weapons. The defection of a key scientist from the former Soviet Union in the 1990s revealed that significant research programs into biological weapons continued to exist even though the U.S.S.R. had signed the BTWC (Alibek, with Handelman 1999). Disclosures such as these demonstrate the difficulty involved in monitoring the development of biological weapons. In November 2003, the Central Intelligence Agency released a report that warned that "advances in biotechnology, coupled with difficulty in detecting nefarious biological activity, have the potential to create a much more dangerous biological warfare threat" (Central Intelligence Agency 2003). While concerns about the threat from nefarious uses of biological weapons have received a great deal of policy and media attention, especially in the period after the September 11 attacks and in the lead-up to the 2003 War in Iraq, it is important to note that as of 2008, instances of terrorist or criminal activity involving biological agents have caused mortality (death) and morbidity (illness) in relatively low numbers of people (Torok et al. 1997; Tucker 2000; WHO 2007d).

Despite a great deal of public and policy attention to nefarious biological threats in recent years, many more people are impacted on a daily basis by chronic infectious disease threats and problems like malnutrition and a lack of clean water, highlighting the fact that efforts to ensure human security from global health threats must address both natural infectious diseases and potential nefarious uses of biological agents. Popular media coverage of weaponized biological agents and their potential use tends to focus on the gruesome aspects of their use, but specialists urge that we be mindful that "the revulsion evoked by these weapons does not push us to take actions with unacceptable adverse effects on competing interests, including the promotion of legitimate research, civil liberties and public health" (Stern 2002, 123). In its 2007 World Health Report, the World Health Organization identifies preparing for deliberate disease outbreaks (along with the potential for health impacts from accidental or deliberate chemical or nuclear incidents) as one of a much broader range of challenges that face the global public health community including naturally occurring disease, accidental contamination of food and water systems, severe weather events, industrial accidents, environmental change, and the potential use of diseases intentionally harnessed to serve nefarious ends (WHO 2007d). Global health and security communities should not let preparing for the possibility of nefarious infectious disease threats impede efforts to make real progress on more pervasive threats to global health and human security.

While numerous factors are responsible for the spread and impact of infectious disease, the nature of threats from infectious disease has been accelerated by development of an increasingly interconnected world. Not only have technological innovation and globalization processes increased flows of people and goods, but they have also led to a considerable reduction in the time required to travel from one part of the world to the next.

Global Health in a Networked World

Processes of economic, political, and social globalization have brought increased interconnectedness, mobility, and access for transnational flows of people, information, and goods. Ulrich Beck describes globalization as "processes through which sovereign national actors are crisscrossed and undermined by transnational actors with varying prospects for power, orientations, identities, and networks" (2000, 11). Changes brought by globalization, combined with reduced capacity of governments to address pressing issues, and an increasing role of nonstate actors in national and international politics have produced a considerable amount of turbulence in world affairs (Rosneau 1990). This global turbulence, as well as globalization processes themselves, has also led to transformations in the landscape of global security threats. There is also a growing sense that some contemporary security challenges—such as infectious disease, terrorism, and trafficking in drugs, people, or illegal goods—operate in different ways than traditional challenges in that they are transnational, meaning they cross borders but generally cannot be directly linked to foreign policies and state behaviors (Matthew and Shambaugh 1998, 163).

In response to globalization's promoting closeness of previously disparate places and people, the notion of a "network" has gained increasing salience with scholars who use it to clarify the complexities of this evolution in global connectivity and describe the evolving structure of relations among people, places, and things. Many types of networks exist, from information networks like the World Wide Web to transportation networks like the air transit system. Physicist Albert-László Barabási writes, "Today we increasingly recognize that nothing happens in isolation. Most events and phenomena are connected, caused by, and interacting with a huge number of other pieces of a complex universal puzzle. We have come to see that we live in a small world, where everything is linked to everything else" (2003, 7). The impact of these connections, Barbasi continues, is that "we have come to grasp the importance of networks" (7). Networks impact many areas of daily life from transportation, to judicial practices, to health and security (Matthew and Shambaugh 1998; Matthew, McDonald, and Rutherford 2004; Slaughter 2004).

Our increasingly networked world provides tremendous advantages for the exchange of information, capital, and people, but increased global interconnectedness has also resulted in a closer connection among the world's populations, economies, and ecologies. This connectivity facilitates the rapid spread of diseases and amplifies other threats to global health. Where human populations once interacted at the speed of travel by foot or animal, they move by automobiles and airplanes. In its 2007 World Health Report, the World Health Organization writes, "2.1 billion airline passengers travelled in 2006; an outbreak or epidemic in any one part of the world is only a few hours away from becoming an imminent threat somewhere else" (WHO 2007d, x). Airline travel is only one indicator of the growing web of connections among people in disparate parts of the world.

The global food system has also been impacted by the increasing speed and scale of connections. Largely a source of safe and healthful food, the global food system is a major connector between many different peoples and places and it can also be a vector for the transmission of disease. In 2003, for example, one-third of global meat exports (6 million tonnes) were affected by an animal disease outbreak (FAO 2004). Contamination of food supplies can sicken large numbers of people over a vast geographic area in a relatively short period of time (Ryan et al. 1987). Infectious diseases are often closely related to food systems and, even in the absence of direct impacts on human populations, can cause tremendous economic, political, and social harm. For example, avian influenza A (H591) is only one of a series of livestock disease outbreaks that have caused losses of more than $100 billion (not including HIV/AIDS) over the past fifteen years (Karesh and Cook 2005).

The development of a more networked world has coincided with significant changes in the patterns of human habitation on the planet. The United Nations predicts that by the end of 2008 half of the world's population will be living in urban areas, and urban areas will absorb almost all the projected global population increase through 2050 (United Nations 2008). The rates of urbanization will vary widely and will largely occur in cities that currently have a population of less than 500,000 inhabitants (United Nations 2008). An increase in urban populations will lead to a continuation, if not acceleration, of trends associated with rapid urban growth in the twentieth century, including insufficient sanitation, education, and public health systems (this topic is discussed in greater detail in chapter 4).

Although more and more people are living in urban areas and peri-urban areas, many people, especially poor people, continue to live in rural environments, and their lifestyles and settlement patterns are also a significant factor in shaping the global health landscape. According to the World Bank, 75 percent of poor people in developing countries live in rural areas, and these people are increasingly forced onto degraded or marginal land in an effort to survive (World Bank 2007, 1). In these marginal spaces, many rural poor seek food sources from wild animal populations, and these interactions between humans and wild animal species are an important factor in the emergence of new infectious diseases. Over

60 percent of identified infectious diseases can affect both humans and animals, and many diseases transfer to humans through processes involved in the killing, processing, and consumption of animals (Karesh and Cook 2005).

Shifting patterns of human habitation also create new edge zones and intermingling population compositions that create fertile ground for the emergence and spread of infectious diseases. The rapid pace of modern transportation means that diseases that emerge in one location can move rapidly into others. In such an urbanized and interconnected world, it is unlikely that spatial distance or geographic barriers, such as mountain ranges or oceans, will provide much protection from infectious disease.

There is also an important distributional nature of health challenges that must be considered when developing health solutions. Globalization has led to increasing levels of connectivity, but the impacts of this connectivity are not equally distributed. Timothy W. Luke writes that while globalization is a long-running series of processes that have led to real increases in material progress, not all of the improvements are being shared equally (2001). Increasing numbers of people, in both developed and developing countries, face health threats related to their diet and lifestyle such as obesity, heart disease, and diabetes. Concurrently, others face health threats from infectious disease, poor sanitation, inadequate nutrition, and lack of clean water.

Efforts to improve global health must take into account these basic inequalities, with awareness that too often solutions are debated and developed in rich countries and applied to poor countries. In recent years, there has been a growing focus on the way that developments in science and technology may make possible great improvements in human health and well-being (Luke 2001). Many of these solutions rely on high-technology approaches such as genetically reengineering the genome of mosquitoes to make them unable to serve as a vector for the spread of malaria parasites or the development of new generations of genetically modified crops that could be used to distribute vaccines. Despite the focus on the promise and potential of high-technology solutions to improve global health, "improvements in overall health measures for most of humanity will not come from 21st century medicine, but rather from 19th century public health practices" (Luke 2001, 15). Achieving improvements in global health will require strategic partnerships that reduce threats from infectious disease by supporting general increases in public health and well-being.

Global Environmental Change and Global Health

Changes in environmental conditions have been a major driver of the changing landscape of health threats impacting human societies; it is important to recognize that the current era is not alone in facing a shifting landscape of health challenges. The relationship between humans and diseases has not been static, and even the nature of what is considered a disease has altered over time. As historian William McNeill comments, "Nearsightedness and a dull sense of smell, which we regard as compatible with good health, would probably have been classed as crippling disease by our hunting ancestors...a person who can no longer perform expected tasks because of bodily disorder will always seem diseased to his fellows" (1998, 27).

While disease has remained a constant factor in human history, it is possible to identify important shifts in the relationship between humans and diseases. Demographer Abdel Omran (1971) recognized that due to the development of better public health measures, improvements in nutrition, and advances in medicine, there had been what he called an "epidemiological transition" where major causes of death in most industrialized nations shifted from infectious diseases to diseases of civilization like cancer, diabetes, and clogged arteries. Anthropologist George Armelagos (1998) and his colleagues have extended Omran's work to suggest that human activities have led to three major epidemiological transitions. The first transition occurred around ten thousand years ago as humans first began shifting from hunter-gatherers to agricultural societies. Omran's work was based on a second transition that began with the Industrial Revolution in the eighteenth century where technology, urban planning, infrastructure development, and modern medicine seemed to be winning the war against infectious disease. The third epidemiological transition centers around recognition that proclamations of a golden age of public health might have been premature, as rapid population growth, accelerating urbanization, global environmental change, and the increasing rapidity of movement of goods and people have given rise to new concerns about infectious disease (Armelagos 1998).

Throughout human history, changes in environmental conditions have been a major driver of the changing landscape of health threats impacting human societies (Crosby 1990; Diamond 1999). Local and global changes to the earth's ecological systems accelerate interactions and extend the range of vectors that spread infectious diseases (Brower and

Chalk 2003; Smolinski, Hamburg, and Lederberg 2003). Perhaps the most widespread and far-reaching set of changes are those related to global climate change. There is general agreement that human activities have contributed to changes in the earth's climate system. The Intergovernmental Panel on Climate Change warned, "Warming of the climate system is unequivocal, as is now evident from observations of increases in global average air and ocean temperatures, widespread melting of snow and ice, and rising global average sea level" (2007). The *Stern Review* (2007) identifies a number of threats from climate change to the basic component of human livelihoods, including melting glaciers, declining crop yields, ocean acidification, rising sea levels, and a variety of impacts on ecosystems and species.

Based on these expected impacts, prominent global leaders have called for recognizing climate change as one of the highest-priority issues facing the international community. Speaking in 2006, former UN Secretary-General Kofi Annan stated, "Global climate change must take its place alongside those threats—conflict, poverty, the proliferation of deadly weapons—that have traditionally monopolized first-order political attention" (2006). The impacts of climate change are expected to be widespread and felt in a range of systems and sectors including water resources, health, and food production. Yet, the impacts from climate change will not be equally distributed. While regions of Africa and Asia will face increasing levels of water scarcity, compromised food production, and impacts to coastal areas that could reduces fisheries and tourism revenues, regions like North America could see a 5–20 percent increase in agricultural yields, at least in the near term (Intergovernmental Panel on Climate Change 2007).

Climate change could have a number of impacts directly related to global health, the most significant being an alteration in the range of pathogens and hosts and an increase in extreme weather events. "Climate can directly impact disease transmission through its effects on the replication and movement (and perhaps evolution) of disease microbes and vectors" (National Research Council 2001). Diseases are most devastating when they first encounter populations that have not developed any resistance or immunity to the disease, and climate change could contribute to exposing many people to new diseases for the first time by extending the range of pathogens and carriers of pathogens. For example, "a slight overall temperature increase would allow the mosquitoes that carry dengue fever to survive as far north as New York City"

(Armelagos 1998, 28). Localized climate variability has been linked to the emergence of diseases in areas where it was previously unknown, such as an outbreak of hantavirus in the United States in 1993 that has been tied to an El Niño event where increased rainfall and warmer temperatures contributed to an abundance of deer mice, the carriers for hantavirus (Smolinski, Hamburg, and Lederberg 2003).

Climate change could also contribute to disease by increasing the frequency, intensity, and duration of extreme weather events (Intergovernmental Panel on Climate Change 2007). Events such as hurricanes, monsoons, and landslides disrupt social, economic, health, and sanitation systems, and create conditions favorable to the spread of disease (Brower and Chalk 2003). Already, the impacts of climate change are linked to increasing severity of weather patterns such as the heat wave that struck Europe in 2003 and claimed the lives of 35,000 people (WHO 2007d, 8). Beyond direct impacts, climate change could also impact the incidence and severity of infectious diseases indirectly, such as the potential for climate change that produced a drop in food production, "thereby producing undernourished human populations more vulnerable to disease" (Smolinski, Hamburg, and Lederberg 2003, 65). As this discussion reveals, the potential impacts, both direct and indirect, of climate change on global health are complex and far-reaching. Such effects could be even more disruptive given that their scope would not be limited to human populations, but could also increase biodiversity loss through impacts on plant and animal populations (Harvell et al. 2002).

In addition to changing the global climate system, other human-induced environmental changes have had a significant and widespread effect on the global environment. Through processes such as land clearance and deforestation, human activities have had a significant impact on land resources; the UN estimates that such human activity has negatively affected the productivity of almost a quarter of arable land (United Nations Environment Programme 2002). Human impacts have been equally significant with regard to forests, oceans, and populations of animal and plants species.

The changes that humans make to environmental systems affect the magnitude and type of diseases they encounter. Efforts to lessen or reverse effects of deforestation often involve efforts to restore vegetation to cleared areas. Merely restoring vegetation without the complex ecosystem that was replaced can lead to problems with increased incidence of diseases. For instance, reforestation in the northeastern United States led to an increase in the white-tail deer populations and a resulting growth in population of deer ticks that are a primary vector for the spread of Lyme disease. As humans entered reforested areas for recreational purposes or built suburbs near these areas, Lyme disease increased in incidence in areas and populations where it was previously unknown (Barbour and Fish 1993).

Environmental changes have also created new edge zones where disease and environments meet and mix, often with lethal results. An example of this phenomenon can be found in the 1991 cholera outbreak in Latin America that was traced to the ballast water of a ship from Asia offloaded in the harbor of Callao, Peru. The epidemic spread to Peru's neighbors, ultimately infecting over 320,000 people and killing 2,600, and was particularly virulent as it involved a strain of cholera resistant to antibiotics thought to have emerged in the highly polluted waters of major seaports (Brower and Chalk 2003).

Processes of global environmental change will make efforts to improve global public health more complex as they will continue to change the landscape of health threats facing human populations. These threats may come directly through increases in the range of vectors that spread infectious disease. Impacts on global health may also be indirect, such as reduced agricultural productivity, increased water scarcity, or biodiversity losses to animal and fish populations that provide key sources of nutrition. The impact of environmental changes on agricultural systems will be diverse and widespread, and could include changes such as shifts in the ecological and economic viability of raising crops and animal species in a given environment, but also much more subtle changes such as impacts on species of soil bacteria that help fix nitrogen or encourage water intake or through loss of species such as honeybees and song birds that play key roles as pollinators.

Addressing Global Health Threats to Human Security

Recent high-profile health events have focused attention on the possibility of the rapid emergence and spread of a health threat of global significance. This attention has resulted in a number of concrete steps to prepare states and the global community to better work together to address health threats. In the United States, for example, the 2001 anthrax incidents motivated a significant increase in funding available to the U.S.

Centers for Disease Control and state and local public health departments (U.S. Centers for Disease Control 2008). While the funding resulted in significant improvements across a range of public health preparedness indicators, a 2008 assessment from the U.S. Centers for Disease Control found that states and cities still faced considerable challenges in their efforts to improve preparedness and response (U.S. Centers for Disease Control 2008). In addition to efforts to improve domestic preparedness, recognition that disease threats are a global issue has motivated the development of global systems, such as the United States Department of Defense's (2008) Global Emerging Infections Surveillance and Response System, to support global surveillance, training, research, and response to emerging infectious disease threats.

To improve international coordination and cooperation on global health issues, the World Health Assembly unanimously adopted a revised version of the International Health Regulations (IHR) on May 23, 2005, as a framework to guide global public health security. This framework "includes a commitment from WHO and from each of its 193 member states to improve capacity for disease prevention, detection, and response and provides ground rules to address national public health threats that have the potential to become global emergencies" (Rodier et al. 2007, 1448). The 2005 IHR updates a global framework that was adopted in 1969 and previously applied only to three infectious diseases: cholera, plague, and yellow fever. Rather than focusing on specific diseases, the revised IHR lays out requirements for notification of any health event that might have international significance. As well as providing a legal framework of requirements and expectations, these revised regulations also identify the important role that the development of strong and agile national-level health capabilities plays in addressing global health needs. The IHR recognizes that different countries have different capacities to develop, fund, and staff national public health institutes, and that actual development of capabilities will vary by country (Rodier et al. 2007).

While globalization has generated new types and magnitudes of health challenges, is has also created new possibilities for solutions and empowered the rise of new actors in global health efforts. States and international organizations such as the World Health Organization and the World Bank remain key participants in global efforts to improve health and well-being, but nonstate actors play an increasingly important role. Since its establishment in 2000, the Bill and Melinda Gates Foundation has provided $16.3 billion in grant commitments and has amassed an as-set trust endowment of $38.7 billion (Gates Foundation 2008). In con-trast, the World Health Organization, which serves as the directing and coordinating authority for health within the United Nations system, had a budget of just over $3 billion for the 2006–2007 operating year (WHO 2007c). The significance of an infusion of resources aimed at tackling global health problems has been recognized, but there is some debate about the lasting impact these resources will have on global health chal-lenges. Laurie Garrett writes that due to an "extraordinary and unprece-dented rise in public and private giving, more money is being directed toward pressing health challenges than ever before" (2007, 14). How-ever, Garrett finds that because the efforts funded by this increased giv-ing are uncoordinated, "there is a grave danger that the current generosity could not only fall short of expectations but actually make things worse on the ground" (14). The full impacts of nonstate actors taking on roles traditionally reserved for the state, such as provision of basic services like food and health, are unclear. If uncoordinated or at odds with the efforts of states and international organizations, efforts by nonstate actors could exacerbate the very problems they seek to alleviate.

Already, the impact of nongovernmental organizations like the Gates Foundation has been a subject of some debate. In February 2008, the *New York Times* provided a glimpse into the debate on the impact of the Gates Foundation when it published excerpts from a 2007 memo from the chief of the WHO's malaria program to the WHO's director complaining that the funding from the Gates Foundation aimed at fight-ing malaria could have "far reaching, largely unintended consequences," including "implicitly dangerous consequences on the policy making pro-cess in world health" (McNeil 2008). It is likely far too soon to pass judgment on the legacy and impact of organizations such as the Gates Foundation. Some critics charge that the focus of the foundation on a specific disease has had a number of unintended consequences that have contributed to a continued lack of meeting basic health needs. A 2007 investigation by the *Los Angeles Times*, for example, found "programs the foundation has funded...have had mixed influences on key mea-sures of societal health" (Piller and Smith 2007, 1). Others have argued that the Gates Foundation can play an important role in providing a needed independent voice in international health discussions through efforts such as the collection and dissemination of data that does not rely on often the unreliable data released by countries who may seek to downplay bad news (Economist 2008).

It is also important to recognize parallels in the debate about the accountability of nongovernmental actors in global health with similar debates about their role in issues such as the international effort to ban landmines (Matthew, McDonald, and Rutherford 2004) and in the environmental arena (Wapner 1996, 2002). As with the role of states, it is unhelpful to simply criticize the actions of nonstate actors, especially actors who are making real efforts to address major global health challenges. More helpful are critiques that seek to ensure that the efforts of all actors—be they state, international, or nonstate—are transparent, are participatory, and do not get overly focused on goals such as the elimination of a particular disease. Instead, these actors should concentrate on the need to invest the resources necessary in an effort that will likely take decades, or perhaps even generations, to improve health care across a range of areas—including needs such as public health capacity, infrastructure, staffing, training, and retention of personnel—that will foster general improvements in health and well-being (Wapner 2002; Garrett 2007).

A topic of considerable significance to efforts to address health threats to human security will be the degree to which efforts by actors at various levels and in various sectors can be brought together to increase health and human security. Increased global attention on the likely impacts of climate change and efforts to mitigate and adapt to coming changes could provide a key unifying theme, especially for efforts to reduce health threats that have environmental components. Improving health can be an integral component of efforts to improve living conditions for all the world's peoples. Efforts to promote community-level investment through strategies like microcredit financing can also involve the creation of community-based health insurance programs to help reduce the impact of poor health on individuals and families. Strategic conservation and sustainable development initiatives could also be used to create ecologically robust buffer zones, cleaner waterways, and resilient ecosystems that help keep disease-carrying organisms in check. While new technologies may offer promise and potential, efforts to develop and implement them should not distract from the many real gains to health that can be achieved through strategies such as improvements in basic nutrition, vitamin intake, and the development of water and sanitation systems.

Conclusion

A cornerstone of conceptualizations of human security is that all people must have the ability to address the things that create disruptions in their daily lives and present threats to their health and well-being. This chapter has focused on discussing the evolving nature of threats to global health with a focus on two primary dimensions: the implication of increasing connections among the world's populations, economies, and ecologies; and the way global environmental change is reshaping the landscape of global health threats. These two dimensions are not intended to be a complete mapping of the landscape of global health threats.

Indeed, there are many sources of threat and vulnerability involved in maximizing global health; however, the preceding discussion demonstrates that as people and places in our world grow more closely linked, it becomes more and more difficult to distinguish health concerns from global environmental change. Timothy W. Luke observes, "Health and the environment cannot be divided in the 21st century" (2001, 15). Recognizing this interdependence between health and environment is essential to developing meaningful strategies to address threats to global health. This interdependence is also integral to conceptualizations of human security "as something that is achieved when and where individuals and communities have the options necessary to end, mitigate or adapt to threats to their human, environmental and social rights" (GECHS 1999). In our turbulent, transnational, and networked world, meeting global health needs will involve state and nonstate diplomatic, security, health, and development organizations working together to achieve goals that none of them are able to achieve independently.

Addressing global health challenges must also be done in ways that are mindful of the goals of human security to protect and empower individuals and communities by creating conditions where people "have the capacity and freedom to exercise these options; and actively participate in pursuing these options" (GECHS 1999). Too often, "the structuring of the future is taking place indirectly and unrecognizably in research laboratories and executive suites, not in the parliament or in political parties. Everyone else—even the most responsible and best informed people in politics and science—more or less lives off the crumbs of information that fall from the planning tables of technological sub-politics" (Beck

1992, 223). One of the essential functions of efforts to address health threats to human security is that they elevate discussions about how to reduce threat and vulnerability from subpolitical arenas into political forums where individuals and communities can be involved in defining problems, prioritizing efforts, and developing solutions.

The promise of public health in the twentieth century was a world free from disease and ill health. While the lessons of past decades may have dimmed hopes that health challenges and infectious disease will ever be part of humanity's past, the magnitude of impacts on human livelihood and well-being from global health threats like infectious disease and environmental change make it clear that improving the health of people around the world is a necessary component of efforts to maximize human security.

References

Alibek, Ken, with Stephen Handelman. 1999. *Biohazard: The chilling true story of the largest covert biological weapons program in the world—told from the inside by the man who ran it.* New York: Delta.

Annan, Kofi. 2006. Annan stresses climate threat at UNFCCC conference. http://www.unep.org/Documents.Multilingual/Default.asp?DocumentID=495&ArticleID=5424&l=en (accessed November 15, 2008).

Armelagos, George J. 1998. The viral superhighway. *The Sciences* (January/February): 24–29.

Barabási, Albert-László. 2003. *Linked: How everything is connected to everything else and what it means for business, science, and everyday life.* New York: Plume.

Barbour, A. G., and D. Fish. 1993. The biological and social phenomenon of Lyme disease. Science 260 (11): 1610–1616.

Beck, Ulrich. 1992. *Risk society: Towards a new modernity.* London: Sage.

Beck, Ulrich. 2000. *What is Globalization?* Cambridge, UK: Polity Press.

Brower, Jennifer, and Peter Chalk. 2003. *The global threat of new and reemerging infectious disease: Reconciling U.S. national security and public health policy.* Arlington, VA: RAND.

Central Intelligence Agency. 2003. The darker bioweapons future. www.fas.org/irp/cia/product/bw1103.pdf (accessed November 15, 2008).

Commission on Human Security. 2003. *Human security now.* New York: Commission on Human Security.

Crosby, Alfred. 1990. *America's forgotten pandemic: The influenza of 1918.* Cambridge, UK: Cambridge University Press.

Diamond, Jared. 1999. *Guns, germs and steel: The fates of human societies*. New York: W. W. Norton.

Economist. 2008. The side effect of doing good. *The Economist*, February 21. http://www.economist.com/world/international/displaystory.cfm?story_id= 10729975 (accessed November 15, 2008).

Federal Bureau of Investigation. 2008. Amerithrax investigation. http://www.fbi .gov/anthrax/amerithraxlinks.htm (accessed November 15, 2008).

Food and Agriculture Organization of the United Nations (FAO). 2004. Animal disease outbreaks hit global meat exports: One-third of global meat exports affected—losses could be high. http://www.fao.org/newsroom/en/news/2004/ 37967/index.html (accessed November 15, 2008).

Garrett, Laurie. 2005. The next pandemic? *Foreign Affairs* 84 (4): 3–23.

Garrett, Laurie. 2007. The challenge of global health. *Foreign Affairs* 86 (1): 14–38.

Gates Foundation. 2008. Foundation fact sheet. http://www.gatesfoundation.org/ MediaCenter/FactSheet/ (accessed November 15, 2008).

GECHS. 1999. *Global Environmental Change and Human Security: GECHS science plan*. IHDP: Bonn.

Harvell, C. Drew, et al. 2002. Climate warming and disease risks for terrestrial and marine biota. *Science* 296 (June 21): 2158–2162.

Hennessy, T. W., et al. 1996. A national outbreak of Salmonella enteritidis infections from ice cream. *New England Journal of Medicine* 334:1281–1286.

Intergovernmental Panel on Climate Change. 2007. *Fourth assessment report. Climate change 2007: Synthesis report. Summary for policymakers*. http://www .ipcc.ch/pdf/assessment-report/ar4/syr/ar4_syr_spm.pdf (accessed November 15, 2008).

Jones, Kate, et al. 2008. Global trends on emerging infectious diseases. *Nature* 451 (21): 990–993.

Karesh, William B., and Robert A. Cook. 2005. "The Human-Animal Link." *Foreign Affairs* 84 (4): 38–50.

Luke, Timothy W. 2001. World health and the environment: Globalization's ambiguities. Presented at the Third Annual Staff Development Conference, University of Wisconsin System Institute of Global Studies, Lake Geneva, WI, October 28–30.

Matthew, Richard A., Bryan McDonald, and Ken Rutherford, eds. 2004. *Landmines and human security: International politics and war's hidden legacy*. Albany: SUNY Press.

Matthew, Richard A., and George E. Shambaugh. 1998. Sex, drugs and heavy metal: Transnational threats and national vulnerabilities. *Security Dialogue* 29 (2): 163–175.

McNamara, Peter J. 2007. Infectious disease. http://www.accessscience.com (accessed November 15, 2008).

McNeil, Donald G. 2008. "Gates Foundation's Influence Criticized." *The New York Times*. February 16. http://www.nytimes.com/2008/02/16/science/16malaria .html (accessed March 3, 2009).

McNeill, William H. 1998. *Plagues and peoples*. New York: Anchor Books.

National Intelligence Council (NIC). 2000. *National intelligence estimate: The global infectious disease threat and its implications for the United States*. http:// www.dni.gov/nic/special_globalinfectious.html (November 15, 2008).

National Research Council. 2001. *Under the weather: Climate, ecosystems, and infectious disease*. Washington, DC: National Academies Press.

Omran, Abdel. 1971. The epidemiologic transition: A theory of the epidemiology of population change. *Milbank Memorial Fund Quarterly* 29:509–538.

Piller, Charles, and Doug Smith. 2007. Unintended victims of Gates Foundation generosity. *Los Angeles Times*, December 16. http://www.latimes.com/news/ nationworld/nation/la-na-gates16dec16,0,3743924.story?coll=la-home-center (accessed March 3, 2009).

Rodier, Guenael, et al. 2007. Global public health security. *Emerging Infectious Diseases* 13 (10): 1447–1452.

Rosneau, James N. 1990. *Turbulence in world politics: A theory of change and continuity*. Princeton: Princeton University Press.

Ryan, C. A., et al. 1987. Massive outbreak of antimicrobial-resistant samolnellosis traced to pasteurized milk. *Journal of the American Medical Association* 258:3269–3274.

Slaughter , Anne-Marie. 2004. *A new world order*. Princeton: Princeton University Press.

Smolinski, Mark S., Margaret A. Hamburg, and Joshua Lederberg, eds. 2003. *Microbial threats to health: Emergence, detection, and response*. Washington, DC: National Academies Press.

Stern, Jessica. 2002. Dreaded risks and the control of biological weapons. *International Security* 27 (3): 89–123.

Stern Review. 2007. *The economics of climate change*. Cambridge, UK: Cambridge University Press.

Torok, T. J., et al. 1997. A large community outbreak of salmonellosis caused by intentional contamination of restaurant salad bars. *Journal of the American Medical Association* 278 (5): 389–395.

Tucker, Jonathan B., ed. 2000. *Toxic terror: Assessing terrorist use of chemical and biological weapons*. Cambridge, MA: MIT Press.

Tucker, Jonathan B. 2001. *Scourge: The once and future threat of smallpox*. New York: Grove Press.

United Nations. 2008. *World urbanization prospects: The 2007 revision*. http:// www.un.org/esa/population/unpop.htm (accessed November 15, 2008).

United Nations Development Programme (UNDP). 1994. *Human development report 1994.* New York: Oxford University Press.

United Nations Environment Programme. 2002. *Global environmental outlook 3: Past, present and future perspectives.* London: Earthscan.

United Nations Programme on HIV/AIDS and World Health Organization. 2007. AIDS epidemic update: December 2007. http://www.unaids.org/en/KnowledgeCentre/HIVData/EpiUpdate/EpiUpdArchive/2007default.asp (accessed November 15, 2008).

United States Department of Defense. 2008. Global emerging infections surveillance. http://www.geis.fhp.osd.mil/ (accessed November 15, 2008).

U.S. Centers for Disease Control. 2000. Biological and chemical terrorism: Strategic plan for preparedness and response, recommendations of the CDC strategic planning working group. *Morbidity and Mortality Weekly Report* 49:5–8.

U.S. Centers for Disease Control. 2001a. Recognition of illness associated with the intentional release of a biological agent. *Morbidity & Mortality Weekly Report* 50:893–897.

U.S. Centers for Disease Control. 2001b. Update: Investigation of anthrax associated with intentional exposure and interim public health guidelines. *Morbidity & Mortality Weekly Report* 50:889–893.

U.S. Centers for Disease Control. 2005. Basic information about SARS. http://www.cdc.gov/ncidod/sars/factsheet.htm (accessed November 15, 2008).

U.S. Centers for Disease Control. 2007. CDC investigation of traveler with multidrug-resistant tuberculosis (MDR TB): Questions and answers for passengers and flight crew on the same flight. http://www.cdc.gov/tb/flightQA.htm (accessed November 15, 2008).

U.S. Centers for Disease Control. 2008. *Public health preparedness: Mobilizing state by state.* http://emergency.cdc.gov/publications/feb08phprep/ (accessed November 15, 2008).

U.S. Department of Health and Human Services. 2004. Pandemics and pandemic scares in the 20th century. http://www.hhs.gov/nvpo/pandemics/flu3.htm#9 (accessed November 15, 2008).

U.S. Food and Drug Administration. 2003. Risk assessment for food terrorism and other food safety concerns. http://www.cfsan.fda,gov/~dms/rabtact.html (accessed November 15, 2008).

Wapner, Paul. 1996. *Environmental activism and world civic politics.* Albany: SUNY Press.

Wapner, Paul. 2002. Defending accountability in NGOs. *Chicago Journal of International Law* 3 (1): 197–205.

Whitby, Simon and Paul Rodgers. 1997. Anti-crop biological warfare: Implications of the Iraqi and U.S. programs. *Defense Analysis* 13 (3): 303–318.

World Bank. 2007. *World development report 2008: Agriculture for development.* Washington, DC: The World Bank.

World Health Organization (WHO). 2002. *Scaling up the response to infectious disease, a way out of poverty: Report on infectious diseases 2002.* http://www .who.int/infectious-disease-report/ (accessed November 15, 2008).

World Health Organization (WHO). 2007a. Malaria. http://www.who.int/ mediacentre/factsheets/fs094/en/index.html (accessed November 15, 2008).

World Health Organization (WHO). 2007b. Tuberculosis. http://www.who.int/ mediacentre/factsheets/fs104/en/index.html (accessed November 15, 2008).

World Health Organization (WHO). 2007c. *Working for health: An introduction to the World Health Organization.* http://www.who.int/about/brochure_en .pdf (accessed November 15, 2008).

World Health Organization (WHO). 2007d. *The World Health Report 2007: A safer future: Global public health security in the 21st century.* Geneva: World Health Organization.

World Health Organization (WHO). 2008. Infectious diseases. http://www .who.int/topics/infectious_diseases/en/ (accessed November 15, 2008).

World Hunger Education Service. 2006. World hunger facts 2006. http://www .worldhunger.org/articles/Learn/world%20hunger%20facts%202002.htm (accessed November 15, 2008).

4

The Vulnerability of Urban Slum Dwellers to Global Environmental Change

Laura Little and Chris Cocklin

The United Nations (UN) estimates that, over the next thirty years, the number of people living in urban areas will increase by 2 billion globally (United Nations Department of Economic and Social Affairs/Population Division 2004, 1; UN-HABITAT 2003, 5). The vast majority of this population growth is anticipated to occur in developing countries (United Nations Department of Economic and Social Affairs/Population Division 2004). Many of these new urban residents are expected to settle in slums, defined generally as settlements where "the inhabitants are characterized as having inadequate housing and basic services" (Expert Group Meeting on Slum Indicators 2002, 8). Indeed, the UN projects that the global population of slum dwellers will rise from the current level of 924 million people[1] to about 2 billion over the next thirty years, "if no firm and concrete action is taken" (UN-HABITAT 2003, xxv). Contemporaneously, human activities are having profound impacts on the environment, leading to problems such as climate change, acid rain, loss of biodiversity, and soil erosion (Goudie and Viles 1997; Morris et al. 2003).

What are the relationships between global environmental change, the process of urbanization, and cities? In particular, how will global environmental change affect the well-being of a growing urban population? These questions are explored in this chapter, against the backdrop of two fundamental propositions. The first is that the impacts of global environmental change are differentiated socially and that this differentiation is the result of underlying social, political, and economic conditions (see, e.g., Sanderson 2000; Cutter, Mitchell, and Scott 2000; Pelling 1999; Adger 1999). The lens of "human security" enables us not simply to identify the potential threats to urban dwellers arising from global environmental change, but to highlight the fact that the *vulnerability* of urban dwellers is socially differentiated. This is achieved through a consideration of slum dwellers' exposure, sensitivity, and capacity to cope with the effects of global environmental change.

The second proposition is that much of the literature on global environmental change fails to adequately probe the human dimensions, with the result that vulnerability is too often expressed in broad generalities. It is insufficient, for example, to simply assert that poverty correlates with higher levels of vulnerability to global environmental change (GEC). If the underlying objective is to intervene in the interests of improved human security, finer-grained analyses of the human dimensions of GEC—the social, political, economic, and institutional factors that influence vulnerability—is necessary. This proposition is substantiated through this chapter's focus on the issue of access to adequate housing. The chapter identifies the conditions and structures that inhibit slum dwellers' access to housing, with a view to exposing some of the underlying factors that lead to differentiated vulnerability to GEC. The analysis of the housing problem reveals that (1) there are multiple stressors that contribute to vulnerability, and (2) these stressors operate at a range of levels, ranging from what we refer to as "fundamental" to "proximate" causes (see also Moser 1998; Pelling 2002). While this chapter analyzes only one dimension of urban poverty, we suggest that the conditions underpinning housing stress are common to other aspects of vulnerability to GEC in cities.

Our discussion begins by considering, in general terms, the relationships among GEC, cities, and the process of urbanization. The analysis then turns to slum dwellers, with the aim of substantiating the point that vulnerability is socially differentiated. This is followed by a more detailed consideration of the factors affecting adequacy of housing.

Global Environmental Change and Urbanization

There are complex and multi-directional links between global environmental change, the process of urbanization, and cities. On the one hand, the demographic shift toward cities—urbanization—can be a driver of global environmental change. For example, the growth of cities can lead to pollution of local seas and waterways and place stress on surrounding ecosystems (World Resources Institute, United Nations Environment Programme, United Nations Development Programme, and World Bank 1996; UNCHS 1996; Leitmann 2003). While the effects of these phenomena are generally realized at a local scale, they are occurring internationally and therefore have global impacts. Additionally, urban areas are major centers of resource consumption and waste generation, so urbanization can, in turn, lead to increases in greenhouse gas emissions and other forms of environmental degradation (World Resources Institute, United Nations Environment Programme, United Nations Development Programme, and World Bank 1996).[2] On the other hand, global environmental change may drive urbanization, though the exact link between environmental degradation and rural-urban migration is disputed (Lonergan 1998; Bilsborrow 2002).

A further dimension of the relationship between cities, urbanization, and the environment is the impact of global environmental change on urban residents. The nature and incidence of these impacts, and peoples' exposure to and ability to cope with them, is the subject of discussion in the remainder of this chapter.

Human Security, Global Environmental Change, and Urban Areas

Urbanization and GEC have significant implications for human security (Brennan 1999; Pirages 1997). This book draws principally upon a definition of human security that emphasizes options—the option to end, mitigate, or adapt to threats, the freedom to exercise these options, and the ability to participate in attaining these options (Lonergan 1999). For the purposes of this chapter, we approach human security from the reverse side—namely, through the concept of "vulnerability." More specifically, to address the implications for human security of urbanization we draw, broadly, on Cutter's (1996) and Bohle's (2001) conceptions of vulnerability, as well as Pelling's work on the vulnerability of urban residents to floods (1997, 1999, 2002). These representations broaden the focus beyond physical hazards to include an analysis of the social factors that shape *how* people are impacted by hazards. Pelling (1999), for example, sought to demonstrate how social and economic assets need to be considered alongside physical resources in assessing vulnerability to environmental stresses. Figure 4.1 brings together some of the main elements of these models. Drawing from Cutter (1996), Cutter et al. (2000), and Pelling (1999), the diagram indicates that vulnerability has both biophysical and socioeconomic dimensions, which collectively define the vulnerability of people in a particular place. The diagram also indicates that

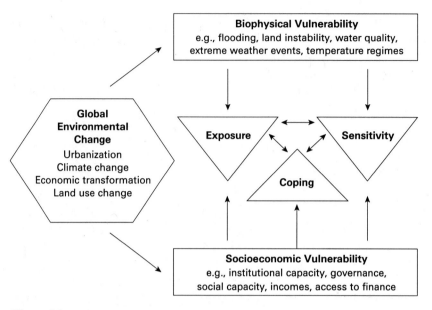

Figure 4.1
Vulnerability in the context of global environmental change

exposure, sensitivity, and coping constitute vulnerability, which borrows from and extends Bohle's (2001) concept of the "double structure" of vulnerability. In this chapter, the emphasis is on the socioeconomic dimensions of vulnerability. As Blaikie et al. (1994) explain, an analysis of these social factors and their root causes is important in understanding *why* people face hazards differently and should enable us to craft more effective policies to mitigate, reduce, or avoid the impacts of hazards (see also Pelling 2002; Moser 1998).

Accordingly, our analysis of the vulnerability of urban residents to the effects of global environmental change involves

1. identifying the ways in which global environmental change poses risks to cities;
2. assessing the potential impact of GEC through an analysis of

• the differentiated exposure of urban residents to GEC,
• the type and degree of damage or loss urban residents are likely to suffer,
• the variable abilities of urban residents to cope with and recover from this damage or loss.

Our emphasis, therefore, is on how environmental change might contribute to increased social vulnerabilities. Accordingly, in the next sections we briefly outline the risks, in general, to cities that might arise from global environmental change and then indicate how the attendant environmental changes could give rise to specific social vulnerabilities. Implicit in the analysis is the view that reducing vulnerability improves human security, which in the context of urban poverty is a perspective that is consonant with much of the UN human security discourse, which sought to associate welfare and poverty issues with security.

Risks Arising from Global Environmental Change
The effects of global environmental change are wide-ranging and vary from place to place. This chapter does not attempt to canvass all the effects of GEC—an enormous and complex task—and it does not aim to explain the underlying causes and the links among various environmental changes. Suffice to say that the causes of GEC and the relationships among various 'environmental phenomena are overlapping and interrelated. Some of the aspects of global environmental change that are likely to impact significantly on urban areas include the following:

• *Increased flooding,* which can cause property and infrastructure damage, result in loss of life or injury, and increase the incidence of waterborne diseases (e.g., Pelling 1999).
• *Decreased water availability,* based on UN estimates that up to 7 billion people in sixty countries could face water shortages by the middle of this century (UNESCO 2003, 10).
• *Decreased water quality,* which is linked to the spread of waterborne diseases, such as cholera and typhoid. It can also cause increased levels of toxins in marine and freshwater species, which can then bioaccumulate in human beings and affect health.
• *Increased range of vector-borne diseases such as malaria and dengue fever,* leading to increased incidence of these and other infectious diseases.
• *Higher maximum temperatures,* with the attendant risk of increased incidence in heat stress illness and mortality.
• *Increased incidence of landslides, mudslides, and land subsidence,* contributing to property and infrastructure damage and loss of life or injury.
• *Increased intensity and frequency of tropical cyclones,* which poses risks to life and has the potential to facilitate the spread of infectious diseases.

• *Higher levels of air pollution*, which can lead to respiratory and cardio-vascular problems (Intergovernmental Panel on Climate Change 2001).

In summary, the *direct* effects of GEC on urban residents are likely to arise predominantly from risks to human safety and infrastructure (e.g., as a result of flooding) and those related to health impacts. There will, of course, be a wide range of social and economic dislocations that would then arise. Sanderson (2000), for example, shows how disasters them-selves contribute to poverty. Other consequences of environmental change, increased disasters, and health effects would include individual and community stress, economic costs at levels ranging from the individ-ual to industry sectors, the costs of disaster relief, infrastructural costs (e.g., increased need for health services), and so forth (see, e.g., Moser 1998; Cutter, Mitchell, and Scott 2000; Pelling 1999; Adger 1999). As we will argue next, the attendant impacts will be socially differentiated.

Vulnerability to the Effects of Global Environmental Change

As Adger (1999) observed, social vulnerability has been underempha-sized in assessments of the impacts of environmental change, and, ac-cordingly, he argues for the explicit consideration of the exposure of individuals and groups to climate change and variability. One of our main propositions is that vulnerability to GEC is socially differentiated and, more specifically, that urban slum dwellers are especially vulnera-ble. In putting forward this proposition, we acknowledge that there are limitations to making generalized statements about slums and poverty (see, e.g. Wratten 1995). Internationally, there is significant variability across areas classified as slums, including differences in the location of slum areas within cities and the level of services and other features (UN-HABITAT 2003). Consequently, while the UN has indicated hous-ing conditions and inadequate services as the most universal indicators, in fact definitions of slums vary from place to place (UN-HABITAT 2003).

This chapter relies broadly on an operational definition of slums, recently recommended by the United Nations Expert Group Meeting, which seeks to draw together common characteristics.[3] Utilizing this def-inition, it is possible to identify several characteristics of slums that underlie vulnerability to GEC.

One characteristic is location, in the sense that slums are often located in hazardous areas such as floodplains and land subject to subsidence

(Pelling 1997; UN-HABITAT 2003; World Resources Insitute, United Nations Environment Programme, United Nations Development Programme, and World Bank 1996). For example, in Rio de Janeiro, the *favelas* are frequently built on steep hillsides subject to landslides, while in Dhaka many slum settlements are located on land that floods regularly (Hamza and Zetter 1998). Slum dwellers are therefore particularly exposed to the increased risks of flooding, landslides, mudslides, and land subsidence—risks that will be amplified by global environmental change.

A second characteristic is the quality of housing; slum housing is typically substandard. Structures are built with nonpermanent materials, such as plywood or metal scraps, that may be unsuited to the location and climate (World Resources Institute, United Nations Environment Programme, United Nations Development Programme, and World Bank 1996; UN-HABITAT 2003). The poor standard of housing puts slum dwellers particularly at risk of suffering property damage, injury, or loss of life associated with flooding, cyclones, landslides, and mudslides (Satterthwaite 2003). Inadequate insulation also exposes slum dwellers to risks of heat mortality, a danger that may be increased as a consequence of rising maximum temperatures (IPCC 2001; World Resources Institute, United Nations Environment Programme, United Nations Development Programme, and World Bank 1996).

Slums are also characterized by overcrowding, with "low space per person, high occupancy rates, cohabitation by different families and a high number of single-room units" (UN-HABITAT 2003). This overcrowding facilitates the spread of infectious diseases (World Resources Institute, United Nations Environment Programme, United Nations Development Programme, and World Bank 1996), making slum dwellers sensitive to the increased incidence of infectious diseases such as malaria, dengue fever, and yellow fever.

Access to water and sanitation is another consideration. Only 40 percent of households in informal settlements have access to clean water (UN-HABITAT 2003, 113). The majority lack access to potable water and many with access face inadequate supply (World Resources Institute, United Nations Environment Programme, United Nations Development Programme, and World Bank 1996; UN-HABITAT 2003). Consequently, slum residents are often forced to rely on open waterways and wells, communal standpipes, and bottled water for their needs (World Resources Institute, United Nations Environment Programme, United Nations Development Programme, and World Bank 1996). The reliance on local waterways and wells exposes slum dwellers to the health risks associated with reductions in water supply and decreases in water quality (World Resources Institute, United Nations Environment Programme, United Nations Development Programme, and World Bank 1996; Leitmann 2003).[4] The inadequate sanitation that is a feature in the majority of slums (Leitmann 2003), such as a lack of sewer connections and an insufficient number of latrines, exacerbates these health risks by promoting the spread of disease.

There is also a lack of other basic services such as drainage and garbage collection. According to a UN report, in the lowest-income countries "perhaps only 10–20 percent of solid waste is collected" (UNCHS 1996, 270) Problems of solid waste collection are most acute in illegal or informal settlements, partly because it is difficult for collection vehicles to access these areas through what are often narrow and poorly made roads (UNCHS 1996). Inadequate waste collection heightens the exposure of slum dwellers to the risk of increased incidence of infectious diseases because it can lead to the establishment of local garbage dumps that then promote the growth and spread of disease in the area. At the same time, inadequate drainage in slums makes these areas particularly sensitive to increased flooding, along with its adverse impacts (Leitmann 2003; Intergovernmental Panel on Climate Change 2001; Pelling 1997, 1999).

As explained earlier, the degree of vulnerability of a person or group to the risks of global environmental change is a function not only of exposure and sensitivity to those risks but also of the capacity to deal with them (figure 4.1). A key determinant of the vulnerability of slum dwellers to GEC is their limited capacity, in many cases, to reduce exposure and sensitivity to risks and to cope when risks materialize. There are a number of factors that commonly underlie this limited capacity and that arise as both a cause and a result of living in slums.

First, residents of slums usually have low incomes (UN-HABITAT 2003). Second, many slum residents lack assets, or have assets that are not recognized by the formal legal system. While slum residents may hold land or land-related assets, they often lack security of tenure (UN-HABITAT 2003). As a result, they cannot use their existing assets as capital to generate income (De Soto 2000). Third, slum dwellers tend to lack formal education and other attributes that shape life chances and opportunities (UN-HABITAT 2003). Low incomes and a lack of assets lead to slum residents being unable to afford safe, well-located, and well-serviced housing (UNCHS 1996) and thereby limiting their exposure to many of the risks associated with GEC. Lack of formal education means that slum dwellers may not be able to access information that could help them avoid or limit risks, such as information about the hazards associated with a site (Blaikie et al. 1994). Low incomes result in many slum residents being unable to afford health care or to take time off from work when suffering from health problems (Satterthwaite 2003). Collectively, low incomes, limited assets, and a lack of education make it difficult for slum residents to deal with the property damage or loss of assets that can result from global environmental change (Blaikie et al. 1994).

The previous analysis indicates that the vulnerability of slum residents to GEC is, to a significant extent, a manifestation of various aspects of poverty. Yet merely stating that vulnerability is linked to poverty does not provide a sufficiently nuanced explanation. As Blaikie et al. would point out, what is missing is an analysis of how the "very *widespread conditions*" of poverty leads to "very *particular vulnerabilities*" (1994, 12). It is therefore necessary to identify the social, political, and economic conditions that give *the meaning of "poverty" to particular circumstances* and that translate poverty into *specific conditions* that create vulnerability. The relevance of broader social, political, and economic conditions in shaping vulnerability is demonstrated through the example of access to housing.

Access to Housing and Vulnerability

The preceding discussion points out that one of the factors typically underlying vulnerability of slum dwellers to GEC is low incomes, which can make it difficult to afford adequate housing. While this information is useful, a focus on income alone does not provide a complete picture of the housing problem. Importantly, it does not explain *why* the incomes of slum residents are insufficient to access housing. Income is relative to the costs of goods and services, which are, in turn, shaped by supply and demand. So the fact that incomes of slum residents are too low to afford adequate housing suggests that a gap exists between demand for housing and supply by the formal market (UNCHS 1996).

In some cities, such as Hong Kong, this gap between demand and supply can be explained by topographical features, which constrain land supply and therefore contribute to relatively high housing prices. More often, the gap between demand and supply is shaped by a mix of social,

economic, and political conditions. In this section we focus on some of
the key conditions that are present in many cities, albeit to varying
degrees, and that influence access to housing. The discussion refers principally to the formal housing sector, although it is noted that self-help
housing is influenced by many of the same factors.

Urban Population Growth

A key factor shaping access to housing is the sheer demand arising from
the scale and pace of urbanization in the developing world (UNCHS
1999, 2001). According to the UN, eighteen million additional units
(equivalent to 5 percent of existing stocks) are required *per annum* to
meet the demand for housing globally (UNCHS 2001, 30). Governments
and the private sector face enormous challenges in supplying sufficient
adequate housing to meet the demand. Where they cannot meet the demand, the price premium for formal housing increases. Those who cannot afford to pay this premium must resort to housing in the informal
market (including self-help housing).

Costs of Housing Construction

A major constraint on the supply of adequate, affordable housing is the
high cost of construction. This is the result of a number of factors.
According to UN-HABITAT, "In most countries in Africa, Asia and
Latin America," building materials are "prohibitively expensive," in
"scarce supply," or are "of low quality" (UNCHS 1996, 225). Indeed,
in "many countries in the South, the formal construction industry
depends almost exclusively" on imported materials, which tend to command high prices (UNCHS 1996, 225). The costs and availability of construction materials present a significant constraint on the housing supply
because "building materials generally constitute the single largest input
into the construction of housing, accounting for as much as 80 per cent
of the total value of a simple house" (UNCHS 1996, 225).

While local production of materials could reduce costs and increase
supply of materials, many countries have faced challenges in developing
such capabilities. Factories face difficulties operating in unstable markets
that lack reliable supplies of energy and inputs. At the same time, small-
scale producers—although effective in meeting demand—face constraints, such as lack of management skills, that prevent development of
larger, more efficient enterprises. Additionally, while effective utilization

of low- cost materials could reduce construction costs, lack of knowledge or skills creates barriers to doing this (UNCHS 1996, 226).

Another important factor contributing to the high costs of construction is inappropriate building standards relating to, for example, construction materials and infrastructure. While minimum standards for health and safety are important, standards are sometimes higher than is arguably necessary. For example, in some countries, regulations "date back to colonial times" (Choguill 1995, 406) and reflect the standards that applied to the housing of colonial rulers rather than the urban poor (UNCHS 1996, 253).

The absence of a well-developed competitive construction industry also contributes to the high costs of construction. According to UN-HABITAT, there are a number of constraints on the development of the construction industry. First, "the sector is not viewed and planned in a holistic manner," leading to "wastage, duplication [and] inefficiency." Second, key inputs such as finance, equipment, and skilled labor are lacking (UNCHS 1996, 225). Transportation costs are also high in many developing countries due to inadequate infrastructure (UNCHS 1996). This can increase the costs of construction directly, as well as indirectly, by constraining the development of the construction sector.

Costs of Land Acquisition, Development, and Transfer

The cost of acquiring, developing, and transferring land are high, constraining the supply of affordable housing. Several factors lead to these high costs. One is that there is significant land speculation in many cities in the developing world—a function of inequality, a lack of other good investment options, and an absence of regulation (Gilbert and Gugler 1992, 126; Bhattacharya 1990). This land speculation can result in the poor "being priced out of the land market" (Gilbert and Gugler 1992).

Similar to the issue of building standards discussed earlier, in many countries regulations relating to plot sizes reflect colonial standards that are unnecessarily restrictive (UNCHS 1996). As a result, even the minimum legal plot size can be too expensive for low-income earners.

A key factor determining the costs of land is the availability of land for development. In some countries, governments have failed to make land accessible for housing development. In India, for example, large amounts of vacant land were withheld from the market for years or released only in small quantities, driving up land prices (Singh 1992). Reasons for this include ineffective bureaucracies, a lack of political will (Battacharya 1990), and, in some instances, land speculation by government agencies (Singh 1992).

In many developing countries, customary land tenure systems still apply to large areas of urban land, sometimes overlapping with European-style land tenure models (UNCHS 1996, 2001). These kinds of legal arrangements can increase the costs of acquiring land in a number of ways. First, as information about customary land rights is often not centrally recorded (De Soto 2000), persons outside a community may have to incur significant costs to find out who has rights to a particular piece of land and the nature of those rights. Second, customary tenure systems can restrict land transfer. This decreases land supply and can thereby lead to increases in land prices. Third, as the relationship between customary and formal land tenure systems is not always clear, the use of these two land systems can lead to uncertainty about *who* owns land (UN-HABITAT 2003).

Additionally, the administrative procedures for registration, development, and transfer of land are complex and time-consuming in many developing countries. For example, registration of land titles in Cameroon can take from two to five years (UNCHS 1996, 252). These administrative procedures can add significantly to the costs of obtaining land through the formal market (UNCHS 1996; De Soto 2000).

The failure of governments, or private operators, to provide basic services, such as piped water and sanitation, can increase land costs by creating a "scarcity premium" on land with infrastructure and services (UNCHS 1996, 209). Similarly, failure to provide cheap and efficient public transportation, particularly to periurban areas, can increase land costs by limiting the amount of land within a reasonable distance of employment opportunities (UNCHS 1996).

Inaccessibility of Housing Finance

In most developing countries, housing finance is largely unavailable for low- and middle-income earners (UNCHS 1996; Singh 1992).[5] Rather, these groups have to rely on their own savings and/or informal loans to pay for housing (UNCHS 1996, 2001). Consequently, they can find it difficult to afford adequate housing. Additionally, the unavailability of housing finance can exacerbate other aspects of the housing problem. Specifically, the resulting lack of demand for formal sector housing can constrain the development of the housing construction sector and thereby lead to increases in housing prices. There are a number of reasons for the unavailability of housing finance. For example, commercial lenders generally require borrowers to have a stable income, at a reasonable level, to reduce the risks of default (UNCHS 1996, 2001). Also, lenders often require borrowers to have collateral in the form of property that has a clear title and readily ascertainable value (UNCHS 1996, 2001). Low-income earners face difficulty in meeting these lending criteria. They often work in the informal sector where incomes can be unstable and difficult to verify. Also, they often lack the required collateral (UNCHS 1996).

More generally, there is reluctance among many finance institutions to lend to low-income earners due to a perception (unsubstantiated) that this group is at high risk of default (UNCHS 1996, 2001). Lenders are likely to be particularly reluctant to take this perceived risk in certain developing countries, where "less developed regulatory and legal frameworks for mortgages" mean they cannot "easily convert mortgaged property into liquid funds in the case of default" (UNCHS 2001, 38–39).

The availability of housing finance for low-income earners has also been an issue in wealthier countries and has been addressed by the establishment of specialized lending institutions (UNCHS 1996). While measures have been taken in developing countries to create specialized lending institutions, these efforts have often failed, with institutions becoming ineffective or collapsing altogether (UNCHS 1996, 2001). Reasons for this failure include the impact of external economic shocks and domestic macroeconomic policies, poor management, and political interference (UNCHS 1996, 2001).

Other Failures of Government Policy

There are problems in discussing "failures" of government policies because, first, there is significant debate as to which policies should be used to address the housing problem. Second, the policies that are appropriate to address the housing problem vary from place to place, and cities face differing constraints on the type of policies they can use. Nevertheless, there are some government policies that have clearly failed to address, and sometimes even exacerbated, the problems outlined earlier. According to Kilmartin, there is a "continuing belief" in some countries that "government investment should be in the 'productive' sectors of the economy rather than in sectors like housing" (1992, 13). Consequently the proportion of resources devoted to housing has been inadequate.

Government housing subsidies, which can assist low-income earners in affording to rent or buy housing, are often poorly targeted. According to Rakodi, subsides are "often confined to civil servants and public officials and [are] often highly regressive" (1992, 42–43). Similarly, many public housing programs have allocated housing to middle- and upper-income groups rather than low-income earners (UNCHS 1996). Even where programs have targeted low-income earners, the eligibility criteria for public housing has "often excluded the poorest households—especially women-headed households" (UNCHS 1996, 219).

Housing and Vulnerability to Global Environmental Change

This brief analysis of access to housing reveals that the problem is shaped by a broad range of factors—from the cost of building materials to transportation infrastructure and housing finance. These factors are, in turn, shaped by underlying social, political, and economic structures. As Adger (1999) points out, social vulnerability is linked to the political economy of markets and institutions. Pelling (2002) makes a similar point, in suggesting that there has been too much focus on "proximate" as opposed to underlying causes. Many of the issues we have highlighted previously are linked to domestic macro- and microeconomic conditions, the structure of the international economic system and governance, including capacity of public servants, the degree of corruption, responsiveness of government, and political representation, particularly of poorer groups. Emerging from this analysis and drawing on the observations of other authors (e.g., Adger 1999; Pelling 2002; Cutter, Mitchell, and Scott 2000), we suggest a causal chain that extends from broad structural factors to specific vulnerabilities, as represented in table 4.1.

It is important to note that the discussion of the housing problem has analyzed only *one aspect* of the vulnerability of *one* particular group to GEC. Other aspects of vulnerability to GEC are also underpinned by a complex set of factors, each with its own chain of causation (Adger 1999; Pelling 2002). What this analysis highlights is the complex array of forces that shape vulnerability to GEC. At the same time, though, delving into the causal chain reveals that many of the forces leading to vulnerability have common underlying causes.

Table 4.1
The causal chain of slum dwellers' vulnerability to GEC

Fundamental causes	Drivers	Proximate causes	Outcomes
Globalization	Legal failures	Lack of basic infrastructure and services	High exposure to risks of GEC such as flooding, landslides, and heat mortality.
Population growth	Market failures		
	Political will		
Political ideologies	Corruption	Poor quality of housing	Sensitivity to increased incidence of disease
Governance structures	Lack of human capital	Poor location of housing	
Cultural factors	Lack of resources	Low incomes and lack of assets	Lack of ability to access safe housing
Distribution of resources		Lack of education	Lack of ability to cope with loss or damage

Note: It is not intended that the table contents are to be read across the rows.

As Blaikie et al. (1994) explain, there is often reluctance to look at these deep structural causes of vulnerability. This reluctance stems from factors including the difficulty in gathering reliable evidence establishing causal linkages, particularly further back in the causal chain, as well as a view that root causes are "too diffuse or deep-rooted to address" (Blaikie et al. 1994, 29–30). While we acknowledge the challenges in tackling root causes of vulnerability, the focus on "outcomes" in policy circles has arguably obscured some of the benefits that can result from looking at underlying structural causes. Exposing underlying structural causes and exploring how these create vulnerability can yield a number of benefits (see, e.g., Moser 1998; Cutter, Mitchell, and Scott 2000). First, it can facilitate development of more effective policies that solve multiple problems by addressing common root causes. Second, it can highlight how addressing one cause of vulnerability can create positive flow-on effects elsewhere. The ability to demonstrate multiple benefits of a specific policy may be particularly valuable in a neoliberal policy environment, where there is often pressure to prove the cost effectiveness of social policies. Finally, a focus on underlying causes can strip away some of the surface complexity that often makes issues seem too overwhelming to tackle. The ability to view problems with greater clarity may be particularly valuable in dealing with issues arising from GEC and urbanization.

Importantly, if it is possible in a particular location (city) to link proximate causes and outcomes to specific fundamental causes and drivers, this would provide a strategic roadmap for tackling the sources of vulnerability and assist in identifying interventions that would improve human security.

Conclusion

Urbanization and GEC are large-scale, interrelated issues with profound implications for human well-being. The sheer scale and complexity of the issues raises challenges in determining how to intervene effectively to address vulnerability. This chapter has focused on one aspect of the relationship between GEC and urbanization—the impacts of GEC on urban residents—and has emphasized that impacts are socially differentiated and that this differentiation is shaped by underlying social conditions. We have highlighted the importance of looking at fundamental causes of vulnerability as a way of dealing with the complexity of urbanization and GEC. We acknowledge that there are difficulties as well as limitations in taking this approach. There is frequently uncertainty about both what causes the problems and how different issues are causally linked. Also, even if fundamental causes can be recognized, there are considerable challenges in addressing general issues such as "market failures." At the same time, an improved understanding of the structural causes of vulnerability raises the potential for devising more lasting and effective policy responses. We believe that these potential benefits make further investigation of structural causes, at the very least, a worthwhile exercise.

Notes

1. This figure is equivalent to 31.6 percent of the world's urban population.

2. It is important to note that although there is a tendency toward higher consumption in urban areas, urban residents do not necessarily consume significantly more resources than their rural counterparts. In fact, the urban poor in developing countries consume a fairly low amount of resources and energy (World Resources Institute, United Nations Environmental Programme, United Nations Development Programme 1996; UN-HABITAT 1996). This group of urban poor makes up a growing proportion of the urban population.

There is a tendency to assume that the shift toward cities will necessarily lead to increased resource consumption because the processes of urbanization and industrialization have historically gone hand in hand. In other words, groups of rural poor have moved to cities, become better off economically, and increased their resource consumption. However, if urbanization in some countries occurs without corresponding industrialization, the assumption that it will lead to higher resource consumption may not hold.

3. The operational definition of a slum as "an area that combines...the following characteristics: inadequate access to safe water: inadequate access to sanitation and other infrastructure; poor structural quality of housing; overcrowding; insecure residential status" (UN-HABITAT 2003, 12).

4. There are health risks associated with both decreased water supply as well as decreased water quality. For example, Satterthwaite refers to a group of diseases known as "water-washed" diseases "because they are associated with a lack of water supplies for washing." Diseases include "various skin and eye infections such as scabies and trachoma" (Satterthwaite 2003, 7).

5. While this chapter discusses the issue of housing finance, it is important to note that there are considerable gaps in data regarding housing finance in many countries; therefore, any conclusions are necessarily tentative.

References

Adger, Neil. 1999. Social vulnerability to climate change and extremes in coastal Vietnam. *World Development* 27 (2): 249–269.

Bhattacharya, K. P. 1990. Housing in India. In *Housing policy in developing countries*, ed. Gil Shidlo, 67–103. London and New York: Routledge.

Bilsborrow, Richard E. 2002. Migration, population change and the rural environment. *The Woodrow Wilson Environmental Change and Security Project Report* 8:69–94.

Blaikie, Piers, Terry Cannon, Ian Davis, and Ben Wisner. 1994. *At Risk: Natural hazards, people's vulnerability and disasters*. London and New York: Routledge.

Bohle, Hans-Georg. 2001. Vulnerability and criticality: Perspectives from social geography. *IHDP Update (Newsletter of the International Human Dimensions Programme on Global Environmental Change)* 2 (1): 1–4.

Brennan, E. 1999. Population, urbanization, environment and security: a summary of the issues. *The Woodrow Wilson Environmental Change and Security Project Report* 5:4–14.

Choguill, Charles L. 1995. The future of planned urban development in the third world. In *Housing the Poor*, ed. Brian C Aldrich and Ranvinder S. Sandhu, 403–414. London and New Jersey: Zed Books.

Cutter, S. 1996. Vulnerability to environmental hazards. *Progress in Human Geography* 20:529–539.

Cutter, S., J. Mitchell, and M. Scott. 2000. Revealing the vulnerability of people and places: a case study of Georgetown County, South Carolina. *Annals of the Association of American Geographers* 90 (4): 713–737.

De Soto, Hernando. 2000. *The mystery of capital: Why capitalism fails in the west and triumphs everywhere else.* London: Bantam.

Expert Group Meeting on Slum Indicators (organized by UN-HABITAT, Urban Secretariat and Shelter Branch). 2002. *Secure tenure, slums and global sample of cities.* Revised draft report, Nairobi.

Gilbert, Alan, and Josef Gugler. 1992. *Cities, poverty and development: Urbanization in the third world,* 2nd ed. New York: Oxford University Press.

Goudie, Andrew, and Heather Viles. 1997. *The earth transformed: An introduction to the human impacts on the environment.* Boston: Blackwell.

Hamza, Mohamed, and Roger Zetter. 1998. Structural adjustment, urban systems and disaster vulnerability in developing countries. *Cities* 14 (4): 291–299.

Intergovernmental Panel on Climate Change (James J. McCarthy, Ozvaldo F. Canziani, Neil A. Leary, David J., Dokken, Kasey S. White, eds). 2001. *Climate change 2001: Impacts, adaptation and vulnerability.* Cambridge, UK: Cambridge University Press.

Kilmartin, Leslie. 1992. Introduction: Analyses, contexts and solutions. In *Housing in the third world: Analyses and solutions,* ed. Leslie Kilmartin and Harjinder Singh, 13–24. New Delhi: Concept Publishing.

Leitmann, Josef. 2003. Urbanization. *AVISO: An Information Bulletin on Global Environmental Change and Human Security* 11:1–11.

Lonergan, Steve. 1998. The role of environmental degradation in population displacement. *Global Environmental Change and Human Security Project, International Human Dimensions Program on Global Environmental Change, Research Report 1.*

Lonergan, Steve. 1999. *Global Environmental Change and Human Security—Science Plan.* IHDP Report 11. Bonn, Germany: International Human Dimensions Programme on Global Environmental Change.

Morris, Dick, et al., eds. 2003. *Changing environments.* London: John Wiley and Sons.

Moser, C. 1998. The asset vulnerability framework: Reassessing urban poverty reduction strategies. *World Development* 26 (1): 1–19.

Pelling, M. 1997. What determines vulnerability to floods: a case study in Georgetown, Guyana. *Environment and Urbanization* 9 (1): 203–226.

Pelling, M. 1999. The political ecology of flood hazard in urban Guyana. *Geoforum* 30 (3): 249–261.

Pelling, M. 2002. Assessing urban vulnerability and social adaptation to risk—Evidence from Santo Domingo. *International Development and Planning Review* 24 (1): 59–76.

Pirages, D. 1997. Demographic change and ecological security. *The Woodrow Wilson Environmental Change and Security Project Report* 3:37–46.

Rakodi, Carole. 1992. Housing market in Third World cities: Research and policy into the 1990s. In *Housing in the Third World: Analyses and solutions*, ed. Leslie Kilmartin and Harjinder Singh, 27–61. New Delhi: Concept Publishing.

Sanderson, D. 2000. Cities, disasters and livelihoods. *Environment and Urbanization* 12 (2): 93–102.

Satterthwaite, David (International Institute for Environment and Development). 2003. The links between poverty and the environment in urban areas of Africa, Asia and Latin America. *The Annals of the American Academy of Political and Social Science* 590:73–92.

Singh, Harjinder. 1992. Urban housing policy in India: Contexts, shifts and implications. In *Housing in the third world: Analyses and solutions*, ed. Leslie Kilmartin and Harjinder Singh, 62–78. New Delhi: Concept Publishing.

UN-HABITAT. 2003. *The challenge of slums: Global report on human settlements 2003*. London: Earthscan Publications.

United Nations Centre for Human Settlements (UNCHS). 1996. *An urbanizing world: Global report on human settlements 1996*. New York: Oxford University Press.

United Nations Centre for Human Settlements (UNCHS). 1999. *Basic Facts on Urbanization*. HS/568/99E, Nairobi.

United Nations Centre for Human Settlements (UNCHS). 2001. *State of the World's Cities Report*. HS/619/01E, Nairobi.

United Nations Department of Economic and Social Affairs/Population Division. 2004. *World urbanization prospects: The 2003 revision*. New York: United Nations.

United Nations Educational, Scientific and Cultural Organization (UNESCO) 2003. *Water for people, water for life, the UN world water development report*. Paris: UNESCO Publishing/Berghahn Books.

World Resources Institute, United Nations Environment Programme, United Nations Development Programme, and World Bank. 1996. *World resources: A guide to the global environment*. New York: Oxford University Press.

Wratten, E. 1995. Conceptualizing urban poverty. *Environment and Urbanization* 7 (1): 11–36.

5

Environmental Change, Disasters, and Vulnerability: The Case of Hurricane Katrina and New Orleans

Victoria Basolo

Hurricane Katrina barreled into the Louisiana coast early on the morning of August 29, 2005. This category 4[1] hurricane swept through the city of New Orleans pushing water from Lake Pontchartrain to the north of the city over levees, leaving trees toppled, and damaging structures. These consequences of a major hurricane were manageable and familiar to residents and response personnel along the Gulf Coast. However, for New Orleans, the full effect of Katrina was delayed a few hours. Late in the morning of August 29, the 17th Street canal levee was breached, sending a torrent of water through the city. Other levee breaches during and after the storm added to the virtual drowning of New Orleans.

The days following the storm revealed the scope of New Orleans's vulnerability to disasters. Not only was the physical site of the city vulnerable to a major storm, but so too were many residents of the city. New Orleans was home to a number of vulnerable populations including minorities, the poor, and the elderly. Many within these populations had evacuated to the Superdome, a shelter of last resort, while others were in health facilities or in their homes. In a flooded city without power and a lagging institutional response, hundreds died and thousands languished for days in unhealthy and unsafe conditions; vulnerable populations were hit especially hard.

Early results of a mapping project at Louisiana State University indicate that deaths occurred across neighborhoods, including relatively affluent, predominately white areas. However, this research shows that the Lower Ninth Ward, a predominately African American neighborhood in New Orleans, had one of the highest death tolls from Katrina (Connolly and Roig-Franzia 2005). In addition, there are numerous accounts of the elderly dying in hospitals, their homes, and evacuation centers (see, e.g., Evans and Susman 2005; *Essence* 2005).

This chapter examines environmental change resulting from the physical and social development of New Orleans, as well as more recent atmospheric change, and how these changes moved the city toward disaster. In addition, it considers the exposure of vulnerable populations to disaster, including factors contributing to lack of preparedness by individuals and the consequences of inadequate government planning and response to disaster. In doing so, the New Orleans case exemplifies the concept of human security in terms of social differentiation and vulnerability as discussed by Little and Cocklin (see chapter 4). This section is followed by a brief discussion of the recovery of New Orleans. Finally, I conclude by summarizing the observations made in this chapter and contemplating the future of New Orleans and the implications for human security in this context.

Physical Development and Environmental Change

The unusual geography of New Orleans, which is situated largely below sea level surrounded by large bodies of water, made it an unlikely site for development. However, New Orleans possessed other unique qualities that made it attractive to the various countries that controlled it beginning in the early 1700s. From the start, the physical development of New Orleans required manipulating the Mississippi River and the Delta's environment. As a result, human actions over the centuries created vulnerabilities to natural hazards such as Hurricane Katrina.

The city of New Orleans began as a French settlement over three hundred years ago. Behind a natural levee built by the Mississippi River and nestled in a crescent-shaped crook of the river's meander, the city was a site exploited for its location between two important bodies of water, the river and Lake Pontchartrain. Jean-Baptiste Le Moyne (also known as Bienville), the champion of the site for the French capital of Louisiana, envisioned a city with the promise of future fortunes. As Ari Kelman writes of Bienville: "He saw only a magnificent system of watery roads, a tapestry of commercial empire woven from the strands of the river system's watercourses" (2003, 4).

The establishment of New Orleans, the promotion of agriculture in the river's delta, and the importation of black slaves spurred development and, therefore, the need for protection from the river and its flooding (Kelman 2003; Morris 2000). Thus, humankind began a struggle with the river and a frustrating history of levee augmentation, flooding, and levee building, repeated throughout each period of development of the city.

The French only modestly developed New Orleans relative to the Spanish and the United States. When France ceded a portion of Louisiana, including New Orleans, to Spain in 1763, the politics of transition included violence and uncertainty. Spain ruled a hostile physical and social environment but nonetheless promoted the growth of New Orleans.

After fewer than five decades under Spanish control, the French again took possession and ultimately sold Louisiana and the city of New Orleans to the United States in 1803 (Din and Harkins 1996; Lewis 2003). It was under U.S. possession and eventually statehood that the Louisiana Territory, especially New Orleans, would experience extraordinary growth and environmental change.

The United States continued a practice of levee building and maintenance to protect the reclaimed land in the Mississippi Delta. Care of the levees along the Mississippi River, however, was uneven and crevasses (levee breaks), which had caused regular flooding, including the inundation of New Orleans in 1735 and 1775 during French and Spanish rule, continued to be a problem in the 1800s (Davis 2000). Near the mid-nineteenth century, the Louisiana state engineer cautioned that the levee system was insufficient, the riverbed had risen due to the levees, and flooding was a threat. However, the state failed to make the substantial investment to address the problems, and eventually the federal government assumed responsibility for river flood control in Louisiana (Colten 2005).

Federal management of flood control created a less fragmented approach and consistent standards for building and maintaining the levee system. Flooding, however, was not eliminated as crevasses continued to appear, allowing water to flow into the inhabited areas along the levee system, including New Orleans (Davis 2000). Despite periodic floods and outbreaks of yellow fever spawned from the mosquito habitats of the backswamps, New Orleans had grown to over 240,000 people by 1890, almost nine times its population in 1820 (Colten 2005; Davis 2000). By the end of the century, a drainage plan and reclamation of backswamps were priorities. Craig E. Colten (2002) writes about this period: "The city council expressed concern that many areas were unoccupied because 'they are practically swamps' and therefore were impediments to urban growth and prosperity." The city installed pumps around 1900 and replaced them less than twenty years later with more efficient pumps, and it embarked on an ambitious drainage plan to open up new land, address sewage problems, and improve water quality (Campanella, Etheridge, and Meffert 2004; Colten 2002).

The engineering feats performed in New Orleans gave confidence to city residents. Large levees, better drainage, and powerful pumps provided a system of protection for the first time in the history of the city. The system, however, experienced a sudden shock in April 1927 when a lightening strike damaged the power station feeding the pumps in the city. With heavy rainfall and without working pumps, the city, situated in a bowl created by its substantial levees, began to fill with water (Kelman 2003). The flooding was significant and fears of continued flooding rippled through the city. Businesspeople were alarmed and observed that "investors were pulling out of the local markets, consumers were fleeing, shops were closing their doors, and commerce was grinding to a halt" (Kelman 2003, 161). They proposed a plan, supported by the governor of Louisiana and approved by the federal government, to cut the levee downriver to relieve pressure on New Orleans (Gomez 2000). The subsequent "release value" along the levee flooded the rural, poor, less powerful residents of St. Bernard Parish. While New Orleans rebounded relatively quickly from the flooding of 1927, St. Bernard Parish's recovery was much slower and fueled with resentment toward its urban neighbor (Gomez 2000; Kelman 2003).

New Orleans's prosperity would sputter over the next few decades, negatively affected by the Great Depression and an economic upsurge following World War II. Changes in technology and the growth of other Sunbelt cities in the post-war period challenged New Orleans's economy (Lewis 2003). The environment was also changing during the period. The drainage system created in the early part of the century removed water from the soils causing compaction and subsidence in New Orleans (Campanella, Etheridge, and Meffert 2004).

In the 1950s, economic competition spurred the Mississippi River Gulf Outlet project. This project again reworked the natural environment by cutting a channel through the delta, reducing ships' voyages from New Orleans to the Gulf of Mexico by forty miles (Lewis 2003; Shallat 2000). This project, completed in 1963, would be blamed, although erroneously, for the damage delivered in 1965 by Hurricane Betsy, a category 3 storm that flooded the Lower Ninth Ward of New Orleans and its neighbor, St. Bernard Parish (Gilgoff 2005; Shallat 2000). Betsy revealed the threat to New Orleans's area and its economic interests, including oil, gas, and shipping. The federal government responded to the threat with $56 million and the expertise of the Army Corps of Engineers. The plan was for new flood controls, including new levees to open up development in New Orleans East, a swampy area northeast of downtown along Lake Pontchartrain (Shallat 2000).

Centuries of challenges and disasters failed to discourage development, even in areas well below sea level. Time merely delivered more sophisticated efforts to control the environment around New Orleans. However, human actions changed the environment of the Delta and New Orleans. The levees grew in number and height to compensate for the river's response to manipulation, the city continued to sink as a result of drainage control, and the Delta's wetlands shrank from sediment starvation due to upriver canals and dams (Campanella, Etheridge, and Meffert 2004).

Global changes in the environment pose even more threat to New Orleans. Climate change due to global warming is thought to be increasing storm activity, suggesting greater vulnerability to catastrophic hurricanes. Based on their research of the North Atlantic Ocean region, Holland and Webster find "the increasing number of tropical cyclones also results in a strong trend in major hurricane numbers that is directly associated with greenhouse warming" (2007, 2713). Local and global environmental changes provided the conditions for a hurricane disaster in New Orleans. Katrina brought death and devastation to the city and also exposed to the world the inequalities embedded in the city's social development and structure.

Social Development and Residential Patterns

The area around New Orleans attracted and was inhabited by many racial and ethnic groups prior to the Civil War. These groups included Native Americans, Europeans, individuals of African descent and mixed races, and a broad range of persons identified as Americans (Somers 1974). Nonetheless, racially, New Orleans has been viewed largely in black and white terms. In fact, the relationship between blacks and whites is critical to understanding the city's social development and the residential patterns that made African Americans particularly vulnerable to the destruction of Hurricane Katrina.

In the eighteenth century, the French exploited economic opportunities and controlled the Mississippi River by importing thousands of African slaves into the area.[2] Many of these slaves worked in agriculture, domestic service, and levee building (Morris 2000). Due to the demand for slaves and the location of New Orleans on the river, the city became the "largest slave-trading center in the United States" (Spain 1979, 83).

Slavery influenced the residential patterns in New Orleans in the early years. Racial segregation was not evident, because slaves tended to live on the property of their owners. Even free blacks working as domestics often lived close to their white employers (Lewis 2003). This pattern of residential integration is described by Daphne Spain: "The richest whites were located along the major boulevards, which were in turn separated by ten or fifteen smaller streets. Blacks who lived behind the big house lived several blocks behind the main boulevard on one of the interior streets" (1979, 86). According to Spain (1979), not all whites could afford the grand houses, and thus interior streets also were home to less affluent whites.

The number of free blacks increased under Spanish rule at the end of the eighteenth century, and the slave trade was ended by the United States in the first decade of the nineteenth century (Ingersoll 1991). While the practice of slavery was not abolished until 1865, in New Orleans the relatively large number of free blacks resulted in some residential segregation. Furthermore, extremely poor blacks had few options and, as a result, tended to locate in the least desirable areas including the backswamps and the river side of the levee (Lewis 2003; Spain 1979).

The postbellum period witnessed successful black activism aimed at desegregation of public facilities. However, by the late 1870s, legally sanctioned discrimination began limiting the freedoms of blacks in Louisiana. The Jim Crow laws effectively denied blacks many previously available opportunities and contributed significantly to increasing residential segregation in the early part of the twentieth century (Colten 2002; Spain 1979). Spain (1979) argues that two technological innovations contributed to rising residential segregation in New Orleans during this period. First, public transportation improvements allowed blacks and whites more mobility and the ability to distance themselves from one another. Second, the development of the wood pump allowed draining of swampy areas around New Orleans and fostered residential development. Jim Crow laws, however, limited these housing opportunities to whites. Colten offers a similar perspective about the public works improvements to drainage in New Orleans and their interaction with Jim Crow laws. He writes:

City ordinances and later deed restrictions were the primary agents of residential segregation toward the lakefront. While they may not have caused segregation, they legally obstructed desegregation. Vast tracts of lakefront property drained after 1920 became entirely new subdivisions, and ordinances and racially restrictive deeds effectively closed them to African-Americans. (2002, 283)

Spain (1979) documents increased residential segregation (as measured by the index of dissimilarity) between 1930 and 1960. Several factors contributed to increased segregation over the post–World War II period. First, according to Martha Mahoney, "federally subsidized 'private' housing was closed to blacks and [was] one of the factors increasing black ghettoization during this period" (1990, 1276). Second, blacks were concentrated in public housing within the city. Finally, suburbanization, particularly "white flight," resulted in demographic change in the city.

New Orleans Demographics

New Orleans grew in population over most of its history and the proportion of blacks to whites varied from a majority during slavery times to a substantial, but lower, proportion through the first half of the twentieth century. Population trends, however, changed beginning in the 1960s. The population of New Orleans hit a peak in 1960 with 627,525 persons, but each decade thereafter, the city lost population with about a 23 percent decline between 1960 and 2000 (U.S. Census Bureau 2005a). Whites were leaving the city resulting in minorities, predominantly African Americans, comprising a majority share of the total population by 1980 (see figure 5.1).[3]

Since 1980, the New Orleans metropolitan area has exhibited a relatively high degree of racial, residential segregation. In 1980, the dissimilarity index for blacks in the New Orleans Metropolitan Statistical Area (MSA) was 0.698, higher than the index value of 0.660 for the South (based on 114 MSAs) as a whole. The index decreased for New Orleans and the South in 1990 (0.679 and 0.605, respectively), but increased again for New Orleans in the following decade. In 2000, the dissimilarity index for the New Orleans MSA was 0.684, while the South at 0.581 exhibited continued decline in residential segregation (Iceland, Weinberg, and Steinmetz, 2002; U.S. Census Bureau 2005b). The dissimilarity index for New Orleans in 2000 indicated 68.4 percent of blacks would have to change locations to achieve an even racial distribution across the MSA.[4]

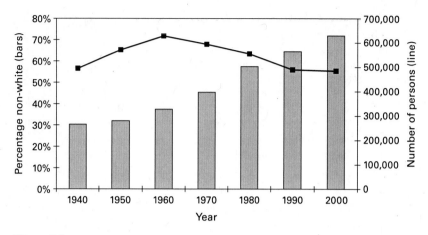

Figure 5.1
Incorporating human vulnerability's "double structure"

Data for New Orleans suggest an aging population. The median age in the city increased from 28.7 years in 1980 to 33.1 years in 2000 (U.S. Department of Commerce, Bureau of the Census 1988; U.S. Census Bureau 2005a). Much of this increase has been due to the aging of the baby boomer population, with persons 65 years and older (elderly) actually decreasing in numbers over the last decade. Despite this decrease, in 2000, 56,000 elderly persons, approximately 11.7 percent of the total population of New Orleans, lived in the city (U.S. Census Bureau 2005a).

Socioeconomic indicators from the 2000 U.S. Census reveal New Orleans residents were relatively worse off compared to the nation as a whole. Slightly more than a quarter of New Orleans residents (25 years and older) did not have a high school diploma or equivalent. While this proportion was similar to the state of Louisiana as a whole, it was higher than the national figure of 19.6 percent. The unemployment rate[5] for the city in 2000 was 9.5 percent, higher than the state (7.3%) and the nation's (5.8%) rates. In 2000, the home ownership rate in New Orleans at 46.5 percent was much lower than the state and national rates, 67.9 percent and 66.2 percent, respectively. On all these indicators, the differences between blacks and whites in New Orleans are striking[6] (see table 5.1). Over 32 percent of blacks lacked a high school diploma or equivalent, compared to 11.4 percent of whites. Unemployment also was noticeably higher among blacks (13.1%) than whites (3.6%). The home

Table 5.1
Socioeconomic characteristics by race

Socioeconomic characteristics	Black #	Black % within race	White #	White % within race
Less than high school education	59,593	32.6%	11,843	11.4%
Unemployment	16,853	13.1%	2,678	3.6%
Home ownership	47,053	41.6%	37,400	55.4%
Below poverty	110,215	35.0%	15,004	11.5%
Median family income	$25,017	—	$61,448	—

Source: U.S. Census Bureau 2005a.

ownership rate for blacks (41.6%) was almost 14 percent lower than the rate for whites (55.4%) (U.S. Census Bureau 2005a).

New Orleans population has endured decades of relatively high poverty. The percentage of persons in poverty[7] within the city has seesawed over the last three decades: decreasing from 1969 to 1979; increasing between 1979 and 1989; and decreasing by about 4 percent from 1989 to 1999 (U.S. Department of Commerce, Bureau of the Census 1973; 1988; U.S. Census Bureau 2005b). Despite the decrease in the poverty rate in 1999, New Orleans had a much higher poverty rate (27.9%) than the state of Louisiana (19.6%) or the nation as a whole (12.4%). Moreover, in 1999, the percentage of blacks in poverty was much higher than for whites (see table 5.1). This disparity between races is also reflected in the substantial difference in median family incomes between blacks and whites in 1999 (U.S. Census Bureau 2005a).

Poverty also affected a substantial proportion of the elderly population. In 1999, while only about 8 percent of the total population in poverty was elderly, over 19 percent of all elderly were in poverty. Among the elderly in poverty, blacks represented an alarmingly high proportion of the population. Elderly whites comprised 22.7 percent of all elderly in poverty, while blacks comprised 73.5 percent of this group (U.S. Census Bureau 2005a).

High-poverty neighborhoods are common in New Orleans. Using Paul Jargowsky's (1997) definition of high poverty being a poverty rate of 40 percent or higher, over one quarter of the neighborhoods (49 of 181) in New Orleans in 1999 were high poverty. These neighborhoods tended to

Table 5.2
African Americans and elderly in high poverty neighborhoods in New Orleans
compared to all neighborhoods in the city

Neighborhood characteristics	High poverty Mean	City Mean
African Americans	85.0%	63.4%
Elderly	10.5%	12.4%

Source: U.S. Census Bureau 2005a.

be heavily African American (see table 5.2). In fact, high poverty neighborhoods, on average, are about 85 percent African American, while the mean percentage for all neighborhoods in the city is slightly greater than 63 percent (U.S. Census Bureau 2005a). High poverty neighborhoods tend to have a smaller percentage of elderly compared to city neighborhoods in general. However, these neighborhoods, on average, are home to 10.5 percent of the elderly population.

The demographic overview reveals population change and disparities between blacks and whites, and between the young and the elderly. Coupled with the city's history of physical and social development, the socio-demographics of New Orleans expose the vulnerabilities of the city to natural disaster and human insecurity. They also illuminate the stark inequalities in the city and help explain, in part, the lack of preparedness by individuals and local government.

Vulnerability, Disaster, and Preparedness

The physical environment of New Orleans is undeniably vulnerable to natural hazards. The city resides in hurricane country, is nestled between major water bodies, and is crossed by water channels. Moreover, much of the city is below sea level including nearly all of the northern part of the city. To combat these vulnerabilities, the city possesses a man-made defense system of levees to keep water from the city and powerful pumps to remove water that gets into the city.

Hurricane Katrina tested the city's defense system and revealed *its* vulnerabilities. Levees breached and the pumps failed, allowing water to fill the city. Much of the city was flooded including the low-lying Lakeview and New Orleans East neighborhoods in the northern section of the city (E. Thomas 2005). The Lower Ninth Ward in the southeastern corner of the city was also extensively flooded, just as it had been during Hurricane Betsy in 1965 (Greater New Orleans Community Data Center 2002; E. Thomas 2005).

Katrina also exposed the social inequalities within New Orleans and the vulnerabilities of specific groups to this environmental disaster. Little and Conklin (chapter 4) state that vulnerability relates to both exposure to risks and the capacity to handle them. A clear understanding of this is found in the case of Katrina and New Orleans. Vulnerable populations[8] —the poor, mostly blacks, and the aged—with little means to evacuate the city stayed behind in shelters of last resort, the Superdome and the Convention Center, or in their homes. When the city flooded and power and water service failed, tens of thousands of people were stranded in the city in the summer heat and without proper supplies. Hundreds died in New Orleans and others suffered for days in fetid, unhealthy conditions waiting for relief (E. Thomas 2005; Thomas and Susman 2005; Zucchino 2005).

Katrina revealed a population and multiple levels of government that were unprepared for disaster. Based on extant research, it is not surprising that vulnerable populations in New Orleans were unprepared for Katrina. Studies have found that minority and lower-income households are less prepared for disasters compared to white and higher-income households (Fothergill, Maestas, and Darlington 1999; Mileti and Darlington 1995; Tierney 1993; Turner, Nigg, and Heller-Paz 1986). Results on age and preparedness suggest a positive relationship (Sattler, Kaiser, and Hittner 2000); however, some studies have found an inverse relationship (see Heller et al. 2005). Furthermore, given that the recommended action to the approach of Katrina was evacuation, many observers have used census data to show that blacks were far less likely to have access to a car to evacuate. Jason DeParle, for example, explains, "The divides in the city were evident in things as simple as access to a car. The 35 percent of black households that didn't have one, compared with just 15 percent among whites" (2005, 1). In an ecological analysis of New Orleans neighborhoods, Basolo (2005a) finds that the percentage of blacks, the poverty rate, and percentage of elderly (65 and over) living alone explain about 79 percent of the variation in the percentage of housing units with at least one car available.[9]

The research evidence suggests institutional preparedness for disaster should give special attention to vulnerable populations. The city of New Orleans, the state of Louisiana, and the federal government were well aware of the vulnerability of the city to major flooding and had created plans in the event of a disaster. The city plans included an evacuation protocol that specifically states, "Approximately 100,000 Citizens of New Orleans do not have means of personal transportation" (City of New Orleans n.d. a, n.d. b.).[10] Despite acknowledgment of many residents' limited access to vehicles in the plan, as well as acknowledgment of special needs populations, actions to protect vulnerable populations mainly involved provision of a shelter of last resort.

City plans also called for risk and preparedness communication to city residents. Information on the level of the city's outreach concerning disaster preparedness and planning is unavailable at this time; therefore, it is not known whether vulnerable populations received adequate information on disaster preparedness. However, recent analyses of 1999 survey data on hurricane preparedness by residents in parts of New Orleans and St. Bernard Parish suggest that vulnerable populations did not receive adequate information. The analyses indicate that preparedness actions and exposure to preparedness information sources are positively associated. However, these data also show that blacks and low-income households are exposed to fewer information sources (Basolo 2005b). Thus, it may be that these vulnerable populations were unaware of the actions to take in preparation for the disaster.

Planning for disaster resulted in mixed results. Eighty percent of the city evacuated to safety; however, many of the city's residents, mainly from vulnerable populations, were left to suffer the brunt of the disaster. Furthermore, post-disaster response was slow from higher levels of government and again had negative consequences for vulnerable populations. In the aftermath of Katrina, blame for ineffective planning and response was aimed at all levels of government (Murdock 2005; C. B. Thomas 2005). Regardless of the ultimate division of responsibility for failures, it is clear that vulnerable populations, blacks, the poor, and the elderly suffered disproportionately from the devastation wrought by Katrina and that human security was a neglected concern in the city.

The Recovery of New Orleans

Recovery is central to New Orleans and its residents today. Yet, the recovery process has different interpretations depending on the focal object. A simple recovery might be restoration of the pre-Katrina population. New Orleans lost more than 50 percent of its population between

2000 and 2007 (U.S. Department of Commerce, Bureau of the Census 2008). The composition of the population also appears to have changed. According to the Census Bureau, 62 percent of the population living in New Orleans today is black, about a 6 percentage point decrease from the pre-Katrina figure. Furthermore, the population appears to be older, on average[11] (*Louisiana Weekly* 2008). However, mere population restoration seems too superficial upon which to make recovery claims.

The strengthening of levees and physical rebuilding in the city appear to be the critical recovery concerns of government. The U.S. Army Corps of Engineers (2008) has improved flood protection in New Orleans and estimates completion of one-hundred-year flood protection by 2011. The city's Web page invites readers to "Track our recovery process"; offers a list of public improvements, such as building rehabilitation and park development, in various stages of completion; and announces "the New Orleans economy is being driven by more than $1 billion in federal money on bricks-and-mortar hurricane recovery projects" (City of New Orleans 2008). While the public infrastructure is an important element of the city's revitalization process, it is only one dimension of recovery.

Recovery of New Orleans's distinctive neighborhoods is an important goal of residents. Katrina razed some neighborhoods and caused major and minor damage in others. The differential impact of the storm translates into variation in recovery, both in terms of structures (houses and businesses) and the neighborhood social fabric. While the former can be rebuilt, the latter may never be retrieved in some neighborhoods.

Recovery, in part, includes better disaster planning and preparedness (beyond flood walls, pumps, and levees). In late August 2008, the city's current approach to avoiding human loss related to storms was tested by Hurricane Gustav. As Gustav approached Louisiana, official city communication was persistent and unambiguous. Officials issued a mandatory evacuation order, offered transportation out of the city to all residents, provided no shelter of last resort within the city, and announced "you are on your own" if you decided to ignore the evacuation order. Reports suggest that most New Orleanians left the city. While Gustav did not land a direct hit on the city, its threat shows that local officials learned from the previous disaster and responded effectively to protect residents.

These forms of recovery are essential to issues of human security in New Orleans. I return to these issues in discussing the future of New Orleans in my conclusion.

Conclusion

The physical and social vulnerabilities of New Orleans led to disaster. Human actions over a long period shaped the physical and social environments of the city. Development, driven by economic interests, spread into areas particularly susceptible to flooding. Human actions also created a social structure that placed some groups at greater risk than others. The poor, mainly black, tended to be located in areas of low elevation prone to flooding. This group also had fewer resources to avoid the consequences of disaster. Lack of transportation to evacuate the city left this group in harm's way. Many elderly also had limited mobility and were left behind in their homes or evacuated to inadequate shelters of last resort.

Institutional response, particularly by government, failed the vulnerable populations of New Orleans. While official planning documents acknowledged the limited resources of a significant proportion of the city's population, actions directly prior to Katrina and in her wake were largely inadequate to protect vulnerable populations. Moreover, disaster response to residents stranded in the city after the storm was slow and disheartening.

Lessons can be learned from the lack of preparedness and inadequate response displayed during the Katrina event. Better risk communication and preparedness training for vulnerable populations could reduce the impact of future environmental hazard events. Moreover, improved planning and coordination among intergovernmental agencies is necessary. Blame assignation, especially when it sounds more like "passing the buck" instead of identifying the weaknesses in the system, does little to produce positive change. While the recent threat of Hurricane Gustav displayed a more confident and definitive management of evacuation procedures, many disaster preparedness researchers still identify a need for an intergovernmental planning and preparedness system overhaul with emphasis on reducing risks for people and special attention to the needs of vulnerable populations.

The future of New Orleans is uncertain at this point. Throughout its history, the city has flooded and the response has been higher levees and more sophisticated engineering. The engineering response has been no different post-Katrina. Of course, raising the levees and strengthening flood walls in the past have not eliminated disaster. In fact, the city has many conditions that suggest disaster cannot be averted in the long term:

the city is subsiding, so increasing the height of the levees makes New Orleans a deeper bowl susceptible to filling with water; pumps are expected to remove water from the city but can fail due to fatigue and storm effects; the erosion of wetlands between the Gulf of Mexico and the city makes New Orleans more vulnerable to hurricanes; and climate change due to global warming increases the threat of catastrophic hurricanes.

New Orleans geographic and topographic vulnerability to hurricanes puts the whole population at risk. However, research and experience show some groups such as minorities, the poor, and the elderly are likely to have fewer resources available to mitigate the risks of a major storm, before and after the event. In other words, they have a lower capacity to protect themselves from harm and are more vulnerable to a hurricane than others in the population. Thus, while hurricanes are threats to human security, they present a more complex and challenging problem for vulnerable populations and leadership seeking to provide protection to all. Recovery for New Orleans, therefore, requires more than stronger levees, bricks and mortar, and rebuilding of neighborhoods. It also means increasing the capacity of vulnerable populations to ensure their security and well-being under environmental change. At the very least, capacity building would include better preparedness education for vulnerable populations, but a longer-term plan to reduce inequalities (socially, economically, and politically) is ultimately the only way to truly strengthen capacity over the long term.

New Orleans is a distinctive case for the United States because of its development history *and* the revelations Katrina made about the city's vulnerable populations. It is not distinctive, however, in that other areas within the United States and throughout the world have environmental risks and vulnerable populations. For this reason, New Orleans is an instructive case for policymakers globally as they design and implement policies aimed at human security.

Notes

1. The intensity of hurricanes is described using the Saffir-Simpson scale. The rating ranges from low (1) to high (5). According this scale, a category 4 storm produces winds of 131–155 mph with a storm surge of 13–18 feet. Extensive damage including flooding of low-lying areas is expected with this level of hurricane (National Weather Service, National Hurricane Center, Tropical Prediction Center 2005).

2. The French attempted to enslave Native Americans in the region; however, this scheme failed and the next strategy was to exchange Native Americans for African slaves from the West Indies (Spain 1979). Moreover, under French rule, slaves had limited opportunity to buy their freedom. Spanish policies, however, supported emancipation of Blacks in the territory (Ingersoll 1991).

3. The U.S. Census Bureau changed categories and its reporting of racial categories through time; therefore, exact counts of the black population in New Orleans are not used in figure 5.1. However, comparing the decennial counts for which black (alone) is reported with years that the Census reports nonwhites and mixed race suggests that non-whites is a good proxy for the black population over time.

4. The dissimilarity index was calculated using white, non-Hispanics as the reference group. This index can range from 0 (fully integrated) to 1 (fully segregated) (Massey and Denton 1988).

5. Unemployment rates were calculated as civilian, unemployed persons in the labor force divided by all civilian persons in the labor force.

6. For the racial comparisons in this section of the chapter, I use the census categories "white alone" and "black alone."

7. The federal poverty measure was developed in the 1960s based on the cost of food to maintain an adequate diet times three to account for other expenses. This measure has many shortcomings but continues to be used despite recommendations for an improved measure of poverty (see Citro and Michael 1995).

8. The term "vulnerable populations" is used commonly in medical research, although a consensus on a single definition of the concept has not been reached. Many of the definitions implicitly or explicitly associate vulnerability with marginalized or disadvantaged groups (see Ruof 2004). In hazards research, social vulnerability has been defined as a combination of social and place inequalities. As Cutter, Boruff, and Shirley explain, social vulnerability includes "social factors that influence or shape the susceptibility of various groups to harm and that also govern their ability to respond [and] characteristics of communities and the built environment such as the level of urbanization, growth rates, and economic vitality, that contribute to the social vulnerability of places" (2003, 243).

9. These results, based on a multiple regression analysis, identify the poverty rate as the strongest predictor of the lack of a car, followed by percentage of blacks and elderly living alone.

10. The author previously downloaded the plans from the web in 2005. However, a later visit to the city site found a request for registration to access the city's Comprehensive Emergency Management Plan and when registration was attempted, access was denied. Parts of the comprehensive plan are available on other web sites (see, e.g, http://www.freerepublic.com/focus/f-news/1478607/posts).

11. These population numbers are contested by city officials who claim an undercount of the total population. Other experts in the city argue that the methodology used to estimate the composition of the population in 2007 is flawed and

more accurate counts will have to wait for the 2010 Census (*Louisiana Weekly* 2008). The Decennial Census also will provide more detailed socioeconomic data such as poverty rates and level of residential segregation.

References

Basolo, Victoria. 2005a. Vulnerability and disaster: Individual and structural explanations of the differential impacts of Hurricane Katrina. Unpublished manuscript.

Basolo, Victoria. 2005b. Why do households fail to prepare for disasters? Citizen perceptions of local government response and their exposure to preparedness information. Paper presented at the HUD Urban Scholars Symposium, Washington, DC, November 7.

Campanella, Richard, Daniel Etheridge, and Douglas J. Meffert. 2004. Sustainability, survivability, and the paradox of New Orleans. *Annals of the New York Academy of Sciences* 1023:289–299.

Citro, Constance F., and Robert T. Michael, eds. 1995. *Measuring poverty: A new approach*. Washington, DC: National Academies Press.

City of New Orleans. 2008. City website. http://www.cityofno.com/ (accessed November 15, 2008).

City of New Orleans. n.d. a. City of New Orleans comprehensive emergency management plan. http://www.cityofno.com/portal.aspx?portal=46&tabid=26 (accessed November 15, 2008).

City of New Orleans. n.d. b. Emergency guide for citizens with disabilities. http://www.cityofno.com/portal.aspx?portal=46&tabid=4 (accessed November 15, 2008).

Colten, Craig E. 2002. Basin street blues: Drainage and environmental equity in New Orleans, 1890–1930. *Journal of Historical Geography* 28 (2): 237–257.

Colten, Craig E. 2005. *An unnatural metropolis: Wresting New Orleans from nature*. Baton Rouge: Louisiana State University Press.

Connolly, Ceci, and Manuel Roig-Franzia. 2005. Grim map details toll in 9th ward and beyond. *Washington Post*, October 23, A14.

Cutter, Susan L., Bryan J. Boruff, and W. Lynn Shirley. 2003. Social vulnerability to environmental hazards. *Social Science Quarterly* 84 (2): 242–261.

Davis, Donald W. 2000. Historical perspective on crevasses, levees, and the Mississippi River. In *Transforming New Orleans and Its Environs*, ed. Craig E. Colten, 84–105. Pittsburgh: University of Pittsburgh Press.

DeParle, Jason. 2005. Broken levees, unbroken barriers. *New York Times* September 4, sec. 4, 1.

Din, Gilbert C., and John E. Harkins. 1996. *The New Orleans cabildo: Colonial Louisiana's first city government, 1769–1803*. Baton Rouge: Louisiana State University Press.

Essence. 2005. Voices from the Gulf. November, 195.

Evans, Martin C., and Tina Susman. 2005. Katrina: The search continues. *Newsday*, September 5, A4.

Fothergill, Alice, Enrique G.M. Maestas, and JoAnne DeRouen Darlington. 1999. Race, ethnicity and disasters in the United States: A review of the literature. *Disasters* 23 (2): 156–173.

Gilgoff, Dan. 2005. Big blow in the Big Easy. *U.S. News & World Report*, July 18, 46.

Gomez, Gay M. 2000. Perspective, power, and priorities. In *Transforming New Orleans and Its Environs*, ed. Craig E. Colten, 109–120. Pittsburgh: University of Pittsburgh Press.

Greater New Orleans Community Data Center. 2002. Lower ninth ward neighborhood snapshot. http://www.gnocdc.org/orleans/8/22/snapshot.html (accessed November 15, 2008).

Heller, Kenneth, Douglas B. Alexander, Margaret Gatz, Bob G. Knight, and Tara Rose. 2005. Social and personal factors as predictors of earthquake preparation: The role of support provision, network discussion, negative affect, age, and education. *Journal of Applied Social Psychology* 35 (2): 399–422.

Holland, Greg J., and Peter J. Webster. 2007. Heightened tropical cyclone activity in the North Atlantic: Natural variability or climate trend? *Philosophical Transactions of the Royal Society A* 365 (1860): 2695–2716.

Iceland, John, Daniel H. Weinberg, and Erika Steinmetz. 2002. Racial and ethnic segregation in the United States, 1980–2000. Paper presented at the annual meetings of the Population Association of America, Atlanta, GA, May 9–11. http://www.census.gov/hhes/www/housing/housing_patterns/working_papers.html (accessed November 15, 2008).

Ingersoll, Thomas N. 1991. Free blacks in a slave society: New Orleans, 1718–1812. *The William and Mary Quarterly* (3rd Ser.) 48 (2): 173–200.

Jargowsky, Paul A. 1997. *Poverty and place: Ghettos, barrios, and the American city.* New York: Russell Sage Foundation.

Kelman, Ari. 2003. *A river and its city: The nature of landscape in New Orleans.* Berkeley: University of California Press.

Lewis, Pierce. 2003. *New Orleans: The making of an urban landscape.* Sante Fe, NM, and Harrisonburg, VA: Center for American Places in association with the University of Virginia Press.

Louisiana Weekly. 2008. Census says New Orleans is Still a "Chocolate" *Metropolis*, August 11. http://www.louisianaweekly.com/news.php?viewStory=257 (accessed November 15, 2008).

Mahoney, Martha. 1990. Law and racial geography: Public housing and the economy in New Orleans. *Stanford Law Review* 42 (5): 1251–1290.

Massey, Douglas S., and Nancy A. Denton. 1988. The dimensions of residential segregation. *Social Forces* 67 (2): 281–315.

Mileti, Dennis S., and J. D. Darlington. 1995. Societal response to revised earthquake probabilities in the San Francisco Bay Area. *International Journal of Mass Emergencies and Disasters* 13:119–145.

Morris, Christopher. 2000. Impenetrable but easy: The French transformation of the lower Mississippi valley and the founding of New Orleans. In *Transforming New Orleans and Its Environs*, ed. Craig E. Colten, 22–41. Pittsburgh: University of Pittsburgh Press.

Murdock, Deroy. 2005. Multi-layered failures. *National Review Online*, September 13. http://www.nationalreview.com/murdock/murdock200509130839.asp (accessed March 3, 2009).

National Weather Service, National Hurricane Center, Tropical Prediction Center. 2005. The Saffir-Simpson hurricane scale. http://www.nhc.noaa.gov/aboutsshs.shtml (accessed November 15, 2008).

Ruof, Mary C. 2004. Vulnerability, vulnerable populations, and policy. *Kennedy Institute of Ethics Journal* 14 (4): 411–425.

Sattler, David N., Charles F. Kaiser, and James B. Hittner. 2000. Disaster preparedness: Relationships among prior experience, personal characteristics, and distress. *Journal of Applied Social Psychology* 30 (7): 1396–1420.

Shallat, Todd. 2000. In the wake of Hurricane Betsy. In *Transforming New Orleans and Its Environs*, ed. Craig E. Colten, 121–137. Pittsburgh: University of Pittsburgh Press.

Somers, Dale A. 1974. Black and white in New Orleans: A study in urban race relations, 1865–1900. *The Journal of Southern History* 40 (1): 19–42.f

Spain, Daphne. 1979. Race relations and residential segregation in New Orleans: Two centuries of paradox. *Annals of the American Academy of Political and Social Science* 441:82–96.

Thomas, Cathy Booth. 2005. New Orleans today: It's worse than you think. *Time*, November 28, 30–37.

Thomas, Evan. 2005. The lost city. *Newsweek*, September 12, 42.

Thomas, Katie, and Tina Susman. 2005. Katrina evacuations. *Newsday*, September 4, A3.

Tierney, Kathleen J. 1993. Disaster preparedness and response: Research findings and guidance from the social science literature. Preliminary Paper #193. Newark: University of Delaware Disaster Research Center.

Turner, Ralph H., Joanne M. Nigg, and Denise Heller-Paz. 1986. *Waiting for disaster: Earthquake watch in California*. Berkeley: University of California Press.

U.S. Army Corps of Engineers. 2008. New Orleans hurricane and storm damage risk reduction system 2008 facts and figures (released August 28, 2008). http://www.mvn.usace.army.mil/hps2/index.asp (accessed November 15, 2008).

U.S. Census Bureau. 2005a. Census 2000. Summary Files 1 and 3. http://factfinder.census.gov/servlet/DatasetMainPageServlet?_program=DEC&_lang=en&_ts (accessed November 15, 2008).

U.S. Census Bureau.2005b. Housing and Household Economic Statistics Division. 19 measures of residential housing patterns, metropolitan area (MSA/PMSA).   http://www.census.gov/hhes/www/housing/housing_patterns/gettable_msa.html (accessed November 15, 2008).

U.S. Department of Commerce, Bureau of the Census. 1973. *County and city data book 1972*. Washington, DC.

U.S. Department of Commerce, Bureau of the Census. 1988. *County and city data book 1988*. Washington, DC.

U.S. Department of Commerce, Bureau of the Census. 2008. U.S. Census Bureau News, press release, July 10. http://www.census.gov/Press-Release/www/releases/archives/population/012242.html (accessed November 15, 2008).

Zucchino, David. 2005. Katrina's aftermath: 'They just left us here to die.' *Los Angeles Times*, September 4, A23.

III

Global Environmental Change, Conflict, and Cooperation

6

Environmental Change, Human Security, and Violent Conflict

Jon Barnett and W. Neil Adger

This chapter examines the interconnections between environmental change and the risk of violent conflict. It also examines the role of states in human security and peace building. We argue that environmental change causes security problems for some individuals and social groups by reducing access to, and the quality of, natural resources that are important to sustain their livelihoods. Environmental change may also, through a range of largely indirect effects, undermine the capacity of states to provide the opportunities and services that help people to sustain their livelihoods. These effects on livelihood are one of numerous coexisting factors that increase the risk of violent conflicts.

Change for the Worse

The development of modern industrial societies has ushered in a historically unprecedented increase in the impacts of human activity on the biosphere. Fossil fuel use, resource use, the production of waste, and human population worldwide have all grown exponentially since the beginnings of the Industrial Revolution in the latter half of the eighteenth century (Ponting 1991). The growth of modern industrialized societies has caused excess consumption and waste generation in the industrialized world, poverty and debt in the industrializing world, and environmental changes of a scale and magnitude that put at risk the economic, cultural, spiritual, and social needs and values of communities.

The types of environmental changes that societies now contend with include but are not limited to deforestation, land degradation, water pollution and scarcity, biodiversity losses, and coastal and marine degradation (including coastal erosion, coral loss and coral bleaching, contracting artisanal fisheries, pollution of lagoons, and overfishing of oceanic stocks). The extent and nature of these stresses are determined by the level of dependence on natural resources and ecosystem services, and the capacity to adapt to changes in these resources and services. In other words, the more people directly depend on natural capital for their livelihoods, other things being equal, the more immediate are the risks they face from environmental change (Millennium Ecosystem Assessment 2005). However, all social-ecological systems are interdependent and no part of the world, social group, or economic system can insulate itself from global change.

There is now a considerable body of evidence that environmental change is a cause of human insecurity that we define here as the risk of loss or injury to one or more of an individual or community's core needs, rights, or values. This definition is informed by the Global Environmental Change and Human Security project, which defines human security as being "achieved when and where individuals and communities have the options necessary to end, mitigate, or adapt to threats to their human, environmental, and social rights; have the capacity and freedom to exercise these options; and actively participate in attaining these options" (Lonergan et al. 1999). We talk of needs, rights, and values as a means to highlight the imperative for some stability in the provision of the needs required for a person to function as an equal member of a society, the fundamental rights to which people are entitled, and the unique things that people and communities value for themselves.

Thus far the focus of research on environmental change and human security has been on the largely local economic and institutional dynamics that limit individuals' and groups' access to environmental, financial, and social resources necessary to respond to variability and environmental change. Much of the knowledge in this research area has pertained to individual and collective vulnerability to observed and forecasted climate changes, but it also concerns land use changes as well as the globalization of economies, disasters, and other phenomena (see reviews in Turner et al. 2003; Pelling 2003; Adger 2006; Leichenko and O'Brien 2008). A similar social vulnerability approach to these climate-specific applications has been applied in anthropology, development, and disasters research (reviewed in Blaikie et al. 1994; see also chapter 5 by Victoria Basolo and chapter 2 by Mike Brklacich, May Chazan, and Hans-Georg Bohle in this volume). In the field of environmental security many case studies, for example from Northern Pakistan (Matthew 2001), South Asia (Najam 2003), the Niger Delta (Mochizuki 2004), the Pacific

Islands (Cocklin and Keen 2000), and Ethiopia (Haile 2004) show that environmental change can be a significant factor that undermines human security.

However, a clear message of this research is that environmental change does not undermine human security in isolation from a broader range of social factors. These include, among other things: poverty, the degree of support (or conversely discrimination) communities receive from the state, their access to economic opportunities, the effectiveness of decision-making processes, and the extent of social cohesion within and surrounding vulnerable groups. These factors determine people's and communities' entitlements to economic and social capital that in turn determine their capacity to adapt to environmental change so that the things they value are not adversely affected.

The way environmental change undermines human security varies across the world since entitlements to natural resources and services vary across space, and the social determinants of adaptive capacity are similarly varied. For example, in East Timor some 85 percent of the population is dependent on agriculture as its sole or main source of income, and the majority of the population is engaged in subsistence farming so that 46 percent of rural people live below the poverty line of US$0.55 per day (UNDP 2002). There is no effective state-directed system of income support in East Timor, but there may be customary and church-lead processes whereby food, and in some places labor, is shared. There is a modest public education system and a very basic public health system. Therefore, most rural Timorese have little or no alternative sources of food beyond their own production. Maize is the most important source of food supply, but nowhere is it an irrigated crop. Therefore, in times of low rainfall, maize production can be reduced by up to one third, resulting in widespread hunger and child malnutrition (see Barnett, Dessai, and Jones 2006). The health and well-being of rural Timorese are therefore vulnerable to environmental changes such as land degradation, and if climate change results in less rainfall in the dry season, then this may negatively affect a number of resources that rural Timorese value, such as sufficient food and good health.

While the focus of human security is the individual, the processes that undermine or strengthen human security are often beyond the geographical and political scope of individuals. In terms of environmental change, for example, upstream users of water, distant atmospheric polluters, multinational logging and mining companies, regional-scale climatic processes, and a host of other distant actors and larger-scale processes influence the security of individuals' entitlements to natural resources and services. Similarly, social determinants of vulnerability, warfare, corruption, trade dependency, macroeconomic policies, and a host of other larger-scale processes shape the so-called architecture of entitlements (Adger and Kelly 1999) that are necessary to reduce an individual's vulnerability (or increase their ability to adapt) to environmental changes. Furthermore, the determinants of human security are as temporally as they are spatially complex: past processes such as colonization and war shape present insecurities, and ongoing processes such as climate change and trade liberalization shape future insecurities.

These trends, such as economic changes in trade regimes, economic integration of regions, and liberalization of some but not all markets, create new insecurities. Leichenko and O'Brien (2008) suggest that many places are doubly exposed to economic globalization and environmental degradation. Similarly Adger, Eakin, and Winkels (2009) suggest three mechanisms of interdependence linking vulnerabilities and resilience of socioenvironmental systems around the world. First, they suggest that owing to the accelerating and increasingly global nature of environmental change processes, the impacts of environmental change in one locality are often connected to other parts of the world through human action and response. Second, Adger and colleagues, in line with Leichenko and O'Brien (2008), argue that economic market linkages can themselves be a driver of interdependent vulnerabilities. The processes of global environmental change amplify the social, political, and economic trends of globalization. Economic policies such as trade liberalization and the integration of economies into world markets can make the incomes of the poor insecure, open to vagaries and price fluctuations, and ultimately more vulnerable when other shocks and stresses come along. Third, they point to the closer connections among places around the world through the movements of people and resources. This mechanism has several consequences, both positive and negative in terms of vulnerability. Demographic changes and migration flows produce new forms of sensitivity to risk, while providing some populations with new opportunities or access to resources that enable them to mitigate vulnerability. The "follow-on" effects of the decline of certain sectors and the responses of those who depend on them for their livelihoods may in turn impact other places; for example, rural decline can cause migration to urban areas, placing increasing demand on urban services and increasing political pressure on the state.

The state itself is an important provider of various entitlements such as education, health care, law and order, credit, and protective security. If through economic contraction and increasing unemployment the revenues available to the state decline, then its ability to continue to provide certain important entitlements may weaken, which in turn may compound human insecurity for some marginalized members of its population. The extent to which system-wide impacts transpire will be determined in part by the degree to which any given national economy is dependent on natural resources, and the robustness and resilience of social institutions in managing change. In both these direct and indirect ways environmental change may be a national security issue (Barnett 2003). The risk to national security may be both a cause and consequence of human insecurity.

Table 6.1 summarizes some of the key arguments in this chapter about the ways in which environmental change may undermine human security and may, in conjunction with an array of other factors, increase the risk of violent conflict. Table 6.1 builds on what is known about the vulnerability of individuals and groups to environmental change. It is important to stress that environmental change will not undermine human security or increase the risk of violent conflict in isolation from other important social factors. And environmental change does not cause violent conflict, but it can affect some parameters that are sometimes important in generating violent conflict. Therefore human security is a function of multiple processes operating across space, over time, and at multiple scales, and hence environmental change is one important cause of human insecurity. What is less clear, however, are the ways human insecurity leads to violent conflict, which is itself a powerful cause of human insecurity and vulnerability to environmental change (Barnett 2006).

Processes of Violent Conflict

It is axiomatic that violent conflict increases human insecurity for many if not all of a population exposed to it. Among other things, violent conflict kills people, maims bodies and traumatizes minds, destroys assets and infrastructure, displaces people, disrupts families and social networks, degrades natural capital, and is strongly associated with economic

Table 6.1
The relationship between determinants of human insecurity, violent conflict, and environmental change

Factors affecting violent conflict	Processes that environmental change could affect/exacerbate
Vulnerable livelihoods	Environmental changes impact on water quality and quantity, fisheries and aquaculture, agricultural productivity, the abundance of forest resources, the frequency and intensity extreme events, and the distribution of diseases. These affect livelihoods by exposing people to risks, thereby increasing their vulnerability. The impacts are more significant in sectors of the population with high resource-dependency, and located in more environmentally and socially marginalised areas.
Poverty (relative/ chronic/ transitory)	Poverty (and particularly relative deprivation) is affected by the nature and spatial differentiation of environmental impacts and the sensitivity of places to them. Environmental can directly increase absolute, relative, and transient poverty by undermining access to natural capital. It can indirectly increase poverty through its effects on resource sectors and the ability of governments to provide social safety nets. Stresses from environmental change interact with political and economic processes such as liberalisation of markets for agricultural commodities to create inequalities in vulnerability.
Weak states	The impacts of environmental change can increase the costs of providing public infrastructure such as water resources, and services such as education, and may decrease government revenues. So it may decrease the ability of states to create opportunities and provide important freedoms for citizens.
Migration	Migration is one response of people whose livelihoods are undermined by environmental change. However environmental change is unlikely to be the sole, or even the most important factor in migration decisions. Yet large-scale movements of people seem to increase the risk of conflict in host communities.

Source: Adapted from Barnett and Adger 2007.

contraction. Not surprisingly, there is therefore a close association between low levels of human development and violent conflict (Stewart and Fitzgerald 2001).

However, beyond considering these and other impacts of violent conflict on human well-being, for the most part the issues of human security and violent conflict are treated as separate entities in research. Instead, most research into the cause of violent conflicts, including most of the greed-versus-grievance debate (see Berdal and Malone 2000), focuses on the structural conditions that increase the risk of conflict rather than the decisions of actors to engage in violent acts (Cramer 2002; Goodhand 2003; Gough 2002; Gleditsch 1998; Hauge and Ellingsen 2001; McDonald and Gaulin 2002). Yet violence happens for a number of reasons, including: because leaders are more able to mobilize some groups of people under certain conditions such as the presence of a weak state (Chossudovsky 1998); because of the "lootability" of natural resources (Collier 2000); and because to varying degrees individuals choose to engage in both violence (excluding those who are forcibly conscripted into armed groups) and peace (Cramer 2002; Gilgan 2001).

The role of individuals in initiating, sustaining, resisting, or solving violent conflicts is a major lacuna in the literature on development and violent conflict, and on environmental change and violent conflict. There are few studies that explain in any detail the ways in which human insecurity increases the risk of violent conflict (but see chapter 7 by Matthew and Upreti in this volume). This section explores the connections between human insecurity and the risk of violent conflict.

A common factor in many internal wars is that armed groups are comprised of young men whose expectations for a better life have been frustrated owing to contractions in their livelihoods (Ohlsson 2000). This makes joining an armed group a relatively more rational option to achieve some status in society, particularly when the group leaders are able to ascribe the young men's poverty to the actions of other ethnic or political groups (Goodhand 2003). Ohlsson juxtaposes the situation of declining livelihoods with a more stable state of affairs, arguing that "young men do not (at least not in significant numbers) regularly seek immediate rewards in illegal activities and looting, as long as the society they live in can provide livelihoods and a social position" (2000, 8). Indeed, poor men may have a "comparative advantage" in violence because the opportunity costs of joining armed groups are low (Goodhand 2003). The opportunity costs for women, in contrast, are relatively higher; their reproductive and domestic obligations arguably mean they are less likely to engage in acts of organized violence because this would mean forsaking those who may be dependent on them (Ohlsson 2000). The gendered division of labor in most countries also makes women the first to suffer from the direct and indirect depredations wrought by violent conflict (Brittain 2003). Perhaps for these reasons, women often are the most important actors in peace-building endeavors (Mochizuki 2004).

Some research hypothesizes that it is not so much chronic poverty per se, but rather the risk or realization of sudden poverty that increases people's propensity to join armed groups (Goodhand 2003; Ohlsson 2000). Stewart and Fitzgerald (2001) point to uncertainty about the future as being a critical factor here, and in this sense it is not just potential or actual insecurity that increases the risk of conflict, but also the perception of future insecurity. In this respect the provision of aid, and, importantly, some certainty that aid will arrive, can help reduce the recourse for people to use violence to provide for their needs (Gough 2002). In many developed countries, established and effective welfare systems perform this function, which in part helps explain why these countries experience relatively less frequent and less intense violent conflicts than developing countries do.

The causes of livelihood contraction are often but not exclusively owing to declining access to natural capital caused by, for example, deforestation; land degradation; natural disasters such as drought and flood; and population displacement related to agricultural expansion, industrial development, or the building of roads and dams. Declining access to land, or rather to the returns from human uses of land, is seen as a key process that causes livelihood contraction and hence increases the risk that people will join armed groups (de Soysa et al. 1999). Other non-ecological factors such as the rolling back of state services and declining terms of trade also matter, and often interact with natural resources use and people's access to these resources in complex ways (Reed 1996). For example, in his analysis of land invasions in a district of Chiapas, Mexico, Bobrow-Swain (2001) shows that declining agricultural production owing to economic and political forces (rather than environmental scarcity) was an important factor in land conflicts. Population growth may be a contributing factor in declining livelihoods, but it is rarely the most significant (Hartmann 1998). War itself is a significant cause of livelihood contraction: violence tends to escalate in part because it generates new causes of grievance and increased impoverishment. These factors rarely operate in isolation.

There is no consensus on whether income inequality causes violent internal conflict. Collier (2000) finds no strong association between income inequality and civil wars. However, many others argue that either vertical (class-based), horizontal (geographical or spatial), or age-based inequalities are a cause of grievance that leads to direct action to redress inequality and to take revenge, or at least makes it possible for leaders to mobilize the poor under the common cause of grievance (Cramer 2003; Goodhand 2003; Hage 2003; Stewart 2000). It is relative rather more than absolute poverty that seems to matter. Because contraction in the livelihoods of some sections of society most often implies increasing inequality (since others are not affected, or may indeed prosper), then this can create conditions more conducive to the outbreak of violence.

It is not just relative, absolute, and transient poverty that can increase the risk of violent conflict, but also a lack of opportunities for individuals and groups to act to improve their lives. Of particular importance here is access to education since it is critical for self-empowerment and increasing the prospects of employment, higher wages, and social mobility. Education enables people to improve their lives. Poverty of opportunities has been seen to be a major factor in the decisions of people—particularly young men—to join militias in Palestine, and street gangs in Managua (e.g., Hage 2003; Maclure and Sotelo 2004).

This focus on agents' decisions reinforces the arguments of Collier (2000), Duffield (2001), and others that wars are not irrational, but rather are the product of a set of rational decisions that lead to a violent reordering of economic and political systems and social relations. However, there are serious limitations to understanding agents only as rational economic actors (Cramer 2002). Joining armed gangs can serve a host of psychosocial needs, by delivering an often badly needed sense of power and status, the prospects of some social mobility (Stewart and Fitzgerald 2001), excitement, and a sense of belonging and social recognition (Hage 2003; Maclure and Sotelo 2004). The decision to join an armed gang may also be motivated by a genuine sense of grievance, frustration, and desire for revenge (Scheper-Hughes 2004); by identification with a common cause, a need for protection from violence, and denial of economic freedoms (Mwanasali 2000). "Generation gaps" between youth and elders can also be a source of frustration and alienation, pointing to the need for inclusive decision making and conflict-resolution processes (Kriger 1992). Once in a violent group, the doing of violence may in part be because of obedience to authority (Milgram 2004) and fear of exclusion from the group, and in large part because of training within armed groups and discursive processes that construct and dehumanize others (Spillmann and Spillmann 1991).

So, on the basis of the arguments and evidence already presented, it appears that human insecurity increases the risk of violent conflict. There is no single explanation for why individuals that are insecure are more likely to join armed groups and engage in violent acts. However, while the connection between human insecurity and an increased risk of violent conflict seems reasonably strong, this is not by any means to suggest (a) that the presence of widespread human insecurity, even when coupled with every other possible risk factor, means violence is more likely than not; (b) that over history the majority of directly violent acts that have caused trauma and death have been committed by the poor; (c) that the forms of structural violence that are the major cause of morbidity and mortality emanate from the decisions and actions of the poor; (d) that violent conflicts in developing countries are entirely local and caused exclusively by endogenous factors. It does suggest, however, that under certain circumstances, at the same time as it negatively affects human security, environmental change may also increase the risk of violent conflict. Livelihood security seems to be an important factor in peace, or, in Gough's words: "human security depends on a system where each rational individual calculates that it is more profitable not to rebel" (2002, 154). Of course, if it is true that human insecurity increases the risk of violent conflict, and bearing in mind that conflict certainly increases human insecurity, then this raises the prospect of iterative downward cycles of conflict, human insecurity, and conflict: in other words, conflict may be both a cause of and a product of human insecurity.

We now turn to discuss some of the larger structural circumstances—in particular the operation of states—that both shape the degree of human security as well as affect the risk of violent conflict, and the ways some of these factors may be affected by environmental change.

What Governments Can Do

Human security cannot be separated from the operation of states. An important insight from the human security perspective is that national security, narrowly defined, traditionally secures the state, but often at the expense of people (see Booth 1991). Yet states may be agents of human security too. They are critical to providing economic opportunities, creating and providing a stable environment so that livelihoods can be pursued with confidence, and providing measures to protect people when livelihoods contract; furthermore, states can exercise their sovereign rights to mediate between global flows in ways that enhance or undermine all or certain groups' livelihoods. So the state is a critical institution for the support of livelihoods. Yet given that few if any conflicts are entirely local, and that most often there are important regional and global forces at work (such as arms trading, the presence of private security forces, cross-border movements of people and goods, foreign investors, and degrees of third-party intervention), the role of the state is also central to understanding the causes of and solutions to violent conflict (Reno 2000).

States play critical roles in creating the conditions whereby people can act in ways to pursue the kind of lives they value (Sen 1999). States can provide protective guarantees to assist people when their livelihoods suddenly contract, for example through income support, food aid, or short-term local employment programs. They can provide economic freedoms that are important for people to seek employment and to interact to seek mutually advantageous outcomes in terms of consumption and production. The state can provide political freedoms such as the freedom of speech, freedom of the media, civil liberties, and the freedom to vote for parties, leaders, and policies. Provision of social opportunities such as education and health care is another important state role. States can institute transparency guarantees to ensure openness and accountability in transactions to mitigate corruption and to maintain faith in market processes. These state functions are interconnected; they "supplement" and "reinforce" each other (Sen 1999, 40), and their instrumentality is maximized when all are in place. When all these functions are extensive and effective states are legitimate, people have opportunities to develop and have less anxiety about the future; conflict-resolution mechanisms tend to be effective; and economies tend to grow and poverty levels tend to fall (Sen 1999). These are characteristics of "strong states" that have effective administrative hierarchies, control the legitimate use of force, can mediate impending conflicts before they turn violent, and are capable of managing environmental degradation and change (Esty et al. 1999). In strong liberal-democratic states both the structural conditions and livelihood factors that increase the risk of violent conflict are reduced.

The risk of violent conflict increases when states cannot provide all these functions. Thus internal wars are more likely in countries where the revenue-raising opportunities for the state are constrained. State functions that seem to be of particular importance to mitigate against the generation of violent conflicts include the provision of health care and education, protection of human rights, establishment and maintenance of a strong and independent judiciary, accountable and transparent police services and armed forces, and protection of democratic processes (Goodhand 2003; Gough 2002). Democracy, for example, gives people power to act to affect change—it creates opportunities that reduce the need for violent action to cause change, and it tends to ensure a minimal level of welfare such that people are less likely to die from, for example, famine (Sen 1999). For these reasons, groups that fall outside of the state or live beyond its protection, for reasons of geographic but also social distance, are often more likely to experience violent conflict. Goodhand (2003) points to the emergence of many violent conflicts in ecologically and economically marginal regions as evidence that relative poverty and poverty of opportunities owing to inadequate access to the state may be a key cause of violence. Bax's (2002) detailed description of the emergence of violent conflict in a Bosnian village shows that contraction of the state and the economy heightened perceptions of inequality within the village, which led to a progressive reduction of a previously pluralistic community into two groups who respectively dehumanized and ultimately began to kill each other.

Of course, where states actively deny entitlements, or deliberately repress and abuse people, violence becomes a more likely tool of resistance (Nafziger and Auvinen 2002). There can be distinct environmental factors in this process. For example, dispossession of land for mining with subsequent environmental impacts and inadequate returns to landholders was a key factor in the formation of the Bougainville Revolutionary Army in Bougainville by individuals who sought independence from Papua New Guinea (Böge 1999); and inadequate distribution of the returns from resource extraction activities has been a factor in violence in West Kalimantan in Indonesia (Peluso and Harwell 2001) and the Niger Delta (Mochizuki 2004; Watts 2001).

There are good grounds to think that when states contract—for example, as a consequence of World Bank and International Monetary Fund structural adjustment and good governance programs—so that the freedoms and opportunities they provide subsequently contract, violent conflict is more likely (Bax 2002; Bobrow-Strain 2001; Gough 2002; Gourevitch 1998). So, understanding the way environmental change increases the risk of violent conflict therefore also requires understanding the way such change may weaken (or strengthen) the capacity of states to provide or deny opportunities for people, and to manage globalization.

Other factors that increase the risk of violent conflict include: the availability of weapons; a history of conflict (according to Collier 2000, a country that has recently emerged from civil war has a 40 percent chance of another war); resource dependence (de Soysa 2000); a "youth bulge" among the working population (Cincotta 2004); and in-migration. In terms of migration, the influx of migrants into new areas has been a significant factor in many "environmental conflicts" (see Baechler 1999; Percival and Homer-Dixon 2001; Peluso and Harwell 2001). So, large migrations have at times led to conflict, and large migrations may be a consequence of environmental change (van Ireland et al. 1996). However, it is the political and institutional responses to new migrants—rather than the existence of migrants per se—that seems to be most important in cases where migration is a factor in violent conflict (Goldstone 2000), so these social dynamics of host communities are important areas for study. Further, people rarely migrate for environmental reasons alone, so understanding the way environmental change may induce more migration also requires understanding the way it will interact with other factors. It also requires understanding the strategies people use to adapt to environmental changes, of which temporary, and ultimately permanent, migration is but one (Mortimore 1989).

Conclusions

We argue in this chapter that environmental change poses risk to human insecurity principally through its potentially negative effects on individual human well-being. Because the actual or perceived insecurity of people owing to a wide range of processes—including livelihood contraction—is a factor in many violent conflicts, human insecurity caused in part by environmental change may in turn lead to more conventional security problems.

Both security and environmental change problems are determined by complex interactions across global, regional, national, and local institutions. Understanding the processes whereby environmental change leads to security problems requires having a sound understanding of the ways in which environmental change may affect localities, and the extent to which people are vulnerable to such effects. It requires understanding not just these social-ecological interactions in places, but also the many economic, political, cultural, and social interactions among different places and the ways these are altered by environmental changes. These changes are speeding up. The potential for dramatic and potentially catastrophic climate changes in the twenty-first century, in particular, increases with each passing year of inaction on reducing emissions, and as a result of this continued inaction, the prospects for the worst-case scenarios of climate change impacts on agriculture, ecosystems, and environmental services are high (Barnett and Adger 2007; Lenton et al. 2008). Social science research on human security therefore needs to directly assess radical potential changes in development trajectories and major shifts in where people choose to live as the climate changes. The challenge on insecurity requires understanding different groups' capacities to adapt to change, and the limits of those capacities. It requires understanding the potential for violent outcomes when these capacities fail. Critically important among the larger-scale institutions is the state. So, what is required is a multilevel, cross-scale, and longitudinal research approach that enables understanding of the political economy of environmental insecurities, and management of these insecurities. Research of this kind can inform decision makers of ways in which both human security and peace can be sustained.

References

Adger, W. N. 2006. Vulnerability. *Global Environmental Change* 16:268–281.

Adger, W. N., H. Eakin, and A. Winkels. 2009. Nested and teleconnected vulnerabilities to environmental change. Forthcoming in *Frontiers in Ecology and the Environment* 7.

Adger, W. N., and P. M. Kelly. 1999. Social vulnerability to climate change and the architecture of entitlements. *Mitigation and Adaptation Strategies for Global Change* 4:253–266.

Baechler, G. 1999. Environmental degradation in the south as a cause of armed conflict. In *Environmental change and security: A European perspective*, ed. A. Carius and K. Lietzmann, 107–130. Berlin: Springer-Verlag.

Barnett, J. 2003. Security and climate change. *Global Environmental Change* 13 (1): 7–17.

Barnett, J. 2006. Climate change, insecurity and justice. In *Fairness in adaptation to climate change*, ed. W. N. Adger, J. Paavola, M. J. Mace, and S. Huq, 115–129. Cambridge, MA: MIT Press.

Barnett, J., and N. Adger. 2007. Climate change, human security and violent conflict. *Political Geography* 26 (6): 639–655.

Barnett, J., S. Dessai, and R. Jones. 2006. Vulnerability to climate variability and change in East Timor. *Ambio* 36 (5): 372–378.

Bax, M. 2002. Violence formations and "ethnic cleansing" at a Bosnian pilgrimage site. In *Conflict in a globalising world: Studies in honour of Peter Kloos*, ed. D. Kooiman, A. Koster, P. Smets, and B. Venema, 69–87. Royal Van Gorcum: Assen.

Berdal, M., and D. Malone, eds. 2000. *Greed and grievance: Economic agendas in civil wars*. Boulder, CO: Lynne Rienner.

Blaikie, P., T. Cannon, I. Davies, and B. Wisner. 1994. *At risk: Natural hazards, people's vulnerability, and disasters*. London: Routledge.

Bobrow-Strain, A. 2001. Between a ranch and a hard place: Violence, scarcity, and meaning in Chiapas, Mexico. In *Violent environments*, ed. N. Peluso and M. Watts, 155–188. Ithaca, NY: Cornell University Press.

Böge, V. 1999. Mining, environmental degradation and war: The Bougainville case. In *Ecology, politics and violent conflict*, ed. M. Suliman, 211–227. London: Zed Books.

Booth, K. 1991. Security and emancipation. *Review of International Studies* 17 (4): 313–326.

Brittain, V. 2003. The impact of war on women. *Race and Class* 44 (4): 41–51.

Chossudovsky, Michel. 1998. Global poverty in the late 20th century. *Journal of International Affairs* 52 (1): 293–311.

Cincotta, R. 2004. Demographic security comes of age. *Environmental Change and Security Project Report* 10:24–29.

Cocklin, C., and M. Keen. 2000. Urbanization in the Pacific: Environmental change, vulnerability and human security. *Environmental Conservation* 27 (4): 392–403.

Collier, P. 2000. *Economic causes of civil conflict and their implications for policy*. Washington, DC: World Bank.

Cramer, C. 2002. Homo economicus goes to war: Methodological individualism, rational choice and the political economy of war. *World Development* 30 (11): 1845–1864.

Cramer, C. 2003. Does inequality cause conflict? *Journal of International Development* 15 (4): 397–412.

de Soysa, I. 2000. The resource curse: Are civil wars driven by rapacity or paucity? In *Greed and grievance: Economic agendas and civil wars*, ed. M. Berdal and D. Malone, 113–136. Boulder, CO: Lynne Rienner.

de Soysa, I., N. Gleditsch, M. Gibson, and M. Sollenberg. 1999. To cultivate peace: Agriculture in a world of conflict. *Environmental Change and Security Project Report* 5:15–25.

Duffield, M. 2001. *Global governance and the new wars: The merging of development and security.* London: Zed Books.

Esty, D., J. Goldstone, T. Gurr, B. Harff, M. Levy, G. Dabelko, P. Surko, and A. Unger. 1999. State Failure Task Force report: Phase II findings. *Environmental Change and Security Project Report* 5:49–72.

Gilgan, M. 2001. The rationality of resistance: Alternatives for engagement in complex emergencies. *Disasters* 25 (1): 1–18.

Gleditsch, N. 1998. Armed conflict and the environment: A critique of the literature. *Journal of Peace Research* 35 (3): 381–400.

Goldstone, Jack A., et. al. 2000. *State Failure Task Force report: Phase III findings.* McLean, VA: Science Applications International Corporation.

Goodhand, J. 2003. Enduring disorder and persistent poverty: A review of linkages between war and chronic poverty. *World Development* 31 (3): 629–646.

Goodin, R., ed. 1996. *The theory of institutional design.* Cambridge, UK: Cambridge University Press.

Gough, M. 2002. Human security: The individual in the security question—The case of Bosnia. *Contemporary Security Policy* 23 (3): 145–191.

Gourevitch, P. 1998. *We wish to inform you that tomorrow we will be killed with our families: Stories from Rwanda.* New York: Farrar, Strauss and Giroux.

Hage, G. 2003. "Comes a time we are all enthusiasm": Understanding Palestinian suicide bombers in times of exighophobia. *Public Culture* 15 (1): 65–89.

Haile, S. 2004. Population, development, and environment in Ethiopia. *Environmental Change and Security Project Report* 10:43–51.

Hartmann, B. 1998. Population, environment and security: A new trinity. *Environment and Urbanization* 10 (2): 113–127.

Hartmann, B. 2001. "Will the circle be unbroken?" In *Violent environments*, ed. N. Peluso and M. Watts, 39–64. Ithaca, NY: Cornell University Press.

Hauge, W., and T. Ellingsen. 2001. Causal pathways to conflict. In *Environmental conflict*, ed. P. Diehl, and N. P. Gleditsch, 36–57. Boulder, CO: Westview Press.

Kriger, N. 1992. *Zimbabwe's guerrilla war: Peasant voices.* Cambridge, UK: Cambridge University Press.

Leichenko, R., and K. L. O'Brien. 2008. *Environmental change and globalization: Double exposures.* Oxford: Oxford University Press.

Lenton, T. M., H. Held, E. Kriegler, J. W. Hall, W. Lucht, S. Rahmstorf, and H. J. Schellnhuber. 2008. Tipping elements in the earth's climate system. *Proceedings of the National Academy of Sciences* 105:1786–1793.

Lonergan, S., M. Brklacich, C. Cocklin, N. Gleditsch, E. Gutierrez-Espeleta, F. Langeweg, R. Matthew, S. Narain, and M. Soroos. 1999. *GECHS Science Plan.* IHDP Report No. 11. http://www.ihdp.uni-bonn.de/html/publications/reports/report11/gehssp.htm (accessed November 15, 2008).

Maclure, R., and M. Sotelo. 2004. Youth gangs in Nicaragua: Gang membership as structured individualization. *Journal of Youth Studies* 7 (4): 417–432.

Matthew, R. 2001. Environmental stress and human security in Northern Pakistan. *Environmental Change and Security Project Report* 7:21–35.

McDonald, B., and T. Gaulin. 2002. Environmental change, conflict, and adaptation: Evidence from cases. Paper presented at the annual meeting of the International Studies Association, New Orleans, LA, March 24–27.

Milgram, S. 2004. Behavioral study of obedience. In *Violence in war and peace: An anthology*, ed. N. Scheper-Hughes and P. Bourgois, 145–150. Oxford: Blackwell.

Millennium Ecosystem Assessment. 2005. *Millennium ecosystem assessment, ecosystems and human well-being: Synthesis*. Washington, DC: Island Press.

Mochizuki, K. 2004. Conflict and people's insecurity: An insight from the experiences of Nigeria. In *Conflict and human security: A search for new approaches of peace-building*, ed. H. Shinoda and H. Jeong, 207–228. IPSHU English Research Report Series no. 19. Institute for Peace Science: Hiroshima University.

Mortimore, M. 1989. *Adapting to drought: Farmers, famines, and desertification in West Africa*. Cambridge, UK: Cambridge University Press.

Mwanasali, M. 2000. The view from below. In *Greed and grievance: Economic agendas in civil wars*, ed. M. Berdal and D. Malone, 137–153. Boulder, CO: Lynne Rienner.

Nafziger, E. Wayne, and Juha Auvinen. 2002. Economic development, inequality, war, and state violence. *World Development* 30 (2): 153–63.

Najam, A. 2003. The human dimensions of environmental insecurity: Some insights from South Asia. *Environmental Change and Security Project Report* 9:59–74.

Ohlsson, L. 2000. *Livelihood conflicts: Linking poverty and environment as causes of conflict*. Stockholm: Environmental Policy Unit, Swedish International Development Cooperation Agency.

Pelling, M., ed. 2003. *Natural disasters and development in a globalizing world*. London: Routledge.

Peluso, N., and E. Harwell. 2001. Territory, custom, and the cultural politics of ethnic war in West Kalimantan, Indonesia. In *Violent environments*, ed. N. Peluso and M. Watts, 83–116. Ithaca, NY: Cornell University Press.

Percival, V., and H. Homer-Dixon. 2001. The case of South Africa. In *Environmental conflict*, ed. P. Diehl and N. P. Gleditsch, 13–35. Boulder, CO: Westview Press.

Ponting, C. 1991. *A green history of the world*. London: Penguin Books.

Reed, D., ed. 1996. *Structural adjustment, the environment, and sustainable development*. London: Earthscan.

Reno, W. 2000. Shadow states and the political economy of civil wars. In *Greed and grievance: Economic agendas in civil wars*, ed. M. Berdal and D. Malone, 43–68. Boulder, CO: Lynne Rienner.

Scheper-Hughes, N. 2004. Who's the killer? Popular justice and human rights in a South African squatter camp. In *Violence in war and peace: An anthology*, ed. N. Scheper-Hughes and P. Bourgois, 253–266. Oxford: Blackwell.

Sen, A. 1999. *Development as freedom*. New York: Anchor Books.

Spillmann, K., and K. Spillmann. 1991. On enemy images and conflict escalation. *International Social Science Journal* 43 (1): 57–76.

Stewart, F. 2000. Crisis prevention: Tackling horizontal inequalities. *Oxford Development Studies* 28 (3): 245–263.

Stewart, F., and V. Fitzgerald. 2001. Introduction: Assessing the economic costs of war. In *War and underdevelopment: Volume 1. The economic and social consequences of conflict*, ed. F. Stewart and V. Fizgerald, 3–38. Oxford: Oxford University Press.

Turner, B. L. I., R. E. Kasperson, P. A. Matson, J. J. McCarthy, R. W. Corell, L. Christensen, N. Eckley, J. X. Kasperson, A. Luers, M. L. Martello, C. Polsky, A. Pulsipher, and A. Schiller. 2003. A framework for vulnerability analysis in sustainability science. *Proceedings of the National Academy of Sciences US* 100:8074–8079.

UNDP (United Nations Development Program). 2002. *Ukun Rasik A'an: East Timor human development report 2002*. UNDP, Dili, East Timor.

van Ireland, E., M. Klaassen, T. Nierop, and H. van der Wusten. 1996. *Climate change: Socio-economic impacts and violent conflict*. Dutch National Research Programme on Global Air Pollution and Climate Change, Report No. 410 200 006, Wageningen, Netherlands.

Watts, M. 2001. Petro-violence: Community, extraction, and political ecology of a mythic commodity. In *Violent environments*, ed. N. Peluso and M. Watts, 189–212. Ithaca, NY: Cornell University Press.

7

Environmental Change and Human Security in Nepal

Richard A. Matthew and Bishnu Raj Upreti

Kathmandu Valley has been the site of continuous human settlement for some nine thousand years, but it was not until 1768 that the Ghurka ruler Prithvi Narayan Shah unified the tiny kingdoms of Kathmandu, Patan, and Bhaktapur into what is today the sovereign state of Nepal.[1] During most of its modern history, Nepal was an isolated and largely peaceful monarchy. Boundary disputes with the British East India Company culminated in the brutal Anglo-Nepalese War (1814–1816), which left Nepal with a much-diminished territory, but also a reputation for great military valor. Quarrels within the royal family occasionally turned violent. But on the whole, Nepal received attention from the rest of the world mainly because of a tectonic drama that has been unfolding under its surface over many millennia. The slow-motion collision of the Indian landmass and Eurasian continent created the world's highest mountains—eight of which are located in Nepal, including Mt. Everest. The first two people to climb Everest—the New Zealander Sir Edmund Hillary and Nepali native Tenzing Norgay—had a major role in shaping the world's perception of this country as the planet's premier destination for high-level mountaineering.

As we write this chapter, however, Nepal is receiving considerable attention from the global community as the site of the world's most recent experiment in democracy. Elections held in April 2008 had an unexpected and dramatic outcome as the Communist Party of Nepal-Maoist (CPN-M), which had just laid down its arms after waging a ten-year civil war against the government, won a plurality of seats. The following month the monarchy was formally abolished and Nepal became a republic. In June, King Gyanendra—who had ascended to the throne in 2001 after Crown Prince Dipendra shot and killed the previous king, the queen, and himself, owing, apparently, to his parents' refusal to allow him to marry a woman who was not Nepalese—vacated the Royal Palace, which will eventually become a national museum. In August 2008 the Maoist leader known by his nom de guerre Prachanda (a former teacher, born Pushpa Kamal Dahal to an impoverished farming family in the Annapurna region) was elected Nepal's first prime minister. As 2008 came to an end, the people of Nepal were both exuberant and hopeful; now the new CPN-M government must address the country's high expectations, largely created by itself, for rapid and significant land reform and poverty alleviation, and for closing socioeconomic gaps linked to gender and caste.

In developing its reform agenda, the new government will have to operate in a world that is reeling from a global financial crisis owing, in large measure, to the dramatic breakdown of the U.S. banking system, a breakdown generally tied to the massive and ill-conceived processes of deregulation begun in the United States during the early 1990s. Nepal's government will have to operate in the fragile space between two rousing giants, China and India, for whom Nepal represents a thin barrier and a convenient and abundant source of fresh water. It will have to operate during the era of accelerating global climate change, which will melt its glaciers and disrupt its monsoon season. And it will have to operate in the complicated context of endogenous demographic and environmental pressures that threaten human security throughout the new republic and which, according to our analysis, were major factors in triggering and sustaining the events that, over the past two decades, transformed a quiet two-century-old monarchy into a front-page-news-dominating war-torn society, and ultimately into a new and hopeful republic.

Our argument is not intended to be an alternative to the more familiar story of contemporary democratization. According to some analysts, for example, Nepal is experiencing a typical pattern of post–Cold War conflict and change. Technology has made it almost impossible for authoritarian regimes to hide freedom and human rights from their people. Wherever political participation is sharply circumscribed, dissent, agitation, and global attention are virtually inevitable. But, while democracy encourages high expectations for personal freedom and economic gain, the processes of political change can be far slower and more turbulent than anticipated. Hence, a society's early efforts to democratize can produce widespread discontent that may erupt into civil violence, and that may be used to justify a return to authoritarian rule.

In fact, since the early 1990s and until their recent electoral success, the Maoists criticized the government of Nepal for not doing enough to address social and economic inequalities, and generally refused to participate in elections and other political reform efforts. They contended that the slow and superficial pace of reform through the first half of the 1990s compelled them to initiate the "People's War" in 1996 (Seddon and Adhikari 2003). Meanwhile, on the other side of the political spectrum, and despite the fact that it was the monarchy itself that legalized political parties in 1990, the royalists also expressed concerns about Nepal's experiments with democracy. Indeed, King Gyanendra justified his coup d'etat on February 1, 2005, by criticizing the elected government's inability to resolve the Maoist issue, which he promised—but clearly failed—to do within three years (Timilsina 2005).

While the story of Nepal's erratic progress toward democracy may, in broad outline, be a familiar one, it does not tell us much about those factors underlying and shaping the discontent that fueled the civil war, or about the war's direct and indirect socioeconomic effects. For this more case-specific analysis, we must place the events of the past two decades in a broader context that considers the turbulence endemic to a rapidly growing, youthful, and extremely unequal society, in which millions of undereducated and desperately poor people were (and still are) struggling to eke out their daily existence from a declining natural resource base. Ironically, Nepal's increasingly violent civil struggle undermined development initiatives and caused tourism—a key source of revenue—to drop by 40 percent. The result was a vicious cycle: the violence was limiting economic opportunity, thereby encouraging higher levels of desperation and migration, which in turn facilitated recruitment into more violence.

In this chapter, we review the broad dynamics of Nepal's recent civil conflict. We argue that environmental stress and population factors played significant roles in creating the underlying conditions for acute insecurity and instability.[2] Through a brief case study of the Koshi Tappu Wetland area, we show that this situation was evident not just in the Maoist strongholds of western Nepal, but even in remote areas of the east, thus encircling the capital region. We conclude that in the post-war period, reducing the prospect of a return to violent conflict requires careful attention to underlying demographic and environmental conditions.

In making this argument, we link to another familiar post-Cold War narrative—the persistence of certain civil wars, from Sudan and the Democratic Republic of the Congo through Cambodia and Sri Lanka to Haiti and Peru. In spite of substantial investments in peacekeeping and peace building in many of the world's chronic conflict sites, work by Paul Collier (2000a and 2000b) and others suggests that about half of all civil wars recur within ten years of a peace settlement. Peace building efforts have not been systematized in the United Nations, but they nonetheless tend to focus on a common set of objectives: disarming rebel and paramilitary groups, repatriating refugees and resettling internally displaced persons (IDPs), holding elections, establishing rule of law and public safety, kick-starting the economy and creating an environment conducive to attracting foreign investment, and organizing reconciliation processes.[3] Remarkably little attention is paid to environmental issues, although as this volume demonstrates the environment is linked in multiple ways to human security and, under certain conditions, to violent conflict as well (Matthew, Halle, and Switzer 2002).[4]

In the introduction to this volume, the literature on the linkages between environmental change and violent conflict is reviewed. The goal of the Global Environmental Change and Human Security project is to explore a related but different approach to linking the environment and security by shifting away from the state and national security as the referent and toward human security, where the referent is people. In making this connection, human security is defined "as something that is achieved when and where individuals and communities have the options necessary to end, mitigate, or adapt to threats to their human, environmental, and social rights; have the capacity and freedom to exercise these options; and actively participate in pursuing these options" (see chapter 1). Nepal is a case that straddles both camps, as it weaves together environmental change, human security, and violent conflict.

Background to the Conflict

About the size of Arkansas, Nepal is a landlocked country of almost thirty million people, located in the Himalayas between China and India. During the four decades following the establishment of India and Pakistan as independent states—a period of tremendous upheaval, turbulence, and violent conflict throughout South Asia—the kingdom of

Nepal seemed largely immune to the instability that surrounded it (Pokhrel 2001). Although many of its inhabitants were desperately impoverished—indeed, Seddon and Adhikari (2003, 11) claim that only "20 percent of those who live in rural areas are considered [food] secure in 'normal' times"—the feudal system of agriculture and government remained stable for decades after World War II. In fact, in 1975 the late King Birendra sought to have Nepal declared a Zone of Peace, perhaps as a way of fortifying it against internal dissent, as well as maintaining its independence from its two big neighbors (Pokhrel 2001).

Nepal comprises three major bioregions that run east to west, transected by a system of north-to-south rivers including the Kosi, Naranyi, and Karnali. The fertile river plain known as the Terai lies in the south along the border with India; the central hills region or Pahad is formed by two low mountain ranges (the Mahabharat Lekh and the Shiwalik) and encompasses the densely populated Kathmandu Valley; and the Himalaya mountain range forms the northern strip of the country and includes eight of the world's ten highest mountains. The economy is agrarian, although most households are not self-sufficient and rely on some nonagricultural sources of revenue (Seddon and Adhikari 2003). Nominal per capita GDP is estimated (IMF 2008) to be less than US$400; 47 percent of the population is unemployed and 42 percent lives below the poverty line. In 2007 Nepal ranked one hundred forty-second on the Human Development Index. The median age is 20; life expectancy is 59.8; and the population growth rate is 2.2 percent. Nepal is the last officially Hindu country in the world, with about 81 percent of its population identified as such. It also has a significant Buddhist population of about three million people; the combination is culturally distinctive. The literacy rate is 45.2 percent overall, which hides the enormous gender gap (27.6 percent of women are literate compared to 62.7 percent of men) common to many aspects of Nepali society (CIA 2005). About 60 percent of the population speaks a variant of Nepali, but all languages spoken in the country are recognized as official languages.

The roots of modern Nepal extend back to 1768, when Prithvi Narayan Shah, the leader of a small hill state called Gorkha or Gurkha, conquered and unified the Kathmandu Valley. The expansionism of the Shah kings was thwarted during the 1814–1816 war against the British, from which a smaller, but fiercely independent, Nepal emerged. A Shah king, regarded as an incarnation of Vishnu, governed until 1846, when the Rana family gained control of the kingdom, took over the office of prime minister, married into the royal family, and ruled behind a symbolic monarch until 1950 (Gayley 2002, 2).

Nepal's contemporary political history begins in 1950, when the Nepalese people and King Tribhuvan overthrew the ruling Ranas with support from the government of India. A Nepali democratic movement had emerged alongside India's struggle to establish itself as an independent and democratic state in the 1940s. After King Tribhuvan sought refuge from the Ranas in India in 1950, the dissidents increased their agitation for democracy, leading to the "Delhi compromise," under which the king, the prime minister, and the Nepali congress agreed to hold elections (Gayley 2002). Even with India's support, Nepal's experiment with multiparty democracy was brief. When King Tribhuvan's son, Mahendra, came to power in 1962, he introduced the *panchayat* system, a form of democracy in which the king ruled with the support of numerous councils, or *panchayats*.

But democratic forces continued to demand change in Nepal. Student demonstrations led to a 1980 referendum in which 55 percent of the electorate voted to maintain a form of the controversial *panchayat* system. External events further politicized Nepal, including the collapse of the Soviet Union, the 1989 Tiananmen Square protests, expanding global support for democracy, and India's 1989 decision to restrict trade after the Nepali government signed an arms deal with China, which placed considerable hardship on the Nepali economy. By 1990, persistent protests forced the government to agree to a new constitution reestablishing a multiparty democracy, which spurred the creation of more than one hundred political parties and many non-governmental organizations (NGOs), newspapers, and other politically engaged entities (Gayley 2002). Despite these political changes, social change was slow, and the political left—the United People's Front—fragmented in 1994, when Comrade Prachanda (whose name means "the fierce one") founded the Communist Party of Nepal-Maoists or CPN-M (CIA 2005; Watchlist on Children and Armed Conflict 2005). The "Maoists claim to have prepared for (1994–96), launched (1996) and undertaken their People's War in response to this failure of development" (Seddon and Adhikari 2003).

From 1996 to 2006, when the war ended, the collapse of Nepali society was truly dramatic, resulting in close to 13,000 deaths, more than 200,000 people displaced internally, and the emigration of about 1.8

million. This decade of violence captured world attention, especially for its impact on women and children. For example, according to the NGO Watchlist on Children and Armed Conflict (2005), during the war as many as twelve thousand girls were trafficked across the border into India each year, primarily to work in dangerous settings and in the sex trade; a cascade of reports accused Maoist and government forces of raping girls; approximately two hundred children were (and still are) killed by landmines each year; and an unknown number of children were recruited by both sides of the conflict to provide military services. Hundreds of schools were destroyed or disrupted during the conflict, and teachers were targeted and harassed as well as students. Although human trafficking has plagued Nepal for decades, the scale of many of these human rights failures can be directly related to the civil war. From a human security perspective, the conflict in Nepal became increasingly brutal over the course of ten years, and hence was closely scrutinized by the United Nations and numerous human rights groups.

The Dynamics of the Conflict

According to Dev Raj Dahal (2004), the conflict in Nepal emerged from two factors. First, the conflict was generated by important structural dimensions, such as the rural-urban disparity—which was aggravated by the government's focus on the urban economy of the Kathmandu Valley—and deeply embedded discriminatory practices that defied progressive laws, such as the persistence of an "untouchable" class—the Dalits—and the marginalization of indigenous groups and women. Second, these structural conditions underlay and shaped the contrasting ideologies and practices of the liberals, monarchists, and communists. These interconnected structural and ideological factors gave rise to or reinforced political problems including corruption, politicization of public service, and human rights abuses by police and military personnel (for a more elaborate analysis, see ICG 2003; Thapa and Sijapati 2003; Upreti 2001, 2003a, 2003b, 2004a).

Shobhakar Budhathoki (2004) notes that the vested interests of the conflict's key players made resolving it extremely difficult. According to Dhruba Adhikary (2004), the key players in the conflict were:

• *The monarchy* King Gyanendra's strength was based in part on the loyalty of the "unified command" that includes the Royal Nepali Army (78,000 troops), the Nepal Police (50,000), and the Armed Police Force

(15,000). On February 1, 2005, the king declared a state of emergency and was able to assume command of the country.

• *The army*   The fight against the Maoists allowed the Royal Nepal Army—historically a ceremonial entity—to modernize its weapons, beef up its training, and gain battle experience.

• *The political parties*   During the 1990s, a dozen progressive parties gained support among the Nepali people, who continued during the war to see them as the only viable platform for democratization; however, infighting and corruption, especially following the king's dissolution of parliament in May 2002, alienated some of the population.

• *The Maoists*   The outlawed CPN-M was regarded as a terrorist organization by the state, a position to which the United States quickly and unthinkingly added its support, and CPN-M was certainly willing to act in brutal ways against unarmed civilians, but it nonetheless wielded considerable control and support in much of the countryside.

Beyond these indigenous actors, the United Nations, the United States, the United Kingdom, neighboring countries such as China and India, NGOs, and donor agencies became embroiled in the conflict through their attempts to help broker a peace agreement. The end result was a complicated political landscape of scrappy, entrenched interests, none of which appeared able to win the civil war or spearhead the formation of an alliance that could achieve peace and restore good governance. Because of this, many assessments of Nepal prior to 2006 were quite bleak (Budhathoki 2004; Pokhrel 2001; Asia Development Bank 2005), although some observers did believe a peaceful settlement was possible (Dahal 2004).

Consideration of demographic and environmental factors was absent from most analyses of the conflict. Their significance, however, affirms many of the arguments made over the past fifteen years in the literature on environment and security (see, among others, Deudney and Matthew 1999; Homer-Dixon 1999; Peluso and Watts 2001).

Demographic Factors

As other chapters in this volume point out (e.g., chapter 10 by Betsy Hartmann), simple relationships among population growth, resource scarcity, and security have been a mainstay of the environmental security literature, providing concise but woefully incomplete and misleading analyses that obscure or exclude issues of inequality and can be marshaled to support draconian and unjust policies. Still, in the case of Nepal the broad effects of the rapid growth in population experienced in the past few decades merit consideration in the contexts of the multiple forms of exclusion, marginalization, and inequity that have been central features of the country's political and economic institutions and practices.

Much of the population of Nepal is young, underemployed, undereducated, and insecure. According to the 2001 census, 40 percent of the population is under age 15 and the median age of the population is 20.1, compared to the global average of 26 (United Nations 2002). More than 40 percent of the people live below the poverty line, and unemployment and underemployment are 17.4 and 32.3 percent, respectively (National Planning Commission 2003, 58, 99). The official literacy rate, which differs from other sources, is 65.5 percent for men and 42.8 percent for women (Central Bureau of Statistics [CBS] 2003). Approximately 12,700 people have been killed in the ten-year civil war.

Population in this resource-thin country has increased more than fivefold in less than a century. Between 1911, when the first census was taken, and 2001, Nepal's population increased from 5.6 million to 23.2 million, and population density rose from 38.3 to 157.3 people per square kilometer (CBS 2003, 3). In 2001, the population growth rate was 2.25 percent and the total fertility rate was 4.1 per woman. Although agricultural output has kept pace with population growth (Seddon and Adhikari 2003), human welfare has not improved in many areas of Nepal, which was ranked one hundred forty-second in the 2007 Human Development Index—and last in South Asia. Indeed, while in terms of population, Nepal ranks fortieth in the world, it ranks ninety-third in terms of land size (most of it unusable for human settlement of agriculture) and one hundred sixty-seventh in terms of per capita income.

Population growth has not been uniform across the country, which is understandable given the relative scarcity of natural resources in the northern mountainous area. The rapid growth of the population in the Terai (plains) has resulted from a combination of births and migration from mountains and hills, as people are lured by better physical facilities such as electricity, transportation, communications, education, and health; more productive agriculture land; and other job opportunities in the plains. The 2001 census summarizes internal migration: 62.8

percent rural-to-rural, 25.5 percent rural-to-urban, and 3.5 percent urban-to-urban migration (CBS 2003, 141). The rate of urbanization is also faster in the Terai than elsewhere in Nepal. Because the Terai is situated along the border with India, it also experiences informal and seasonal immigration. Finally, it is estimated that 200,000 to 300,000 people were internally displaced owing to the armed conflict and most of them moved into district headquarters and urban areas.

The situation in Nepal reflects the principal findings of Phase III of the State Failure Task Force, which found "the odds of failure to be *seven times* as high for partial democracies as they were for full democracies and autocracies." Moreover, "low levels of material well-being" doubled the odds of state failure, and "countries with larger populations and higher population density had 30–percent and 40–percent greater odds of state failure, respectively" (Goldstone et al. 2000, vi).

Environmental Factors

Nepal is experiencing significant environmental pressures. About 48.4 percent of the population lives in the Terai, which constitutes about 17 percent of the total land (Subedi 2003). This land is the most productive in the country: the average yield of Nepal's major crops (barley, maize, millet, paddy, wheat, and potatoes) is 1.71 metric tons per hectare in the mountains, 2.08 in the hills, and 2.61 in the Terai (Subedi 2003). In fact, only 20 percent of the entire country is suitable for agriculture, upon which 78 percent of the total population relies for subsistence. Arable land is scarce in Nepal, and its cost is out of the reach of most people. The *Nepal Human Development Report 2004* indicates that the bottom 47 percent of households own only 15 percent of the total arable land, whereas the top 5 percent own around 37 percent (UNDP 2004). According to the same report, 29 percent of the people are landless and more than 70 percent of the peasants own less than one hectare of arable land. This skewed distribution of land in favor of elites was a focus of criticism by the Maoist insurgents—who also promised that once in power they would oversee massive land reform and poverty alleviation.

In fact, during the civil war the CPN-M developed detailed analyses of Nepal's economic structure, which it characterized as "semi-feudal" and "semi-colonial," along with clear recommendations for change (International Crisis Group 2005). The proposed reforms included "changing production relations" by "confiscating land from feudals," "mixed ownership" of land, "a protected and regulated economy," "planned development" on the Maoist model, and "balanced development"(6).

Terai areas are highly prone to flooding—facilitated by deforestation—during the rainy season, which compels people to move. According to UNDP (2005, 61), forest cover declined from 37 percent to 29 percent between 1990 and 1995, a trend that appears to be continuing. The growing population depends primarily on traditional energy sources, 90 percent of which is provided by burning wood for fuel. In fact, the use of fuel wood increased slightly from 1995 to 2003, while other traditional energy sources such as cow dung declined; kerosene use remained constant; and petroleum gas (LPG) jumped from 0.99 percent of energy in 1995 to 8.2 percent in 2004 (UNDP 2005, 66). The extremely high dependency on wood for fuel has also created air pollution and respiratory problems, in addition to producing deforestation. Flooding, land scarcity, and wood collection cause people to encroach on ecologically fragile areas such as Siwalik (CBS 1998).

The general environmental trends in Nepal are well-summarized by L. P. Sharma:

The Midland region of Nepal is at present under the serious attack of environmental maladies. The deforestation has already been severe, so in most of the places, there is acute shortage of wood, fuel wood, and fodder to run daily life. The soil erosion has been non-stop phenomena [sic] aggravated floods and landslides. In most of the hill districts of Nepal, there is shortage of food supply on account of low productivity and ultimately the carrying capacity of the land has been seriously distorted. The out migration process to the valleys, plain lands and urban areas for better opportunities has been a regular practice. (1998, 23)

On the whole, environmental governance in Nepal is uneven and often ineffective, a reflection of the broader political processes that have afflicted the country (Upreti 2001). There have, however, been improvements in some environmental indicators. Land protected to maintain biological diversity increased threefold from 1995 to 2004 (UNDP 2005, 61). The proportion of the population with sustainable access to safe drinking water increased from 46 percent in 1990 to 81 percent in 2005, and the proportion with sustainable access to improved sanitation has jumped from 6 percent in 1990 to 39 percent in 2005, a gain realized primarily in urban areas (UNDP 2005, 70). Ironically, in some cases conservation efforts exacerbated the environmental scarcity experienced by the growing population of poor and landless, making them more receptive to the rhetoric of the CPN-M. This is clear in our case study of Koshi

Tappu, but it is also validated by our work throughout the region with the International Union for the Conservation of Nature (IUCN 2005).

Case Study: Koshi Tappu Wetland

A case study was conducted in 2004 in the Koshi Tappu area by an IUCN research team (including the authors). This wetland area, located on the eastern Terai plains near the border with India, includes the Koshi Tappu Wildlife Reserve and the sixteen villages surrounding it. People moved into this remote and sparsely inhabited wetland only in the mid-twentieth century, a migration designed by the Nepali government with the explicit goal of reducing population pressure on the resource base of Kathmandu Valley. Today some 78,000 people live in an area where the resources they depend upon are steadily becoming less available owing to changes in land tenure, poor conservation practices, and depletion. Primary resources include gathering grass for roofing and fodder; fishing; collecting fuel, including dung and driftwood; irrigation farming; collecting rocks for construction; grazing livestock; and gathering cattails for mattresses (Bastola n.d., 4–5). The region's population growth rate is 2.8 percent, adding more pressure on resources (3).

Nepal leased five thousand hectares of the wetland to India in 1954 to permit the construction of a dam so that water could be diverted to irrigate farms in the Indian state of Bihar. A wildlife reserve, established in 1976 and expanded in 1979, is now classified as a Ramsar Wetland of International Importance.[5] Little or no compensation was offered for the residents' decreased access to resources and the Maoists channeled frustration with this situation into support for their insurgency.

During in-depth interviews conducted on site, representatives of the nineteen ethnic groups dependent on the case study area's natural resources explained that their traditional or customary rights to local natural resources have been curtailed or denied (Upreti 2004b; Matthew 2005).[6] Consequently, their livelihoods have become increasingly perilous, and their willingness to engage in protest and crime has increased.

The problem has at least three interactive causes. First, local people have seen few benefits from the development of the dam, the Koshi Barrage, in part owing to barriers such as language and lack of information but also because the government felt no obligation to share the benefits of this project or provide compensation for the losses it caused. For example, the construction of the dam relied heavily on labor imported from India. Second, in the 1950s, the availability of abundant natural resources and fertile land attracted a large number of migrants from nearby hilly regions. Even as population pressure on the resources mounted, the construction of the East-West Highway made the area accessible to more migrants from other parts of the country (Heinen 1993; Sharma 2002). Finally, conservation efforts, including the decision to protect the area as a Ramsar site owing to its remarkable biodiversity, further restricted the local population's access to essential resources, including fish, birds, forest products, and grasses. Reserve wardens soon introduced the political corruption endemic throughout the country, allowing some people to access the reserve's resources for a fee or other considerations. The resources that are available to the residents are woefully underserviced. Since irrigation facilities are inadequate, farmers depend upon rainwater. Much of the area lacks a reliable means of transportation, making it extremely difficult to reach the market, schools, and hospitals, especially during the rainy season. During the civil war, the Maoist insurgents promised to return the reserve land to the local inhabitants, thus underscoring their appeal to the beleaguered residents.

Conclusions

As in the rest of the world, the population of Nepal increased by sixfold during the course of the last century. This rapid growth occurred in a mountainous and land-locked area with few natural resources. There is no doubt that this growth also occurred in a context of inequality and political exclusion (Cincotta, Engelman, and Anastasion 2003; Upreti 2004a). But the Gini index for Nepal, in the mid-1940s throughout the past decade, is roughly the same as in the United States—on this basis the country is a little more inegalitarian than the developed countries with the lowest Gini indices, but by no means one of the least equal countries in the world. If we base our calculations simply on land size, and assume a constant value, then the ratio between those who are among the top five percent of the nation (with 37 percent of the land) and those who are in the bottom 47 percent (with 15 percent of the land) is 24 to 1. Unequal, certainly, but not in itself an adequate basis for explaining why it is that 42 percent of the population is living below the poverty line. The proximate answer is that the resource base is not able to support an agricultural economy of this magnitude. Under conditions of scarcity such as these, elites may not see a way to protect their privileged position and also raise the living standards of non-elites.

The situation in Nepal is loosely akin to what historians call "feudal anarchy." This particular type of social breakdown occurred in Europe when land holdings became smaller and smaller under the burden of population growth, to the point where they could no longer support the people who depended upon them, but alternative livelihoods did not emerge quickly enough to meet demand. The lag between the erosion of traditional livelihoods and the creation of new ones was exaggerated by the behavior of elites who, through culture or calculation, resisted socio-economic change. The end result, of course, was a massive power shift away from the royalty toward the emerging merchant class, risk-taking entrepreneurs willing to displace traditional power holders and also to help serfs transform themselves into proletarians, a transformation made possible by the massive and unsustainable use of natural resources, and especially energy.

It may be, as Francis Fukuyama has suggested, that liberal democracy is simply a superior form of social organization, and all societies will gradually gravitate toward its political and economic forms. It may be that the processes of decolonization, democratization and liberalization, promoted by the United States after World War II, placed pressure to conform on all parts of the developing world, including Nepal. But it may also be the case that the processes of political change that began in Nepal in the 1950s were in an important sense a response to endogenous demographic and environmental pressures of the kind that linked Kathmandu Valley to Koshi Tappu.

Insofar as this is true, the new government of Nepal may discover that violence itself is not enough to trigger constructive processes of social change, and that foreign models to emulate are in short supply. What does an agrarian economy do to accommodate the livelihood needs of some twelve million destitute people? Especially when there is no new land available to cultivate and climate change threatens traditional agricultural practices. The only proven strategies for agricultural intensification are costly ones, like irrigation and fertilizer use, designed to reduce environmental risks, but prone to create new types of problems, such as soil exhaustion, within a few years. The answer must lie in cultivating new livelihoods, which in Nepal means developing sectors such as hydroelectric energy, water harvesting, and tourism, none of which appear likely to deliver millions of new jobs quickly.

The challenges Nepal faces are shared by other densely populated, resource-poor, war-torn countries such as Cambodia, Rwanda, and Haiti. Once peace has arrived, these places have tended to become magnets for donor countries and NGO activity, and the danger has been that a bubble of foreign aid will act like an antibiotic administered to an individual suffering from both malnutrition and parasites: a rapid improvement followed by a relapse into illness.

The excitement in today's Nepal is widespread and sincere. In short order, the violence has largely come to an end; the monarchy has been removed; the population has voted in reasonably fair and open elections; and a new regime has been put in place. These are remarkable accomplishments, and many observers thought them impossible ones just two years ago. But in terms of human security, much remains to be done. People have voice, and the Maoist regime may well succeed in diminishing gender and caste discrimination, dismantling the costly dowry system, and redistributing land. But these measures will only be the first step toward providing people with the "options necessary to end, mitigate or adapt to threats to their human, environmental and social rights [and] the capacity and freedom to exercise these options" (see chapter 1) Nepal needs also to find a pathway to human security and from there on to sustainable development.

Notes

1. Adapted and updated with permission from Richard Matthew and Bishnu Upreti (2006).

2. For a general discussion of the relationship among population factors, environmental stress, and state failure, see Goldstone et al. 2000.

3. This analysis is based largely on Matthew's personal involvement with the new UN Peacebuilding Commission and his direct participation in UNEP post-conflict assessment activity in Africa.

4. Our analysis is based in part on the extensive personal experience of Upreti with many aspects of this issue, as a researcher, consultant, and policy advisor living in Nepal throughout the period under consideration; and in part on two field research trips to Nepal made by Matthew.

5. The Convention on Wetlands, signed in Ramsar, Iran, in 1971, is an intergovernmental treaty that provides a framework for national action and international cooperation for the conservation and use of wetlands and their resources. There are presently 147 contracting parties to the convention, with 1,524 wetland sites, totaling 129.2 million hectares, designated for inclusion in the Ramsar List of

Wetlands of International Importance. For more information, see http://www
.ramsar.org/.

6. The main ethnic groups are Sunaha, Khanwas, Mallahs, Bote, Mushahars,
Bantar, Gongi, Mukhia, Dushad, Sahani, Kewat, Danuwars, Darai, Kumal, Bar-
hamus, Dhangar, Pode, Kushars, and Majhi.

References

Adhikary, Dhruba H. 2004. *Contemporary conflict dynamics in Nepal.* http://
www.fesnepal.org/reports/2004/seminar_reports/paper_conflict-reporting/paper
_dhruba.htm (accessed November 15, 2008).

Asian Development Bank. 2005. Nepal. *Asian development outlook 2005* (part
2, South Asia). http://www.adb.org/Documents/Books/ADO/2005/nep.asp (accessed November 15, 2008).

Bastola, Rabin. n.d. *Ramsar sites: Threats and opportunities for community development.* http://www.fern.org.np/publications/ramsar.htm (accessed November
15, 2008).

Budhathoki, Shobhakar. 2004. The King's Communist conundrum. *Asian
Affairs.* http://www.asianaffairs.com/oct2004/nepal.htm (accessed September 22,
2005).

Central Intelligence Agency (CIA). 2005. *Nepal.* http://www.cia.gov/cia/
publications/factbook/geos/np.html (accessed September 22, 2005).

Central Bureau of Statistics (CBS). 1998. *A compendium on environmental statistics of Nepal.* Kathmandu: CBS.

Central Bureau of Statistics (CBS). 2003. *Population monograph of Nepal,* vol.
1. Kathmandu: CBS. http://www.cbs.gov.np/Population/Monograph/volume1_
contents.htm (accessed November 15, 2008).

Cincotta, Richard, Robert Engelman, and Danielle Anastasion. 2003. *The security demographic: Population and civil conflict after the Cold War.* http://www
.populationaction.org/resources/publications/securitydemographic/index.html
(accessed September 22, 2005).

Collier, Paul. 2000a. Economic causes of civil conflict and their implications for
policy. Paper for the World Bank Group. http://www.worldbank.org/research/
conflict/papers/civilconflict.pdf (accessed November 15, 2008).

Collier, Paul. 2000b. Doing well out of war: An economic perspective. In *Greed
and grievance: Economic agendas in civil wars,* ed. Mats Berdal and David
Malone, 91–111. Boulder, CO: Lynne Rienner.

Dahal, Dev Raj. 2004. *Conflict dynamics in Nepal.* http://www.fesnepal.org/
reports/2004/seminar_reports/report_conflict-mangmt_decont.htm (accessed November 15, 2008).

Deudney, Daniel, and Richard A. Matthew, eds. 1999. *Contested grounds: Security and conflict in the new environmental politics.* Albany: SUNY Press.

Gayley, Holly. 2002. Gyanendra's test: Nepal's monarchy in the era of democracy. *Harvard Asia Quarterly VI* (1). http://www.fas.harvard.edu/~asiactr/haq/200201/0201a009.htm (accessed September 22, 2005).

Goldstone, Jack A., et al. 2000. *State Failure Task Force report: Phase III findings.* http://www.cidcm.umd.edu/inscr/stfail/SFTF%20Phase%20III%20 Report%20Final.pdf (accessed September 22, 2005).

Heinen, J. T. 1993. Park-people relations in Koshi Tappu Wildlife Reserve, Nepal: A socio-economic analysis. *Environmental conservation* 20 (1): 25–34.

Homer-Dixon, Thomas. 1999. *Environment, scarcity, and violence.* Princeton: Princeton University Press.

International Crisis Group (ICG). 2003. *Nepal: Back to the gun* (Asia Briefing No. 28). Kathmandu/Brussels: ICG.

International Crisis Group (ICG). 2005. *Nepal's new alliance: The mainstream parties and the Maoists* (Asia Report No. 106). Kathmandu/Brussels: ICG. http://www.crisisgroup.org/home/index.cfm?id=3810andl=1 (accessed November 15, 2008).

International Monetary Fund (IMF). 2008. Nepal. World Economic Outlook Database. http://www.imf.org/external/pubs/ft/weo/2008/02/weodata/index.aspx (accessed March 3, 2009).

International Union for the Conservation of Nature (IUCN). 2005. *Livelihood security in South Asia.* http://www.iucn.org/places/asia/livelihood/index.html (accessed November 21, 2005).

Matthew, Richard A. 2005. Sustainable livelihoods, environmental security and conflict mitigation: Four cases in South Asia. Poverty, Equity and Rights in Conservation Working Paper Series. Geneva: IUCN. http://www.iucn.org/themes/ spg/Files/IUED/Case%20Study%20South%20Asia.pdf (accessed September 22, 2005).

Matthew, Richard, Mark Halle, and Jason Switzer, eds. 2002. *Conserving the peace: Resources, livelihoods, and security.* Geneva: IISD.

Matthew, Richard, and Bishnu Upreti. 2006. "Environmental Stress and Demographic Change in Nepal: Underlying Conditions Contributing to a Decade of Insurgency." *Environmental Change and Security Project Report* 11:29–39.

National Planning Commission. 2003. *Tenth five-year plan.* Kathmandu: National Planning Commission.

Peluso, Nancy, and Michael Watts, eds. 2001. *Violent environments.* Ithaca, NY: Cornell University Press.

Pokhrel, Gokul. 2001. History of conflict in Nepal. http://www.fesnepal .org/reports/2004/seminar_reports/paper_conflict-reporting/paper_gokul.htm (accessed November 15, 2008).

Seddon, David, and Jagannath Adhikari. 2003. *Conflict and food security in Nepal: A preliminary analysis.* Kathmandu: Rural Reconstruction Nepal. http:// europa.eu.int/comm/external_relations/cpcm/mission/nepal_food03.pdf (accessed September 22, 2005).

Sharma, L. P. 1998. Geography. In *A compendium on environmental statistics of Nepal*, Central Bureau of Statistics, 20–27. Kathmandu: CBS.

Sharma, R. K. 2002. *Conservation and sustainable use of wetland resources in Nepal: Socio-economic and cultural dimensions*. Kathmandu: IUCN Nepal.

Subedi, Bhim Prasad. 2003. Population and environment: A situation analysis of population, cultivated land and basic crop production in Nepal in 2001. In *Population monograph of Nepal*, vol. 2, 1–36. Kathmandu: CBS. http://www.cbs .gov.np/Population/Monograph/volume2_contents.htm (accessed November 15, 2008).

Thapa, Deepak, and Bandita Sijapati. 2003. *A kingdom under siege: Nepal's Maoist insurgency, 1996 to 2003*. Kathmandu: The Printhouse.

Timilsina, Amga R. 2005. *A plan for the post-conflict reconstruction of Nepal* (FPIF Policy Report). Silver City, NM, and Washington, DC: Foreign Policy in Focus. http://www.fpif.org/fpiftxt/683 (accessed November 15, 2008).

United Nations. 2002. Population ageing: facts and figures. *Building a society for all ages*. http://www.un.org/ageing/prkit/factsnfigures.htm (accessed November 21, 2005).

United Nations Development Programme (UNDP). 2003. *Human development report*. New York: United Nations.

United Nations Development Programme (UNDP). 2004. *Nepal human development report*. Kathmandu: United Nations Development Programme.

United Nations Development Programme (UNDP). 2005. *Nepal Millennium Development Goals: Progress report 2005*. http://www.undp.org.np/publications/ mdg/index.html (accessed September 15, 2005).

Upreti, Bishnu Raj. 2001. *Conflict management in natural resources: A study of land, water and forest conflict in Nepal* (published doctoral dissertation). Wageningen, Netherlands: Wageningen University.

Upreti, Bishnu Raj. 2003a. Social exclusion, centralism and conflict: Challenges for conflict transformation in Nepal. Paper presented at the Social Science Baha conference, The Agenda of Transformation: Inclusion in Nepali Democracy, Kathmandu, Nepal, April.

Upreti, Bishnu Raj. 2003b. *Management of social and natural resource conflict in Nepal: Reality and alternative*. New Delhi: Adroit Publishers.

Upreti, Bishnu Raj. 2004a. *The price of neglect: From resource conflict to the Maoist insurgency in the Himalayan Kingdom*. Kathmandu: Brikuti Academic Publications.

Upreti, Bishnu Raj. 2004b. Sustainable livelihoods, environmental security, and conflict mitigation in protected areas of Nepal: Trend and challenges (preliminary draft report). Kathmandu: IUCN.

Watchlist on Children and Armed Conflict. 2005. *Caught in the middle: Mounting violations against children in Nepal's armed conflict*. New York: Watchlist on Children and Armed Conflict (January). http://www.watchlist.org/reports/ nepal.report.20050120.pdf (accessed September 25, 2005).

IV

Human Security and Sustainable Development

8

Global Environmental Change, Equity, and Human Security

Karen L. O'Brien and Robin M. Leichenko

Global environmental change has been described as a collection of transformations to the coupled human-environment system that threatens the sustainability of both ecological and social systems (Steffan et al. 2004; Turner et al. 2003). References to an "endangered planet Earth" and "our common future" help frame global environmental change as a unifying threat that demands international responses, backed by universal commitments to protect the environment (World Commission on Environment and Development 1987; Gore 1992, 2007). Global environmental change is often portrayed as a major threat to human security, in that all humans will be affected by the impacts of climate change, biodiversity loss, land use changes, ozone depletion, and other global environmental problems (World Resources Institute et al. 2000; United Nations Environment Programme 2002; Worldwatch Institute 2005; Leichenko and O'Brien 2008).

Yet in recent years environmental change issues have been increasingly framed in relation to equity, drawing on some of the debates originating in the environmental justice movement. Among equity-based analyses of climate change, the focus is typically on questions of equity in mitigation of greenhouse gas (GHG) emissions; equity in terms of impacts, vulnerability, and adaptation; and intergenerational equity (Müller 2002; Kemfert and Tol 2002; Tonn 2003; Brown 2003; Gardiner 2004; Adger et al. 2006; Farber 2007; Roberts and Parks 2007; Beckman 2008; Beckman and Page 2008; Paavola 2008). A growing awareness of the equity issues surrounding environmental change is not surprising, given widespread recognition that the effects are likely to be highly uneven. Some individuals, households, communities, or regions will experience significant negative effects, such as the loss of life and property resulting from climate extremes, a rise in skin cancer because of stratospheric ozone depletion, the loss of agricultural productivity, increased stress on water resources, and so on, whereas others may experience only minor negative effects, and still others may experience net benefits, such as lower winter heating costs owing to warmer temperatures, a longer agricultural growing season, increased forest productivity, or an expansion of tourism owing to land use changes. In other words, global environmental change is likely to create both winners and losers (O'Brien and Leichenko 2003).

Equity-based responses or "solutions" to global environmental change nonetheless require approaches that are quite different from responses that address general, undifferentiated threats to humankind. When framed in terms of equity, global environmental change is transformed from a unifying discourse for responding to environmental problems that threaten the security of all humans, into an issue of differential vulnerability that draws attention to some key questions, such as "Whose security is at stake, and why?" and "What are the underlying factors contributing to differential vulnerability?"

In this chapter, we show that an equity-based discourse on global environmental change demands much broader and comprehensive responses than those based on a "global" framing. Whereas global framings tend to directly address the physical drivers of environmental change (e.g., control of pollution through regulation of emissions), equity-based approaches must first and foremost address human security, and in particular, the underlying social, economic, political, and cultural relations that contribute to inequities and insecurities. While equity concerns pervade all facets of global environmental change, we focus on climate change to illustrate some of the most pressing equity issues. In the following section, we discuss some definitions and interpretations of equity, emphasizing that equity has both procedural and distributional components. In the next section, we explore some of the recent literature that addresses equity in relation to climate change, and we consider related procedural and distributional equity issues. We emphasize here that equity is not simply a North-South issue—particularly in light of globalization processes—but it is rather an issue that cuts across national boundaries and needs to be addressed comprehensively, at different scales and units of analysis (Leichenko and O'Brien 2008). We conclude by considering the direct and indirect implications for policy responses to environmental change.

What Is Equity?

Equity is a term that has many meanings and interpretations. To describe global environmental change as an issue of equity, rather than as simply a general threat to the security of human and ecological systems, it is first necessary to clarify what we mean by equity. In a very general sense, the concept of equity is associated with the freedom from bias or favoritism, or something that is fair to all concerned. The idea of equity is often closely related to justice. Rawls (1971), for example, correlates justice with fairness, which is essentially equal treatment for equal cases. While there are many scholarly debates about the relationship between equity and justice, it is clear that equity is a key component of social justice, where the term *social justice* includes both fairness and equity in the distribution of a wide range of attributes (Rawls 1971; Smith 1994; Ikeme 2003; Adger et al. 2006; Paavola 2008).

One important distinction to note is that equity does not necessarily imply equality in the distribution of attributes. As Boulding (1978) notes, "Equality in an absolute sense would be advocated by nobody. On the other hand, it is very clear that there are degrees of inequality in a society which threaten its legitimacy and stability." These varying degrees of inequality in a society are reflected in some of the different interpretations of equity. Equity is influenced by the availability and access to opportunities, which in some cultures is closely linked to the notion of meritocracy, where "inequality is accepted if everyone has had equal opportunity at initial allocation and differentials is only accounted for by difference in effort and hard work" (Ikeme 2003, 199). Equity is also associated with the full realization of human potential, which "may be much more a function of the average wealth and status of the society than it is of any internal distribution" (Boulding 1978). Equity has also been approached through the "no envy" principle, represented by an equal opportunity of consumption, whereby no agent would prefer someone else's "bundle of consumption" to his or her own (Ikeme 2003). This contrasts with the minimum standard or basic need approach, which addresses the needs of the poorest of society. Finally, equity is reflected in the concept of "just deserts," which seeks remedies in proportion to the weight of the injustice, and ensures that remedy to one injustice should not engender a second injustice. Regardless of how equity is interpreted, there is a consensus among political philosophers and social scientists that more equality in a society is better than less equality (Smith 1994).

While social equity has long been an issue of discussion and debate, concern about environmental equity has emerged as a major area of study only in the past few decades. Areas of research that devote considerable attention to equity include environmental economics, environmental policy, and normative political theory, all of which emphasize the linkages between equity, fairness, and justice in the search for appropriate responses to environmental problems. Each of these fields has paid considerable attention to equity issues, with an emphasis on intergenerational equity, discounting, and issues related to scale and aggregation (Rose et al. 1998; Dore and Mount 1999; Toth 2000; Beckman and Page 2008). As noted by Rose and Kverndokk (1998, 4), within the context of environmental economics, "Equity is not only a normative concept, but a positive one. That is, equity is worthy of pursuit not only because of fairness, but because it may enhance the likelihood of agreement between parties." Within the environmental policy literature, equity concerns arise not only in relation to the outcomes, such as the distribution of environmental externalities, but also through the process of developing fair policies: "Equity is not just about how societies distribute resources. It is also the basis for generating social capital necessary, alongside economic, natural, and intellectual capital, for sustainability.... Fairness is integral to the establishment and maintenance of social relations at every level from the micro to the macro, from the local to the global" (Rayner and Malone 2001, 199).

Gender and the environment is another field where equity issues play a central role. Research on gender and environment provides critical analyses of gender-differentiated contributions, impacts, and responses to global environmental change, with equity issues a recurring theme. Studies on gender and environment have shown how gender mediates the use of the environment through roles, responsibilities, expectations, norms, and the division of labor, including livelihood strategies (Seager and Hartmann 2004). Gender-related equity concerns arise in relation to all aspects of climate change, including the driving forces, the impacts or consequences, and the responses (Skutch 2002; Cutter 1995a). Women in particular have been identified as disproportionately vulnerable to the consequences of climate change as the result of unequal access to and control over resources (Denton 2002).

Another key area of research that addresses equity issues is environmental justice. Within this literature, the terms *justice* and *equity* are often used interchangeably (Ikeme 2003; Kütting 2004). The environmental justice literature initially focused on the location of hazardous industrial waste sites in advanced countries, demonstrating that these sites tended to be disproportionately located in areas where poor and minority residents live (Cutter 1995b; Cutter and Solecki 1996). However, the idea of environmental justice is increasingly being applied in an international context to address issues including the disposal of hazardous wastes in developing countries and the effects of consumption in advanced countries on the environment in developing countries (Ikeme 2003; Agyeman, Bullard, and Evans 2003; Leichenko and Solecki 2008). Rees and Westra (2003, 110) in discussing the linkages between consumption patterns and environmental justice comment that "consumption by the world's wealthy causes much ecological destruction around the world, but... distance and wealth insulate the rich from the negative consequences of their consumer lifestyles."

An important insight from the environmental justice literature are the distinctions among different types of environmental equity, including outcome equity and process equity (Cutter 1995b). Outcome equity entails equitable (i.e., random) distribution of environmental hazards or environmental amenities, while process equity entails an equitable procedure for deciding both where to site environmental hazards (or amenities) and on production of the burdens that require distribution (Lake 1996; Leichenko and Solecki 2008). More recently, the environmental justice movement has appealed to both "justice as outcome" and "justice as recognition," with the latter referring to "the right to be heard in debates and to have a fair influence on decisions" (Adger 2004, 1713). As discussed in the next section, a definition of equity that includes outcome (distributional) and process (procedural) considerations is useful when considering policy responses to climate change, as it addresses the processes driving climatic changes, the impacts of these changes, and strategies to both mitigate and adapt to climate change.

Framing Climate Change as an Equity Issue

Many arguments can be made to support the contention that the collective security of humankind is at risk as the result of climate change.

Indeed, changes to ocean currents, rapid sea-level rise, and other catastrophic events could have global consequences (IPCC 2007; Lenton et
al. 2008). Yet it is increasingly evident that not every "global citizen"
contributes equally to climate change, and/or will be equally affected by
climate change. While climate change mitigation has already raised many
equity-related issues concerning international negotiations to reduce
greenhouse gas emissions, equity perspectives on climate change drivers,
impacts, and adaptations are also beginning to frame international
debates about climate change (Brown 2003; Ikeme 2003; Adger 2004;
Adger et al. 2006). This can be seen through the emerging "climate justice" movement within civil society, which is an increasingly visible force
for action on climate change (Pettit 2004). This movement seeks to link
climate change and human development, presenting the issue in the language of rights and focusing attention on inequitable economic relations
(Athanasiou and Baer 2002; Pettit 2004).

Climate justice inevitably demands distinguishing the different types of
equity. Adger (2004) identifies several aspects of equity related to climate
justice. The first relates to welfare, such as the impacts of climate change
on human health and material well-being. The second relates to the right
to avoid increased impacts, or the right to development pathways uncon-
strained by new climatic risks (Adger 2004). From a distributional standpoint, equity in outcomes would require that each individual, household,
social group, or region might have an equal chance of either benefiting
from or being harmed by climate change. From a process perspective,
equity would require that those groups that are affected by climate
change have a voice in debates about policies and responses, including a
voice in decisions about the processes that are causing global environmental change. These multiple facets of equity can be seen in many contemporary debates about mitigation, impacts, and adaptation in relation
to climate change.

Equity in Climate Change Mitigation

Much of the discussion of equity and climate change focuses on issues
associated with climate change mitigation. Within these discussions,
there is a growing consensus that equity is a prerequisite for success at
reducing GHG emissions. Brown (2003, 233), for example, suggests
that we need to take equity into account in order to arrive at a unified
strategy for responding to global warming: "the nations of the world
are only likely to agree on equitable sharing of the burdens and benefits

of protecting the global environment if they feel they are being treated fairly... equity is an indispensable element to a global solution to climate change." Adger (2004, 1714) makes a similar argument regarding acceptance by developing countries of post-Kyoto emissions targets: "Without regard to justice as outcome and justice as recognition, there is little prospect of these countries accepting post-Kyoto emissions targets."

Within the context of international negotiations on GHG emissions, a key process-related inequity entails differential negotiating capacity across countries. While some countries were able to send delegations consisting of dozens of lawyers and diplomats to the Kyoto negotiations, other countries could only afford to send single-person delegations with limited experience and expertise on international negotiations on climate change (Gupta 2000). From a distributional equity standpoint, a critical issue for GHG emissions targets is the perception of equity in outcomes. The 1992 Kyoto Protocol's approach to mitigation via reduction of emissions of greenhouse gases is based on an implicit equity principle of "common but differentiated responsibilities" (Tonn 2003, 297). This means that countries that are most responsible for emitting GHGs and most able to pay the costs of reducing GHG emissions are expected to bear most of the responsibility for reducing GHG emissions (Ringuis, Torvanger, and Underdal 2000; Tonn 2003, 298). Yet some nations argue that the outcomes of Kyoto are inequitable. The United States, in particular, has argued that Kyoto is inequitable because developing countries are excluded from emissions limitations. At the same time, developing countries argue the opposite, that Kyoto is inequitable because it keeps emissions higher in developed countries, thereby perpetuating economic inequalities (Tonn 2003, 297). Issues of equity are likely to play a major role in discussions about post-Kyoto climate agreements following the 2012 expiration of the Kyoto Protocol (Michaelowa, Tangen, and Hasselknippe 2004; Schmidt et al. 2008).

While equity debates about climate change mitigation have emphasized process-related issues such as differential negotiating capacity *across* nations, there are also many relevant process equity considerations among different groups *within* nations. Questions arise, for example, about who has a voice in national decisions about emissions targets. And who decides how emissions targets are met? Because Kyoto was negotiated among national governments, the agreement does not necessarily take into account the views of dissenting or marginalized groups within different nations. In many cases, these groups have a limited voice at the national level in either decisions about emissions targets or plans for mitigation. In the United States, for example, the resistance to the Kyoto agreement at the federal level belies significant support for reduction of GHGs within many communities (Slocum 2004b). As a result of dissatisfaction with the U.S. position on Kyoto, a number of U.S. city governments have adopted their own policies to reduce GHG emissions (Slocum 2004a).

Concerning distributional equity in the context of climate change mitigation, questions arise about who pays the costs and who bears the burdens for emissions reductions. These types of equity issues arise, in part, "because of the qualitative differences in the effects of climate change and climate change policy on the poor and those who are better off" (Rayner and Malone 2001, 178). In less-developed countries, GHG mitigation may create restrictions on the use of certain types of fuel, such as wood in urban areas, which differentially affects poor residents. Within more affluent countries, GHG mitigation may entail requirements for lower-emission vehicles. Such vehicles are typically newer and more expensive, making them harder to afford for lower-income groups. As with other efforts to reduce air pollution and increase energy efficiency, middle- and higher-income consumers often are more easily able to make lifestyle adjustments to meet these requirements than are poorer consumers.

Another equity-related limitation of the Kyoto agreement is that it does not address issues of intergenerational equity, including obligations of fairness, maintaining options, and ensuring quality of life (Tonn 2003). Fairness requires not imposing on future generations risks that present generations would deem unacceptable. Maintaining options entails keeping the future world as free of human-made constraints as possible (see Gardiner 2004). Quality of life implies ensuring that future generations enjoy the most important aspects of life such as "peace and security, a healthy environment, a small risk of preventable catastrophe, stable governance, conservation of knowledge, a good life for children, and opportunities for living" (Tonn 2003, 300). An alternative, equity-first framework based on the premise that every person should have an equal share of the world's allowable GHG emissions has been proposed, with "allowable" defined as a level of emissions that would not lead to unacceptable consequences (Athanasiou and Baer 2002; Tonn 2003; Baer, Athanasiou, and Kartha 2008). This rights-based approach, which is based on a principle of equity as equality, attempts to address both present and intergenerational questions of distributional equity.

Equity in Climate Change Impacts and Adaptation

Despite the emphasis on inequities associated with mitigation of climate change, it is the inequities in impacts of climate change that perhaps raise more critical concerns for human security. As noted by Müller (2002, 4), "The cardinal climate change inequity is consequently not the potentially unfair allocation of mitigation targets but the inevitably unfair distribution of climate impact burdens." If there were a sufficient "veil of uncertainty"—to paraphrase Rawls (1971)—as to who would benefit from climate change and who would experience losses, a convincing argument could perhaps be made to suggest that the outcomes of climate change are just. However, a just outcome is dependent upon the outcomes being randomly distributed across regions, sectors, social groups, and ecosystems. In reality, outcomes are neither random, nor determined by physical factors (e.g., magnitude of drought), social factors (e.g., education or income), or individual factors (e.g., behavior or initiative) alone. Instead, differential outcomes that result from processes of climate change are generated, in large part, by combinations of inequitable social, economic, environmental, and political conditions (O'Brien and Leichenko 2000, 2003; Dow, Kasperson, and Bohn 2006; Barnett 2006; Leichenko and O'Brien 2008).

Research on climate change vulnerability has contributed to a better understanding of equity issues in climate change impacts and adaptations (Kasperson Kasperson, and Dow 2001; Füssel and Klein 2006). For example, in assessing the impacts of climate change on Indian agriculture, O'Brien and colleagues (2004) found that economically marginal regions often faced greater sensitivity and exposure to climate change, and at the same time had much lower adaptive capacity than better-off regions. Adaptive capacity was calculated as a composite index of social, environmental, technological, and economic indicators, many of which tended to be systematically lower in regions that were relatively more exposed to climate change. By contrast, relatively better-off regions tended to be less likely to experience the negative effects of climate change as the result of both lower sensitivity and exposure, and higher adaptive capacity. Other studies of climate vulnerability have reached similar conclusions, demonstrating that differential vulnerability across regions or social groups typically reflects underlying socioeconomic, political, and environmental inequities (Vásquez-León, West, and Finan 2003; Adger and Kelly 1999; Thomas and Twyman 2006). What these studies suggest is that climate change will further increase inequities, rather than diminish them.

Adaptation to climate change presents a series of dilemmas related to both distributive and procedural justice (Paavola and Adger 2002; Paavola, Adger, and Huq 2006; Adger et al. 2006). It is clear that some countries, regions, and social groups are much better able to adapt to the impacts of climate change. Some unresolved distributive issues relate to the amount and allocation of funding for adaptation in developing countries, as well as to the distribution of the benefits and the negative consequences of any adaptive response (Paavola and Adger 2002). From the perspective of procedural justice, issues of interests, influence, and participation in the adaptation process remain unsettled (Pavavola and Adger 2002). Decisions about what adaptation strategies to pursue are likely to exclude many groups who might be affected by these decisions. This is of particular concern in cases where one group's adaptation increases another group's vulnerability.

In considering inequities associated with adaptation to climate change, it is especially important to emphasize that inequities are not limited to the international scale; they also appear at other scales of decision making and planning. Lack of participation in local- or regional-level decisions about how to respond to climate change may also be interpreted as a procedural inequity. Referring back to the example of Indian agriculture, village-level case studies revealed that some groups—particularly larger farmers—had more influence over strategies for responding to climate change than others, including the ability to access irrigation for continued production of export crops (O'Brien et al. 2004). However, increased water withdrawals in semiarid areas—particularly those areas likely to become drier as the result of climate change—were found to have long-term sustainability implications for all farmers, raising still other questions about equity in the distribution of the impacts of efforts to adapt to climate change.

Further, it must be underscored that the local and regional inequities related to climate change impacts and adaptation are not exclusive to developing countries. Although developed countries are often assumed to have low vulnerability and a high adaptive capacity based on GDP, technological development, education, institutions, and other factors, there are often regions, communities, or social groups that are considerably more vulnerable and have a lower capacity to adapt to changing climate conditions (O'Brien et al. 2004). In relation to climate change vulnerability and adaptation in Norway, O'Brien and colleagues found that some municipalities have relatively lower capacities to adapt to changes in the agricultural and tourism sectors resulting from climate change (O'Brien, Sygna, and Haugen 2004; O'Brien et al. 2006). These municipalities were generally characterized as having less-diversified economies that were already strained by a limited tax base and demographic shifts toward a more elderly population. Although the Norwegian government has for many decades promoted regional equality through rural polices and government transfers schemes, inequalities remain and are likely to be exacerbated through the unequal impacts of climate change. As will be discussed, this recognition of local and regional inequities associated with climate change in both developing and advanced countries suggests that equity considerations in the context of climate change and human security need to move beyond rigid North-South distinctions.

Moving Beyond the North-South Divide

Climate change has frequently been framed as an equity issue between the developed countries of the North and the developing countries of the South (Müller 2002; Tonn 2000; Ikeme 2003). The North typically views equity issues in terms of fair allocation of emission reduction targets, while the South sees the key equity questions as pertaining to responsibility for climate change and experiences of the negative impacts from climate change (Müller 2002). These differing views on climate change equity are related to different perceptions about how climate change may affect human security. In the North, climate change is not seen as a critical threat to human security, but instead is characterized as an environmental pollution problem that involves lifestyle changes, and can be addressed through lifestyle changes and pollution control policies. In the South, by contrast, climate change is considered a life-threatening human welfare problem that circumscribes the potential for development (Ikeme 2003).

However, the emphasis on inequities across nations, and particularly between advanced and developing countries, disguises many other critical equity issues related to climate change, with broader relevance to questions of human security. As described earlier, procedural and distributive inequities that influence human security can be found within all countries and across all regions. Indeed, there are many regions or groups that contribute little to greenhouse gas emissions, have no voice in climate change negotiations, and no influence on key policies, which are disproportionately vulnerable to climate change and are unable to respond or adapt. For example, gender-based analyses show differential vulnerability for women, as well as differential ability to respond (Seager and Hartmann 2004). If climate change is to be truly framed as an equity issue, then inequities within countries and across different social and gender groups also need to be acknowledged: "In fact, if we differentiate between rich and poor *people*, rather than rich and poor *countries*, we find that the human insecurities world-wide may look more alike" (O'Neill 1997, 10). Furthermore, these inequities between rich and poor are becoming greater as the result of globalization, with disproportionately negative impacts on women. This new geography of inequity was illustrated in the case of Hurricane Katrina, which flooded the city of New Orleans in 2005 and exposed differential vulnerability (Leichenko and O'Brien 2008).

Although distinctions based on income or gender do not sufficiently capture all equity aspects of climate change, the point is that there are differences across the globe, not just between the North and the South. As noted by Rayner and Malone (2001), there is very little positive relationship between a country's average income and its level of poverty, citing the United States as a case in point. By the same token, the problem of overconsumption is not exclusive to the industrialized world. There are growing middle classes in the developing world and many members of these classes are increasingly adopting high-consumption, energy-intensive suburban lifestyles similar to those that have become commonplace in industrialized countries (Leichenko and Solecki 2005).

Globalization processes in particular have transformed the nature of the global economy, with implications for equity that extend beyond the North-South divide. It is widely recognized that there are both winners and losers from economic globalization (O'Brien and Leichenko 2003), and the distribution no longer follows the traditional axes of North-South or developed-developing (Friedman 2005). While it can indeed be argued that most of the world's poor live in developing countries of the global South, and that they are likely to experience negative outcomes from processes that are to a large extent generated or dictated by the North, this generalization is becoming increasingly less valid as globalization—and market liberalization in particular—creates a new "social architecture" that cuts across national and geographic boundaries and rearranges the world into what can be considered the winners and losers of globalization (Castells 1998; Hoogvelt 1997; Held and McGrew 2002) . This proliferation of networks of inclusion/exclusion has been associated with a greater concentration of power and affluence, where the majority of the world's population is left behind.

The North-South divide on both mitigation and adaptation has arguably served to oversimplify the equity aspects of climate change, presenting them as issues of development or poverty, and responsibility or victimization. Yet a closer examination of the process and outcome inequities associated with climate change reveals a much more complex picture, where alliances across the North-South divide may better mobilize action on climate change. As argued by Rayner and Malone (2001, 199–200, emphasis added):

simultaneously addressing gross distributional inequities *within* both the North and the South seems to be both an equity requirement and a necessary political condition for the success of any global climate policy...climate change...provides an arena for debating a wide variety of social, economic, and political issues that society finds difficult to address directly. These include the unequal distribution of wealth within and among nations and the tension between the imperatives of independence and interdependence at all levels of social organization. Much of the debate about equity in climate change mitigation [as well as in impacts and adaptation] is an extension of the broader debate about international economic development and political empowerment.

In short, binaries such as "North-South" and "developed-developing" are become increasingly inappropriate as global environmental change and globalization transform the conditions that characterize these divisions, fragment traditional groupings, and create new coalitions and alliances. Although some authors (e.g., Kydd 2002) distinguish between globalizing and nonglobalizing developing countries, this binary is equally unsatisfying, as it hides the fact that even within globalizing developing countries such as China and India, significant parts of the population are excluded from the benefits of globalization. And within nonglobalizing developing countries, there are some who experience the benefits of globalization, through offshore savings and investments, increased consumption, or market opportunities. Meanwhile there is a growing class of poor and marginalized people in developed countries who share many concerns with their counterparts in developing countries

(Ehrenreich 2001). Likewise, within both globalizing and nonglobalizing countries in the North and South, there are some who are disproportionately vulnerable to environmental change. Leichenko and O'Brien (2008) show that the synergistic interactions between global environmental change and globalization may compound existing inequities, but that these are not necessarily confined to the North-South divide.

Global Environmental Change, Equity, and Human Security

Human security, broadly defined, includes having the means to secure basic rights, needs, and livelihoods, and to pursue opportunities for human fulfilment and development (Khagram, Clark, and Firas Raad 2003). From another perspective, "human security is achieved when and where individuals and communities have the options necessary to end, mitigate, or adapt to threats to their human, environmental and social rights; have the capacity and freedom to exercise these options; and actively participate in attaining these options" (GECHS 1999, 26). The inequities that are created or exacerbated through differential drivers, outcomes, and responses to global environmental change thus have considerable implications for human security.

Climate change, as it is currently being researched, debated, and addressed in international science and policy arenas, has been represented as an issue of global concern that can be resolved through improved environmental management if the broader implications for development are simultaneously addressed (Berkhout, Leach, and Scoones 2003; Adger et al. 2001). Although global arguments are significant and should be reason enough for actions to address global environmental change, issues such as a gradual changes in temperature and precipitation patterns, loss of biodiversity, and the thinning of the ozone layer often do not resonate with the day-to-day experiences of individuals, communities, and regions. Equity issues, on the other hand, often generate both attention and action. The value of an equity-based framing of environmental issues is illustrated by the success of the environmental justice movement, particularly in terms of raising awareness and fostering cleanup of industrial waste sites. Viewing climate change as an issue of equity may make global environmental change more relevant to many who now see it as a distant, "global" problem.

In considering the broader linkages between global environmental change and human security, it also critical to recognize that threats to human security come not only through the direct consequences of climate change, biodiversity loss, and other environmental transformations (i.e., through increased resource scarcity and changing access or control), but also through the underlying processes that create vulnerability. Research on local and regional vulnerabilities to climate change has demonstrated that inequities that exist within and across nations can very often be attributed to unequal economic relationships, unequal access to entitlements, differential social capital, unequal power relationships, and institutional factors (Leichenko and O'Brien 2008). Global environmental change may increase inequities and potentially create new ones, but the fact that inequities existed in the first place must nonetheless be recognized. The potential for overlaps of these new and emerging inequities with underlying and longer-term inequities across nations, regions, and social groups, poses a critical threat to human security and should be a priority area for policy attention. Policies that respond to the environmental aspects of climate change without addressing underlying equity issues are likely to both create and perpetuate inequities and insecurities.

Recognition of global environmental change as an issue of equity that selectively undermines human security in some regions and groups is essential. This means elaborating on the "global" discourse, and moving beyond the North-South equity divide. If enhanced human security is an objective, then policy responses must address the underlying factors that influence vulnerability among individuals and communities around the world. An emerging global movement demands justice, equity, and rights in relation to environmental problems, and this has helped to place the notion of human security on the global environmental change agenda. Nevertheless, the quest for and implementation of equitable solutions remains a key challenge for policymakers, negotiators, and civil society. Research can support a transformation toward an equity-based understanding of global environmental change by asking and investigating probing questions related to environmental change, equity, and human security.

Acknowledgments

Some of the material presented in this chapter is based on an article by O'Brien and Leichenko (2006) that appeared in *Die Erde*. We thank the original reviewers of the article and the three reviewers of this chapter.

References

Adger, Neil. 2004. Commentary: The right to keep cold. *Environment and Planning A* 36:1711–1715.

Adger, Neil, and Mick Kelly. 1999. Social vulnerability to climate change and the architecture of entitlements. *Mitigation and Adaptation Strategies for Global Change* 4:253–266.

Adger, Neil, Jouni Paavola, Saleemul Huq, and M. J. Mace, eds. 2006. *Fairness in adaptation to climate change*. Cambridge, MA: MIT Press.

Adger, W. N., T. A. Benjaminsen, K. Brown, and H. Svarstad. 2001. Advancing a political ecology of global environmental discourses. *Development and Change* 32:681–715.

Agyeman J., R. D. Bullard, and B. Evans, eds. 2003. *Just sustainabilities: Development in an unequal world*. Cambridge, MA: MIT Press.

Athanasiou, Tom, and Paul Baer. 2002. *Dead heat: Global justice and global warming*. New York: Seven Stories Press.

Baer, Paul, Tom Athanasiou, and Sivan Kartha. 2008. The right to development in a climate constrained world: The greenhouse development rights framework. http://www.ecoequity.org/GDRs (accessed November 15, 2008).

Baer, Paul, J. Harte, B. Haya, J. Herzog, N. E. Hultman, D. M. Kammen, R. B. Norgaard, and L. Raymond. 2000. Equity and greenhouse gas responsibility. *Science* 289:2287.

Barnett, Jon. 2006. Climate change, insecurity, and injustice. In *Fairness in adaptation to climate change*, ed. W. Neil Adger, Jouni Paavola, Saleemul Huq, and M. J. Mace, 115–129. Cambridge, MA: MIT Press.

Beckman, Ludvig. 2008. Do global climate change and the interest of future generations have implications for democracy? *Environmental Politics* 17:610–624.

Beckman, Ludvig, and Edward A. Page. 2008. Perspectives on justice, democracy and global climate change. *Environmental Politics* 17:527–535.

Berkhout, Frans, Melissa Leach, and Ian Scoones. 2003. Shifting perspectives in environmental social science. In *Negotiating environmental change: New perspectives from social science*, ed. Frans Berkhout, Melissa Leach, and Ian Scoones, 1–31. Cheltenham, UK: Edward Elgar.

Boulding, Kenneth E. 1978. *Stable peace*. Austin: University of Texas Press.

Brown, Donald. 2003. The importance of expressly examining global warming policy issues through an ethical prism. *Global Environmental Change* 13:229–234.

Castells, M. 1998. *End of millennium*. Malden, MA: Blackwell.

Cutter, Susan. 1995a. The forgotten casualties: Women, children, and environmental change. *Global Environmental Change* 5 (3): 181–194.

Cutter, Susan. 1995b. Race, class and environmental justice. *Progress in Human Geography* 19:107–118.

Cutter, Susan, and William Solecki. 1996. Setting environmental justice in space and place: Acute and chronic airborne toxic releases in the southeastern United States. *Urban Geography* 17:380–399.

Denton, Fatma. 2002. Climate change vulnerability, impacts, and adaptation: Why does gender matter? *Gender and Development* 10 (2): 11–20.

Dore, Mohammed H. I., and Timothy D. Mount. 1999. *Global environmental economics: Equity and the limits to markets.* Cambridge, MA: Blackwell.

Dow, Kirstin, Roger E. Kasperson, and Maria Bohn. 2006. Exploring the social justice implications of adaptation and vulnerability. In *Fairness in adaptation to climate change,* ed. W. Neil Adger, Jouni Paavola, Saleemul Huq, and M. J. Mace, 79–96. Cambridge, MA: MIT Press.

Ehrenreich, Barbara. 2001. *Nickel and dimed: On (not) getting by in America.* New York: Metropolitan Books.

Farber, Daniel A. 2007. Basic compensation for victims of climate change. *University of Pennsylvania Law Review* 155:1605–1656.

Friedman, Thomas. 2005. *The world is flat: A brief history of the Twenty-First Century.* New York: Farrar, Straus and Giroux.

Füssel, Hans Martin, and Richard J. T. Klein. 2006. Climate change vulnerability assessments: An evolution of conceptual thinking. *Climatic Change* 75:301–329.

Gardiner, Stephen M. 2004. Ethics and global climate change. *Ethics* 114:555–600.

GECHS. 1999. *Global Environmental Change and Human Security (GECHS) Science Plan.* IHDP Report No. 11. Bonn, Germany: IHDP.

Gore, Albert. 1992. *Earth in the balance: Forging a new common purpose.* London: Earthscan Publications.

Gore, Albert. 2007. *An inconvenient truth: The crisis of global warming.* New York: Viking.

Gupta, Joyeeta. 2000. "On behalf of my delegation,...": A survival guide for developing country climate negotiators. Washington, DC: Center for Sustainable Development in the Americas. http://www.cckn.net/pdf/my_delegation_en.pdf. (accessed November 15, 2008).

Held, David, and Anthony McGrew. 2002. *Globalization/anti-globalization.* Cambridge, UK: Polity Press.

Hoogvelt, Ankie. 1997. *Globalization and the postcolonial world.* Baltimore, MD: Johns Hopkins Press.

Homer-Dixon, Thomas. 1994. Environmental scarcities and violent conflict: Evidence from cases. *International Security* 19:5–40.

Ikeme, Jekwu. 2003. Equity, environmental justice and sustainability: Incomplete approaches in climate change politics. *Global Environmental Change* 13:195–206.

IPCC. 2007. *Impacts, adaptation and vulnerability. Contribution of Working Group II to the fourth assessment report of the Intergovernmental Panel on Climate Change*, ed. M. L. Parry, O. F. Canziani, J. P. Palutikof, P. J. van der Linden, and C. E. Hanson. Cambridge, UK: Cambridge University Press.

Kasperson, Roger E., Jeanne X. Kasperson, and Kirstin Dow. 2001. Vulnerability, equity, and global environmental change. In *Global environmental risk*, ed. Jeanne Kasperson and Roger Kasperson, 247–272. London: Earthscan Publications.

Kemfert, Claudia, and Richard Tol. 2002. Equity, international trade, and climate policy. *International Environmental Agreements: Politics, Law and Economics* 2:23–48.

Khagram, Sanjeev, William C. Clark, and Dana Firas Raad. 2003. From the environment and human security to sustainable security and development. *Journal of Human Development* 4 (2): 289–313.

Kütting, G. 2004. Environmental justice. *Global Environmental Politics* 4:115–121.

Kydd, Jonathan. 2002. *Agriculture and rural livelihoods: Is globalization opening or blocking paths out of rural poverty?* Agricultural Research and Extension Network Paper No. 121. London: Overseas Development Institute.

Lake, Robert. 1996. Volunteers, NIMBYS, and environmental justice: Dilemmas of democratic practice. *Antipode* 28:160–174.

Leichenko, Robin, and Karen O'Brien. 2008. *Environmental change and globalization: Double exposures.* New York: Oxford University Press.

Leichenko, Robin, and William Solecki. 2008. Consumption, inequity, and environmental justice: The making of new metropolitan landscapes in developing countries. *Society and Natural Resources* 21:611–624.

Leichenko, Robin, and William Solecki. 2005. Exporting the American dream: The globalization of suburban consumption landscapes. *Regional Studies* 39:241–253.

Lenton, Timothy M., Hermann Held, Elmar Kriegler, Jim W. Hall, Wolfgang Lucht, Stefan Rahmstorf, and Hans Joachim Schellnhuber. 2008. Tipping elements in the earth's climate system. *Proceedings of the National Academy of Sciences* 105:1786–1793.

Michaelowa, Axel, Kristian Tangen, and Henrik Hasselknippe. 2004. Issues and options for the post-2012 climate architecture—An overview. *International Environmental Agreements: Politics, Law and Economics* 5:1573–1553.

Müller, Benito. 2002. *Equity in climate change: The great divide.* Oxford: Oxford Institute for Energy Studies, with support of Shell Foundation.

O'Brien, Karen, and Robin Leichenko. 2006. Climate change, equity, and human security. *Die Erde* 137:165–179.

O'Brien, Karen, and Robin Leichenko. 2003. Winners and losers in the context of global change. *Annals of the Association of American Geographers* 93:99–113.

O'Brien, Karen, and Robin Leichenko. 2000. Double exposure: Assessing the impacts of climate change within the context of economic globalization. *Global Environmental Change* 10:221–232.

O'Brien, K., R. Leichenko, U. Kelkar, H. Venema, G. Aandahl, H. Tompkins, A. Javed, S. Bhadwal, S. Barg, L. Nygaard, and J. West. 2004. Mapping vulnerability to multiple stressors: Climate change and economic globalization in India. *Global Environmental Change* 14 (4): 303–313.

O'Brien, K. L., L. Sygna, and J. E. Haugen. 2004. Resilient or vulnerable? A multi-scale assessment of climate impacts and vulnerability in Norway. *Climatic Change* 64:193–225.

O'Brien, K. L., S. Eriksen, L. Sygna, and L. O. Næss. 2006. Questioning European complacency: Climate change impacts, vulnerability and adaptation in Norway. *Ambio* 35 (2): 50–56.

O'Neill, Helen. 1997. Globalisation, competitiveness and human security: Challenges for development policy and institutional change. *The European Journal of Development Research* 9 (1): 7–37.

Paavola, Jouni. 2008. Science and social justice in the governance of adaptation to climate change. *Environmental Politics* 17:644–659.

Paavola, Jouni, and W. Neil Adger. 2002. Justice and adaptation to climate change. Tyndall Centre for Climate Change Research, *Working Paper 23*. Norwich: Tyndall Centre for Climate Change Research.

Paavola, Jouni, W. Neil Adger, and Seleemul Huq. 2006. Multifaceted justice in adaptation to climate change. In *Fairness in adaptation to climate change*, ed. W. Neil Adger, Jouni Paavola, Saleemul Huq, and M. J. Mace, 277–363. Cambridge, MA: MIT Press.

Pettit, Jethro. 2004. Climate justice: A new social movement for atmospheric rights. *IDS Bulletin* 35 (3): 102–106.

Rawls, John. 1971. *A theory of justice*. Oxford: Oxford University Press.

Rayner, Steve, and Elizabeth L. Malone. 2001. Climate change, poverty, and intragenerational equity: The national level. *International Journal of Global Environmental Issues* 1 (2): 175–202.

Rees, William, and Laura Westra. 2003. When consumption does violence: Can there be sustainability and environmental justice in a resource-limited world? In *Just sustainabilities: Development in an unequal world*, ed. Julian Agyeman, Robert Bullard, and Bob Evans, 99–124. Cambridge, MA: MIT Press.

Ringuis, Lasse, Asbjorn Torvanger, and Arild Underdal. 2002. Burden sharing and fairness principles in international climate policy. *International Environmental Agreements: Politics, Law and Economics* 2:1–22.

Roberts, J. Timmons, and Bradley C. Parks. 2007. *A climate of injustice: Global inequality, north-south politics, and climate policy*. Cambridge, MA: MIT Press.

Rose, Adam, and Snorre Kverndokk. 1998. Equity in environmental policy: An application to global warming. In *Handbook on environmental and resource economics*, ed. J. van den Bergh, 352–379. London: Edward Elgar.

Rose, A., B. Stevens, J. Edmonds, and M. Wise. 1998. International equity and differentiation in global warming policy. *Environmental and Resource Economics* 12:25–51.

Schmidt, Jake, Ned Helme, Jin Lee, and Mark Houdashelt. 2008. Sector-based approach to the post-2012 climate change policy architecture. *Climate Policy* 8:595–515.

Seager, Joni, and Hartmann, Betsy. 2004. *A gender assessment of DEWA and UNEP: Final report to DEWA*. Nairobi: Division of Early Warning and Assessment.

Skutch, Margaret. 2002. Protocols, treaties and action: The "climate change process" viewed through gender spectacles. *Gender and Development* 10 (2): 30–39.

Slocum, Rachel. 2004a. Consumer citizens and the cities for climate protection campaign. *Environment and Planning A* 36 (5): 763–782.

Slocum, Rachel. 2004b. Polar bears and energy-efficient light bulbs: Strategies to bring climate change home. *Environment and Planning D: Society and Space* 22 (3): 413–438.

Smith, David. 1994. *Geography and social justice*. Cambridge, MA: Blackwell.

Steffen, Will, et al., eds. *Global change and the earth system: A planet under pressure*. Berlin: Springer Verlag.

Thomas, David S. G., and C. Twyman. 2006. Adaptation and equity in resource dependent societies. In *Fairness in adaptation to climate change*, ed. W. Neil Adger, Jouni Paavola, Saleemul Huq, and M. J. Mace, 223–237. Cambridge, MA: MIT Press.

Tonn, Bruce. 2003. An equity first, risk-based framework for managing global climate change. *Global Environmental Change* 13:295–306.

Toth, Ferenc. 2000. Intergenerational equity and discounting. *Integrated Assessment* 1 (2): 127–136.

Turner, Billie Lee II, et al. 2003. A framework for vulnerability analysis in sustainability science. *Proceedings of the National Academy of Science* 100 (14): 8074–8079.

United Nations Environment Programme. 2002. *Global environment outlook 3*. London: Earthscan Publications.

World Commission on Environment and Development. 1987. *Our common future*. New York: Oxford University Press.

Vásquez-León, Marcela, Colin Thor West, and Timothy J. Finan. 2003. A comparative assessment of climate vulnerability: Agriculture and ranching on both sides of the US-Mexico border. *Global Environmental Change* 13:159–173.

World Resources Institute et al. 2000. *World resources 2000–2001*. Washington, DC: WRI.

Worldwatch Institute. 2005. *State of the world 2005: Global security*. Washington, DC: Worldwatch Institute.

9

Approaches to Enhancing Human Security

Marvin S. Soroos

Most of the research being conducted on global environmental change and human security seeks to increase knowledge on how an expanding human population is altering and degrading the natural environment and the ways in which these changes threaten the welfare, if not the very survival, of human societies. Less consideration has been given to what humans can do, either individually or collectively, to *enhance their security* in the face of threatening environmental changes. This chapter looks at the basic options that humanity has for addressing the challenges posed by global and international environmental problems, such as climate change, depletion of the ozone layer, marine pollution, depletion of fisheries, loss of biological diversity, water scarcity, and desertification.

Current generations are by no means the first to confront the challenge of securing themselves against environmental change. For as long as they have inhabited the planet, humans have had to contend with threatening natural phenomena such as storms, floods, tidal waves, droughts, volcanoes, earthquakes, pestilence, and predatory animals. History provides compelling examples of civilizations that have survived and flourished through their ability to anticipate and adapt to changing natural conditions, while others that have been less adept at foreseeing and coping with environmental changes have declined and even completely disappeared (Diamond 2005). Such adaptations have tended to take place in a spontaneous way rather than by a conscience policy process (Smithers and Smit 1997, 132). Nevertheless, many insights can be gleaned from these historical experiences of societies that have succeeded or failed in adjusting to the natural world (Tol, Fankhauser, and Smith 1998, 116–117). The environmental threats that now confront humanity are arguably more severe, complex, and of a greater scale geographically than those faced by earlier generations. Furthermore, current environmental changes are to a greater extent human-induced, and thus potentially susceptible to strategies designed to manage threats as opposed to simply adapting to naturally occurring ones. Modern civilizations may also be better equipped to secure themselves against environmental threats, given their technologies, scientific knowledge, and economic resources, while those at lesser stages of development can do little to reduce their vulnerabilities to environmental changes.

Basic Approaches to Enhancing Human Security

Humans experience *security* to the extent that their insecurities are minimized if not totally avoided or eliminated. An *insecurity* arises when two basic conditions are present—a threat and a related vulnerability. A *threat* is present when circumstances exist that have the potential for significant adverse impacts on humans. A *vulnerability* exists when humans are exposed to potentially harmful developments and lack the means to effectively prevent, limit, or cope with the damage that may occur from them (Dow 1992, 419–420). For example, human communities have long been confronted with military insecurities when there is a combination of a threat posed by the armed buildup by a neighboring society and a vulnerability arising from a lack of means to mount an effective defense. Similarly, global climate change jeopardizes the security of small-island states and low-lying states that are susceptible to being inundated by rising sea levels and storm surges, while having few if any realistic options for limiting the resulting damage.

This definition of insecurity suggests two potential strategies for enhancing security. The first is to take steps to *manage threats* by preventing them from arising in the first place, or, if they do materialize, to limit, reduce, or eventually eliminate the threats. In a military context, a threat might be prevented or eliminated by a preemptive attack on a potential adversary that is designed to keep it weak. Environmental threats might be averted or minimized by reducing the emissions of pollutants that could endanger the health of a community. Some threats are more susceptible to being managed than others, in particular those that arise from human activities and therefore can at least in theory be altered or terminated. Naturally occurring environmental threats, such as earthquakes and volcanoes are clearly impossible to prevent or contain, and thus other strategies must be used to avoid or limit harmful consequences.

The second major strategy for enhancing human security is to *reduce vulnerabilities*. In some cases, it may be possible to avoid exposure to threatening circumstances; in other words to "stay out of harm's way." For example, an individual may elect to stay away from crime-infested neighborhoods, especially in the dark of night, or from countries where terrorist acts are frequent. People may be able to reduce exposure to natural forces by choosing not to live in earthquake-prone areas, near potentially active volcanoes, or in flood plains. Vulnerability can also be reduced by erecting protective barriers that buffer a community from impending harms, as was once done by building thick walls around ancient cities, or more recently, by constructing sea walls to protect against rising ocean levels and storm surges. Another possible strategy is to take steps to reduce the impact of potentially harmful developments that take place. For example, buildings can be reinforced to withstand earthquake shocks or hurricane winds. Vaccination programs can be implemented to limit the spread of infectious diseases. Finally, societies are less vulnerable to threats to the extent of their capacity to *cope* with impacts of damaging developments (see Soroos 1999, 46–50). Coping capacity refers to the resilience of a society, in particular its ability to absorb impacts and continue functioning somewhat normally despite potentially disruptive events, or to recover from losses, such as by rebuilding after a war or natural catastrophe (Dow 1992, 421).

Timing of Security-Enhancing Strategies

Ideally, efforts to enhance human security are *anticipatory* in the sense of being undertaken before threatening circumstances come to fruition, such as in the form of an extreme event. Anticipatory efforts may be directed either toward preventing or limiting threats to human security or to reducing the vulnerabilities of societies to these threats. Anticipatory strategies require foresight to identify the threats that could arise and the specific impacts that they have on humans as well as advanced planning and implementation of measures that will minimize the threats or vulnerabilities. An anticipatory response toward reducing vulnerability might include emergency-preparedness planning, such as early warning systems, evacuation instructions, and assembling relief supplies that could minimize the number of casualties in the event of a natural disaster. The hundreds of billions of dollars that are invested annually on armed forces and weaponry, when they are not engaged in fighting wars, are indicative of the emphasis that states put on anticipatory response to military security. Governments have been less inclined to commit such large amounts of resources toward securing their populations from environmental threats. An anticipatory response is more likely when the threatening developments are both highly probable and potentially very harmful or disruptive.

In the absence of an effective anticipatory strategy for enhancing security, individuals or societies are left with option of *reactive* responses to harmful or disruptive developments that evolve from threatening circumstances. In contrast to anticipatory actions, which are consciously planned, reactive responses are more likely to be ad hoc or spontaneous adaptations to devastating events, as was the case with responses to the Asian tsunami of 2004 and the major earthquakes in Pakistan in 2005 and in China in 2008. Generally speaking, reactive responses are less likely to be effective in enhancing human security than anticipatory ones, and may be considerably more expensive to implement. Some circumstances may even preclude an effective reaction.

Reactive responses seek to reduce the extent and severity of harmful impacts, for example by providing relief to those who are most seriously affected, such as flood victims. By definition, threats cannot be completely averted by reactive strategies. However, it may be possible to take steps to keep harmful developments from getting worse or to diminish if not ultimately eliminate them, as is the thrust of international efforts to contain the AIDS pandemic. Likewise, signs of the decline of a fishery may trigger the imposition of limits on the catch or even a moratorium on fishing to enable the stock to regenerate to earlier levels. Reactive as opposed to anticipatory responses are more likely when the probability of the threat materializing into a damaging development is perceived to be very low even if the potential impacts could be severe and widespread.

Societal Levels of Security-Enhancing Strategies

Efforts to enhance human security can be made at all levels of social organization ranging from the individual or family unit to global organizations, such as the United Nations. Those undertaken by individuals have been referred to as *autonomous* responses (Tol, Fankhauser, and Smith 1998, 110–111). For example, at the height of the Cold War in the 1960s, some individual families built bomb shelters under their homes in hopes of having a safe refuge in the event of a nuclear attack. Another example: individuals can avoid the harmful health effects of ultraviolet radiation from the sun by applying liberal doses of sun screen or by minimizing time spent in the sun. It is impossible or too costly, however, for individuals to secure themselves against many of the threats to their well-being. Thus, they may enter cooperative arrangements in which they work with others to jointly enhance their security. Such is the case with contributions to group insurance programs for calamities such as fires, automobile accidents, health problems, and premature death. These arrangements provide compensation to individuals suffering costly losses, thereby spreading the risk.

One of the principal functions of governments is to provide its citizenry with security from certain types of threats. Local police forces are a means for securing the lives and property of residents by providing a deterrent to crime. National governments have traditionally assumed the primary responsibility for securing their citizens from military aggression from hostile states or violence by terrorists. Governments are also expected to provide economic security by carrying out policies that stabilize the economy or by guaranteeing a social safety net for the disadvantaged sectors of their societies. Within governments, for example, environmental ministries seek to control pollutants that jeopardize the health of a population.

Some threats to human security are dealt with most effectively internationally, and in some cases even globally. Thus, in recent decades numerous international institutions have been created to collectively enhance the security of their member states. The UN Security Council has the responsibility for responding to aggression by one state against another. The World Health Organization seeks to reduce the threats to human health from contagious diseases that do not respect international boundaries. The International Monetary Fund lends stability to the global economy and assists countries facing financial crises. The United Nations Environment Programme has facilitated negotiations on treaties designed to lessen environmental threats to human security, such as preventing further deterioration of the ozone layer.

Security and Global Environmental Change

The options that human beings have for enhancing their security in the face of global environmental change are too numerous and diverse to

Table 9.1
Options for enhancing security

	National	International/Global
Reduce threats	I	II
Reduce vulnerabilities	III	IV

inventory in a chapter. They range from what individuals can do personally to limit their impact on the environment or to adapt to environmental changes all the way to efforts of the global community to negotiate treaties and establish international programs through the United Nations. Thus, this chapter maps only a part of the terrain of options for enhancing security, specifically those basic approaches defined by the four combinations defined by two pairs of alternative paths. In the first pair is the distinction between strategies designed to manage the threats associated with environmental change, and those designed to reduce vulnerabilities. In the second pair is the distinction between those efforts undertaken by states or subnational groups on their own, and those requiring a measure of international or global cooperation (see Soroos 1994, 1997). These options are diagramed in table 9.1.

National Efforts to Reduce Threats

The first option is for states to act on their own to avert, limit, or reduce the threats associated with environmental change, an example being an American law adopted in 1977 that banned domestic nonessential uses of chlorofluorocarbons (CFCs) in the interest of preserving the ozone layer. These unilateral actions may be effective in addressing more localized environmental problems caused largely by activities taking place within that country, but may do little to address the threats posed by global environmental changes that are the cumulative effect of practices taking place in many countries. Isolated, unilateral measures adopted by larger countries, such as the United States, which are responsible for a significant share of global threats, will have a greater impact than those of smaller states. Such steps toward environmental responsibility may also set an example that spurs others to follow suit. Such was part of the motivation for the Nordic countries making commitments in the mid-1980s to reduce their sulfur dioxide emissions by 80 percent, well beyond the 30 percent reductions mandated by the Helsinki Protocol on

Sulphur Emissions adopted by most European countries in 1985. In most cases, however, few countries respond to the unilateral acts of environmental responsibility of others, thus opting to play the role of "free riders" who benefit from the restraint of others while making no sacrifices on their own. Anticipating the free rider problem, most countries are reluctant to absorb significant costs to create or maintain a global pubic good—in this case preservation of the environment—until they are assured that other countries contributing to the threat make comparable commitments.

International Efforts to Reduce Threats

The second approach to enhancing human security requires international cooperation to minimize environmental threats. Recent decades have seen numerous international treaties developed to lessen environmental threats, such as climate change, ozone depletion, various forms of atmospheric and marine pollution, overharvesting of fisheries, and loss of biodiversity. The primary thrust of these treaties, which are the products of international negotiations that are often protracted and contentious, is to limit or curtail those activities that are contributing to the threats they address. In recent decades, the typical pattern has been first to agree on a framework treaty (or legal convention) that sets goals and spells out general principles, but requires few sacrifices by the states become parties. Examples of framework treaties are the Vienna Convention on Protecting the Ozone Layer (1985) and the United Nations Framework Convention on Climate Change (1992) Continuing negotiations may lead to the adoption supplemental protocols that require ratifying countries to limit their environmental damaging activities, in some cases by quantified amounts within a specified time frame. Accordingly, the Kyoto Protocol (1997) was a first step in addressing global climate change by mandating specific limits on greenhouse gas emissions by the developed countries by the years 2008 to 2012. The record of the international community in establishing effective regimes has been mixed. Significant progress has been made toward preserving the stratospheric ozone layer by means of the Montreal Protocol and subsequent amendments and adjustments. These agreements have dramatically reduced the flow of CFCs and other ozone-depleting substances into the atmosphere and offer the prospect that the ozone layer will recover to preindustrial levels later in the current century. By contrast, negotiations on limiting emissions of climate-altering greenhouse gases into the atmosphere have been fraught with conflict, and thus relatively little has been done thus far to mitigate the threats posed by global climate change.

National Efforts to Reduce Vulnerability

If environmental threats cannot be sufficiently moderated by either national or international means, states may have no other option but to try to lessen their vulnerabilities. Countries may act on their own to reduce exposure to environmental threats, such as avoiding disasters by relocating people from harm's way. Barriers to the impacts of climate changes might be constructed, such as sea walls around low-lying metropolitan areas. Steps can also be taken to provide timely warnings of imminent environmental threats, to speed emergency relief to those whose lives are abruptly disrupted by the impacts of environmental change, and to facilitate longer-term recovery. National investments in reducing vulnerability have the advantage of not being dependent upon the uncertain prospects of protracted international negotiations among nations with contrasting and conflicting interests. Moreover, from a political standpoint, it may be easier to persuade an electorate to make sacrifices for outcomes that it will enjoy exclusively, as opposed to contributing to a global public good. However, there may be not be a practical way for nations to reduce vulnerabilities to some threats to acceptable levels, as is the case with depletion of the ozone layer.

International Efforts to Reduce Vulnerability

Efforts to reduce vulnerability can also take the form of international cooperation and assistance, which is especially important for smaller and less-developed countries that are less able to cope with environmental change. This approach was encouraged by the 1990s International Decade for Natural Disaster Reduction, coordinated by the United Nations Development Programme and the Department of Humanitarian Affairs, which sought to facilitate assessment of vulnerabilities, enhance early warning systems, and strengthen planning for disaster mitigation at the national and local levels. Such efforts most often take the form of development or humanitarian assistance to developing countries that lack the means to effectively address their vulnerabilities. Such assistance is generally more available for dealing with disaster-induced emergencies than for making more deliberate adaptations to more gradually unfolding threats. Developing countries that are highly vulnerable to environmental threats but have limited capacity to deal with them, as in the case of African nations heavily impacted by global warming, argue that the industrialized countries responsible for their plight bear a moral responsibility to assist them in adapting to environmental changes.

Will it be possible to achieve the level of international cooperation that would be needed to limit environmental threats to a manageable level and to assist smaller and less-developed countries to lessen their vulnerabilities? Such a combination of approaches will tend to be more prevalent in countries that contribute little to global environmental changes, but nevertheless are heavily impacted by them, such as small-island states facing rising sea levels. Countries that contribute disproportionately to creating the problem, while being less impacted, will be inclined toward self-help strategies of adjusting to them. Environmentalists and internationalists tend to look askance at proposals that would have countries invest heavily in national strategies aimed at reducing vulnerabilities out of concern that they may displace efforts to prevent or minimize human-induced environmental changes (Pielke 1998, 162). Those skeptical of the seriousness of environmental threats and the efficacy of international cooperation are more inclined to explore possibilities of nationally based ways of reducing vulnerabilities and adapting to whatever changes take place.

The Challenge of Reducing Vulnerabilities

As previously suggested, much more has been done to investigate prospects for international cooperation designed to prevent or limit environmental threats. However, there have been alternative currents of thought arguing for exploring the possibilities for reducing vulnerabilities, centering on the term *adaptation* both on the grounds of feasibility and cost. The following subsections outline considerations that should be kept in mind if a decision is made to invest more heavily in such defensive strategies, especially at the expense of continuing efforts to minimize threats.

The Increasing Variety, Intensity, and Complexity of Impacts
Reducing vulnerabilities entails coping effectively with the many and diverse impacts of environmental changes on natural systems and human societies. Furthermore, complex interrelationships that will inevitably arise among these impacts and feedback loops may accelerate or counteract certain impacts. Timing is also a critical factor, as the various impacts

will become manifest at different times and intensify at different rates. It may be possible over the next few decades to anticipate some of the early impacts and to adapt somewhat effectively to many of them, but the pace and complexity of the effects of some environmental changes, such as global warming, are likely to accelerate over time. Rapid, unanticipated changes may prove to be highly disruptive and pose sudden, daunting challenges for social adaptations (Smithers and Smit 1997, 130–131). In this latter regard, there is growing concern in the scientific community that climate changes may be approaching critical tipping points that would abruptly alter the environmental challenges confronting humanity (National Research Council 2003; Cox 2005).

Persisting Scientific Uncertainties on the Nature and Interrelatedness of Impacts

Skeptics have seized upon scientific uncertainties about the nature and severity of environmental threats, such as those associated with global warming, to justify putting off a potentially costly program for managing threats. The science of the impacts of environmental changes, especially those of a secondary or tertiary nature (such as economic and social impacts), tends to be even more diverse and uncertain. Thus, if the science pertaining to impending environmental threats has not been conclusive enough to spur effective preventive action, the even more inadequate knowledge of the impacts of global warming or other environmental changes is even less likely to trigger substantial investments in schemes designed to reduce vulnerability.

Vulnerability as a Local or Regional Problem

Steps taken to avoid or mitigate global environmental threats contribute to the security of nations and human communities generally. By contrast, the diverse array of potential vulnerabilities arising from these changes tends to be specific to regions and even localities. Thus, enhancing human security by reducing vulnerabilities becomes more of a bottom-up rather than a top-down challenge. Accordingly, dealing with vulnerabilities is likely to be a much more complex undertaking than minimizing the threat in the first place. While tailoring responses to smaller social units increases the likelihood that vulnerability-reducing strategies are well adapted to local circumstances, questions arise about how to effectively mobilize, coordinate, and facilitate such activities among a vast number of localized districts or regions.

Different Types and Degrees of Exposure to Environmental Change

States and regions differ greatly in their exposure to environmental changes and their impacts. Developing countries are prone to higher losses of life and greater relative economic losses, while absolute monetary losses tend to be higher in developed countries (Dow 1992, 418–419). The very survival of numerous small island states is jeopardized by rising sea levels and increase in the frequency of tropical storms. Other countries with major cities or agricultural regions lying at sea level, such as Egypt and Bangladesh, are also likely to be heavily impacted by climate change. Environmental changes pose more of a threat to developing countries whose economies and export revenues are heavily dependent on agricultural production. By contrast, landlocked and more highly developed countries would be less seriously impacted.

Differing Capacities to Reduce Vulnerabilities

States and societies differ considerably in their capacities to deal with their vulnerabilities. Wealthy, highly developed countries have far more options and resources available to apply to security-enhancing projects to anticipate impacts, provide emergency relief, and facilitate recovery. Such measures also tend to be more feasible for large states in which most impacts are relatively small in proportion to the size of their territory, population, and economy. Less-impacted areas in a large country may assist devastated localities to cope with a natural disaster. Such burden sharing may not an option for smaller, more homogeneous countries, as was the case with the devastation that Hurricane Mitch wreaked on Honduras and Nicaragua in 1998. Unfortunately, the countries that are the most threatened by environmental changes are often among not only the most vulnerable but also the least able to adapt.

Defensive Strategies that Intensify or Compound Environmental Threats

Ideally, the steps taken to reduce vulnerabilities do not aggravate the threats they are designed to address or raise other environmental problems. This may not be the case with some coping strategies, however. In the United States and other developed countries, people can easily adjust to markedly warmer summer temperatures by increasing their use of air conditioners powered with electricity produced by burning fossil fuels, thereby accelerating the buildup of greenhouse gases in the atmosphere. Exploiting groundwater resources in the face of droughts may contribute to even greater water crises in the future. Large dams constructed to lessen the threats from floods can have serious environmental consequences and add significantly to the insecurities of large numbers of displaced people.

Defensive or Adaptive Strategies that Adversely Affect Other States or Regions

What each country or society does to address its environmentally related vulnerabilities may create problems for others (Smithers and Smit 1997, 138). For example, the common practice of building levies to protect land along flood-prone rivers may increase the water levels that threaten other communities. Alternatively, if droughts lead to reduced stream flows, upstream states may hold water back in more reservoirs to meet their needs, thus cutting further the amount of water available to downstream neighbors. States experiencing substantially reduced agricultural yields owing to climate changes may increase imports of food to the extent that world food prices rise sharply, making it impossible for poorer countries to afford needed food imports.

Complications Resulting from Continued Population Growth

While global population growth rates have declined considerably since peaking at just over 2 percent in the 1960s to about 1.2 percent currently, approximately 80 million people are still being added to the world's numbers each year. As a result, the world's population is projected to increase from 6.7 billion in 2007 to 9.4 billion in 2050 (U.S. Census Bureau 2008). Most of this increase will continue to take place in developing countries, which are among the most vulnerable to the harmful effects of environmental changes and have the least resources for adapting to them. The population of Africa alone is on track to double within the next fifty years (Population Reference Bureau 2007). The large numbers of additional people in such regions will not only compound the insecurities, as land, water, and other natural resources become more scarce, but they will also greatly complicate the task of adapting to environmental changes with the already limited resources that are available.

The Complexity of Decisions about Adaptive Strategies

In view of the broad range of potential impacts of environmental changes both in the short and long term, and given the regional variability, policy makers will be faced with a vast array of policy choices as they try to reduce vulnerabilities or enhance their societies' capacities to adapt or recover. Reaching agreements on a portfolio of such responses could be extraordinarily difficult, especially in democratic societies in which competing groups aggressively pursue their own interests. It may be possible to settle on strategies for dealing with immediate impacts, especially in a reactive way where the problems are readily apparent, as was the case with damage from Hurricane Katrina in 2005. Decision making may be more complicated in the case of distant future threats that are inherently more uncertain, but potentially much more catastrophic, and may be addressed in a greater variety of ways, including anticipatory approaches. Without an immediate sense of urgency and given the tendency of decision makers and the general public more generally to discount future threats, it is less likely that societies can reach a broad-based agreement on how to reduce their vulnerabilities.

Conclusion

Environmental changes threaten human security in many ways, and some states and subnational units are much more vulnerable to them than are others. These threats and vulnerabilities are likely to intensify as the world's human population continues to grow rapidly, especially in developing regions, with associated stresses on the planet's natural resources and environment. Communities and nations worldwide face several basic questions as they seek to enhance their security in the face of these threats. How much emphasis will they place on averting or limiting environmental threats, as opposed to acting defensively by trying to reduce their vulnerabilities to these threats? How much are they willing to invest in anticipatory measures either to lessen environmental threats or prepare in advance for their impacts, as opposed to relying on their innate capacity to cope reactively with whatever adverse circumstances arise? And finally, to what extent are human societies or nations going to rely on self-help strategies for advancing their security as opposed to working cooperatively with others on an international or global basis?

Limiting major environmental threats requires an approach that is both anticipatory and global. While such a response has been accomplished in the case of preserving the stratospheric ozone layer through the Montreal Protocol (1987) and a series of amendments, such a high level of international cooperation has proven to be elusive in addressing other environmental threats, such as global climate change. As environmental changes become increasingly manifest and trigger increasingly disruptive impacts, human communities will need to devote more of their resources to reducing their vulnerabilities and improving their capacities to cope with and recover from whatever adverse contingencies arise. Such defensive responses will encounter daunting complexities and uncertainties about impacts, and many countries, especially developing ones, lack the economic and technical resources to respond to these challenges. While international cooperation is generally recognized as a prerequisite to any serious effort to mitigate many environmental threats, when it comes to adaptive responses the more highly developed societies may see little reason to assist even the most heavily impacted developing countries to cope with the mounting difficulties their people inevitably will face. It is imperative that greater attention be given to avoiding a situation in which countries act to address their own vulnerabilities with little regard for how their actions may contribute to the insecurities of other societies or may further aggravate environmental problems that give rise to other types of human insecurities.

References

Cox, John D. 2005. *Climate crash: Abrupt climate change and what it means for our future.* Washington, DC: Joseph Henry Press.

Diamond, Jared. 2005. *Collapse: How societies choose to fail or succeed.* New York: Viking Press.

Dow, Kirsten. 1992. Exploring differences in our common future(s): The meaning of vulnerability to global environmental change. *Geoform* 32 (3): 417–436.

National Research Council (Committee on Abrupt Climate Change). 2003. *Abrupt climate change: Inevitable surprises.* Washington, DC: National Academies Press.

Pielke, Roger A., Jr. 1998. Rethinking the role of adaptation in climate policy. *Global Environmental Change* 8 (2): 158–170.

Population Reference Bureau, 2007. *2007 world population data sheet.* http://www.prb.org/pdf07/07WPDS_Eng.pdf (accessed August 25, 2008).

Smithers, John, and Barry Smit. 1997. Human adaptation to climate variability and change. *Global Environmental Change* 7 (2): 129–146.

Soroos, Marvin S. 1994. Global change, environmental security, and the prisoner's dilemma. *Journal of Peace Research* 31 (3): 317–332.

Soroos, Marvin S. 1997. *The endangered atmosphere: Preserving a global commons.* Columbia: University of South Carolina Press.

Soroos, Marvin S. 1999. Strategies for enhancing human security in the face of global change. In *Environmental change, adaptation, and security*, ed. Stephen C. Lonergan, 41–56. Dordrecht: Kluwer Academic Publishers.

Tol, Richard S. J., Samuel Fankhauser, and Joel B. Smith. 1998. The scope for adaptation to climate change: What can we learn from the impact literature? *Global Environmental Change* 8 (2): 109–123.

United States Census Bureau, 2008. International data base. http://www.census .gov/ipc/www/idb/worldpop.html (accessed August 25, 2008).

10

Rethinking the Role of Population in Human Security

Betsy Hartmann

The "population explosion" of the last century is over. Worldwide population growth rates are declining more rapidly than anticipated. Since 1965, the world's annual population growth rate has fallen from 2.04 to 1.2 percent. According to the UN's 2004 medium projection, world population will grow from its present level of around 6.5 billion to 9.1 billion in 2050 and will then begin to stabilize. Total fertility is expected to decline from approximately 2.6 children per woman today to just over two per woman in 2050 (UN Population Division 2004).

The lingering perception that we are still experiencing a population explosion stems from the fact that a large proportion of the population in developing countries is comprised of young men and women entering their reproductive years, but over time this demographic momentum will slow. In fact, there is a growing convergence between the average family size in developed and in developing nations (Wilson 2001). Ironically, many demographers now worry about population aging and the possibility of a "population implosion" (Eberstadt 2001). A *New York Times* article about China's "time bomb" population crisis focuses not on population growth but on the perils of rising longevity and falling fertility (Kahn 2004).

Despite these changing demographic realities, fears of overpopulation still drive many Western perceptions of the menacing Third World masses. In 2003 Population Action International, a prominent population advocacy organization, released a report on *The Security Demographic: Population and Civil Conflict after the Cold War* (Cincotta, Engelman, and Anastasion 2003) that sets out to prove that population pressure in the Third World is a major contributor to violent conflict through generating environmental stresses, a "youth bulge" of potentially volatile young men prone to terrorism, and rapid urbanization. It calls for military and intelligence agencies to develop better demographic expertise.

This report is old wine in a new bottle, stamped with the vintage of the current war on terror. Since the end of World War II, concerns about overpopulation in the Third World have strongly influenced both foreign policy and public consciousness in the West, especially in the United States. Neo-Malthusian narratives about the negative impact of population growth on security, the environment, food production, and economic development have achieved the status of "hegemonic myths" (Thompson and Rayner 1998) with remarkable staying power and legitimacy in popular, academic, and policy circles. Their dominance, despite a lack of scientific rigor, has often marginalized conflicting evidence and research, excluding alternative narratives from policy debate (Stott and Sullivan 2000; Hartmann 2003).

While at its core neo-Malthusian orthodoxy is conservative, blaming the fertility of poor women for all manner of social ills, it appeals to many liberals for a variety of interrelated reasons including its concern for the environment and its support for family planning. These are particularly contentious issues in the U.S. political context where there is strong conservative opposition to birth control and abortion as well as to environmental regulation. More recently, neo-Malthusianism has been linked closely to women's rights. At the 1994 UN International Conference on Population and Development (ICPD) in Cairo, women's health activists and population agencies, both concerned about fundamentalist threats to family planning, forged the strategic "Cairo consensus" (Hodgson and Watkins 1997). This consensus maintains that rapid population growth is still a major cause of poverty and environmental degradation, but that women's empowerment and reproductive health programs are the solution to high birth rates, instead of the coercive population control programs of the past. Although the Cairo consensus has helped spark many necessary reforms, it has also provided renewed legitimacy to neo-Malthusianism in U.S. liberal policy circles, as one can now supposedly support women's rights and population control at the same time.[1]

The embrace of neo-Malthusianism by liberal policy elites has enabled it to influence alternative conceptions of security, including human security. While the Global Environmental Change and Human Security (GECHS) definition of human security that frames this volume does not focus on population growth,[2] other key conceptualizations of human security do. For example, the UN's *Human Development Report 1994* puts unchecked population growth first on its list of threats to human security. On the local level, the report claims, population growth causes people to move to marginal areas where they are vulnerable to natural disasters; on the global level it is "at the root of global poverty, international migration and environmental degradation" (UNDP 1994, 36).

The Canadian government, which includes human security as an important part of its foreign policy framework, has stated on the subject of population: "Canada's approach to population issues is guided by the recognition that they are integral to the security of Canadians and the stability of the international community. The government statement on foreign policy, Canada and the World, recognized that population growth *and related issues* [my emphasis], including mass and involuntary migration, poverty, social inequity, environmental degradation, and the abuse of human rights, are challenges to human security and to peace and security at the regional and international level" (Government of Canada 1998). Although it may seem like a minor semantic point, relating all these grave issues to population growth implies a causal relationship. The Japanese government, which also embraces human security as a key perspective in its foreign policy, makes a more explicit claim: "The population issue induces the problems of food shortage, unemployment, urban slums, deterioration of environment, etc., and is the biggest factor that precludes economic and social development" (Government of Japan n.d.).

This chapter argues that such assumptions about population growth undermine the human security agenda by reinforcing stereotypes about the destructive and dangerous Third World poor. In so doing, they impede more productive avenues of research and policy, including collaborative efforts between North and South, and potentially expand the reach of military and intelligence agencies. The first section takes a historical look at a set of core neo-Malthusian narratives—what I call "degradation narratives"—that have unduly influenced conceptualizations of human security and environmental security. These narratives greatly oversimplify complex relationships among population growth, poverty, environmental degradation, migration, and conflict. The second section outlines a critique of degradation narratives and related neo-Malthusian arguments. The third section offers a cautionary note on how human security, if not carefully defined and differentiated from neo-Malthusian views of the poor, could end up serving the interests of defense and intelligence agencies in much the same way that the concept of environmental security has done.

The Destructive Peasantry: History of Degradation Narratives

In Western international development policy and environmental advocacy, degradation narratives have largely shaped understandings of the relationships among population, poverty, and environmental degradation in the global South. The basic story line is that population pressures and poverty precipitate environmental degradation. More recently, environmental conflict theorists have extended the causal chain to include migration and violent conflict.[3] The result is that peasants and pastoralists are viewed not only as destroyers of the environment, but also as instigators of political instability.

These biases have roots in colonial policies that blamed peasant agricultural practices and population pressure for soil erosion, deforestation, and desertification. In areas of settler agriculture in eastern and southern Africa, for example, British land-expropriation policies were predicated on the perceived backwardness of African peasants and the superiority of Western knowledge (MacKenzie 1995; Rocheleau, Steinberg, and Benjamin 1995; Leach and Mearns 1996). In Kenya, European settlers mounted a campaign in the 1920s and 1930s to depict African agriculture as a scourge upon the land. "The African people have never established a symbiotic relationship with the land," stated a witness before the Kenyan Land Commission. "They are, in the strict scientific sense, parasites on the land, all of them" (cited in Rocheleau, Steinberg, and Benjamin 1995, 1042).[4]

This image of not only a backward, but also a destructive peasantry carried over into post–World War II development thinking (Escobar 1995, 53). Neo-Malthusianism assumptions became increasingly prominent from the 1960s on, serving as a common explanation, for example, for famines in Ethiopia and the Sahel (Franke and Chasin 1980). Within large international agencies like the World Bank, degradation narratives became a rationale for both rural development and population control interventions. Ignoring the great variety and complexity of African agricultural practices, the World Bank characterized them mainly as slash and burn and nomadic livestock raising, both of which can become destructive under conditions of rapid population growth. The solutions set forward were the introduction of Green Revolution technologies, privatization of land rights, and contraceptives—all requiring Western finance and expertise. Meanwhile, the World Bank neglected the ecologically damaging impact of the mechanized, chemical-intensive farming it was promoting (Williams 1995).[5]

Degradation narratives have persisted despite important challenges from within the development field. One of the earliest was Ester Boserup's book *The Conditions of Agricultural Growth* (1965), which argued that population growth was the driving factor behind agricultural revolutions and increases in productivity. In 1987, Blaikie and Brookfield's book *Land Degradation and Society* offered a systematic analysis of the causes of land degradation across regions and time periods, challenging the common hypothesis that population pressure on resources was chiefly to blame. While this critical literature had an impact on the development field, it had little influence on the emerging concept of sustainable development. The ideological roots of sustainable development were not in development theory, but rather in Northern environmentalism with its quite limited understanding of Third World political economy and ecology (Adams 1995).

Liberal sustainable-development advocates, from popular writers such as Paul Harrison to advocacy organizations such as the Worldwatch Institute, were more willing to acknowledge the role of social and economic disparities, such as unequal land distribution, in the creation of rural poverty, so on first inspection their analyses appeared more sympathetic to the poor. As the argument proceeded, however, these inequalities would often fade from view. The poor made themselves even poorer by having too many children, setting in motion a vicious downward spiral of increasing poverty and environmental degradation. "[I]t is through population that inequality and expropriation work their impact on the environment," wrote Harrison. "They confine the oppressed to a smaller area, and artificially boost population density. Natural population growth goes on to feed that density, and worsens the problem. In most countries population growth is now the main factor pushing people into marginal areas" (1992, 131).

In the mid-1980s, sustainable development incorporated the problematic notion of "environmental refugees" into its lexicon, expanding the degradation narrative in the process (Black 1998).[6] Indeed, it was the addition of migration, particularly from the countryside to the city, which gave the degradation narrative its security dimension: the migration of poor people to other rural areas incites ethnic tensions; their young unemployed sons become a "youth bulge" that gravitates to political extremism in already overcrowded cities;[7] and when they cross international borders, they threaten national social and cultural cohesion.

In the period leading up to the end of the Cold War, the degradation narrative became a common feature of articles and reports rethinking security in environmental terms. The influential 1987 report of the UN World Commission on Environment and Development, commonly known as the Brundtland Report, identified poverty-induced environmental stress as an important source of conflict, noting in particular the destabilizing effects of "environmental refugees." It advocated the use of the most sophisticated surveillance technology to establish an early warning system to monitor indicators of environmental risk and conflict, such as "soil erosion, growth in regional migration, and uses of commons that are approaching the thresholds of sustainability" (World Commission on Environment and Development 1987, 28).

These findings of the Brundtland Report presage the development of the environmental security field in the 1990s. The end of the Cold War extended the concept of security in what Emma Rothschild calls a geometry of "dizzying complexity." The concept of security was extended downward from nations to groups and individuals, upward to the international system and biosphere, and horizontally to include not just military but also "political, economic, social, environmental, or 'human' security" (Rothschild 1995, 55). In this process, the concept of environmental security came to occupy pride of place, especially models of environmental conflict developed by Canadian political scientist Thomas Homer-Dixon (Florini and Simmons 1998).

Homer-Dixon's work is heavily influenced by degradation narratives. He argues that scarcities of renewable resources such as cropland, fresh water, and forests, induced in large part by population pressure, contribute to migration and violent intrastate conflict in many parts of the developing world. Around the globe, he asserts: "Population growth and unequal access to good land force huge numbers of rural people onto marginal lands. There, they cause environmental damage and become chronically poor. Eventually, they may be the source of persistent upheaval, or they may migrate yet again, helping to stimulate ethnic conflicts or urban unrest elsewhere" (Homer-Dixon 1999, 155). This conflict, in turn, can potentially disrupt international security as states fragment or become more authoritarian.

Homer-Dixon's ideas seized the imagination of the U.S. liberal foreign policy establishment in the mid-1990s, propelling degradation narratives into the high rhetoric and politics of national security. His particular rendering of the degradation narrative found its way almost verbatim into speeches of top officials from the White House, State Department, CIA, and U.S. Department of Defense, as well as into many academic, popular, and policy publications on population, environment, and security (see Hartmann 2003). In 1994 and 1995, the Clinton administration's *National Security Strategy of Engagement and Enlargement*, which is considered an important blueprint for foreign and defense policy, stated boldly in the preface, "large-scale environmental degradation, exacerbated by rapid population growth, threatens to undermine political stability in many countries and regions" (White House 1995, 47).

While it is difficult to measure their direct policy impact, Homer-Dixon's ideas proved useful to defense and intelligence agencies. They figured in the U.S. Department of Defense's strategy of "preventive defense" as concerns about environmental security became an "engagement tool" to build bridges with military officials and civilian institutions in strategic areas such as the Middle East, Horn of Africa, and Central Asia. They also served as a rationale for the use of U.S. military expertise and weaponry in the policing of nature reserves. In the intelligence community his ideas served multiple objectives: supporting the establishment of the CIA's environment center; facilitating engagement with NGOs and academics; providing an interface between environmental scientists and intelligence agencies in the design of early warning systems; and justifying continuing expenditures on expensive satellite surveillance systems developed during the Cold War (Hartmann 2003).

In the heyday of environmental security, the continual repetition of the degradation narrative, a virtual litany of blaming the poor, reinforced its truth claims and helped block from view the considerable body of alternative research that challenges it. However, the hegemony of the degradation narrative also came with a price: Northern environment and security advocates, eager to expand their networks in the South, found resistance there to an ideology steeped in old colonial and neo-Malthusian prejudices. "Current efforts to translate the environment, population and conflict debates into a positive, practical policy framework for environmental cooperation and sustainable peace have not enjoyed broad success," the Environment, Development and Sustainable Peace Initiative (EDSP) noted in advance of the World Summit for

Sustainable Development. "More importantly, these efforts have failed to engage a broad community of stakeholders, particularly in the global South" (EDSP 2002).

Challenging the degradation narrative is thus essential to advancing a human security and environmental agenda that meaningfully bridges divides between North and South. The following section offers the elements of a critique.

Beyond Degradation: Elements of a Critique

A critique of degradation narratives must start with the obvious point that simplistic causal narratives rarely do justice to complex social, economic, and environmental processes. Degradation narratives ignore the great diversity in both social systems and ecological conditions in the global South. Context, contingency, agency, and specificity are sacrificed to a universalizing "one size fits all" model. Other key problems with the degradation narrative will be examined in turn.

Faulty Data

Degradation narratives often distort the way research is conducted. For example, sometimes neo-Malthusian assumptions are built into the way data are collected and presented, skewing the results. In their study of six West African nations, Fairhead and Leach found that the extent of deforestation had been exaggerated in each, in part owing to lack of attention to historical evidence and the resulting assumption that at the beginning of the twentieth century, West African forests existed in a state of pristine equilibrium, essentially undisturbed by human use (Fairhead and Leach 1998). Moreover, in the absence of other data, many analyses of forest change in West Africa have utilized a model that links population increase to land clearance, and hence vegetation change. As a result, "neo-Malthusian assumptions about local population-forest relations are thus embedded in the forest statistics themselves" (Leach and Fairhead 2000, 24). In some studies, such as a 1999 UNEP report on Africa, increases in population density are used as a proxy for the location of emerging environmental threats, assuming that population growth is necessarily negative for the environment (Singh et al. 1999).[8] At the very least, such findings indicate that the data that undergird degradation narratives should be carefully interrogated, and that a healthy dose of skepticism is in order.

Localization of Blame

In focusing on poor peasants and pastoralists as the destroyers of the environment, degradation narratives do not take into account powerful social, economic, and political forces that may be strongly implicated. "Effective demand" from elsewhere for a region's natural resources may drive environmental degradation much more than local poverty or population growth. As Dalby (1999, 2002) notes, the demands of rich urban areas in the North for the natural resources of the South create a "shadow economy" of degradation. The crucial role of extractive industries, such as mining, timber, and agribusiness, and the destructive activities of militaries do not figure in the story at all. Also ignored are the complex interactions between resource appropriation and power structures at the local, regional, national, and international levels (Fairhead 2001). In a period of rapid global economic integration, degradation narratives are markedly insular in scope. They essentially describe a closed system where internal stresses may generate movement outward, mainly through mass migration, but the outside is rarely seen to be pressing in.[9] Yet in reality there is no distinct boundary between the inside and the outside, or between the local, regional, national, and global; they are linked through complex patterns of trade, investment, and foreign policy imperatives.

Neo-Malthusian Causality

The uncritical acceptance of neo-Malthusian causality prevents a more complex analysis of the role of population growth in environmental change. Whether or not population pressure is beneficial or damaging to the environment depends on a host of intervening institutional and technological factors as well as the nature of the particular environment in question. Degradation narratives fail to take into account that under some circumstances, population pressure may spur agricultural innovation and intensification. For example, while population growth may decrease the size of landholdings, it can also expand the family labor supply, encouraging more labor-intensive cultivation and conservation techniques. Thus, a study in Rwanda found that declining landholdings were associated with more investments in soil conservation and greater managed tree densities per unit of land (Templeton and Scherr 1999).

In their research in West Africa, Fairhead and Leach document how population increase can lead to greater rather than less forest cover. Farming practices such as gardening and mounding can alter soils in ways that encourage afforestation, while village settlements are associated with the intentional creation of forest "islands" in the savannah as a source of forest products, a means of defense, and a location for cultural activities. Farmers also plant and transplant trees in fields and fallows (Leach and Fairhead 2000; see also Fairhead and Leach 1996, 1998).

These authors caution, however, that one should not simply trade neo-Malthusian assumptions for neo-Boserupian ones. Just as there is no iron-clad law that population growth leads to environmental degradation, it is not axiomatic that population growth automatically spurs agricultural innovation and environmental improvement. "By framing the issue primarily in terms of relationships among aggregate populations, an aggregate 'environment' or resource set, and technology," they write, "both neo-Malthusian and neo-Boserupian perspectives exclude crucial questions relating to social and ecological specificity and history" (Leach and Fairhead 2000, 18).

Depopulation

In focusing only on population growth, degradation narratives ignore the role depopulation can play in environmental degradation. In Brazil, for example, many areas depopulated by poor peasants because of their lack of access to land and agricultural inputs have gone over to ecologically damaging extensive cattle raising, industrial monoculture, and logging (Mello 1997). Similarly, in Mexico the exodus of peasants to urban areas has led to the loss of valuable microhabitats and crop genetic diversity previously sustained by their labor (Garcia-Barrios and Garcia-Barrios 1990). In Africa low population densities and dispersed settlement patterns have been identified as important factors impeding the development of agriculture (Turner, Hyden, and Kates 1993). In general, as Templeton and Scherr observe, decreases in population density can lead not only to declines in cropping frequency, but also "to cessation of labor-intensive methods of replenishing soil fertility, to neglect, abandonment or destruction of terraced landscapes and to soil erosion, downstream siltation and other forms of degradation" (1999, 906).

Livelihood Diversification

Degradation narratives also fail to consider the possibility of livelihood diversification. They tend to promote a one-dimensional view of the peasantry as living solely off the land, ignoring the reality that many peasant households have diversified livelihood strategies. In a village in Bangladesh, for example, one family may have different members engaged in agricultural labor, petty trade, rickshaw driving, teaching, and service in the military. Income derived from nonagricultural activities, meanwhile, is often invested back in productivity-increasing land improvements.

Moreover, degradation narratives do not differentiate types of rural poverty and their relationship to environmental change. Agrarian scholars have pointed out how poverty cannot be treated as a single concept and that assets must be broken down into specific categories. When households are "investment poor," lacking the cash and human resources to invest in maintenance or enhancement of the natural resource base, then environmental degradation is more likely to occur. However, there are many different reasons for investment poverty. Analyses need to be time- and site-specific, and the precise nature of the environmental change in question must be specified (Reardon and Vosti 1995).

Migration

Degradation narratives have a similarly one-dimensional view of migration as distress-generated and generating. However, the causes of migration are extremely complex and context-specific, and there is little evidence to support the view that demographic pressure is at the root of many population movements (Suhrke 1997). Moreover, migration from rural areas is often not a linear phenomenon or a rejection of rural livelihoods. Instead, it can be a vital part of sustaining them. A study in Vietnam found that internal migration is frequently circular and seasonal, with migrants returning to the rural areas at harvest time. Their remittances from urban jobs often help fund investments in agricultural intensification, children's education, and so on, enhancing the ecological and social resilience of the household (Locke, Adger, and Kelly 2000).

Gender Stereotyping

Despite the lack of explicit attention to gender issues, certain views of women are implicit in degradation narratives, especially given the central and negative role they ascribe to population growth. First and foremost, women are seen as reproducers of children—not economic producers. Subsumed into the analytic frame of population pressure, women through their fertility become the breeders of environmental destruction, poverty, and even violence, and controlling their fertility becomes a magic-bullet solution. Women's access to land and property rights, labor obligations, roles in environmental resource management, and relative status in the household and community are not part of the picture, even though gender dynamics can have an important impact on agriculture and the environment. Case studies in Africa note how in many places women are making the day-to-day decisions about agriculture when access to land is still invested in men, a contradiction that can lead to agricultural stagnation (Turner, Adger, and Kelly 1993).

Another stereotype encouraged by the degradation narrative is of the distressed peasant woman battling to collect scarce water and cooking fuel in a desertified environment. As Schroeder notes, the image of the quintessential Third World woman is an African woman carrying a large bundle of firewood on her head. "The wood-gathering icon represents Third World women as Africans, African women as peasants, and peasant women as a single type. There is no geographical detail at either the localized or macropolitical scales that might serve as an explanation for the plight thus portrayed" (1999, 6).[10] Such stereotypes persist despite the fact that there is a large body of feminist political ecology literature, much of it based on intensive fieldwork, which calls them into question and complicates the relationships among gender, class, and the environment.[11]

The impact of neo-Malthusian reasoning extends beyond degradation narratives to include the framing of resource scarcity in terms of population growth overshooting carrying capacity at local, national, regional, and/or global scales. Dryzek (1997) refers to this school of thought as "survivalism." Faddishly, the survivalist focus has shifted from one resource to another: from food shortages in the 1960s, to energy shortages and deforestation in the 1970s and 1980s, to water shortages ("water wars") and biodiversity loss in the 1990s. While there are many genuine concerns associated with resource depletion, neo-Malthusianism invests it with a breathless alarmism, obscuring vast class and institutional differences in resource use through employing aggregate terms like *population* and ignoring the possibility and political economy of both social and technological change. Moreover, as Dryzek points out, survivalist discourses tend to favor authoritarian and hierarchical forms of social control. Recent scholarship has uncovered how Western survivalist thinking heavily influenced the drafters of China's draconian one-child policy, particularly the Club of Rome's famous report *Limits to Growth* (Greenhalgh 2003).

Despite their authoritarian bent, survivalist discourses have exerted considerable influence on alternative visions of security, particularly in Western peace studies circles. In the later Cold War period, in particular, their apocalypticism meshed well with fears of an imminent nuclear holocaust, but even today they continue to flourish (Hartmann 2003; Matthew 2005).

A less alarmist narrative, popular in liberal international population and development circles, is that slowing population growth will "buy time" in which to make the critical decisions and policies necessary to protect the environment (e.g., UNFPA 2001, 4). The underlying assumption is that it is somehow easier and cheaper to change the desired family size of poor people than to reduce the consumption of the rich or to invest in sustainable technologies. In discussions of global warming, the trade-off is presented as curbing population growth versus curbing emissions. *The State of World Population 2001* claims, for example, that reducing population size "would inevitably reduce the need for the most expensive reductions" in greenhouse gas emissions (53). The "buying time" argument begs the question of buying time for whom—for "rogue" states like the United States to comply with environmental agreements such as the Kyoto Protocol?

Whether through degradation narratives, survivalism, or the latest "buying time" arguments, the focus on population serves to obscure critical issues of power—social, economic, and political—that are central to political ecology. Questions of who wins and who loses in relationship to the environment are conspicuous by their absence in most international environment and development policy documents.[12] There are poor people (who make themselves poorer by having too many children), but the rich are virtually invisible except when viewed through the overly aggregated term of *consumption* in the simple population/consumption dichotomy. Today's neoliberal lexicon of *stakeholders* and *partnerships* among civil society, private enterprise, and government also assumes a win-win world where individual agents or collectives of agents wield equal influence when it comes to decision making.

There is typically little relationship presented between the poverty of one group of people and the wealth of another. For example, in UNEP's *Africa Environment Outlook* a photograph of slum dwellings in front of a wealthy house bears the caption "Refugees from a degraded agricultural land living in a slum in Nairobi, Kenya" (UNEP 2002, 271). That the vastly unequal distribution of wealth and power in Kenya

represented by the rich house might have something to do with deteriorating conditions faced by the rural and urban poor is conveniently left
out of the picture. Elsewhere in the document the lack of attention to
power issues is even more notable. In Africa in general, we are told, sociopolitical issues such as "racial segregation, discrimination, colonial,
and other forms of oppression, and foreign domination" have "virtually
been eliminated," though environmental objectives remain compromised
(266).

In contrast to such views, political ecology frames the environment "as
an arena of contested entitlements, a theater in which conflicts of claims
over property, assets, labor and the politics of recognition play themselves out" (Peluso and Watts 2001, 25). Emerging out of this tradition,
the environmental entitlements framework offers a much more complex, historical, and pluralist approach to understanding both the
dynamics of local ecologies and the diverse institutions and differentiated
social actors that affect and are affected by them (Leach, Mearns, and
Scoones 1997). It moves beyond simple cause and effect relationships to
what Black calls "contextualization"—"the examination of complex,
overlapping and sometimes contradictory trends at a range of spatial
scales" that is the hallmark of political ecology (1998, 10). This kind of
contextualization is very different from the determinist logic of degradation narratives.

While this section has offered some suggestions on why *analytically*
one needs to break out of the neo-Malthusian box when examining the
relationship between people and the environment, the final part turns to
why it is *politically* necessary in order to avoid defining human security
in ways that stigmatize poor people and play into the hands of military
and intelligence interests.

Making Peace with Militarism? A Cautionary Note

Using security as a way to frame an alternative environment and development agenda is a risky business. Environmental security is a case in
point. Timura (2001, 105–106) argues that the concept of environmental conflict serves as a boundary object whose power derives in part from
its ambiguity and vagueness, so that players "from all sides of the political spectrum" are able to enter the definitional debate and appropriate it
to serve already-existing agendas. The participation of multiple players
meanwhile increases the credibility of the discourse, helping to ensure its

continual survival and expansion. As we have seen, the prominence of degradation narratives in environmental security made it particularly appealing to defense and intelligence interests looking for new threats to replace old Cold War enemies as well as justifications for continued expenditures on expensive surveillance technologies.

Today, alarmist visions of population, environment, and security continue to circulate in the U.S. defense establishment. A study done for the Pentagon on the potential impact of abrupt climate change on national security portrays a world trapped in a vicious Malthusian cycle: "As abrupt climate change lowers the world's carrying capacity aggressive wars are likely to be fought over food, water and energy. Deaths from war as well as starvation and disease will decrease population size, which overtime will re-balance with carrying capacity" (Schwartz and Randall 2003, 15). In the meantime, large population movements of "unwanted starving immigrants" (18) will seek entry to the United States and wash up on European shores, demanding the strengthening of Western borders. Unfortunately, such alarmist discourses on climate change are gathering steam as not only defense interests, but also a number of population, environment, and development NGOs, international agencies, and prominent pundits are building fears of "climate conflict" and "climate refugees," adopting and adapting many of the same problematic neo-Malthusian narratives that came to dominate the environmental security field (Nordas and Gleditsch 2007; Hartmann 2009).

Could human security, like environmental security, be similarly appropriated by military interests? Could defending human security become a rationale for sending in the troops, just as promoting democracy has been used as a rationale for the U.S. invasion of Iraq? Unfortunately, it is not so hard to imagine, especially if human security is not clearly defined in opposition to militarism and employs stereotypes of the threatening Third World poor. A report on U.S. military programs in Latin America reveals how under the umbrella of human security, the broadening of emerging security threats to include social, economic, and environmental issues is legitimizing the expanding role of U.S.-financed and U.S.-trained militaries in the region and favoring military actors and solutions over civilian ones (Haugaard, Isacson, and Olson 2005).[13] Justifications for the U.S. military's controversial new Africa command, AFRICOM, now include improving human security in the face of climate change and other destabilizing environmental threats (Beebe 2007; Bellamy, Hicks, and Morrison 2008).

In developing and deploying the concept of human security, conceptual clarity and political caution must guide the way. Beware of wolves in sheep's clothing, the old adage goes. Dressed in environmental or women's rights language, neo-Malthusian narratives may appear progressive, but they stand in the way of the kind of progress we need—the kind of creative thinking and dialogue between Northern and Southern environmentalists that acknowledges and addresses disparities in wealth and power, and advances an integrated agenda of social justice, racial and gender equality, environmental protection, and peace.

Notes

1. For example, Population Action International's report calls for investments in women's reproductive health, education, and employment as a means to reduce population growth and hence conflict (Cincotta, Engelman, and Anastasion 2003). Its release rated a Reuters news story: "Study: Women's health linked to unrest: High birth rates, AIDS set stage for global violence" (Reuters News Service 2003). Many women's health activists are disturbed by such reasoning and believe that women's empowerment and reproductive health are worthy goals in and of themselves and should not be pursued in an instrumental fashion (Silliman and King 1999; Silliman and Bhattacharjee 2002). Indeed, linking family planning to national security could help set the stage for the reemergence of coercive population-control programs.

2. According to the GECHS Science Plan, "Human security is achieved when and where individual communities have the options necessary to end, mitigate, or adapt to threats to their human, environmental, and social rights; have the capacity and freedom to exercise these options; and actively participate in attaining these options. Moreover, human security will be achieved through challenging the structures and processes that contribute to insecurities." http://www.ihdp .uni-bonn.de/html/publications/reports/report11/gehssp.htm.

3. Vaclav Smil humorously describes the resulting equation: "eroding slopelands = environmental refugees = overcrowded cities = political instability = violence" (1997, 108). Also see Thompson 2000 for a critique.

4. Colonial administrators overstated the extent of land degradation not only owing to their prejudice against native farmers, but also faulty scientific methodologies. The exclusion of historical data on landscapes led to speculative projections about the past that romanticized previous environmental conditions, or assumed conditions at a particular time were representative of an abiding state of affairs. For example, colonial administrators viewed the low population densities found in East African savannahs at the beginning of the twentieth century as the norm, but in reality they were the result of a severe depopulation of humans and livestock as the result of recent war, famine, and disease (Leach and Mearns 1996).

5. Emery Roe (1995) coined the phrase crisis narrative to describe the stereotypical population/scarcity scenarios applied indiscriminately to different African countries and designed to justify the intervention of Western development agencies. In their book on environmental policy processes in Africa, Keeley and Scoones (2003, 12) note

the remarkable degree of similarity and consistency of approach from the colonial era to the present. . . . Perceptions of crisis, in particular, have informed and shaped environmental policy-making. For example, the issues of soil fertility decline, deforestation and desertification are deeply entrenched as problems for policy concern. Accordingly, project strategies and legislation have consistently been formulated to address such perceived crises. However, the frame of reference for much policy debate is "what tools are there to better attack these problems?," rather than an examination of whether the questions that are being posed are appropriate in the first place.

6. For a detailed genealogy of the concept of environmental refugees and its Malthusian roots, see Saunders 2000. Black (1998) notes that even when refugees resettle, they are frequently stereotyped as "exceptional resource degraders," whether the empirical evidence supports the claim or not.

7. See Hendrixson (2003, 2004) and Hartmann and Hendrixson (2005) for a critique of the "youth bulge" theory of conflict generation. While there is evidence that large youth populations can contribute to political instability in some countries with slow or no economic growth and poor governance, the focus of much youth bulge theory is on the population side of the equation, placing the blame on "too many young men" rather than looking more deeply at the political economy. Moreover, political instability is not always a negative phenomenonthe political activism of youth has often been a positive force for democratic change.

8. Similar critiques exist of research on land degradation and soil erosion. For example, see Keeley and Scoones 2003, Stocking 1996, and Lindert 2002.

9. In this sense they have similar shortcomings to closed ecological system dynamic models. In his critique of such a model for the impact of nomadic pastoralists on the Sahelian environment, Taylor (1992) points to a number of problems, including the choice of what are considered internal or external factors in the particular ecology and how agents are categorized and specified.

10. See Leach 2003 for an analysis of how images of women and the environment have changed over time. The belief that women are somehow closer to nature has also led to the stereotype of women as potential saviors of the environment, often as "unpaid" resource managers.

11. See, for example, Agarwal 1994, Rocheleau, Thomas-Slayter, and Wangari 1996, Schroeder 1999, and Deere and León 2001.

12. See Boyce 2002 for a discussion of winners and losers in environmental degradation.

13. Promoting itself as a defender of biodiversity, the U.S. military is becoming increasingly involved in policing the Mesoamerican Biological Corridor (Griffard, Bradshaw, and Hughes Butts 2002).

References

Adams, W. M. 1995. Green development theory? In *Power of development*, ed. Jonathan Crush, 87–99. London: Routledge.

Agarwal, Bina. 1994. *A field of one's own: Gender and land rights in South Asia.* Cambridge, UK: Cambridge University Press.

Beebe, Shannon. 2007. Guest contributor Shannon Beebe on AFRICOM and environmental security. *The New Security Beat.* Washington, DC: Woodrow Wilson Center Environmental Change and Security Project. http://newsecuritybeat .blogspot.com/2007/07/guest-contributor-shannon-beebe-on.html (accessed November 15, 2008).

Bellamy, Mark, Kathleen Hicks, and J. Stephen Morrison. 2008. Strengthening AFRICOM's case. Washington, DC: Center for Strategic and International Studies. http://www.csis.org/component/option,com_csis_progj/task,view/id,1160/ (accessed November 15, 2008).

Black, Richard. 1998. *Refugees, environment and development.* New York: Longman.

Blaikie, Piers, and Harold Brookfield. 1987. *Land degradation and society.* London: Methuen.

Boserup, Esther. 1965. *The conditions of agricultural growth: The economics of agrarian change under population pressure.* Chicago: Aldine Publishers.

Boyce, James K. 2002. *The political economy of the environment.* Northampton, MA: Edward Elgar.

Cincotta, Richard P., Robert Engelman, and Daniele Anastasion. 2003. *The security demographic: Population and conflict after the Cold War.* Washington, DC: Population Action International.

Dalby, Simon. 1999. Threats from the south?: Geopolitics, equity and environmental security. In *Contested grounds: Security and conflict in the new environmental politics*, ed. Daniel H. Deudney and Richard A. Matthew, 155–185. Albany: State University of New York Press.

Dalby, Simon. 2002. *Environmental security: The geopolitics of colonizing nature.* Minneapolis: University of Minnesota Press.

Deere, Carmen Diana, and Magdalena León. 2001. *Empowering women: Land and property rights in Latin America.* Pittsburgh: University of Pittsburgh Press.

Dryzek, John S. 1997. *The politics of the earth: Environmental discourses.* New York: Oxford University Press.

Eberstadt, Nicholas. 2001. The Population Implosion. *Foreign Policy* 123 (March/April): 42–53.

EDSP. 2002. Invitation to the roundtable on environment, development, and sustainable peace at the World Summit for Sustainable Development, Johannesburg. Received from ecsp-forum@cren.net. http://www.sustainable-peace.org/ download/Roundtable_announcement_logo.PDF (accessed March 3, 2009).

Escobar, Arturo. 1995. *Encountering development: The making and unmaking of the Third World*. Princeton: Princeton University Press.

Fairhead, James. 2001. International dimensions of conflict over natural and environmental resources. In *Violent environments*, ed. Nancy Lee Peluso and Michael Watts, 213–236. Ithaca, NY: Cornell University Press.

Fairhead, James, and Melissa Leach. 1996. Rethinking the forest-savanna mosaic: Colonial science and its relics in West Africa. In *The lie of the land*, ed. Melissa Leach and Robin Mearns, 105–121. London: International African Institute.

Fairhead, James, and Melissa Leach. 1998. *Reframing deforestation: Global analyses and local realities: Studies in West Africa*. London: Routledge.

Florini, Ann M., and P. J. Simmons. 1998. *The new security thinking: A view of the North American literature*. New York: Rockefeller Brothers Fund Project on World Security.

Franke, Richard W., and Barbara H. Chasin. 1980. *Seeds of famine: Ecological destruction and the development dilemma in the West African Sahel*. Montclair, NJ: Allanheld, Osmun and Co.

Garcia-Barrios, R., and L. Garcia-Barrios. 1990. Environmental and technological degradation in peasant agriculture: A consequence of development in Mexico. *World Development* 18 (11): 1569–1585.

Government of Canada. 1998. Population issues. http://www.dfait-maeci.gc.ca/foreign_policy/human-rights/popissue-en.asp (accessed June 9, 2004).

Government of Japan. n.d. Population and AIDS problems are the common issues of all humanity. http://www.mofa.go.jp/policy/pop_aids/gii/common.html (accessed June 9, 2004).

Greenhalgh, Susan. 2003. Science, modernity, and the making of China's one child policy. *Population and Development Review* 29 (2): 163–196.

Griffard, Bernie, Art Bradshaw, and Kent Hughes Butts. 2002. Central American environmental defense program in the Mesoamerican Biological Corridor. Issues Paper 06–02. Carlisle, PA: U.S. Army War College Center for Strategic Leadership.

Harrison, Paul. 1992. *The third revolution: Population, environment and a sustainable world*. London: Penguin Books.

Hartmann, Elizabeth (Betsy). 2003. Strategic scarcity: The origins and impact of environmental conflict ideas. PhD thesis, Development Studies Institute, London School of Economics and Political Science.

Hartmann, Betsy. 2009. From climate refugees to climate conflict: Who's taking the heat for global warming? Forthcoming in *Climate change and sustainable development: New challenges for poverty reduction*, ed. Mohamed Salih. Cheltenham, UK: Edward Elgar Publishers.

Hartmann, Betsy, and Anne Hendrixson. 2005. Pernicious peasants and angry young men: The strategic demography of threats. In *Making threats*, ed. Betsy

Hartmann, Banu Subramaniam, and Charles Zerner, 217–236. Lanham, MD: Rowman and Littlefield.

Hartmann, Betsy, Banu Subramaniam, and Charles Zerner, eds. 2005. *Making threats: Biofears and environmental anxieties*. Lanham, MD: Rowman and Littlefield.

Haugaard, Lisa, Adam Isacson, and Joy Olson. 2005. *Erasing the lines: Trends in U.S. military programs with Latin America*. Washington, DC: Center for International Policy, the Latin America Working Group Education Fund, and the Washington Office on Latin America.

Hendrixson, Anne. 2002. Superpredator meets teenage mom: Exploding the myth of the out-of-control youth. In *Policing the national body*, ed. Jael Silliman and Anannya Bhattacharjee, 231–258. Boston: South End Press.

Hendrixson, Anne. 2004. *Angry young men, veiled young women: Constructing a new population threat*. Dorset, UK: The Corner House.

Hodgson, Dennis, and Susan Cotts Watkins. 1997. Feminists and neo-Malthusians: Past and present alliances. *Population and Development Review* 23 (3): 469–523.

Homer-Dixon, Thomas F. 1999. *Environment, scarcity and violence*. Princeton: Princeton University Press.

Kahn, Joseph. 2004. The most populous nation faces a population crisis. *New York Times*, May 30, section 4: 1, 5.

Keeley, James, and Ian Scoones. 2003. *Understanding environmental policy processes: Cases from Africa*. London: Earthscan.

Leach, Melissa. 2003. Women as natural environmental careers: Earth mother myths and other Ecofeminist fables or how a strategic notion rose and fell. Paper prepared for the workshop on Feminist Fables and Gender Myths, IDS/ University of Sussex, July.

Leach, Melissa, and James Fairhead. 2000. Challenging neo-Malthusian deforestation analyses in West Africa. *Population and Development Review* 26 (1): 17–43.

Leach, Melissa, and Robin Mearns. 1996. *The lie of the land: Challenging received wisdom on the African environment*. Oxford, UK, and Portsmouth, NH: International African Institute with James Currey and Heinemann.

Leach, Melissa, Robin Mearns, and Ian Scoones. 1997. Environmental entitlements: A framework for understanding the institutional dynamics of environmental change. IDS Discussion Paper No. 359. Brighton, UK: University of Sussex Institute for Development Studies.

Lindert, Peter H. 2000. *Shifting ground: The changing agricultural soils of China and Indonesia*. Cambridge, MA: MIT Press.

Locke, Catherine, W. Neil Adger, and P. Mick Kelly. 2000. Changing places: Migration's social and environmental consequences. *Environment* 42 (7): 24–35.

MacKenzie, Fiona. 1995. Selective silence: A feminist encounter with environmental discourse in colonial Africa. In *Power of development*, ed. Jonathan Crush, 100–113. London: Routledge.

Matthew, Richard. 2005. Bioterrorism and national security: Peripheral threats, core vulnerabilities. In *Making threats*, ed. Elizabeth Hartmann, Banu Subramaniam, and Charles Zerner, 237–246. Lanham, MD: Rowman and Littlefield.

Mello, Fatima. 1997. Security, livelihood and the politics of space in Brazil: An interview with Jean Pierre Leroy. *Political Environments* 5:S18–S21.

Nordas, Ragnhild, and Nils Petter Gleditsch. 2007. Climate change and conflict. *Political Geography* 26 (6): 627–638.

Peluso, Nancy Lee, and Michael Watts, eds. 2001. *Violent environments*. Ithaca, NY: Cornell University Press.

Reardon, Thomas, and Stephen A. Vosti. 1995. Links between rural poverty and the environment in developing countries. *World Development* 23 (9): 1495–1506.

Reuters News Service. 2003. Study: Women's health linked to unrest: High birth rates, AIDS set stage for global violence. December 17.

Rocheleau, Dianne E., Philip E. Steinberg, and Patricia A. Benjamin. 1995. Environment, development, crisis, and crusade: Ukambani, Kenya, 1890–1990. *World Development* 23 (6): 1037–1051.

Rocheleau, Dianne, Barbara Thomas-Slayter, and Esther Wangari. 1996. *Feminist political ecology: Global issues and local experience*. London: Routledge.

Roe, Emery M. 1995. Except Africa: Postscript to a special section on development narratives. *World Development* 23 (6): 1065–1069.

Rothschild, Emma. 1995. What is security? *Daedulus* 124 (33): 53–98.

Saunders, Patricia L. 2000. Environmental refugees: The origins of a construct. In *Political ecology*, ed. Philip Stott and Sian Sullivan, 218–246. London: Arnold.

Schroeder, Richard. 1999. *Shady practices: Agroforestry and gender politics in the Gambia*. Berkeley: University of California Press.

Schwartz, Peter, and Doug Randall. 2003. An abrupt climate change scenario and its implications for United States national security. October. San Francisco, CA: Global Business Network. http://www.gbn.com/consulting/article_details .php?id=53 (accessed May 14, 2009).

Silliman, Jael, and Anannya Bhattacharjee, eds. 2002. *Policing the national body: Race, gender and criminalization*. Boston: South End Press.

Silliman, Jael, and Ynestra King, eds. 1999. *Dangerous intersections: Feminist perspectives on population, environment and development*. Boston: South End Press.

Singh, Ashbindu, Amadou M. Dieye, Mark Finco, M. Sean Chenoweth, Eugene A. Fosnight, and Albert Allotey. 1999. *Early warning of selected emerging environmental issues in Africa: Change and correlation from a geographic perspective*. Nairobi, Kenya: UN Environmental Program.

Smil, Vaclav. 1997. China's environment and security: Simple myths and complex realities. *SAIS Review* 17 (1): 107–126.

Stocking, Michael. 1996. Soil erosion: Breaking new ground. In *Lie of the land*, ed. Melissa Leach and Robin Mearns, 140–154. Oxford, UK, and Portsmouth, NH: International African Institute with James Currey and Heinemann.

Stott, Philip, and Sian Sullivan, eds. 2000. *Political ecology: Science, myth and power*. London: Arnold.

Suhrke, Astri. 1997. Environmental degradation, migration and the potential for violent conflict. In *Conflict and the environment*, ed. Nils Petter Gleditsch, 255–272. Dordrecht: Kluwer Academic Publishers.

Taylor, Peter J. 1992. Re/constructing socioecologies: Systems dynamic modeling of nomadic pastoralists in sub-Saharan Africa. In *The right tools for the job: At work in twentieth century life sciences*, ed. Adele E. Clarke and Joan H. Fujimura, 115–148. Princeton: Princeton University Press.

Templeton, Scott R., and Sara J. Scherr. 1999. Effects of demographic and related microeconomic change on land quality in hills and mountains of developing countries. *World Development* 27 (6): 903–918.

Thompson, Michael. 2000. Not seeing the people for the population. In *Environment and security: Discourses and practices*, ed. Miriam R. Lowi and Brian R. Shaw, 192–206. London: Macmillan.

Thompson, Michael, and Steve Rayner. 1998. Cultural discourses. In *Human choice and climate change*, vol. I, *The societal framework*, ed. Steve Rayner and Elizabeth L. Malone, 265–344. Columbus, OH: Battelle Press.

Timura, Christopher T. 2001. Environmental conflict and the social life of environmental security discourse. *Anthropological Quarterly* 74 (3): 104–113.

Turner, B. L., II, Goran Hyden, and Robert W. Kates, eds. 1993. *Population growth and agricultural change in Africa*. Gainesville: University Press of Florida.

UNDP. 1994. *Human development report 1994*. New York: Oxford University Press.

UNEP. 2002. *Africa environment outlook*. UK: Earthprint Limited/UNEP.

UNFPA. 2001. *The state of world population 2001*. New York: UNFPA.

UN Population Division. 2004. *World population prospects: The 2004 revision*. New York: UN Department of Economic and Social Affairs. http://www.un.org/esa/population/publications/WPP2004/2004EnglishES.pdf (accessed August 17, 2006).

White House. 1995. National security strategy of engagement and enlargement, July 1994 and February 1995. Excerpted in *Environmental Change and Security Project Report* 1:47–50.

Williams, Gavin. 1995. Modernizing Malthus: The World Bank, population control and the African environment. In *Power of development*, ed. Jonathan Crush, 158–175. London: Routledge.

Wilson, Chris. 2001. On the scale of global demographic convergence, 1950–2000. *Population and Development Review* 27 (1): 155–171.

World Commission on Environment and Development. 1987. *Our common future*. Oxford: Oxford University Press.

11

Women, Global Environmental Change, and Human Security

Heather Goldsworthy

Many women around the world face pressing challenges to their human security that are unique to their gender. According to the Global Environmental Change and Human Security (GECHS) Science Plan, "[h]uman security is achieved when and where individuals and communities have the options necessary to end, mitigate, or adapt to threats to their human, environmental and social rights, have the capacity and freedom to exercise those options, and actively participate in attaining those options (GECHS 1999)." Within the human security models outlined by GECHS (1999) and the UNDP (1994), the most significant threats to the well-being of individuals and communities are no longer *military* threats to the *national* security of the sovereign state, but *transnational* threats to *human* security, including the spread of pandemic disease, global trafficking in drugs and people, violence and terrorism operating through stateless networks, and environmental degradation that does not respect national borders.

While these dangers imperil the well-being of all men, women, and children around the world to varying degrees, many groups of women experience heightened levels of insecurity unique to their gender owing to their subjugated social position, limited education, and restricted economic freedom and social capital. Some face both sudden and chronic threats to their human security every day in the form of food insecurity, bodily insecurity, restricted freedom, and limited decision-making power. These threats are both structural (endemic within the gender-stratified social structure), and situational (arising from unique situations, such as environmental change, violent conflict, or forced migration). It is when these structural and situational pressures combine that many women experience the most profound challenges to their well-being. Such pressures compromise women's ability to end or adapt to threats to their human and social rights, and limit their capacity to participate in actively creating alternative, more secure structures.

Degradation of the natural environment is one source of insecurity that is made particularly threatening by a unique combination of structural and situational issues. All men, women, and children depend on the natural environment for subsistence and income; however, the poorest of the world rely on nature in a far more immediate sense than people in developed countries who are able to pay for ecosystem services, such as water and energy (UNEP and IISD 2004). So while resource scarcity and degradation may affect all populations, they certainly do not affect them all equally (see chapter 8 by Karen O'Brien and Robin Leichenko). The poor suffer the greatest hardships as resources are depleted. Among the poor, women are made particularly vulnerable by environmental change and its associated consequences owing to their profound reliance upon, and their more frequent and intimate contact with, nature compared to their male counterparts.

This chapter examines the impacts of global environmental change on the human security of those women whose livelihoods and security are dependent on their close relationship with the natural world. The objectives are twofold: (1) to develop a typology of gender-based discrepancies in vulnerability to global environmental change, looking at both natural disasters and gradual, incremental environmental change, and (2) to examine the viability of microfinance as a tool to strengthen women's role in environmental management and disaster relief efforts given the intimate nature of women's contact with the environment and the strength of microfinance as a strategy of poverty alleviation and network building.

Women and Environment

There exists a long and complex dialogue surrounding the relationship of women to the natural environment. Where we position ourselves within that dialogue determines from what perspective we analyze the vulnerabilities created for women by environmental change. One highly influential philosophical camp is often referred to as *ecofeminism*, and is championed most notably by Vandana Shiva, Val Plumwood, and Carolyn Merchant. Theories of ecofeminism argue women, particularly women of developing countries, are closer to nature than men for two reasons: their inherent biological connection, and their mutual devaluation and domination within patriarchal ideology (Shiva 1989; Plumwood 1993; Merchant 1980). According to this discourse women perform roles akin to the services provided by nature, bearing children, nurturing, and providing sustenance. And in the patriarchal society ecofeminism opposes, these "basic" activities are considered inferior to the realm of culture assigned to men. By this life-sustaining activity women are said to be more connected to the natural world and more innately attuned to conservation and preservation of natural resources. From this perspective, women are assigned privileged access to nature as environmental stakeholders, a role that eludes not only men but also women in the developed world who have comparatively less experience with or intimate knowledge of ecological processes.

The ecofeminist perspective has certainly influenced much of gender and environment discourse as it continuously evolves, bringing to the forefront of environmental dialogue the concept of a gender-biased relationship of humans to nature and the mutual subjugation of women and nature, spurring much debate and scholarship. However, the philosophy has sometimes been criticized for its broad essentialization of women in developing countries (see especially Agarwal 1992, 2000). An opposing school of thought with regard to women and environment may be comparatively less essentialist, but still maintains there exists a unique relationship between women and nature based not on patriarchal ideology or biology, but on social, economic, and political inequalities that structure women's interactions with nature (Agarwal 1992; Seager and Hartmann 1994; WEDO 2003). From this perspective, called "feminist environmentalism" by Agarwal, women's unique relationship with nature is defined in fundamental ways by constructed inequality, discrimination, and marginalization in larger structural systems. This inequality, while putting women at greater risk of negative consequences from environmental degradation, also establishes them as experts on local ecology. So while ecofeminism and feminist environmentalism vary on their treatment of the source of the relationship, both argue women and nature are connected by some mechanism unique to their gender.

It can be argued that there are both pros and cons to generalizing women in terms of environment, and it is not the ambition of this chapter to determine which camp is right or wrong. By adopting an intellectually neutral position the aim here is to recognize that regardless of the reason, be it biological predisposition or social constructions of gender roles, women are often in more frequent and intimate contact with nature than the men in the same societies. This is particularly true in subsistence-based societies where everyday existence is characterized by significant interaction with the natural world (UNEP and IISD 2004). In these circumstances many women work not only as caregivers and providers within the domestic sphere, but also as producers and gatherers of food, water, and energy supplies for their families (UNFPA 2001; Population Reference Bureau 2002). While this subsistence-based relationship with the environment is particularly intimate for rural women, their urban and peri-urban counterparts assume similar burdens when raising families in marginalized, impoverished sections of cities where the procurement of clean water and food expends significant amounts of time and energy. Women in both contexts develop a profound understanding of and association with the environment, one that is instrumental in nature and has evolved largely out of the distribution of labor according to traditional social norms (Agarwal 1992). It is the contention of this chapter that the incidence and intimacy of women's contact with nature, along with their comparative disadvantage in many components of human security, make them relatively more vulnerable than men to negative consequences associated with environmental change.

Women, Inequality, and Vulnerability

Having established the perspective from which this chapter will approach questions of gender and environment, it is next helpful to elaborate on the conditions of some women's lives that make environmental change such a credible threat to their human security. It is important to state that this chapter focuses on women and environments in developing countries where restricted governing capacity, highly segregated social systems, and poor economic development create political, social, financial, and environmental insecurity not experienced in the developed world. Not all countries experience the same types of insecurity, and certainly not all people within the same country are subject to the same vulnerabilities. Gender, race, and class are very powerful intervening variables when considering human security. It is the overall position of this chapter, however, that in situations of instability and insecurity, women are comparatively less well off compared to men in their communities owing to their disadvantageous social status and the restrictions of their gender roles.

This section will address women's unique vulnerabilities by analyzing the impact of systemic disenfranchisement on women's daily experience. This disenfranchisement is part of the highly inequitable social stratification by gender that dictates the roles, rights, and responsibilities of women and men, determines what each gender can and must do, and where they are able to act. Even in situations where both men and women's access to education, health care, political action, and financial autonomy is severely restricted, the subordinate position of women in the social stratification leaves them with the *least* access to these services and freedoms, and sometimes subjects them to physical abuse. A social order is thus created that keeps women in the margins of society, creating persistent *structural* threats to their human security by exclusion.

Access to Education, Health Care, and Physical Security

The structural position of women in a society can act directly and indirectly to threaten their livelihoods through violence and discrimination, beginning as early as childhood. In some cultures, ingrained attitudes that female children are liabilities to the family rather than assets contribute to selective abortion, infanticide, and neglect of female children. Reliable statistics on feticide and infanticide are scarce; however, UNICEF and Amnesty International report that discrimination against girls, in the form of prenatal sex selection, abuse, and neglect, is responsible for 60 to 100 million "missing women" that would otherwise be alive (Amnesty International 2004; Hudson and den Boer 2004; UNICEF n.d.a, n.d.b, 2000, 2006).

In some cases the low status of women also makes them frequent targets for abuse and rape. It is estimated that at least one in three women worldwide has suffered some form of violence, including sexual assault and all forms of abuse (UNICEF n.d.a). In areas where dowries are common, particularly India and Bangladesh, stories are reported of wives being murdered when their families cannot pay the cost of a dowry, or so that a husband may remarry and collect another dowry (Amnesty International 2001). Approximately seven thousand "dowry deaths" are reported each year in India, though there are likely many more that go unreported. These murders, along with hundreds of disfiguring acid attacks against women over dowry disputes annually, serve as an indication that women are viewed in these situations as expendable property (Amnesty International 2001; UNIFEM n.d.).

Based on this low valuation compared to men and their heavy burden of domestic responsibilities, female children are often granted less access to education and healthcare than male children (World Bank 2003). Worldwide, of the 104 million school-aged children not enrolled in school, an estimated 54–57 percent, are girls (UN Millennium Project 2005), and nearly two-thirds of the world's illiterate are women (UNICEF n.d.a; UNFPA 2005a). In South Asia, where school enrollment and literacy rates are low for both boys and girls, girls still receive half as much schooling as boys, on average. In sub-Saharan Africa girls' enrollment in primary education is less than 60 percent (World Bank 2003). Even in areas where boys and girls begin school at the same rates, girls are more likely to drop out because of marriage, pregnancy, or domestic responsibilities (World Bank 2003; UNICEF 2006).

Discrimination and gender roles can also contribute to limited access to pediatric health care for girls and prenatal health care for women. Though it must be remembered that malnutrition is a serious problem for both sons and daughters in much of the developing world, boys still often receive more food and better health care than girls (World Bank 2003; UNICEF 2006). As women age, cultural norms may also prevent them from accessing health care services by prohibiting interaction with strangers while unaccompanied. This tradition leaves women without health education that could reduce rates of illness and disease transmission, particularly the rapid spread of HIV/AIDS. Worldwide, women account for nearly half of adults infected with HIV, but the percentage is far higher in many parts of the developing world. In some parts of Africa and the Caribbean, prevalence among women age 15–24 is up to six times higher than among men of the same age (UNICEF 2006). Lack of health education and access to health care also increases the incidence rate of pregnancy—and childbirth-related illnesses and death. Over five hundred thousand women die as a result of childbirth each year; 99 percent of these deaths occur in developing countries as a result of lack of medical care (UNICEF n.d.a.; World Bank 2003).

Restricted Financial Autonomy and Limited Political Influence

In many cultures the socially accepted gender roles, and sometimes explicit law, prohibit women from working outside the home or in the formal employment sector, owning property, accessing credit, and receiving inheritance (UNEP and IISD 2004; UNFPA 2001, 2005a; WEDO 2003; World Bank 2003). These restrictions severely inhibit the ability of women to generate income, making them financially reliant on men (Population Reference Bureau 2002; UNFPA 2001). While both men and women suffer in poverty, women's restricted ability to generate income creates a disproportionate level of financial insecurity, putting them at the leading edge of destitution. Additionally, because women often have little interaction outside the domestic sphere, they also have little political power or influence, holding a total of only 16 percent of national parliament seats worldwide (UNFPA 2005a). In many societies, women do not represent a voting constituency because of their limited public activity and are therefore virtually invisible during policy development (Gupta 2003). Thus, the structural position of women not only limits the contribution they are able to make to policy and decision making, it also limits the recourse or political tools women have to fight back against the myriad abuses they suffer.

Global Environmental Change

These structural threats to the human security of women are exacerbated by the *situational* challenges that accompany environmental degradation. The systematic political, economic, social, and cultural disenfranchisement of women renders them less able to prepare for, and more vulnerable to, the negative consequences of environmental change compared to men. To best address the impacts of these changes on women they must be understood in the context of social, economic, and cultural restriction of women's rights. Deeply embedded structural gender inequalities converge with both catastrophic and incremental situational environmental change to complicate women's interactions with the natural environment, amplifying security risks inherent in vulnerable areas.

Environmental change presents itself in two common ways: as catastrophic natural disasters (tsunamis, hurricanes, earthquakes) and persistent incremental transformation (deforestation, climate change, desertification). Both forms of environmental change present problems for human security for all people; however, the nature of women's contact with the environment begs investigation of their specific vulnerabilities to these environmentally induced threats to well-being.

Women and Natural Disasters

Since the mid-1990s, the number of natural disasters and associated fatalities worldwide has been on the rise. Between 1990 and 1999, nearly six hundred thousand people died as a result of these sudden, and most often unforeseen, events (World Health Organization 2002). The onslaught of natural disasters that have occurred so far in the early years of the twenty-first century—the Indonesian tsunami, Hurricane Katrina, and the earthquakes in Pakistan and China—shed light on the vulnerability to environmental change inherent in many communities, and clearly demonstrate the uneven distribution of impacts along age, race, economic, and gender lines. Populations in developing countries often do not have the benefit of early-warning systems for disasters such as cyclones and tsunamis and face limited resource availability for post-disaster health care and reconstruction. For these reasons, members of communities in the developing world are four times more likely to die as a result of a natural disaster than people in a developed country (World Health Organization 2002). Women in these areas are even less resilient compared to men following natural disasters, as they generally have less access to resources such as information, transportation, and social networks that might help them prepare for and recover from these catastrophes (Bryne and Baden 1995; Pan American Health Organization n.d.). The structural inequalities suffered by women make them more vulnerable to the insecurities created prior to, during, and after disasters.

During the early stages of a disaster, women may be made especially insecure by their inability to receive warnings and evacuation notices, where they are available, owing to the rural location of most homes, the social restrictions that keep women inside the home and prohibit interacting with non-kin men, and the nature of the work most women perform—largely agricultural tasks and self-employment. Gender roles also limit the decision-making power of women, which can lead to delays in evacuation while they wait for their husbands to arrive home and make decisions for the family (World Health Organization 2002). During a disaster women may also have restricted mobility owing to the children, ill, and elderly under their care at home. They may then be left in the path of the disaster, suffering higher rates of death and injury than men. Also, if the culture is one that values sons over daughters, and the disaster is such that quick decisions must be made about assisting one child before another, daughters may suffer higher rates of injury and death compared to sons (World Health Organization 2002).

When social mores prohibit women from interacting with strangers, they have restricted access to any humanitarian aid or development assistance that may be available following a natural disaster (World Health Organization 2002). Even in situations where women are mobile they often receive less assistance after a disaster based on the common practice of distributing aid to male heads of households who then often allocate it unevenly within the family (Byrne and Baden 1995; Enarson and Fordham 2001; World Health Organization 2002). Also, relief supplies are usually thought of as "gender neutral," and are not assembled with sex-specific health issues in mind; thus women's hygiene products such as sanitary napkins and contraception are often unavailable (Byrne and Baden 1995; World Health Organization 2002). All men, women, and children are vulnerable following a natural disaster. However, women are often at the leading edge of destitution post-disaster as a result of aid inequities and their restricted asset base and limited financial resources. The role of women as gatherers and providers of subsistence can make their workloads particularly heavy following a catastrophic event as their ability to meet the needs of their family are compromised or made impossible by scarcity pressures. Natural disasters often damage resources, and can also prohibit access to them through physical blockades. Women may be especially impacted by these catastrophes as resources become harder to find or access, and their ability to meet the food, water, and fuel needs of their family is hindered. Following a catastrophic event women also face even higher rates of physical and sexual violence, as well as greater risk of forced marriage, forced participation in sex trade (sometimes in exchange for aid), and even less control over their education, employment, and migration than before the disaster struck (Byrne and Baden 1995; Enarson and Fordham 2001; Pan American Health Organization n.d.; World Health Organization 2002).

Within the last few years a number of devastating natural disasters have made millions of lives insecure, drawing much attention and providing unfortunate examples of women's unique vulnerabilities to catastrophic environmental events. These recent catastrophic events illustrate that during a natural disaster women face exacerbated vulnerability compared to men owing to their higher relative rates of poverty, their immobility, their roles as mothers and caretakers, their specialized medical needs, and their status in society. Boxes 11.1, 11.2, and 11.3 look at three recent catastrophic natural disasters through a gender lens.

Box 11.1
The Indonesian Tsunami

The December 2004 Indian Ocean tsunami left over 200,000 people dead or missing in South and Southeast Asia and East Africa. While men, women, and children were victims, women have been shown to be particularly affected due to their limited mobility and social standing. In Aceh, Indonesia, women are reported to have been 55–70 percent of all casualties resulting from the tsunami. Those who survived have faced threats to their health as well as their economic and bodily security, but have presented themselves as valuable disaster managers for their communities and families. Many women have taken up roles distributing aid, caring for survivors, and acting as foster mothers to orphaned children. In spite of their strength, women in the tsunami-affected areas face burdens that are often left out of relief planning.

For many women who survived the disaster, the devastating death toll left them as heads of household, facing discrimination, harassment, and physical and sexual violence when seeking aid and shelter. As aid is most commonly distributed to men, women without husbands or adult sons have restricted access, or receive assistance in the form of goods but no cash. In situations where land is owned by a deceased or missing man, women may have difficulty claiming property ownership, leaving them homeless. In addition, many shelters often have not provided adequate facilities for women to bathe and attend to their hygiene needs in private as culturally demanded, putting women's health and dignity at particular risk post-tsunami.

Source: See UNIFEM 2005a, b.

Women and Incremental Environmental Change

In contrast to catastrophic natural disasters, persistent incremental changes in the natural environment develop over time and endure for long periods, perhaps indefinitely. These changes may take decades to be recognized or to present enough of a problem to affect livelihoods. Examples include global climate change, deforestation, desertification, and diffuse pollution of air and water. These types of changes may create threats to subsistence in several ways that will be discussed here: through scarcity, pollution, and displacement.

Persistent environmental change can lead to reduced resource availability and threatened subsistence. Most immediately and directly, reduced resource availability limits the food, water, and fuel wood readily available and accessible for the management of basic needs (UN

Box 11.2
Hurricane Katrina

Hurricane Katrina, the most destructive natural disaster in U.S. history, devastated the Gulf Coast in August 2005. Approximately 1,300 people were killed, thousands went missing, and 770,000 were displaced to temporary shelters all over the southeastern United States. This catastrophic environmental event highlighted not only the profound race and class inequality in the United States, but also made clear the disproportionate burdens thrust upon women following a natural disaster, particularly women with comparatively restricted economic resources. The percentage of women living in poverty in the most devastated area of the hurricane, New Orleans, is nearly twice that of all women in the United States. Women of the Gulf Coast also suffer higher rates of poverty in comparison to men of the region. Many women of New Orleans are single heads of households; more than half of families with children in the city are female-headed. These female-headed households face high poverty, with 41 percent living below the poverty line.

The hurricane increased economic and familial burdens on women by putting them out of work, exacerbating their poverty, and making it increasingly difficult to secure food and shelter for their children. During and after the hurricane the availability of safe food and water was limited, leaving children hungry and infants without formula. Health issues following the hurricane were also a serious concern as hospitals were disabled or closed, leaving victims without access to medical care or medications. Pregnant women, for whom nutrition and infectious disease are particularly important considerations, were left without prenatal care. Women are also a majority of the elderly population in the New Orleans area, and the elderly comprised most of the fatalities caused by the hurricane. Especially disturbing are the anecdotal reports of increased rape and sexual assault on the streets and in the temporary shelters housing evacuees, such as the Superdome.

Source: Gault et al. 2005; White House 2006.

2003). Unsustainable resource extraction, changing weather patterns resulting from global climate change, and land modification all reduce the quantity and quality of these necessities, and degrade land, reducing productivity. As resources are diminished and land is depleted, unsustainable agricultural practices such as increased chemical inputs and reduced fallow periods are necessary to increase crop yields, further damaging the land and creating a cycle of degradation (UNFPA 2001). Women and girls are particularly impacted in situations of reduced

Box 11.3
The Kashmir Earthquake

> The earthquake that rocked northern Pakistan in October 2005 was monumentally devastating to the population of the region; over 70,000 were killed, 140,000 were injured, and approximately 3 million were left without shelter just as the harsh winter was beginning. Hundreds of thousands of men, women, and children in some of the poorest parts of the country were faced with insecurity in many forms, including homelessness, landlessness, loss of access to common property resources, hunger, and loss of jobs and income. However, women and children faced unique burdens post-disaster. Many women's work burdens and family roles were shifted from those of caregivers to heads of household when husbands were killed, a particular problem in a conservative society where women face barriers to property ownership and land access. Post-earthquake violence also increased as populations were displaced, and women faced discrimination, intimidation, rape, and psychological abuse. There is some evidence that cultural customs such as female seclusion kept women from fleeing their homes, resulting in far more deaths of women and girls than men and boys. Twice as many women than men age 25–49 were reported dead. The disaster relief efforts following the earthquake, though significant, did not consider the culture- and gender-sensitive needs of the affected population, leaving women with little access to personal hygiene products, to privacy in bathrooms, or to proper obstetric care for the tens of thousands who were pregnant in the region.
>
> *Source*: See CRPRID 2006; UNDP Pakistan 2006; UNFPA 2005b.

resource supply as their status usually requires them to eat last and least (UNICEF n.d.a.).

Resource scarcity also creates insecurity for women in less direct ways. Perhaps the most commonly discussed impact of reduced resource availability on women's lives is the extra effort required to gather food and water, responsibilities that fall largely in the domestic sphere of women (WEDO 2003). When clean water and fuel wood become difficult to find because of desertification, pollution, or deforestation, women who cannot afford to pay for these resources must travel farther to gather them. Women's physical security may also be compromised when they have to travel farther out to less secure areas, or move their residence, to look for resources. This adds to the time and energy required to complete these tasks, while at the same time other responsibilities are not alleviated (UNFPA 2001). A reduction in fuel wood availability can also lead women to use agricultural residues or animal waste as fuel for cooking fires inside the home. These fuels create indoor air pollution when burned that leads to illness and as many as two million deaths in the developing world every year (World Bank 2003). Women and girls are most often the victims of these conditions as they are responsible for tending the fire and doing the cooking. Reduced fuel wood supplies can also encourage a shift toward foods that do not need to be cooked (Population Reference Bureau 2002). This diminishes the nutritional value of diets, especially for women who eat the least, and can complicate pregnancy and nursing (UNFPA 2001). Shifting diets toward raw foods can be particularly problematic in parts of the world where the diet staples are grains that must be cooked or livestock raised by the families themselves.

Environmental conditions are closely related to incidence rates of infectious and parasitic disease and respiratory illness, and contribute to approximately a quarter of all deaths from communicable disease every year worldwide (UNFPA 2001). Water and soil become polluted by increased use of agricultural pesticides and fertilizers as land productivity decreases, as well as by the irresponsible use and disposal of these products by industry. Land modification can expedite the spread of pollution by increasing irrigation and erosion. Women bear the brunt of the negative health consequences associated with this contamination because of their roles as farmers and water gatherers. Toxic levels of these chemicals accumulate in their body tissues and breast milk, leading to pregnancy complications, miscarriages, and stillbirths, and may be passed on to nursing children (UNFPA 2001).

Persistent environmental degradation also contributes to the forced migration of peoples (Homer-Dixon 1999; Homer-Dixon and Blitt 1998; IFRC 1999; Meyers 2002; UN 2003), and the experience of displacement varies for men and women (Lammers 1999; Martin 2004; Mertus 2003). Unlike political refugees, there are no UNHCR aid programs in place for migrants displaced by environmental degradation, despite their growth in numbers as resource scarcity and land modification progress. The 1999 World Disasters Report by the International Federation of Red Cross and Red Crescent Societies estimated twenty-five million environmental refugees were displaced at the end of the twentieth century, comprising over half of all total displaced persons (IFRC 1999). Scholars at the United Nations University estimate as many as fifty million more in the next five years as the consequences of land degradation, desertification, and flooding are intensified by population growth (BBC News 2005). These "environmental refugees" are on the move toward urban and peri-urban areas, sometimes within the same region, other times across political boundaries. These swollen urban areas are often ill-equipped to accommodate rapidly expanding populations, and the poorest end up settling in marginal areas on unstable land, such as steep hillsides or deforested areas, further escalating environmental depletion. These new refugees must secure their livelihoods, and typically men are drawn away from the home to work in the market economy. This trend increases the number of female-headed households. Thus, during displacement, women are made responsible for an increased schedule of household duties, particularly while men are absent (Martin 2004; Population Reference Bureau 2002; UNDP Pakistan 2006). Women must sometimes take on formal or informal employment when subsistence cannot be achieved through agriculture and gathering, and monetary income becomes essential for the purchase of resources in new urban settlements. As previously discussed, economic aid is rarely available to female-headed households, so a woman's wage-earning ability becomes especially important. However, owing to limited education, formal training, and lack of access to credit and financial services, women are at risk of economic and physical exploitation. They may enter the labor force by performing low-wage work at home, becoming domestic workers, or by taking on dangerous or illegal work as drug traffickers, in sweatshops, or even in the sex industry (Martin 2004; Mertus 2003; UNFPA 2001, 2005a).

In recent years microfinance has garnered growing attention in the government, banking, and non-governmental arenas as an alternative to the highly gendered and largely unsuccessful state-run and multilateral development and aid programs of the past. This heartily embraced form of poverty alleviation is targeted specifically at women in the developing world, and is intended to improve their access to credit, moving them out of poverty and away from dangerous and illegal work.

Microfinance as Capacity Building

The goal of microfinance is to extend financial services, including credit, savings, and insurance to those populations who have historically been excluded from traditional banking, specifically the poorest of the world (Ledgerwood 1999). The majority of activity in the industry is microcredit, which is the provision of very small loans, most often without requiring collateral, to groups of women in the developing world who collectively share the responsibility of repayment (Morduch 1999). These loans are intended to help clients start and grow their small enterprises, which generally involve small-scale trade or domestic production. These loans come with strict regulations, however, such as rapid repayment schedules and very high interest rates by Western standards.[1]

The microfinance industry has reported rather remarkable success over the last three decades of its development. At the end of 2006 the Microcredit Summit Campaign reported over 3,300 microfinance institutions had served more than 133 million new and continuing clients and 464 million associated family members with loan repayment rates typically over 95 percent (Daley-Harris 2007). The industry is able to bring together financial instruments—such as loans, savings, and insurance—with a unique organizational structure to make those instruments work by creating local network systems to support clients in their villages. It presents a tool that allows the poor, particularly women, to turn their assets and skills into income. Microfinance thus has particular relevance to environment in that the assets held by most microfinance clients are in large part comprised of natural resources, and their skill set is rich with environmental knowledge.

Thus, microfinance has the potential to act as a tool of sustainable development in several ways:

First, the majority of the client base of microfinance organizations is poor women, who as previously discussed are uniquely reliant on natural resources for both subsistence and income. Not only do these women have a particular reliance on nature, they also have a wealth of specialized knowledge about natural resources. This specialized knowledge among the pool of microfinance clients could inform microenterprise development in environmentally sustainable ways, thereby creating responsible economic development that protects the natural resource base.

Second, if done responsibly and with cultural context in mind, microfinance could enable women to participate in spheres of society from which they are typically excluded, such as financial markets and household decision making, by giving them a way to market their assets. This participation could lead to the incorporation of women's knowledge into community decisions as they become a more publicly active constituency in the community. Incorporating women's knowledge could lead to increased investment in children's health and education, reduced incidence of catastrophic and incremental environmental change through incorporation of their ecological knowledge in the community, and mitigation of negative effects when those environmental changes do occur (Seager and Hartmann 1994). Women's participation in household and community decision making and asset allocation, enabled by microfinance, is also a challenge to the traditional social structures that keep women subjugated in the home. The freedom to challenge those structures of oppression is considered a major component of achieving human security.

Third, the structure of microfinance (mostly group lending and joint liability) encourages the formation of solidarity groups and friendships among women clients. These social networks can help women gain rights to property and common resources (UNEP and IISD 2004), and provide a safety net in times of hardship. Also, these solidarity groups and networks are more likely to persist than men's or mixed-gender networks as a result of women's daily reliance on them; this mutual dependence can lead women to devise modes of collective action for sustainable development that persists through adversity (Agarwal 2000).

Fourth, microfinance activity allows women to build assets and savings to buffer against seasonal variation in income, to improve living conditions by moving out of areas prone to disaster or fortifying their homes to be sturdier, and to invest in sustainable technologies such as solar cook stoves and water wells that will improve their health and reduce the pressure to use resources unsustainably (Seager and Hartmann 1994).

These four points broadly illustrate the potential of microfinance as a tool, operated largely by women, for achieving sustainable environmental development and broader human security. Through their shared roles as microfinance clients and environmental stewards, women are able to contribute specialized knowledge about how to responsibly engage local environments in their income-generating activities. This not only helps their families and communities to mitigate and adapt to threats to their human, environmental, and social rights, it also builds women's capacity to actively participate in attaining those rights by moving them out of the homes and into the public and economic spheres where they can exercise their capabilities.

For now there is very little knowledge of how microfinance interrelates with environmental issues. There is some attention to microfinance interventions following a natural disaster, and this is followed by a caution to use microfinance as credit rather than aid that has the potential to be misallocated and abused. However, the industry as yet has little knowledge of microfinance's contribution to creating sustainable development plans that address persistent environmental change. It is my contention that there is much potential, as microfinance grows and evolves, to establish it as a great tool for empowering women as environmental managers for their community. It could also become an institutionalized source of sustainable development and ecological information and education for both the poor and those practitioners working in fragile environments. But microfinance is just one tool among many that are crucial to reducing vulnerabilities to environmental change and promoting human security. Sustainable development strategies and an emphasis on human rights are also essential.

Conclusion

Clearly all men, women, and children suffer as the environment is suddenly and chronically modified. The arguments presented in this chapter seek to highlight the unique and amplified vulnerabilities of women in situations of environmental change resulting from the combination of structural inequalities and situational pressures. In closing, three important final points must be made about how women and environment are framed in the international agenda.

First, it must be acknowledged that not only are women made uniquely insecure by environmental pressures, they are also sometimes criticized as culpable for the degradation of the environment, because of their frequent and intimate contact with nature and their role in population growth as bearers of children (Burn 2000; Betsy Hartmann, chapter 10, this volume; Suliman 1999). While these ideas are largely in the process of being replaced by more contextualized understandings of environmental degradation, particularly the topic of overpopulation (see Hartmann 1998), women's role as extractors of natural resources remains an issue that continues to draw attention. Charging women with environmental degradation shifts focus away from their unique vulnerabilities in situations of scarcity, and prevents not only the provision of their needs but also prohibits the incorporation of women into disaster mitigation and environmental planning. If gender and nature are to be addressed together in a productive way, this finger pointing must be resolved.

Second, empirical evidence shows us there exists enormous potential for women as environmental stewards and risk managers during environmental disasters. Fulfilling this potential will require acknowledging women's specialized knowledge of the local ecology and community and their skills as organizers of social networks. This idea privileges women by acknowledging that their relationship with nature has given them a rich understanding of local systems and processes that eludes governments, international development agencies, and NGOs that rely on generalized ecological principles to guide policies that are rarely sensitive to local realities, and whose imposition in decision making can lead to ineffective or even detrimental outcomes. Too often gender is pushed off by governments as an "add on" issue, particularly during disaster relief, and there is still frustration with the idea of mainstreaming gender while preparing for or recovering from a crisis. This unwillingness to grapple with gender issues not only disadvantages women, it also misses the opportunity to tap into their expertise. Empowering women as environmental managers will also require eliminating the construction of women as helpless victims during times of crisis. By framing women's relationship with the environment as one of helplessness, the potential to generate political and social change—by giving women leadership positions and a role in decision making—is wasted. The capacity of women to survive under extreme circumstances, to provide for their families and sustain life when resources are scarce and conflict is overwhelming, is often overlooked by disaster-response and relief agencies that focus their efforts toward male heads of households and fail to include women in aid planning. The failure of the international community to draw sufficient attention to this issue may have severe impacts by perpetuating, even exacerbating, preexisting social and cultural beliefs that women are weak, helpless, and inferior.

Last, we must remember the broader issue to be addressed, that of human security as a whole. Gender-disparate environmental vulnerability is neither solely a gender issue nor solely a nature issue. The framework of human security provides a holistic lens through which to view the relationship of humans to nature. By focusing on human security as a guiding goal, gender and environment are both mainstreamed.

Note

1. Some organizations charge interest rates of up to 60 percent, according to a panel presentation at the Microfinance and Beyond conference at the University of Southern California, May 2006.

References

Agarwal, B. 1992. The gender and environment debate: Lessons from India. *Feminist Studies* 8 (1): 119–158.

Agarwal, B. 2000. Conceptualizing environmental collective action: Why gender matters. *Cambridge Journal of Economics* 24:283–310.

Amnesty International. 2001. Violence against women: A fact sheet. http://www .amnestyusa.org/violence-against-women/stop-violence-against-women-svaw/ violence-against-women-information/page.do?id=1108245 (accessed March 3, 2009). Amnesty International. 2004. *It's in our hands: Stop violence against women*. London: Amnesty International Publications.

BBC News. 2005. Millions "will feel degradation." http://www.newsvote.bbc .co.uk (accessed October 13, 2005).

Burn, S. M. 2000. *Women across culture: A global perspective*. Mountain View, CA: Mayfield.

Byrne, B., and Baden, S. 1995. Gender, emergencies and humanitarian assistance. BRIDGE Report No. 33. Brighton, UK: Institute of Development Studies, University of Sussex.

Centre for Research on Poverty Reduction and Income Distribution (CRPRID). 2006. *Pakistan 2005 earthquake: An assessment of impoverishment risks*. Islamabad: CRPRID.

Daley-Harris, S. 2007. *State of the Microcredit Summit Campaign report 2006*. Washington, DC: Microcredit Summit Campaign.

Enarson, E., and M. Fordham. 2001. From women's needs to women's rights in disasters. *Environmental Hazards* 3:133–136.

Gault, B., H. Hartmann, A. Jones-DeWeever, M. Werschkul, and E. Williams. 2005. *Institute for Women's Policy Research briefing paper: The women of New Orleans and the Gulf Coast: Multiple disadvantages and key assets for recovery, part I. Poverty, race, gender and class*. Washington, DC: IWPR.

GECHS. 1999. *IHDP (International Human Dimensions Programme on Global Environmental Change) Report No. 11*. Bonn, Germany: IHDP.

Gupta, S. 2003. Human security, economic development and gender. In *Human security in South Asia: Energy, gender, migration and globalization*, ed. P. R. Chari and S. Gupta, 52–66. New Delhi: Social Science Press.

Hartmann, B. 1998. Population, environment and security: A new trinity. *Environment and Urbanization* 10 (2): 113–117.

Homer-Dixon, T. 1999. *Environment, scarcity and violence*. Princeton, NJ: Princeton University Press.

Homer-Dixon, T., and J. Blitt, eds. 1998. *Ecoviolence: Links among environment, population, and security*. Lanham, MD: Rowman & Littlefield.

Hudson, Valerie M., and Andrea M. den Boer. 2004. *Bare branches: The Security implications of Asia's surplus male population*. Cambridge, MA: MIT Press.

International Federation of Red Cross (IFRC) and Red Crescent Societies. 1999. *World disasters report*. Geneva: International Federation of Red Cross and Red Crescent Societies.

Lammers, E. 1999. *Refugees, gender, and human security: A theoretical introduction and annotated bibliography*. Utrecht: International Books.

Ledgerwood, J. 1999. *Microfinance handbook: An institutional and financial perspective*. Washington, DC: World Bank.

Martin, S. F. 2004. *Refugee women*, 2d ed. New York: Lexington Books.

Merchant, C. 1980. *The death of nature: Women, ecology and the scientific revolution*. San Francisco: Harper.

Mertus, J. 2003. Sovereignty, gender and displacement. In *Refugees and forced displacement: International security, human vulnerability, and the state*, ed. E. Newman and J. van Selm, 250–273. New York: United Nations University Press.

Meyers, N. 2002. Environmental refugees: A growing phenomenon of the 21st century. *Philosophical Transactions of the Royal Society*. 357:609–613.

Morduch, J. 1999. The microfinance promise. *Journal of Economic Literature* 37:1569–1614.

Pan American Health Organization. n.d. Fact sheet: Gender and natural disasters. http://www.paho.org/English/DPM/GPP/GH/genderdisasters.pdf (accessed March 3, 2009). Plumwood, V. 1990. *Feminism and the mastery of nature*. London and New York: Routledge.

Population Reference Bureau. 2002. *Women, men and environmental change: The gender dimension of environmental policies and programs*. Washington, DC: Population Reference Bureau.

Seager, J., and B. Hartmann. 1994. A gender assessment of DEWA and UNEP. Unpublished report.

Shiva, V. 1989. *Staying alive: Women, ecology and development*. Atlantic Highlands, NJ: Zed Books.

Suliman, M., ed. 1999. *Ecology, politics, and violent conflict*. New York: Zed Books.

UN (United Nations). 2003. *Human security now*. New York: Commission on Human Security.

UNDP. 1994. *Human development report 1994*. New York: UNDP.

UNDP Pakistan. 2006. *Gender mainstreaming in recovery phase—Post earthquake Pakistan*. Islamabad: UNDP Pakistan.

UNEP and IISD. 2004. *Exploring the links: Human well-being, poverty and ecosystem services*. Winnipeg: IISD.

UNFPA. 2001. *The state of the world population 2001*. New York: UNFPA.

UNFPA. 2005a. *The state of the world population 2005*. New York: UNFPA.

UNFPA. 2005b. Press release: Thousands of pregnant earthquake survivors will face life-threatening complications in coming months. http://www.unfpa.org/news/news.cfm?ID=709&Language=1 (accessed November 15, 2008).

UNICEF. n.d.a. The situation of women and girls: Facts and figures. http://www
.unicef.org/gender/index_factsandfigures.html.

UNICEF. n.d.b. Factsheet: discrimination. http://www.unicef.org.

UNICEF. 2000. Press release: UNICEF executive director targets violence against women. http://www.unicef.org/newsline/00pr17.htm (accessed November 15, 2008).

UNICEF. 2006. *State of the world's children 2007*. New York: UNICEF.

UNIFEM. n.d. Facts and figures on violence against women. http://www.unfem
.org/gender_issues/violence_against_women (accessed February 1, 2007).

UNIFEM. 2005a. *UNIFEM responds to the tsunami tragedy, one year later: A report card*. New York: UNIFEM.

UNIFEM. 2005b. News release: Asian tsunami, UNIFEM calls for greater role of women in recovery and reconstruction efforts. http://www.unifem.org.

UN Millennium Project. 2005. *Taking action: Achieving gender equality and empowering women*. Task Force on Education and Gender Equality. Sterling, VA: Earthscan.

WEDO (Women's Environment and Development Organization). 2003. *Common ground: Women's access to natural resources and the United Nations Millennium Development Goals*. New York: WEDO.

White House. 2006. *The federal response to Hurricane Katrina: Lessons learned.* http://www.whitehouse.gov/reports (accessed February 6, 2007).

World Bank. 2003. *Gender equality and the Millennium Development Goals.* Washington, DC: World Bank.

World Health Organization. 2002. *Gender and health in natural disasters.* Geneva: WHO.

12

Human Security as a Prerequisite for Development

Kwasi Nsiah-Gyabaah

Security and development are not new concepts. The right to life and security of all persons are basic rights that were enshrined in article 3 of the 1948 UN Declaration. However, since the publication of the World Commission on Environment and Development report *Our Common Future* by Gro Harlem Brundtland of Norway (WCED 1987), and the United Nation Development Programme's 1994 Human Development Report (UNDP 1994), security and development have been interpreted in many different ways. "Human security" and "sustainable development" have emerged as new paradigms for understanding different threats to security and development. Recently, human security and governance and sustainable development have become important fields of study, which are taught in universities as part of international relations, environmental science, peace, and human rights studies (UNDP 1994; Tadjbakhsh and Chenoy 2006).

In spite of the popularity and extensive use of the human security and "sustainability" concepts in research and development (R&D), there is no consensus on their actual meaning or the links between them (Redclift 1987, 1992; Adelman 2000; UNDP 1994, 1998; Sen 2000). What one country perceives as human security and sustainable development may not be another's perception because of the wide range and complexity of the phenomena that are attributed to both concepts. The quagmire of meanings and ambiguity have not only reduced the practical value of the concepts, but have led to fundamental questions being asked about whether it is possible for them to be fully met, and if it is feasible to implement the human security and sustainable development agendas. Fundamental questions such as "what security?," "whose security?," "whose sustainability?," and "for how long?" have not been adequately addressed regarding the identification of the multiple threats and vulnerability and adaptation to the threats of human security and development (Redclift 1987, 1992; Hyden 1998).

In order to ensure global peace, human security, and cooperation, it is important for researchers and the policy community to understand each other's aspirations and perceptions of security and development. Therefore, this chapter sets out to address three issues. First, it examines the meanings and scope of human security and development. Second, it presents new perspectives of human security and development and the links between them. Third, it establishes prerequisites for achieving human security and sustainable development. The primary objective is to provide an entry point for researchers and the policy community to formulate policies and implement action programs that address the critical and pervasive threats to human security and sustainable development at the international, regional, and local levels.

What Is Human Security?

Human security is a concept that has evolved since the Cold War from the notion of "national security" or the state protecting its borders from external aggression, to include threats to the physical security of the person and human rights, as well as direct and indirect threats to livelihoods, human dignity, and well-being (UN 1948; Berkowitz and Bock 1968; Brock 1991; UNDP 1994; Matthew 2002). The potential for conflict during the Cold War era shaped the notion of threats to a country's borders and the ability to deter or defeat external aggression. Although the majority of people still see security in terms of state security or militarism, this narrow, state-centered definition has been contested because it leaves out the most elementary and legitimate concerns of ordinary people regarding their health, water, energy, livelihoods, environment, and other securities in their daily lives (Rodney 1982; Ullman 1983: Renner 1989; Westing 1989; Gleditsch 1997). In Africa, where the greatest threats to human security are pervasive poverty, inequality, HIV/AIDS, and bad governance, the traditional definition of human security as "state security" or national sovereignty is too narrow and inadequate for policy formulation and implementation (UNDP 1994; Lonergan, Gustavson, and Carter 1999; Dabelko, Lonergan, and Matthew 2000).

Moreover, globalization, information and communication technology (ICT), and rapid economic development have created more opportunities for conflict resolution and new threats such as terrorism, drug abuse, infectious diseases, and environmental degradation that extend beyond state security. The complexities of the array of these human security challenges are not captured and cannot be resolved by state security instruments such as military force and international sanctions. As a result of the limitations of the traditional definition, a human security paradigm has emerged that is "people-centered" and takes account of the complex and multidimensional causes of threats to human security (WCED 1987; Buzan 1991; UNDP 1994).

New Paradigms of Human Security

A new understanding of people-centered security, which incorporates factors such as poverty, environment, infectious diseases, gender, empowerment, freedom from want, and survival, has become extremely important in policy formulation and implementation because in addition to military threats, nonmilitary threats such as human rights abuses, bad governance, and widespread poverty continue to undermine human security and development in many countries, especially Africa. While in some countries such as Sierra Leone and Liberia, the state has failed its security obligation to protect its citizens from violence, in others such as Darfur, the state has become the instrument of oppression and a major source of threat to the safety, rights, and freedoms of its own citizens (Axworthy 2001; Sanjeev, William, and Raad 2003). Therefore, human security is about the ability of the state to protect both its citizens and its borders from external aggression (Heinbecker 1999).

Recent definitions of human security therefore emphasize the protection and safety of individuals, their fundamental rights and freedoms, gender equality, and promotion of their welfare. In this context, human security needs are paramount, rather than the protection of territorial borders. Human security is therefore people centered and goes beyond state protection to the security of individuals, empowering them and addressing the threats to their lives and freedoms and reducing their vulnerability to poverty, disease, and natural disasters (Axworthy 2001; Commission on Human Security 2003; Leichenko and O'Brien 2005). The Universal Declaration of Human Rights (UN 1948) was one of the first attempts to bring together the political and socioeconomic perspectives into one analytical framework for understanding security. It noted that there is security when people have the right to life and are not vulnerable to the constant threats of hunger, disease, crime, famine, environmental degradation, natural disasters, oppression, ethnic cleansing, and political persecution. It noted further that when citizens are killed by their own security forces or cannot walk the streets because of fear of being attacked, their security is threatened (Rodney 1982; Ullman 1983; Renner 1989; Westing 1989).

The United Nations Development Programme (UNDP 1994) gave a broader definition of human security, which included threats in seven areas: economic, political, food, health, environment, community, and personal security. According to the UNDP, freedom from want and freedom from fear for all persons is the best way to address the problem of global human security (UNDP 1994; 1997). Although each of UNDP's seven areas of threats to human security has received international attention, appropriate mechanisms for achieving them have proved illusive. Other proponents of a broader definition of human security such as Mahbub ul Haq and Steve Lonergan have stressed the importance of a human-centered approach, and the application of sustainability, vulnerability, resilience, poverty, and secured livelihoods concepts in understanding human security. Consequently, they have designed people-centered interventions such as poverty reduction, access to income, and sustainable livelihoods to address the enduring and underlying causes of human security problems (Meyers 1989; UNDP 1994; Rothschild 1995; GECHS 1999; Lonergan, Gustavson, and Carter 1999; Sen 2000; King and Murray 2002; RIVM 2002).

In the last decade, the notions of human security are being transformed in the face of climate change (GECHS 1999; Matthew 2002). The Global Environmental Change and Human Security (GECHS) project has become a core area of research of the International Human Dimensions Programme (IHDP). GECHS situates environmental change and the capacity of individuals, communities, and regions to cope with and adapt to environmental change within the larger context of human security. GECHS defines human security broadly not only as freedom from conflict, but also as having the means to secure basic rights, needs, and livelihoods, and to pursue opportunities for human fulfillment and development (GECHS 1999; Matthew 2002; Leichenko and O'Brien 2005). It focuses on gender, equity, and how certain individuals, groups, or regions are supported or constrained in their capacity to respond to the multiple processes of change, which can manifest either as shocks or as structural transformation (Leichenko and O'Brien 2005). The GECHS project's conceptualization of human security argues that "human security is achieved when and where individuals and communities have the options necessary to end, mitigate, or adapt to threats to their human, environmental and social rights; have the capacity and freedom to exercise these options; and can actively participate in attaining these options" (GECHS 1999). Challenging the structures and processes that contribute to insecurities is considered key to achieving human security (GECHS 1999). Moreover, "human security embodies the notion that problems must always be addressed from a broader perspective and must include both *poverty* and issues of *equity* (i.e., social, economic, environmental, or institutional) because they often lead to conflict and human insecurity (GECHS 1999; Lonergan, Gustavson, and Carter 1999).

Human security is now widely used to convey a condition in which individual citizens live in freedom, peace, and safety and can participate fully in the processes of governance and decision making. It includes the protection of fundamental human rights and access to resources and basic necessities of life such as health, decent housing, education, and an environment that is not injurious to people's livelihoods and well-being. Researchers, non-governmental organizations (NGOs), and policy-makers have found the people-centered, comprehensive human security framework a useful approach for poverty reduction and implementation of sustainable development. This chapter supports the notion of human security as a condition in which the rights and freedoms of citizens are respected; where there is rule of law and good governance; where the basic material and survival needs of citizens are met; where people are not constrained by poverty, disease, ignorance, and hunger; and where the poor and vulnerable groups such as women are able to participate meaningfully in decision making and development.

What Is Development?

Development, like human security, has been interpreted in many different ways (Seers 1977; Simon 2003; World Bank 2004). The evolving vision of development has largely overturned the old assumptions of economic growth-oriented strategies as the path to development and a world divided into "rich" and "poor," "developed" and "underdeveloped." For many years, economists used the concept of development to explain why some countries are *rich* or *developed* while others are *poor* or *underdeveloped*, and how the social, economic, political, and cultural conditions in the poor countries could be changed so that they would become rich. The general perception was that the rich countries such as the United States and Great Britain had achieved certain positively evaluated socioeconomic conditions, which needed to be copied by the poor countries so that they could become rich. This meant that changes in the developing countries so that they resembled the developed countries were regarded as development.

As a result of this, many of the developing countries, especially the former colonies, adopted the Euro-American models of development after independence, with emphasis on industrialization, urbanization, and modernization. The blueprint Eurocentric models of development achieved limited results. This approach to development carried a negative connotation by dividing the world in two: the rich *or developed countries* on one hand, and the poor or underdeveloped (also called backward) countries on the other hand. One of the significant adverse impacts of the dichotomy was the exploitation of natural resources from poor countries to rich countries and the unequal terms of trade between the developed and developing countries (Rodney 1982).

Many writers criticized this definition of development as narrow, value laden, and too ethnocentric. The critics considered the Western-style industrialized society as the standard against which the developing countries were measured inadequate (Warwick 1982; Mertus, Flowers, and Mallike 1999). The definition also portrayed the poor countries negatively: not by what they were but by what they were not; and not by what they had, but by what they lacked. Moreover, it overlooked the miserable history and legacy of colonialism, which were believed to be the root causes of poverty and underdevelopment in the former colonies (Harrison 1993). In order to address the immediate economic concerns in developing countries in the 1980s, it became necessary to shift the emphasis on development away from the post-war classic industrialization, modernization, and Western-style approach to the Marxist and neo-Marxist political and economic growth paradigms, which were defined as *economic growth with* or *without equity.* Development was seen in economic terms and income per capita was taken as the key indicator of the standard definition of development. Efforts to measure productive capacity and economic growth were limited to income measurements of one kind or another such as gross national product (GNP) and gross domestic product (GDP) (Marx 1976; Sen 1988; Streeten 1994).

These ideas were never unchallenged. In the late 1970s, advocates for women rights and equality argued that development required empowerment of women so they could enjoy greater freedom, power, and security. In the late 1980s, many writers questioned the theoretical adequacy and empirical validity of the growth-centric model because it ignored the social and demographic dimensions of development (Weaver and Jameson 1981). They argued that development cannot be defined purely in economic terms. Although the critics recognized that increased incomes and national economic growth were important in improving the standard of living, they were not the only preconditions for development (Sen 1988). An alternative "welfare-centric" paradigm emerged. Human welfare and poverty reduction became the overall objective and essence of development. The welfare-centric theorists, therefore, urged the pursuit of much broader goals with emphasis on rural development, poverty alleviation, and improvement in human welfare (Griffen 1981; Streeten 1981; Weaver and Jameson 1981: Dreze and Sen 1989). This led to the development of all kinds of infrastructure including water, roads, and energy systems, reflecting the belief of the state as the main agent of investment and development.

However, since the WCED report and the UN 1994 Human Development Report, development has taken a new outlook and the idea of sustainability has become a useful entry point to understanding the environment, human security, and development. By the early 1990s it was becoming clear that decades of misguided growth in the name of development had manifested in environmental degradation, mostly air, water, and land degradation, which posed serious threats to human security and development (WCED 1987; UNDP 1994; Redclift 1987, 1992; Mannion 1992). Although there are over one hundred definitions of *sustainable development*, the most popular definition was submitted by the Brundtland Commission report, *Our Common Future*, which defined it as: "development that meets the needs of the present without compromising the ability of future generations to meet their own needs" (WCED 1987; Blaikie 1996). Sustainable development implies maintaining a delicate balance among human needs to improve well-being while preserving natural resources and ecosystem in the interest of future generations (Department of Environment 1988).

Even though the Brundtland Commission report represented an important shift from the notion of sustainability as primarily ecological, to a focus on environment and equity, not all advocates of sustainable development considered the environment as a primary concern of the sustainability debate. Others, however, maintained that the sustainability of the environment and the security of future generations were the ultimate goals of sustainable development. They also believed that ecological/environmental, political, economic, technological, and technical sustainability as well as participatory democracy were important (Barbier 1989; Brinkerhoff and Goldsmith 1990; Rees 1990; UNCED 1992; UNDP 2003).

In 1994, the UNDP advanced a broader understanding of the human dimensions of development when it introduced the concept of sustainable human development. Sustainable human development emphasized growth, but growth with rather than at the expense of employment, environment, empowerment, and equity. It is pro-poor, pro nature, pro-jobs, and pro women (UNDP 1993). The creators of the Human Development Movement, led by Mahbub ul Haq, introduced the human development paradigm as a holistic development model that focused on people. Human security was defined simply as "a process of enlarging people's choices" (UNDP 1994). In principle, these choices can be definite and can change over time. According to the UNDP report, people often value achievements that do not show up at all, or not immediately, in income or growth figures, including: greater access to knowledge, better nutrition and health services, more secure livelihoods, security against crime and physical violence, satisfying leisure hours, political and cultural freedoms, and a sense of participation in community activities.

The definition embraces every development issue including economic growth, empowerment, the provision of basic needs and social safety nets, political and cultural freedoms, and all aspects of people's lives. It also includes safety from chronic threats such as hunger, disease, and repression as well as protection from sudden and harmful disruptions in the patterns of daily life—whether in homes, in jobs, or in communities. While no aspect of the sustainable development model falls outside its scope, the vantage point is the widening of people's choices and the enhancement of their lives (UNDP 1994). The Millennium Development Declaration also expanded development and human security to include eight key indicators to be achieved by 2015 (UN 2000).

Causes and Threats to Human Security

There is still much to learn about the threats to human security because the causes are many and the relationships among the drivers and how they influence one another are complex and interdependent. Violent conflict is one of the major threats to human security and a barrier to development in many of the world's poorest countries. The post-World War II era has seen the emergence of other nonmilitary threats resulting from poverty, food insecurity, water shortage, natural and human-made disasters, environmental degradation, and climate change. The United Nations Human Security Report (UNDP 1994) has identified seven critical areas of threats to human security for action. They include:

• *Political insecurity*   Results from conflict, bad governance, and lack of participation in decision making.

• *Economic insecurity*   Mainly owing to the lack of basic needs for a good life and livelihood support for the vulnerable, financial insecurity and volatility, and insecurity of jobs and incomes affecting people in rich and poor countries.

• *Food insecurity*   Lack of access to nutritious, healthy, and well-packaged food for all at all times and in all places.

• *Health insecurity*   Caused by infectious diseases, with HIV/AIDS, malaria, and tuberculosis the most obvious risks.

• *Community/cultural insecurity*   Caused by unbalanced flows of TV, film, and other media that are heavily weighed from rich countries to poor ones.

• *Personal insecurity*   Caused mainly by domestic violence, growing crime areas such as rape, drug abuse, armed robbery, and other acts that affect personal safety.

• *Environmental insecurity*   Caused by natural and human-made disasters, lack of environmental resources, and climate change.

Political insecurity is mainly caused by inter- and intrastate conflict and bad governance, which contribute to making people unsafe and incapable of adapting and coping with changes that affect their livelihoods and survival. According to O'Reilly, because of violent conflict, about 3.6 million people were killed, 24 million were internally displaced, and 18 million became refugees between 1990 and 1998 (O'Reilly 1998). In Rwanda, between 200,000 to 500,000 people died during the conflict. In 2000, about 10.6 million people in Africa were internally displaced by ethnic conflicts.

In Africa, the major threats to human security are violent conflict, bloody coups, poverty, bad governance, and political instability. These threats have led to the loss of millions of lives. Available statistics show that over four million people have died in violent conflict in the Democratic Republic of Congo (DRC). Between 1999 and 2003, an estimated

10,000 people lost their lives and 800,000 were internally displaced as a result of "localized" conflict in Nigeria (Commission for Africa 2005). In many countries, bad governance has led to human rights abuses, political oppression and persecution of opponents, ethnic cleansing, and lack of citizen participation in governance. Human rights abuses, killing of civilians, and human suffering in Kosovo, Liberia, and Iraq under Saddam Hussein show the effects of bad governance on human security and development and the exaggerated belief that state security is a guarantee for achieving human security and prosperity. In countries such as Sudan (Darfur region) where security forces are killing citizens, and people cannot walk the streets for fear of being killed, human security is threatened.

Another threat to human security is climate change and the systematic destruction of natural resources especially water, forests, and marine resources. At a global scale, the destruction of natural resources is undermining the ability of the poor to secure their livelihoods. In the last two decades climate change has become a global human security issue because of its staggering impacts on health, food security, and water supply. Adverse impacts of climate change on water supply are known to lead to conflict, which can undermine human security (Meyers 1989; ERM 2002). Lack of access to safe drinking water and sanitation is also a major threat to human security. It is estimated that around 3.4 million people die annually from water-related diseases (DFID 2002). In many parts of the world, conflict rages over rights to the use and management of water and as a result of the adverse impacts of climate change these conflicts may become more intense (Gleditsch 1997).

Globalization and growing poverty constitute another cause of human insecurity in the developing countries. The increasing marginalization of Africa, critical limitations to industrial development, lack of technology, low and decreasing levels of production, high level of poverty, illiteracy, and minimal trading power affect the economy and livelihoods and pose major indirect threats to human security. In addition, external factors such as high oil prices, unfair trade between the North and South, and mounting external debts and debt servicing affect local economies, livelihoods, and human security. While globalization is creating unparalleled opportunities for wealth creation and sustainable development in the developed countries, it is leading to diminished human security in the poor countries with limited capacity to compete in the global market. The estimated 1.2 billion people, especially the absolutely poor who live on less than one dollar per day and the 800 million people who go hungry each day, without shelter and good health have minimal security. In the Northern Region in Ghana, pervasive poverty and deprivation are major causes of violent conflict and unsustainable use of natural resources, which also undermine livelihoods and human security. Therefore, poverty, including the lack of access to basic needs for survival such as water, food, health, education, and shelter, are important causes of human insecurity in many developing countries.

In many developed and developing countries, particular social vulnerability configurations such as illegal immigration, rapid population growth, and urbanization and the associated problems of armed robbery and organized international crime have become the greatest threat to human security. Other insecurities that people and societies face include natural disasters, climate change, floods, drought, diseases, wildfire, proliferation of weapons—especially the development of nuclear technology—and HIV/AIDS (Bush 2003). In Africa drought has had human security implications for a variety of livelihood activities. In addition, infectious diseases, especially HIV/AIDS, has affected nearly thirty million people, including three million under the age of fifteen. Although violent conflict and war were the major causes of human insecurity in the 1940s, with the demise of the Cold War and demilitarization other factors such as drought, floods, hurricane, poverty, illiteracy, climate change, and political and religious persecution are among the major threats to human security (Ullman 1983; Renner 1989; WCED 1987; Westing 1989, Buzan 1991). Figure 12.1 shows the complex and multidimensional causes of human insecurity. Development is a concept that must be seen within the larger context of household, community, and national economies and, more broadly still within the context of human well-being, human security, basic materials for a good life, good social relations, and freedom of choice or action. Therefore, development and human security are directly and intimately related because the factors that cause human insecurity also undermine the development process and the achievement of development objectives.

However, as new understanding of the meaning and complexity of factors that affect human security and development emerge, establishing the links between human security and development is extremely important for policy formulation and implementation. The main objective of development is to improve human well-being through sustainable livelihoods, and to meet the basic needs of food, water, shelter, clothing, transport, healthcare, education, and productive employment. Other

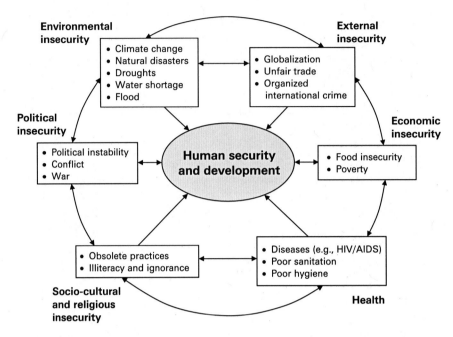

Figure 12.1
The multiple causes and threats to human security and the relationships between human security and development

aims include poverty reduction, environmental security, elimination of drugs and diseases, conflict prevention, and sustainable production and consumption patterns. Human security is enhanced when sustainable development objectives are met. However, it is the first casualty when sustainable livelihoods and other development objectives are not achieved.

In this context, Thomas (2000) argues that human security and development are intimately linked because they aim for the same objectives: ensuring human safety, adequate food, health, education, gender equality, participation in decision making, good governance, human dignity, and control over one's life. According to DFID, human security and sustainable development are possible where people live in peace and have a say in how their community is run, and have access to water, food, shelter, education, and the chance to earn a living and to bring up healthy and educated children (DFID 1997). Both human security and sustainable development are enhanced when there is good governance, rule of law, and active citizen participation in decision making and development.

The links between human security and development can be traced to the post-war efforts of the UN General Assembly on global disarmament and nonproliferation of nuclear weapons and weapons of mass destruction. The UN noted that violent conflict affected both personal safety of citizens and socioeconomic development. In Africa, where violent conflicts have occurred, the links between human security and development are clear. In the war-afflicted countries such as Liberia and Sierra Leone, conflicts have led to the loss of lives, destruction of property and basic infrastructure, and refugee problems. Violent conflict has also contributed to growing poverty, food insecurity, diseases, and underdevelopment (Starr 1991; Annan 2001). The UN argues that human insecurity due to conflict is profoundly damaging to sustainable development because resources meant to provide basic infrastructure and services are sacrificed for the protection of national sovereignty. In 1985, about $900 billion was spent on military purposes. The cost in terms of development is what the same resources could have been used to do—for example, it was estimated that to rehabilitate the degraded tropical forests would cost $1.3 billion; to combat desertification would cost $4.5 billion; to provide water and supply contraceptives for family planning would cost $30 billion and $2 billion respectively (Agarwal et al. 1981; World Bank 1984; ITF 1985; Tolba 1986).

Currently, the war in Iraq and the fight against terrorism cost the United States huge sums of money to protect national security and ensure the safety of U.S. nationals from terrorist attacks. If the money that has been spent since the war had been made available to Africa, the enormous human security and development challenges facing the continent would belong to history. Moreover, the loss of human resources and displacement of people as a result of conflict deprive nations of the human resources they need for development (O'Reilly 1998). Therefore, while human security can promote sustainable development, insecurity and conflict can increase substantially the vulnerability of the poor to diseases and food insecurity and reduce poor people's capacity to mitigate, cope with, and adapt to security threats.

Francis Stewart (2004) has described a three-part relationship for human security and development. First, human security forms an important part of human well-being, which is also an objective of development. Second, human insecurity affects economic growth and development. Third, issues of equity are important sources of conflict, which undermines human security. Therefore, lack of development and growing poverty can lead to conflict and conflict can also lead to lack of development as well as poverty and deprivation. Similarly, high levels of security enhance socioeconomic development, and socioeconomic development promotes human security (ibid.). For example, in Africa, violent conflict, which leads to human insecurity, also results in hunger, poverty, and deprivation. Globally, countries with the highest percentage of poor people are also those that have been affected by conflict. In the 1990s, forty-six countries in the world were involved in armed conflict (primarily civil). This included more than half of the poorest countries (17 out of 33). These conflicts had very high costs because they destroyed development gains, leaving a legacy of damaged assets and mistrust that impeded future gains (UNDP 2003).

As a result of the bidirectional relationships between human security and development, many states and individuals have asserted that human security is the underlying condition and prerequisite for sustainable development. The violent conflicts and human insecurity in countries such as Sierra Leone, Rwanda, Burundi, the DRC, Liberia, Côte d'Ivoire, and Darfur in Sudan best illustrate the direct but complex links between human security and development as well as the importance of ensuring human security as a prerequisite for sustainable development. In these countries, violent conflicts have hampered the development process in many ways. Farmlands have been ruined, houses have been flattened, and basic infrastructure and services, especially schools, hospitals, and water-distribution systems have also been destroyed. The WCED (1987), the 1992 Rio Conference, and the UN Millennium Development Goals (MDGs) (UN 2000) also elaborated, at the highest level, the fundamental relationship between sustainable development and human security when linked to the environment. It was noted that sustainable development and human security largely depend on the creation of a safe and secure environment.

The theories linking development and human security to the environment are based on the feedback that exists between them (Westing 1989). Since many environmental problems are directly linked to human well-being and development, environmental protection has formed the basis for ensuring human security and sustainable development. Environmental problems, particularly air, water, and soil pollution, are seen as a violation of the right to life and a barrier to socioeconomic development. Whether or not we believe that environmental concerns are linked to human security and development, it is difficult to argue that environmental problems have not been important considerations in armed conflicts and peace building, which are important human security and development issues.

Mahbub ul Haq, for example, has noted that sustainable development shares a common vision with human security. "The objectives of development are to enlarge people's choices, protect human freedom and rights, and create an enabling environment for people to enjoy long, healthy and creative lives" (UNDP 1994). For development to occur, people must be free to exercise their choices and to participate in decision making that affects their lives. Development and human security are therefore mutually reinforcing, helping to secure the well-being and dignity of all people, building self-respect and the respect of others. The development aspects of human security relate to poverty eradication, health improvement, education and gender equality, income equality, adequate food and water supply, shelter, employment, and the removal of other types of inequalities. It is in recognition of the direct and intimate relationships between human security and sustainable development that development agencies and advocates for global peace and security must form a strong partnership, with a common agenda, to promote human security and sustainable development.

Human Security as a Prerequisite for Sustainable Development

It is generally acknowledged that on the one hand, sustainable development is impossible in the context of conflict or human insecurity because conflict exposes vulnerable people, particularly women and children, to hunger, poverty, and deprivation. On the other hand, human security is also impossible in the midst of growing poverty, hunger, and deprivation. While threats to human insecurity—especially violent conflict— has led to poverty and deprivation in many other countries, underdevelopment including poverty and the lack of basic infrastructure has increased the vulnerability of individuals, groups, and regions to violent conflict and human insecurity. In addition, threats such as droughts, floods, and storms, which have resulted in loss of lives, displacement, and damage to natural, social, and physical capital, have negatively impacted on development.

While the 1950s witnessed growing recognition that international peace and cooperation were necessary for human security and development, growth-based development models aimed at ensuring long-term sustainability and sharing of economic progress dominated R&D think-ing in the 1980s. After World War II, many people held the view that peace was a precondition for economic growth and development. The link between human security and development was seen in terms of loss of lives and property. However, with the emergence of new definitions and perspectives of human security and sustainable development, the di-rect and indirect links between them have become complex and therefore not clearly understood.

Robert McNamara, who expanded the notion of security to include the promotion of socioeconomic and political development in order to prevent conflicts in Africa and preserve global order and stability, argues that development is a precondition for peace and human security (McNamara 1968). In his opinion, everyone has basic needs for water, food, basic education, and health, which must be available to ensure hu-man security. These basic needs that are the objectives of development enable the poor to take charge of their own future. Consequently, under his leadership as president of the World Bank in the 1970s, the World Bank pursued a policy of massive resource transfers to support socio-economic development in the developing countries in order to promote global peace and security. Others think that, for a start, sustainable de-velopment and progress in ensuring peace cannot be achieved unless everyone's human rights are protected, including those of the poorest and most disadvantaged people (DFID 1997).

Over the years, many African countries have learned from their own experiences that human security is necessary for sustainable development because the countries that have experienced violent conflicts, natural dis-asters, and environmental degradation are poor and underdeveloped. Of the forty poorest countries in the world, twenty-four are either in the midst of armed conflict or have recently emerged from it. In Africa, where armed conflict has led to massive population displacement, socio-economic development has been slow. Therefore, many African countries have pledged their support for global peace, environmental security, and good governance to promote human security and sustainable develop-ment. Other qualitative elements of human security that African govern-ments consider essential and prerequisites for attainment of the goals and objectives of development include the protection of human rights, rule of law, economic stability, good governance, democratic accountability, and democratic institutions for decision making and policy implementa-tion (Brinkerhoff and Goldsmith 1990).

Although human security is a prerequisite to development, the process of development can also threaten aspects of human security. Development can generate friction or create conflict and become a destabilizing force in communities. It can create problems, contradictions, and social upheavals (PRIO 1999). The social grievances, conflict, and disruptions of traditional ways of life arising from modernization, industrialization, and commercialization in Africa have been discussed extensively by writers such as Huntington (1968) and Olson (1963). Recently, development through science and technology has led to the introduction of new technologies such as nuclear weapons and other weapons of mass destruction, which pose a serious threat to human security in many countries. Human security forms an important part of people's well-being and is therefore an objective of development (Stewart 2004). Insecurity cuts life short and thwarts the use of human potential, thereby affecting the achievement of development objectives.

The experience of many countries in Africa—from the DRC to Sierra Leone, from Ethiopia to Liberia, and from Angola to Côte d'Ivoire—best illustrates the importance of human security as a precondition for sustainable development. The violent conflicts in these countries have had huge direct costs in loss of lives, with serious long-term consequences on development. The conflict in Sierra Leone, for example, represents a good example of the direct link between human security and development. The heinous crimes committed against the people led to three thousand deaths and one million refugees. In addition, three thousand children were abducted and over five thousand buildings were destroyed. Moreover, when stocks of food for development agencies were looted, the agencies abandoned development projects and many local and foreign investors left the country (UNICEF 1996; Lansana 2000). Thousands of professionals including medical doctors, engineers, administrators, and academics also fled to Europe and other safe countries in the subregion. Development suffered immensely and post-war reconstruction has remained an unaccomplished task.

According to the UK Department for International Development (DFID 1997), the right to life and security is a basic human right and key for sustainable development. It is impossible to achieve sustainable development and make progress in reducing poverty unless the rights and freedoms of all citizens are protected (ibid.), and without increased investment to reduce threats to security—especially conflict, environmental degradation, and climate change—the developing countries cannot reduce poverty and make the rapid acceleration in development that people aim to achieve. New policy responses and action programs are therefore required to ensure peace and security and integrate human security and sustainable objectives in a bidirectional relationship to ensure peace and security and create a favorable environment for sustainable development.

Recommendations

Different threats to human security and development require different policy and action response strategies. However, the promotion of peace and stability is indispensable if countries are to attract investment and trade and promote pro-poor development. Today's world offers many opportunities and the developing countries—especially in Africa— should form partnerships and networks with the developed countries for a better future. Long-term global cooperation, good governance, and rule of law are necessary conditions for ensuring human security and sustainable development, and governments should be committed to good governance and the rule of law. In the pursuit of sustainable development and human security, the UN, NGOs, and civil society should refocus their development efforts to eliminate poverty in the developing countries. They should support policies that create sustainable livelihoods for the poor, promote human development, and conserve the environment. All appropriate mechanisms must be strengthened and timely prevention and resolution of conflict are necessary to protect individuals from the effects of conflict.

The wealthy countries must show greater commitment to working with the poor countries by creating an enabling environment in which free trade and sustainable development are possible. The wide range of avenues to promote sustainable development and human security include development and transfer of appropriate technology, prevention and control of diseases, especially HIV/AIDS, environmental protection, and participatory democracy. Given the persistence of poverty, accelerated environmental degradation, especially the threat of climate change, violent conflict, and the growing gap between the developed and the developing countries, comprehensive implementation of Agenda 21, which developed out of the 1992 United Nations Conference on Environment and Development in Rio de Janeiro, and the MDGs remain vitally important (UNCED 1992; UN 2000). Development assistance should focus on the root causes of human insecurity including violent conflict, food insecurity, poverty, and environmental degradation and should promote good governance, sustainable environmental development, and global peace and cooperation.

Conclusion

Two of the most pressing issues facing humankind are human security and development. However, they are fundamentally linked because widespread, chronic, and crushing poverty and underdevelopment negatively impact human security; and threats to human security such as climate change, international crime, food insecurity, conflict, infectious diseases, bad governance, and human rights violations negatively impact development. Therefore, sustainable development objectives can be achieved when poverty reduction, global peace, and cooperation are promoted and threats to human security are eliminated or reduced.

The hope for human security lies in a balanced development approach based on poverty reduction, global peace, and cooperation, in which threats to both development and human security are eliminated. Effective conflict prevention, poverty reduction, and environmental security are not only development goals but also central to the challenges for human security, and will require concerted action and commitment from all stakeholders including the UN, NGOs, the media, and civil society. Moreover, gender equality, and participatory, accountable, and efficient governance can facilitate and harness activities toward the achievement of development objectives. New policies, new expertise, and more resources are required in the face of increasing terrorist attacks and accelerating environmental degradation to meet the challenges of global peace, human security, and sustainable development. Concerted effort by governments, civil society, and the diverse range of development partners would ensure the achievement of sustainable development and human security objectives.

References

Adelman, H. 2000. From refugees to forced migration: The UNHCR and human security. *International Migration Review* 35:17–32.

Agarwal, A., J. Kimondo, G. Morena and J. Tinker. 1981. *Water, sanitation, health—for all? Prospects for the international drinking water supply and sanitation decade: 1981–90.* London: IIED/Earthscan Publication.

Annan, Kofi. 2001. *Report to the UN General Assembly*. New York: United Nations.

Axworthy, Lloyd. 2001. Human security and global governance: Putting people first. *Global Governance* 7:19–23.

Barbier, E. 1989. *Economics, natural resource scarcity and development*, London: Earthscan.

Berkowitz, M., and Bock, P. 1968. National security. *International encyclopedia of the social science*, vol. 11. New York: Macmillan and The Free Press.

Blaikie, P. 1996. New knowledge and rural development: A review of views and practicalities. Paper presented at the 28th International Geographical Congress, The Hague, August 5–10.

Brinkerhoff, D. W., and A. A. Goldsmith, eds. 1990. *Institutional sustainability in agriculture and rural development: A global perspective*. New York: Praeger.

Brock, Lothar. 1991. Peace through parks: The environment on the peace research agenda. *Journal of Peace Research* 28 (4): 407–424.

Bush, George W. 2003. *State of the Union Address*. Office of the Press Secretary, The White House, Washington, DC, January 28.

Buzan, B. 1991. *Peoples, states and fears: An agenda for international security studies in the post-Cold War era*, 2d ed. Boulder, CO: Lynne Rienner Publishers.

Commission for Africa. 2005. *Our common interest: Report of the Commission for Africa*. Tony Blair (chair), March.

Commission on Human Security. 2003. *Human security now*. New York: Commission on Human Security.

Dabelko, G., S. Lonergan, and R. Matthew. 2000. *State of the art review of environmental security and co-operation*. Paris: OECD.

Department of Environment. 1988. *Our common future: A perspective by the UK on the report of the World Commission on Environment and Development*. London: HMSO.

Department for International Development (DFID). 1997. *Eliminating world poverty: A challenge for the 21st century—A summary*. London: DFID.

Department for International Development (DFID). 2002. *Poverty and environment*. March. London: DFID.

Dreze, J., and A. Sen. 1989. *Hunger and public action*. New York: Oxford University Press.

Environmental Resources Management (ERM). 2002. *Predicted impact of global climate change on poverty and sustainable achievement of the Millennium Development Goals*. London: Environmental Resources Management.

GECHS. 1999. *Global environmental change and human security: GECHS Science Plan*. IHDP: Bonn.

Gleditsch, N. P. 1997. Environmental conflict and the democratic peace. In *Conflict and the environment*, ed. N. P. Gleditsch, 91–106. Dordrecht: Kluver Academic Publishers.

Griffin, K. 1981. *Land concentration and world poverty*, 2d ed. New York: Holmes and Meier.

Harrison, Lawrence. 1985. *Underdevelopment is a state of mind: The American case*. Cambridge, MA: The Center for International Affairs, Harvard University.

Heinbecker, P. 1999. Human security. *Headlines* 56 (2): 4–9.

Huntington, S. 1968. *Political order and changing societies*. New Haven, CT: Yale University Press.

Hyden, G. 1998. Environmental awareness, conflict genesis and governance. In *Managing the globalized environment: Local strategies to secure livelihoods*, ed. Tina Riita Granfelt, 150–172. London: IT Publications.

International Task Force (ITF). 1985. *Tropical forests: A call for action*. Washington, DC: World Resources Institute.

King, Gary, and Christopher Murray. 2002. Rethinking human security. *Political Science Quarterly* 116 (4): 585–610.

Lansana, Fofana. 2000. Sierra Leoneans know the devastating consequences of conflict on their country's fledging development. *Developments, The International IFPRI Development Magazine* 12 (fourth quarter): 7–9.

Liechenko, R. M., and K. L. O'Brien. 2005. *Double exposure: Global environmental change in an era of globalization*. New York: Oxford University Press.

Lonergan, S. C., K. R. Gustavson, and B. Carter. 1999. *Developing an index of human security*. Global Environmental Change and Human Security Project, Research Report No. 2. University of Victoria, BC (see also *AVISO Bulletin* 6: 1–2).

Mannion, A. M. 1992. Sustainable development and biotechnology. *Environmental Conservation* 19:298–305.

Matthew, Richard. 2002. In defense of environment and security research. *ECSP Report* 8:109–124.

Marx, Karl. 1976. *Capital*, vol. 1. Harmondsworth: Penguin.

McNamara, Robert S. 1968. *The essence of security: Reflections in office*. New York: Harper and Row.

Mertus, Julie, N. Flowers, and D. Mallike. 1999. *Local action, global change: Learning about human rights of women and girls*. New York: UNIFEM.

Meyers, Norman. 1989. Environment and security. *Foreign Policy* 74 (2): 23–41.

National Institute for Public Health and the Environment (RIVM). 2002. Forum for globally-integrated environmental assessment modeling. United Nations University (UNU), Japan, and the National Institute for Public Health and the Environment (RIVM), the Netherlands. http://www.unu.edu/env/GLEAM/ (accessed March 4, 2009).

Olson, M. 1963. Rapid growth as a destabilizing force. *Journal of Economic History* 23 (1): 524–552.

O'Reilly, Siobhan. 1998. Conflict and development: Responding to the challenge. *World Vision* 6 (Spring): 3.

PRIO. 1999. *To cultivate peace: Agriculture in a way of conflict.* Report 1/99. Oslo: International Peace Research Institute (PRIO).

Redclift, M. 1987. *Sustainable development: Exploring the contradictions.* London: Methuen.

Redclift, M. 1992. The meaning of sustainable development. *Geoforum* 23:395–403.

Rees, W. E. 1990. The ecology of sustainable development. *The Ecologist* 20:18–23.

Renner, M. 1989. *National security: The economic and environmental dimensions.* Worldwatch Paper 89. Washington, DC: Worldwatch Institute.

Rodney, W. 1982. *How Europe underdeveloped Africa.* Enugu: Ikenga Publishers.

Rothschild, Emma. 1995. What is security? *Daedalus* 124 (3): 53–93.

Sanjeev, K., C. William, and D. Raad. 2003. From the environment and human security to sustainable development. *Journal of Human Development* 4 (2): 289–231.

Seers, D. 1977. The meaning of development. *International Development Review* 11:2–6.

Sen, Amartya K. 1999. *Development as freedom.* New York: Knopf, and Oxford: Oxford University Press.

Sen, Amartya K. 2000. Why human security? Paper presented at the International Symposium on Human Security, Tokyo, July 28.

Simon, David. 2003. Dilemmas of development and the environment in a globalizing world: Theory, policy and praxis. *Progress in Development Studies* 3 (1): 5–41.

Starr, J. R. 1991. Water wars. *Foreign Policy* 82:17–36.

Stewart, Francis. 2004. Development and security. Centre for Research on Inequality, Human Security and Ethnicity (ORISE), Working Paper 3. London: University of Oxford.

Streeten, P. 1981. *First things first: Meeting basic needs in developing countries.* New York: Oxford University Press.

Tadjbakhsh, S., and A. Chenoy. 2006. *Human security: Concepts and implications.* London: Routledge.

Thomas, C. 2000. *Global governance, development and human security.* London, Pluto.

Tolba, M. K. 1986. Desertification and economic survival. *Land Use Policy,* 6:260–268.

Ullman, R. H. 1983. Redefining security. *International Security* 8 (1): 129–153.

United Nations (UN). 1948. *United Nations Declaration of Human Rights*. New York: United Nations.

United Nations (UN). 2000. *United Nations Millennium Development Goals.* New York: United Nations.

United Nations Conference on Environment and Development (UNCED). 1992. *Agenda 21.* Rio de Janeiro.

United Nations Development Programme (UNDP). 1993. *Heading for change. UNDP annual report.* Oxford: Oxford University Press.

United Nations Development Programme (UNDP). 1994. *Human development report.* Oxford: Oxford University Press.

United Nations Development Programme (UNDP). 1999. *Human development report.* Oxford: Oxford University Press.

United Nations Development Programme (UNDP). 2003. *Re-conceptualizing governance.* Discussion Paper 2. New York: UNDP.

UNICEF. 1996. *The state of the world's children 1996.* Oxford: Oxford University Press.

Warwick, Donald. 1982. *Better pills: Population policies and their implementation in eight developing countries.* Cambridge, UK: Cambridge University Press.

Weaver, J., and Jameson, K. 1981. *Economic development: Competing paradigms.* Lanham, MD: University Press of America.

Westing, Arthur H. 1989. The environmental component of comprehensive security. *Bulletin of Peace Proposals* 20 (2): 129–134.

World Bank. 1984. *World development report.* New York: Oxford University Press.

World Bank. 2004. *Perspectives on development.* Washington, DC: World Bank.

World Commission on Environment and Development (WCED). 1987. *Our common future.* Oxford: Oxford University Press.

13

Free to Squander? Democracy and Sustainable Development, 1975–2000

Indra de Soysa, Jennifer Bailey, and Eric Neumayer

Sustainable development is a process of change in which the exploitation of resources, the direction of investments, the orientation of technological development...are all in harmony and enhance both current and future potential to meet human needs.
(WCED 1987, 46)

We all want to live in sustainable societies, but what form of government is most likely to achieve one? Must we sacrifice democracy in the interests of future generations? This chapter examines the relationship between sustainable economic development and democracy. Previous work has examined the link between democracy and the environment (Lafferty and Meadowcroft 1996; Midlarsky 2001; Reuveny and Li 2004), or democracy and the creation of wealth (economic growth) independently, yielding mixed results (Barro 1998; Gerring et al. 2005); and yet another strain of literature finds democracy to provide higher levels of investment in human capital (Baum and Lake 2003; Deacon 2003). This chapter builds on that work but goes beyond it. We argue that sustainable economic development must capture how society protects the future in terms of *how* it uses its resources (including clean air) and invests in people so that vulnerabilities are reduced (increasing well-being) and future generations are better secured against deprivation and shocks—through the building up of resilience (Adger 2006; Folke 2006). Achieving so-called sustainability requires conscious decisions about how best to augment total capital, including natural, human, and produced capital. To capture this broader range of impacts, we test several different measures of democracy on the World Bank's indicator of weak sustainability (genuine savings), which measures the rate at which investment in manufactured, human, and natural capital exceeds its depreciation on an annual basis (World Bank 2002).[1]

Our results are easy to summarize. Controlling for a range of economic, political, demographic, and social variables, we find that higher levels of political democracy are associated with higher genuine savings because democracies invest more in human capital, create less carbon monoxide (CO_2) damage, and extract fewer natural resources per unit of economic output produced for creating wealth, even if they accumulate manufactured capital at lower rates than do autocracies. We establish that democracies outperform autocracies, results that are consistent across several measures of democracy thought to be noninterchangeable despite high correlations among them (Casper and Tufis 2003). The rest of this chapter is structured as follows: we first discuss the nature of sustainability, and explain why we focus on the notion of weak sustainability. We then discuss how democracy might impact weak sustainability and present the findings of previous empirical studies. We proceed to the presentation of the methods, data, and results of our study, concluding with the discussion of our findings.

Weak Sustainability and Genuine Savings

The natural environment affects the well-being and sustenance of future generations (Dasgupta 2001). Yet a community that emphasizes the preservation of the environment over all other goals is unlikely to be economically, socially, or politically viable because economic deprivation, for example, reduces well-being, increases vulnerability, and often reduces the capacity of societies to deal with shocks. However, a society that ignores the indirect effects of economic and social development on the environment risks jeopardizing current and future well-being. Sustainability, thus, must be achieved along all these dimensions simultaneously. How can we capture the complexity of sustainability? One way forward lies through the concepts of weak and strong sustainability and the economic concept of capital.

Weak sustainability requires maintaining or raising the value of a country's total capital stock, including human, natural, and produced assets, assuming unlimited substitutability among these various forms of capital. *Strong sustainability* also calls for maintaining or raising the value of the overall capital stock, but differs in regarding natural capital as nonsubstitutable, either in its entirety or in certain forms of natural capital, the so-called *critical* natural capital. Strong sustainability therefore requires maintaining critical natural capital. We focus here on weak sustainability for three main reasons. First, it is a necessary condition for strong sustainability. In other words, achieving weak sustainability is a first step toward achieving strong sustainability. Second, there is little excuse for any country if it fails to achieve weak sustainability. Achieving strong sustainability is, however, much more difficult and arguably no country today succeeds in this. Third, on a pragmatic basis, there currently is no good indicator of how far countries are from achieving strong sustainability.

The genuine savings rate, or the genuine investment rate as Dasgupta (2001) prefers to call it, provides a measurement of the concept of weak sustainability. If resources are used recklessly for consumption with no regard at all for the environment—with high rates of pollution and exploitation of resources along with little investment in human capital—then a society clearly is on a weakly, unsustainable path of development. Looking at capital in this way captures the trade-offs policymakers face in the allocation of resources for the maintenance and enhancement of various forms of capital. Moreover, such an indicator is objectively measurable and allows one to gauge the performance of societies along these dimensions over time.

Genuine savings is net national savings (mainly net investment in manufactured capital) minus resource depletion (fuel, minerals, ores, metals, and forests), minus costs of CO_2 pollution, plus investment in human capital.[2] The measurement of investment in human capital is one reason this focus on genuine savings is particularly useful: while traditional national accounting treats government spending on education as consumption, the adjusted savings treats it as a proxy variable for investment in human capital. The overall importance of the genuine savings measurement, however, stems from its ability to capture changes in the total capital stock, which allows for trade-offs among the various forms and facilitates assessment as to whether these are beneficial or detrimental to future well-being. As Dasgupta (2001, 87) has written, "Genuine investment is the social worth of net changes in an economy's capital assets. It is a comprehensive notion, including as it does the social worth of net changes in manufactured and human capital, public knowledge, and natural capital. Thus, ensuring that social well-being is sustainable involves taking care that the economy's assets are managed well."

Thus, our primary research question is: what form of humanly devised system of governance (policymaking) allows better overall management of society's assets?

How Can Democracy Affect Weak Sustainability?

The use of genuine savings suggests that a broad array of socioeconomic policies is highly relevant to weak sustainability. There has, of course, been a good deal of research on the relationship between democracy and socioeconomic outcomes. These have clustered into two general areas. First, scholars have addressed the effect of democracy on public expenditures, investment in manufactured and human capital, and economic development (Baum and Lake 2003; Gerring et al. 2005; Krieckhaus 2004). The second area of research is the direct effect of democracy on the environment and patterns of resource extraction (Midlarsky 1995; Reuveny and Li 2004). Our study is the first to use an indicator that looks in an integrated approach at the various trade-offs inherent in policymaking along both of these rather broad dimensions.

The study of the effects of democracy on economic performance and human welfare has a long and highly political history. The first strand of research focused on the relationship between regime type and development, the latter usually operationalized as economic growth. It focused on public expenditures, investment in manufactured and human capital, and per capita income (Sirowy and Inkeles 1991). An early consensus grew around the idea that low-income countries faced the "cruel dilemma" of having to choose between democracy and development. Democracy was associated with higher levels of development, but as an effect rather than a cause (Lipset 1959, 1993). It might be desirable over the long run, but introducing it into countries with low income levels resulted in too many popular demands upon weak institutions, creating political instability that in turn deterred development (Huntington 1968). Meanwhile, the rapid growth of authoritarian East Asian countries contrasted sharply with democratic "failures" in many parts of the globe. The conclusion was that it was better to let development bring democracy in its train (Barro 1998).

The end of the Cold War, the "rush to freedom," and the general discrediting of state-led development schemes prompted a fresher, more positive focus on democracy's economic impact. This research was also driven by interest in endogenous growth theory in economics, and interest in new institutionalism in several fields of the social sciences. Apparently, good economic outcomes were determined by political institutions as much as by market forces (Barro 1998; Romer 1986). Others argued that democracies promote efficiency because they create political stability for investors and produce higher-quality entrepreneurial talent, thereby promoting technological development (Olson 1993). Communist dictatorships might have sported very high growth rates in the post-war years, but they were ultimately unsustainable because they were inefficient at producing high-quality goods and sustaining high levels of wealth over time. Moreover, the wealth that had been created often came at the expense of environmental quality, as many parts of the old USSR attest to. It may also have come at the expense of social capital. In short, planned economies that pushed growth at the expense of both the environment and consumer preferences were unstable and unsustainable over the long run.

The new round of empirical analyses on the effects of regime type on growth yielded mixed results, but the weight of the evidence suggests that democracy has no direct relationship with growth.[3] Democracy may perhaps influence growth only indirectly, via higher rates of accumulation of human capital (Lake and Baum 2001). There is little evidence thus far for the argument that democracy is superior at creating wealth: in fact, once human capital is accounted for, democracy is associated negatively with growth (Barro 1996). China, on average, does much better than India despite the recent surge in India's growth rates, and Vietnam better than Bangladesh. Still, autocracies do seem to have a higher variability in their growth rates than democracies. Well-run autocracies do better than democracies, but poorly run autocracies also do much worse (Almeida and Ferreira 2002).

Those who see democracy conflicting with economic development argue that democracies succumb to populist tendencies to redistribute wealth, which may reduce investment and destroy entrepreneurial talent (de Schweinitz 1964; Haggard 1990; Keech 1995). Democracy, then, can lead to profligate spending that increases inflation and reduces savings and investment, thereby affecting growth and sustainability (Mueller and Stratmann 2003).[4] Moreover, democratic governments might run high deficits because organized labor will lobby for higher wages at the same time as demand for the provision of public goods in the general population rises. In step with this line of thinking, several scholars show that democracies have larger governments (Boix 2001). High demand for spending and lower ability to collect taxes coupled with low growth could mean a vicious circle leading to unsustainable economic development.[5] Profligate spending patterns may come with high rent seeking and special-interest politics. Such politics leads to larger government spending that may hamper growth and efficient investment. More directly relevant to our question of what form of policymaking allows better overall management of society's assets, such policies may easily result in unsustainable use of resources and environmental damage. In short, democracies may squander their future by succumbing to pressures for present consumption. Ironically, such policies are ultimately counterproductive, because the longer-term survival of a democracy seems to depend on achieving reasonable rates of sustained economic growth (Przeworski et al. 2000).

Contrarily, others argue that autocratic rule has liabilities of its own, including strong incentives to discount the future (to loot the state); a lack of the rule of law that stifles investment; and tendencies to promote population growth, incur public debt, exercise poor fiscal management, and stifle innovation (Acemoglu and Robinson 2006; Olson 1993; Wittman 1995). This work challenges the view that autocracies are more efficient at creating and managing wealth.

Despite the heavy focus on growth, no study to date has addressed the degree to which democracies are able to trade off possible profligate patterns of spending with sustainable allocation of resources over the longer run. While most scholars focus on regime type and the size of the public sector itself, what really matters is how governments spend their money. How do spending patterns look from the vantage point of weak sustainability? Some government expenditures, such as a good deal of military expenditures, or private jets for ministers, or "White Elephant" infrastructure projects are clearly wasteful. However, government expenditures on education are not. In short, the existing empirical evidence on how democracies and autocracies may promote weak sustainability via capital investment and public expenditures does not clearly focus on the trade-offs inherent in the weak sustainability concept.

The second broad area of research focuses on democracy's effects on the environment and ecosystems upon which future welfare depends, as well as on the rate of exploitation of natural resources. Here the arguments made are similar to those made with respect to economic growth. Some have suggested that democracies are likely to sacrifice society's long-term welfare to short-term gains for politically powerful individuals and groups, and that democracies fail to adopt necessary but painful policies of restructuring, pursuing strategies based on electoral considerations, and not coherent policy. They also suggest that democracy is often "captured" by rapacious "capitalists," whose search for profits is granted priority over communitarian interests. Even democracies with strong left-wing governments may be unsympathetic to measures of environmental protection because of electoral pressures to create growth and employment.[6] Moreover, where environmental factors are in most need of attention, democracy may work less than perfectly, so that optimism about participatory environmental protection and natural resource management might be misplaced (Walker 1999).

But it is more common today to argue the opposite. Payne (1995) summarizes the most commonly made arguments as to why democracy benefits the environment: (1) democracy creates a political climate in which information can flow freely and citizens can act on that information to organize and press demands upon government; (2) democratic government is responsive to popular demands; (3) democratic governments are better able to implement innovative policies and draw lessons from successes and failures; (4) democratic governments are more likely to participate in international cooperative ventures to solve global problems, including environmental problems; and (5) democracies are often market-based economic systems and these can be harnessed to provide environmental as well as economic benefits. Note that according to these lines of reasoning, popular demand has a beneficial effect and the dispersion of power acts as a check that is absent in autocratic regimes.

The empirical evidence for a direct impact of democracy on the environment is mixed. Gleditsch and Sverdrup (2002) find that democracy has a positive effect on the environment, although its positive effect on development results in environmental damage that sometimes outweighs its beneficial effects. Democracy's positive effect on the environment comes from the mobilization of counter forces that lobby to lessen environmental problems to some extent. Congleton (1992) finds that democracies produce more methane and more chlorofluorocarbons (CFCs) than their less liberal and/or authoritarian counterparts (although less per unit of income), but are more willing to regulate at home as well as to support global efforts to regulate. Neumayer (2002) finds that democracies are more likely to sign on to stronger international environmental commitment than nondemocracies.

Studies that focus more exclusively on indicators for pollution and environmental quality also report mixed findings. Some find that democracies are associated with reductions in CFC emissions between 1986 and

1989, but that they also have higher absolute levels of CFC emissions (Murdoch, Sandler, and Sargent 1997). Others find that democracies have lower CO_2 emissions per capita, lower nitric oxide $(NO)_x$ emissions per capita, less organic pollution in water, lower deforestation rates, and less land degradation (Li and Reuveny 2004). Deacon (2003) reports that democracies tend to reduce lead in gasoline at faster rates than autocracies. They conclude that democracy reduces the extent of human activities that directly degrade the environment. Yet Midlarsky (1995, 358) found "no uniform relationship between democracy and the environment." For three indicators of environmental quality (deforestation, CO_2 emissions, and soil erosion by water), he found significant negative relationships between democracy and environmental quality, although democracies seem to protect a higher percentage of their land area (Midlarsky 2001).

Another relevant line of research explores the so-called "resource curse" (Hamilton, Atkinson, and Pearce 2003). Some suggest that autocracies have incentives to discount the future since an autocrat has very few checks against squandering the patrimony of future generations and society's wealth. Here scholars argue that corrupt, elitist, and nonaccountable governments extract natural resources rapaciously and channel resource rents into nonproductive, wasteful consumption expenditures as well as private savings of the small ruling elite in foreign bank accounts (Auty 2001). Democratic governments, on the other hand, have to spread the benefits from resource extraction more evenly across society and need to show that they have put these rents to productive use for the social good, or be punished at the ballot box. Some argue that democracies are generally less prone to corruption (Sandholtz and Koetzle 2000), while corruption may explain why resource-wealthy states squander their wealth (Dietz, Neumayer, and de Soysa 2007). Of course, causality may run in both directions, since resource abundance hinders the development of a civil society and democratic forms of governance (Jensen and Wantchekon 2004; Ross 2001). Even so, natural resource abundance does not necessarily imply nondemocratic governance, as Bolivia, Botswana, Chile, Ecuador, Papua New Guinea, Trinidad and Tobago, Venezuela, and other examples attest. However, given the question at hand, we control for resource wealth in order to compute the independent effect of regime type on sustainability—in other words, the net effect of democracy holding constant the independent effect of resource wealth.

How to Measure Weak Sustainability

As the seminal publication on sustainable development by the WCED quoted at the beginning of this chapter suggests, weak sustainability is a process that depends on the nature of investments that a society chooses to make toward the future. The World Bank tries to capture this dimension with the genuine savings rate. It is calculated as follows:

GS = (investment in manufactured capital − net foreign borrowing
    + net official transfers − depreciation of manufactured capital
    + current education expenditures − net depreciation of natural
    capital and cost of atmospheric pollution) / gross national income
    (GNI)

Note that based on this calculation, investment in manufactured capital minus foreign borrowing plus net official transfers minus depreciation of manufactured capital is equal to net national savings. While the traditional national accounting treats government spending on education as consumption, the genuine savings approach treats it as investment. This is regarded as a first approximation to the full value of human capital investment, which is difficult to measure precisely. Capturing human capital investment is critical because it has a major impact on behavior in general and economic activity in particular. A more educated population engages in economic activities that draw less directly on natural resources and the environment, and their demands upon government may also change in a post-materialist direction.

Depreciation of natural capital covers nonrenewable resource extraction such as fossil fuels and minerals as well as forestry and is measured as price minus average cost times the amount of resources extracted. The cost of atmospheric pollution is approximated by the damage caused by carbon dioxide emissions. It is apparent then, from the preceding formula, that negative genuine savings could be driven by high consumption (i.e., low investment in manufactured capital), high resource depletion, and high pollution, while investment in education remains low, a clearly profligate, unsustainable path for a society. On the other hand, higher genuine savings are achieved via investment in manufactured capital with relatively lower depletion of the resource base, higher investment in human capital, and less damage to the environment. Quite simply, then, savings of all forms of capital is the essence of weak sustainability.

The development of the genuine savings rate is the culmination of efforts over many years to capture a broader concept of development while also making cross-country and over-time comparisons possible and meaningful. Economists once viewed the growth of gross domestic product (GDP) as the yardstick of development. Gross domestic product and the investment required for the growth of output were thought of as involving merely manufactured capital (and sometimes human capital). But GDP statistics did not account for the degradation of natural capital in the process of economic activity. Green accounting processes began as an important corrective, in an attempt to make GDP reflect the degradation of the environment and the depletion of natural resources as a result of economic production. In reaction to this, the World Bank embarked on a project to estimate the "Wealth of Nations," and included manufactured, human, and natural capital of countries as a first step toward monitoring the progress of nations in terms of sustainability (World Bank 1997). The changes in the redefined estimates of wealth, therefore, indicate whether the development trajectory of any given country is weakly unsustainable over time. Significantly, however, these data also show that the most important component of most nations' capital stocks is human capital (unfortunately, social capital is left out of the calculations because of the complex issues surrounding its measurability).

An added advantage of the genuine savings rate is that the data are now available for a large number of countries spanning over twenty-five years. Here, genuine savings data are taken from the World Bank's (2002) World Development Indicators (WDI) CD-ROM, where they are called "net adjusted savings." We use this source, but we drop Angola and Sudan from the sample since their data seem to be reported with error as they are often below 100 percent and are inconsistent with other data published at the World Bank's website. In addition, the 1991 value for Kuwait was set to missing as it was unusually low and clearly affected by the Iraq occupation and the ensuing Second Gulf War.

Methods and Data

This study employs pooled time-series cross-section (TSCS) data to gauge the effect of democracy on the genuine savings rate and each of the components of this composite measure. Given our arguments about the importance of gauging democracy's effects on a composite indicator that captures some sense of the trade-offs implicit in policymaking, we focus primarily on the composite genuine savings rate, but also test each of the genuine savings rate components. We think it is useful to know via which of the four components democracy and its institutional features affect sustainability. While ideally we should model each component with relevant controls for each, we keep the models the same for each component using the same control variables, such as when the overall genuine savings rate is the dependent variable. This tactic is not entirely satisfactory since each of the components should be modeled separately. We hope to pursue this further in future research.

The data allow up to 129 countries to be tested with all controls included. We first discuss the control variables in the model and then our operationalization of regime type and institutional design. There are no clear models to guide the determinants of genuine savings. We control for the following factors because of their theoretical connection with our measures of democracy, or their direct effects on the dependent variable. In general, the models account for important factors predicting the net national savings rate, in order to control as fully as possible, but parsimoniously, for its determinants.[7] Note that fiscal policy variables such as government expenditures, tax revenues, and so on, cannot be included in the estimations as explanatory variables since they form part of genuine savings and their inclusion would therefore effectively construct a partial identity between the left and right sides of the equation.

The models control for level of per capita income since richer countries have higher savings rates and supposedly exhibit better environmental standards on several dimensions. We use gross national income (GNI) per capita in purchasing power parity. All the data are obtained from the World Bank (2002) unless noted otherwise.[8] We also include a squared income term to allow for a diminishing effect of per capita income on weak sustainability.[9] We control for the year-to-year change in per capita income levels (economic growth), since it is often thought that higher rates of growth require more intensive use of environmental resources, but it is also often found to be associated with the rate of investment in manufactured capital. However, higher growth may enable increases in other forms of capital, such as manufactured and human capital that reduce the direct dependence of people on natural resources.

The level of democracy, savings rates, and environmental stress can be affected by demographic factors (Dahl and Tufte 1974; MEA 2003).[10]

Thus, population size (total population), population density (people per square kilometer), and the share of urban population in total population are included in the models. Urbanization has important implications for levels of pollution and investment in manufactured capital because it is argued that consumption rises with rising urbanization. Democracy also relates to trade openness (Li and Reuveny 2003). Many argue that democracy increases openness (Milner 1999). Others show that trade openness relates positively with genuine savings (de Soysa and Neumayer 2005). But trade openness is also related to higher government spending on public goods (Garrett 1999; Rodrik 1996). We control for the effects of trade dependence, using simply the sum of imports and exports divided by GDP.

The models include the degree to which countries are dependent on natural resource exports because resource depletion will be higher among these countries. Several early studies on the topic indicate a strong relationship between resource exports and lower genuine savings. Apparently, high resource dependence often leads to low growth, lower than normal investment in human capital, and other maladies that hamper sustainability—the familiar "resource curse" hypothesis (Atkinson and Hamilton 2003). We use a discrete variable that takes the value of one if exports of petroleum are greater than 30 percent of GDP as our control variable.[11] This measure is obtained from an independent source (Easterly and Sewadeh 2001). All these variables are lagged one year to mitigate simultaneity bias and some are logged to mitigate the influence of extreme values.

Finally, we control variables for experience with armed conflict, which presumably influences savings rates and the degree to which extractive activity, corruption, and accumulation of manufactured capital proceeds. We compute a count of peace years since 1946 with the help of the binary time-series-cross-section (BTSCS) method of Beck, Katz, and Tucker (1998) utilizing the Uppsala-PRIO civil war data that uses a threshold of twenty-five or more battle deaths to be counted as war (Gleditsch et al. 2002). We also add the incidence of civil war to account for ongoing civil war, again taken from the Uppsala-PRIO data. The baseline model is then as follows:

$$
\begin{aligned}
GS = {} & \beta_0 + \beta_1 \times \text{income} + \beta_2 \times \text{income}^2 + \beta_3 \times \text{growth} + \beta_4 \\
& \times \text{population} + \beta_5 \times \text{trade} + \beta_6 \times \text{density} + \beta_7 \times \text{urbanization} \\
& + \beta_8 \times \text{fuel exports} + \beta_9 \times \text{mineral exports} + \beta_{10} \times \text{civil war} \\
& + \beta_{11} \times \text{peace years} + \beta_{12} \times \text{year} \ldots
\end{aligned}
$$

To this baseline model containing twelve control variables, we add our regime type and institutional variables selectively. What democracy is and how exactly to measure it are thorny questions (Bollen and Paxton 2000; Gurr and Jaggers 1995). The most popular databases capture somewhat different dimensions of democracy and use more or less objective indicators (Henisz 2000; Vanhanen 2000).[12] The Polity data set is the most frequently used, and contains indicators for the constraints upon the chief executive, the openness and competitiveness of executive recruitment, and the competitiveness of political competition (Marshall and Jaggers 2002, 13). The Freedom House (2004) data constitute the only dataset that focuses exclusively and very directly on political and civil liberties, but it is widely criticized as being highly subjective. In addition, Bollen and Paxton (2000) show that the coding of democracy is systematically biased.[13] Vanhanen's (2000) measure captures Robert Dahl's (2000) conceptualization of democracy as "Polyarchy," which is an equally weighted index of the level of electoral participation and degree of party competition at elections. Vanhanen's data are the only fully objective measures, based as they are on voting turnout and the narrowness of electoral victory, or competition, between parties for control of the government (Vanhanen 2000).[14] Whatever the conceptualization of democracy, the measures currently in use are very highly correlated with each other. Some scholars have warned, however, that even though measures of democracy differently arrived at correlate well, they are not interchangeable (Casper and Tufis 2003). We adopt their advice and follow a strategy of testing several accepted measures that stress one or another theoretical aspect of democracy.

For our purposes, the democracy measure should capture adequately dimensions that reflect such aspects as representation and accountability, which matter for the various issues over sustainability previously discussed. Secondarily, the measure should reflect normative aspects, such as the degree to which people enjoy political and civil rights. People are either free to squander or save; thus, we employ the Polity data as our primary measure of democracy, but we also test Polyarchy (the only measure of democracy that is coded on the basis of actual electoral data), and Freedom House's civil and political liberties index. In short, Polity gauges the nature of the election of government and constraints on executive power, Polyarchy measures objective levels of participation and competition, and Freedom House's data capture the degree of political rights and civil liberties.

The Polity IV (version 2) dataset codes five institutional dimensions of democracy. This version of the data corrects in weighted form the interregnum years that were previously coded as missing. The Polity measure gauges democracy and autocracy along six dimensions:

1. institutional measures regarding transfer of executive power
2. extent to which executive power is subject to competitive elections
3. extent of opportunities for non-elites to gain executive power
4. de facto constraints on the executive
5. extent of opportunity for political expression
6. extent to which non-elites have access to institutional structures for political expression.

We follow the norm by subtracting the autocracy value from the democracy value, adding 11 to create an overall scale of democracy ranging from 1 to 21. Since we are interested in all increases of democracy from a previous level, we utilize the entire scale, but we also test a dummy variable for regime type by assigning the value 1 if democracy ranges from 16 to 21, and 0 if the values are between 1 and 15 (autocracy) to accommodate those who argue that a regime is either democratic or not (Przeworski et al. 2000). This variable correlates almost perfectly ($r = 0.96$) with others who have used the Polity data in a dichotomous manner (Fearon and Laitin 2003). Polyarchy is the degree of competition, derived as 100 minus the share of the largest winning party's vote times the percentage share of votes cast relative to total population. In other words, Polyarchy captures the narrowness of victory by the largest winning party in any general election times the number of people participating in deciding (see Vanhanen 2000 for details). Democracy, thus, is a function of both dimensions. For the Freedom House measure, we use the sum of scores of both dimensions of the Freedom House data—political rights and civil liberties—and invert the scores so that the index of rights stretches from 2 (least free) to 14 (most free).[15]

The analysis of TSCS data generally poses several problems in the estimating process. TSCS models often suffer from serially correlated errors as well as heteroskedasticity. The well-known Parks method based on the feasible generalized least squares method (FGLS), which is close to the ordinary least squares (OLS) method, is discredited for underestimating the true variability of the parameter estimates, which some report to be as high as 200 percent (Beck and Katz 1995). They propose "panel corrected standard errors" (PCSE) as an alternative procedure. We use this method, assuming a first-order autoregressive process (AR1) process to deal with autocorrelation. The Rho coefficient computed in the AR1 process accounts for serially correlated errors in the model (Stata 2003).

Results

Table 13.1 reports the PCSE regression results of regime type on the genuine savings rate for each of the indicators of democracy. The first column reports results with the continuous Polity index. As seen there, democracy has a positive and statistically significant effect on genuine savings, net of the control variables. A one-point increase in the Polity scale increases genuine savings by 0.16 points, which means a shift from a perfect autocracy of value 1 on the index to a perfect democracy of value 21 would mean an increase of 3.6 points of the genuine savings rate. Since the mean genuine savings score is 6.6, this would effectively mean that moving from strict autocracy to perfect democracy increases average genuine savings by roughly 48 percent. For the dummy variable constructed from the Polity index in column 2, moving from an autocracy to a democracy increases the genuine savings rate by 1.8 points, or 27 percent of the average genuine savings rate over the twenty-five year period. In column 3, we see that an increase of 1 percent in the combined level of participation and competition increases the genuine savings rate by .07 points. Raising the polyarchy score from its minimum to its maximum level increases the genuine savings rate by 3.3 points. For the remaining measure of democracy, Freedom House's civil and political liberties index, a one-point increase raises the genuine savings rate by 0.20 points and a move from minimum to maximum by 2.4 points.

The control variables largely test in accordance with theoretical expectations. Higher per capita income raises genuine savings, but at a diminishing rate. Economic growth is not a statistically significant determinant. Greater trade openness and a larger population size and density are associated with higher genuine savings, whereas the opposite is the case for major oil exporters and the urbanization rate. Civil war experience has a negative effect on the genuine savings rate. A longer period of peace years raises the genuine savings rate. These results are plausible and consistent with theoretical expectations.

We now turn to Polity's effects on each of the components of genuine savings, namely net national savings (mainly net investment in manufactured capital), education expenditures, carbon dioxide damage caused, and resource depletion, all relative to a country's GNI.[16] Table 13.2,

Table 13.1
PCSE regressions of regime type on the genuine savings rate, 1975–2000

	(1)	(2)	(3)	(4)
Polity	0.16***			
	(0.04)			
Polity_dummy		1.77***		
		(0.57)		
Polyarchy			0.07**	
			(0.03)	
Freedom House				0.20**
				(0.10)
Ln gni/pc	12.62***	12.78***	13.80***	12.69***
	(4.78)	(4.79)	(4.91)	(4.83)
(Ln gni/pc)^2	−0.48*	−0.48*	−0.53*	−0.46
	(0.29)	(0.29)	(0.30)	(0.29)
Econ. growth	0.02	0.02	0.02	0.00
	(0.03)	(0.03)	(0.03)	(0.03)
Urban pop.%	−0.19***	−0.19***	−0.21***	−0.20***
	(0.03)	(0.03)	(0.03)	(0.03)
Ln trade/gdp	2.30***	2.31***	2.30***	2.31***
	(0.68)	(0.68)	(0.67)	(0.67)
Ln pop.size	0.57**	0.61**	0.66**	0.65**
	(0.28)	(0.28)	(0.27)	(0.28)
Ln pop.density	1.60***	1.61***	1.50***	1.54***
	(0.24)	(0.25)	(0.25)	(0.25)
Oil dummy	−9.46***	−9.67***	−9.45***	−9.52***
	(1.45)	(1.48)	(1.45)	(1.46)
Civil war	−0.93*	−0.90*	−0.91*	−0.76
	(0.49)	(0.49)	(0.50)	(0.50)
Peace years	0.07***	0.07***	0.07***	0.07***
	(0.02)	(0.02)	(0.02)	(0.02)
Year	−0.29***	−0.28***	−0.29***	−0.28***
	(0.07)	(0.07)	(0.07)	(0.07)
Constant	490.33***	482.37***	494.15***	478.22***
	(143.84)	(142.54)	(143.18)	(144.30)
Observations	2564	2564	2563	2572
No. countries	129	129	129	129

Absolute standard errors in parentheses. *significant at 10 percent; **significant at 5 percent; ***significant at 1 percent.

Table 13.2
PCSE regressions on components of genuine savings, 1975–2000 (Polity)

	(1)	(2)	(3)	(4)
	Nns/gni	Educ/gni	CO$_2$dam/gni	Res.depl/gni
Polity	−0.10***	0.01**	−0.00**	−0.20***
	(0.04)	(0.00)	(0.00)	(0.04)
Ln gni/pc	19.06***	0.00	2.00***	3.98
	(4.05)	(0.59)	(0.34)	(3.40)
(Ln gni/pc)^2	−0.94***	0.03	−0.13***	−0.29
	(0.24)	(0.03)	(0.02)	(0.21)
Econ. growth	0.03	−0.00	−0.00	0.01
	(0.03)	(0.00)	(0.00)	(0.02)
Urban pop.%	−0.11***	0.01	0.01***	0.09**
	(0.02)	(0.00)	(0.00)	(0.04)
Ln trade/gdp	3.68***	0.26***	0.10*	1.09*
	(0.64)	(0.08)	(0.06)	(0.58)
Ln pop.size	1.40***	−0.12***	0.09***	0.46*
	(0.27)	(0.04)	(0.03)	(0.26)
Ln pop. density	0.72***	−0.27***	0.00	−1.26***
	(0.23)	(0.05)	(0.02)	(0.31)
Oil dummy	4.16***	−0.18**	0.12***	9.56***
	(1.11)	(0.07)	(0.04)	(1.85)
Civil war	−0.85**	0.02	−0.01	0.38
	(0.42)	(0.05)	(0.02)	(0.37)
Peace years	0.03**	0.00	−0.00**	−0.03*
	(0.02)	(0.00)	(0.00)	(0.02)
Year	−0.32***	−0.01	0.02***	−0.05
	(0.06)	(0.01)	(0.00)	(0.10)
Constant	522.71***	24.54	−55.79***	83.38
	(120.39)	(15.18)	(10.48)	(194.94)
Observations	2564	2564	2564	2564
No. countries	129	129	129	129

Absolute standard errors in parentheses. *significant at 10 percent; **significant at 5 percent; ***significant at 1 percent.

column 1, shows that increasing democracy decreases the net national savings rate. Democracies seem to consume more and invest less in manufactured capital than autocracies. This result is also true for Polyarchy, and Freedom House's political and civil liberties index (see tables 13.3 and 13.4).

Table 13.2, column 2, reveals, however, that democracies as measured by Polity invest more in human capital, measured as education spending. This result holds for the other two indicators of democracy as well. Democracy is also good news for those concerned about CO_2 pollution (see column 3). While the Polity measure and Freedom House are associated with less CO_2 emissions per economic unit produced, the Polyarchy measure has the same negative coefficient, but is not statistically significant. Our results support others who show that democracy reduces atmospheric pollution, net of the level of income (Reuveny and Li 2004). In table 13.2, column 4, Polity democracy is negatively related to resource depletion, and this result is net of the major oil export dummy variable. This result too is common to all the indicators of democracy (table 13.3, column 4; table 13.4, column 4). It seems that democratic politics might be a way to solve problems of resource abuse, but democracy might be hard to achieve given the difficulties of democratization within countries abundant in natural resources, which are also often plagued by political instabilities and civil war (de Soysa 2002; Ross 2004).

We conducted several tests of sensitivity and checks for robustness. We add two variables strongly related to savings, but doing so reduces the sample of countries drastically. These variables are identified in the general savings literature as additional determinants of savings. First, we enter a term for the total money supply (M2), and second, enter the age dependency ratio. Controlling for both variables, which are statistically significant in the models, the reported effects of democracy remain unaffected. We next test only a subsample consisting of developing countries by dropping twenty-one OECD countries from the complete sample (Western Europe, North America, Japan, Australia, and New Zealand). The basic results on democracy remained unchanged. This suggests that the results are quite robust to sample size and specification.

Conclusion

Democracy is ostensibly triumphant, but its benefits to society are questioned on many grounds (Shapiro and Hacker-Cordón 2002). In partic-

Table 13.3
PCSE regressions on components of genuine savings, 1975–2000 (Polyarchy)

	(1)	(2)	(3)	(4)
	Nns/gni	Educ/gni	CO_2dam/gni	Res.depl/gni
Polyarchy	−0.11***	0.01**	−0.00	−0.13***
	(0.03)	(0.00)	(0.00)	(0.03)
Ln gni/pc	16.83***	0.04	1.98***	1.58
	(4.06)	(0.60)	(0.34)	(3.26)
(Ln gni/pc)^2	−0.76***	0.03	−0.13***	−0.12
	(0.24)	(0.04)	(0.02)	(0.20)
Econ. growth	0.03	−0.00	−0.00	0.01
	(0.03)	(0.00)	(0.00)	(0.02)
Urban pop.%	−0.12***	0.00	0.01***	0.10***
	(0.02)	(0.00)	(0.00)	(0.04)
Ln trade/gdp	3.78***	0.27***	0.10*	1.24**
	(0.65)	(0.08)	(0.06)	(0.58)
Ln pop. size	1.48***	−0.11***	0.09***	0.48*
	(0.27)	(0.04)	(0.03)	(0.25)
Ln pop. density	0.65***	−0.28***	−0.01	−1.24***
	(0.23)	(0.05)	(0.02)	(0.30)
Oil dummy	4.07***	−0.18**	0.13***	9.96***
	(1.09)	(0.07)	(0.05)	(1.87)
Civil war	−0.81*	0.03	−0.01	0.38
	(0.42)	(0.05)	(0.02)	(0.38)
Peace years	0.04**	0.00	−0.00**	−0.03*
	(0.02)	(0.00)	(0.00)	(0.02)
Year	−0.34***	−0.01	0.02***	−0.07
	(0.06)	(0.01)	(0.00)	(0.09)
Constant	564.12***	25.68*	−54.16***	122.57
	(120.37)	(15.36)	(10.10)	(183.37)
Observations	2563	2563	2563	2563
No. countries	129	129	129	129

Absolute standard errors in parentheses. *significant at 10 percent; **significant at 5 percent; ***significant at 1 percent.

Table 13.4
PCSE regressions on components of genuine savings, 1975–2000 (Freedom House)

	(1)	(2)	(3)	(4)
	Nns/gni	Educ/gni	CO_2dam/gni	Res.depl/gni
Freedom House	−0.30***	0.02**	−0.01***	−0.35***
	(0.08)	(0.01)	(0.00)	(0.10)
Ln gni/pc	18.48***	−0.07	2.00***	3.72
	(4.10)	(0.59)	(0.34)	(3.41)
(Ln gni/pc)^2	−0.87***	0.04	−0.13***	−0.26
	(0.24)	(0.03)	(0.02)	(0.21)
Econ. growth	0.01	−0.00	−0.00	0.01
	(0.03)	(0.00)	(0.00)	(0.02)
Urban pop.%	−0.13***	0.00	0.01***	0.09**
	(0.02)	(0.00)	(0.00)	(0.04)
Ln trade/gdp	3.68***	0.29***	0.10*	1.16**
	(0.65)	(0.08)	(0.06)	(0.58)
Ln pop.size	1.43***	−0.10***	0.09***	0.45*
	(0.27)	(0.04)	(0.03)	(0.26)
Ln pop.density	0.64***	−0.28***	−0.00	−1.29***
	(0.23)	(0.04)	(0.02)	(0.32)
Oil dummy	4.14***	−0.18**	0.13***	9.81***
	(1.13)	(0.07)	(0.04)	(1.88)
Civil war	−0.69*	0.02	−0.01	0.37
	(0.41)	(0.05)	(0.02)	(0.37)
Peace years	0.05***	0.00	−0.00**	−0.02
	(0.02)	(0.00)	(0.00)	(0.02)
Year	−0.35***	−0.01	0.02***	−0.08
	(0.06)	(0.01)	(0.00)	(0.09)
Constant	590.67***	24.70*	−53.31***	148.21
	(122.69)	(14.66)	(10.20)	(185.99)
Observations	2572	2572	2572	2572
No. countries	129	129	129	129

Absolute standard errors in parentheses. *significant at 10 percent; **significant at 5 percent; ***significant at 1 percent.

ular, there is little evidence that it aids economic development, a factor vital for underwriting the consolidation of recent democratic gains (Barro 1998; Mueller and Stratmann 2003). Others, however, show how democracy enhances future growth indirectly through human capital investment (Lake and Baum 2001). The concept of weak sustainability that calls for maintaining or increasing the total wealth of a society moderates how one views immediate economic benefit, so that raising incomes is balanced with intergenerational equity and the quality of growth (Thomas et al. 2000).

How then does democracy fare when one compares its performance over time for making the trade-offs required for raising current well-being without harming the future? To answer this question, we use the World Bank's measure of genuine savings, which measures the rate of net investment in all forms of capital, including human and natural capital. Democracies are more weakly sustainable than autocracies, even though they invest less in manufactured capital. It seems that democracies spend more on human capital accumulation, create less CO_2 damage, and deplete fewer resources per unit of economic output produced in the creation of wealth. Together these effects are strong enough to compensate for democracy's negative effect on investment in manufactured capital such that democracies have higher overall genuine savings rates than autocracies. Our results thus confirm and yet qualify the effect of democracy found in existing studies. Yes, democracies spend more than autocracies and thus have less investment in manufactured capital. However, at the same time, it matters what public money is spent on and democracies spend more to build up human capital by spending higher levels on education. Democracies might not show better economic performance in the short term as measured by growth rates, but are likely be more protective of the long-term welfare of society. Our main finding that democracy benefits weak sustainability is robust for a variety of specifications and holds for a subsample consisting only of developing countries. In conclusion, we find that democratic policymaking is associated with better prospects for sustainable economic development. Our results, like those of others, may suggest that the general pessimism toward the economic performance of democracies might be highly premature, as others too have suggested (Lake and Baum 2001). Future research should aspire to test the effect of regime type on stronger forms of sustainability to see whether the positive effect of democracy carries over.

Appendix

Table 13A.1
Summary statistics

	N	Mean	Std. deviation	Min.	Max.
Genuine savings	2572	6.6	12.3	−61.4	50.4
Polity	2564	12.5	7.5	1	21
Polyarchy	2563	13.2	13.4	0	47.1
Freedom House	2572	8.5	3.9	2	14
Income (log)	2572	8.0	1.1	5.4	10.4
Economic growth	2572	1.2	5.3	−43.7	35.5
Pop. urban	2572	50.1	24.2	4	100
Trade (log)	2572	4.1	0.6	1.8	6.1
Population (log)	2572	16.1	1.5	12.8	20.9
Pop. density (log)	2572	3.8	1.4	0.3	8.8
Oil export dummy	2572	0.1	0.4	0	1
Civil war	2572	0.2	0.4	0	1
Peace years	2572	20	16.5	0	54

Correlation matrix of variables

	1	2	3	4	5	6	7	8	9	10	11	12
(1) Gen. saving												
(2) Polity	0.29											
(3) Polyarchy	0.29	0.83										
(4) Freedom House	0.30	0.90	0.84									
(5) Income	0.26	0.58	0.70	0.65								
(6) Growth	0.25	0.10	0.11	0.11	0.09							
(7) Pop. urban	0.04	0.45	0.59	0.53	0.82	0.02						
(8) Trade	0.11	0.01	0.08	0.05	0.20	0.06	0.18					
(9) Population	0.02	0.10	0.08	0.05	0.06	0.06	0.05	-0.61				
(10) Pop. density	0.28	0.18	0.20	0.16	0.16	0.11	0.09	0.13	0.18			
(11) Oil export	-0.48	-0.21	-0.17	-0.16	0.04	-0.10	0.16	0.08	-0.01	-0.12		
(12) Civil war	-0.05	-0.02	-0.09	-0.11	-0.12	-0.04	-0.12	-0.26	0.28	0.13	-0.04	
(13) Peace years	0.20	0.26	0.36	0.37	0.39	0.09	0.30	0.14	-0.12	-0.05	-0.05	-0.50

Notes

1. The term *genuine savings* was coined by Hamilton, Atkinson, and Pearce (2003) and subsequently appears as *net adjusted savings* in the World Development Indicators.

2. We discuss the construction of the measure and the data in detail, to follow.

3. Growth, or the increase of income, is strongly associated with the consolidation of democracy (Przeworski et al. 2000).

4. There is little empirical work to date on public and private savings behavior under democratic and authoritarian conditions (Edwards 1995; Loayza, Schmidt-Hebbel, and Servén 1999). The World Bank has an entire research section on this, which thus far has not addressed how democracy associates with savings behavior (Loayza, Schmidt-Hebbel, and Servén 2000).

5. Some find that there is no difference in the tax rates between democracies and autocracies (Cheibub 1998). Others find that democratic resource-wealthy countries have slower growth rates than autocratic countries, due largely to inefficient management of resource wealth under electoral pressures (Collier and Hoeffler 2005) available at http://users.ox.ac.uk/~ball0144/col&hoe_natres.pdf.

6. Of course, growth and job creation and the "greed" of capitalists can drive sustainability by creating wealth, but the question is: at what environmental cost? See Gleditsch and Sverdrup 2002 for a summary of the arguments against democracy, and Neumayer 2003 for a discussion of left-wing politics and environmental issues.

7. We have largely relied on the World Bank's research program on savings across the world to pick several variables found to be associated with public and private savings rates. The basic model employs per capita income, economic growth, and urbanization. For robustness, we also test broad money supply (M2/GDP), and age dependency ratio. Using these variables lowers the sample of countries considerably. The World Bank's research on savings can be accessed at http://www.worldbank.org/research/projects/savings/savinwld.htm.

8. The dataset and Stata data output files to generate the results will be posted at http://www.svt.ntnu.no/iss/indra.de.soysa/card/.

9. There is mixed evidence of the effects of income on pollution and environmental quality (Grossman and Krueger 1995). Some of the dimensions of the sustainability index, such as CO_2 damage, are likely to be negatively affected by income given the logic of the environmental Kuznets curve (EKC), which is that pollution increases with rising income but either falls or diminishes at higher levels.

10. Neo-Malthusian views and antiglobalization views generally coincide on issues of sustainable development. There is a lively debate in the literature between the neo-Malthusians and the cornucopians, or those who think substitution of natural resources with human ingenuity is possible. For the classic debate, see Myers and Simon 1994. Most texts on environmental security and economic sustainability sample this debate (Conca and Dabelko 1998).

11. We have no data for other resources, but note that oil is by far the major natural resource in terms of value.

12. The Polity data are available at http://www.systemicpeace.org/polity/polity4 .htm.

13. The Freedom House data are available at http://www.freedomhouse.org.

14. The Vanhanen Polyarchy data are available at http://www.sv.ntnu.no/iss/ data/vanhanen/.

15. The Freedom House scores for 1981 are scored until August 1982 and scores for 1982 stretch from August to November 1983. Thus we take the 1981 scores for 1982 also (gap between August and December). In this way, the scores from August 1982 to November 1983 become scores for 1983 (one month gap), and scores from November 1983 to November 1984 become scores for 1984, and so on.

16. Note that because in PCSE regressions a separate Rho coefficient of auto-correlation is estimated in each regression, the coefficients of variables in the regressions on the subcomponents of sustainability will not necessarily add up to the coefficient size of variables in the regression on the aggregate sustainability measure.

References

Acemoglu, Daron, and James A. Robinson. 2006. Economic backwardness in political perspective. *American Political Science Review* 100 (1): 115–131.

Adger, W. Neil. 2006. Vulnerability. *Global Environmental Change* 16 (3): 268–281.

Almeida, H., and D. Ferreira. 2002. Democracy and the variability of economic performance. *Economics and Politics* 14 (3): 225–245.

Atkinson, Giles, and Kirk Hamilton. 2003. Savings, growth and the resource curse hypothesis. *World Development* 31 (11): 1793–1807.

Auty, R., ed. 2001. *Resource abundance and economic development.* Oxford: Oxford University Press.

Barro, Robert J. 1996. Democracy and growth. *Journal of Economic Growth* 1:2–27.

Barro, Robert. 1998. Determinants of economic growth: A cross-country empirical study. Cambridge, MA: MIT Press.

Baum, Matthew A., and David A. Lake. 2003. The political economy of growth: Democracy and human capital. *American Journal of Political Science* 47 (2): 333–347.

Beck, Nathaniel, and Jonathan N. Katz. 1995. What to do (and not to do) with time-series cross-section data. *American Political Science Review* 89 (3): 634–647.

Beck, Nathaniel, Jonathan N. Katz, and Richard Tucker. 1998. Taking time seriously: Time-series-cross-section analysis with a binary dependent variable. *American Journal of Political Science* 42 (4): 1260–1288.

Boix, Carles. 2001. Democracy, development, and the public sector. *American Journal of Political Science* 45 (1): 1–17.

Bollen, Kenneth, and Pamela Paxton. 2000. Subjective measures of liberal democracy. *Comparative Political Studies* 33 (1): 58–86.

Casper, Gretchen, and Claudiu Tufis. 2003. Correlation versus interchangeability: The limited robustness of empirical findings on democracy using highly correlated datasets. *Political Analysis* 11 (2): 1–11.

Cheibub, Antonio José. 1998. Political regimes and the extractive capacity of governments: Taxation in democracies and dictatorships. *World Politics* 50 (3): 349–376.

Collier, Paul, and Anke Hoeffler. 2005. *Democracy and resource rents.* Oxford: Centre for the Study of African Economies.

Conca, Ken, and Jeffrey D. Dabelko, eds. 1998. *Green planet blues: environmental politics from Stockholm to Kyoto,* 2d ed. Boulder, CO: Westview.

Congleton R. 1992. Political institutions and pollution control. *Review of Economics and Statistics* 74 (3): 412–421.

Dahl, Robert. 2000. *On democracy.* New Haven, CT: Yale University Press.

Dahl, Robert, and Edward Tufte. 1974. *Size and democracy.* Palo Alto, CA: Stanford University Press.

Dasgupta, Partha. 2001. *Human well-being and the natural environment.* Oxford: Oxford University Press.

de Schweinitz, Karl, Jr. 1964. *Industrialization and democracy.* New York: Free Press.

de Soysa, Indra. 2002. Paradise is a bazaar? Greed, creed, and governance in civil war, 1989–1999. *Journal of Peace Research* 39:395–416.

de Soysa, Indra, and Eric Neumayer. 2005. False prophet, or genuine savior? Assessing the effects of economic openness on sustainable development, 1980–1999. *International Organization* 59 (3): 731–772.

Deacon, Robert T. 2003. *Dictatorship, democracy, and the provision of public goods.* Santa Barbara: University of California, Santa Barbara.

Dietz, Simon, Eric Neumayer, and Indra de Soysa. 2007. Corruption, the resource curse and genuine saving. *Environment and Development Economics* 12 (1): 33–53.

Easterly, William, and Mirvat Sewadeh. 2001. Global Development Network Growth Database. http://www.worldbank.org/research/growth/GDNdata.htm.

Edwards, Sebastian. 1995. *Why are savings rates so different across countries? An international comparative analysis.* Cambridge, MA: National Bureau of Economics Research.

Fearon, James D., and David D. Laitin. 2003. Ethnicity, insurgency, and civil war. *American Political Science Review* 97 (1): 1–16.

Folke, Carl. 2006. Resilience: The emergence of a perspective for social-ecological systems analyses. *Global Environmental Change* 16 (4): 253–267.

Freedom House. 2004. *Freedom in the world 2004: The annual survey of political rights and civil liberties*. Lanham, MD: Rowman and Littlefield.

Garrett, Geoffrey. 1999. Globalization and government spending around the world. Paper presented at the Annual Meetings of the American Political Science Association, at Atlanta, September 1–5.

Gerring, John, Philip Bond, William T. Barndt, and Carola Moreno. 2005. Democracy and economic growth: An historical perspective. *World Politics* 57 (April): 323–364.

Gleditsch, Nils Petter, and Bjørn Otto Sverdrup. 2002. Democracy and the environment. In *Human security and the environment: International comparisons*, ed. E. A. Page and M. R. Redclift, 45–70. Cheltenham: Edward Elgar.

Gleditsch, Nils Petter, Peter Wallensteen, Mikael Eriksson, Margareta Sollenberg, and Havard Strand. 2002. Armed conflict 1946–2001: A new dataset. *Journal of Peace Research* 39 (5): 615–637.

Grossman, Gene M., and Alan B. Krueger. 1995. Economic growth and the environment. *Quarterly Journal of Economics* 110 (2): 353–377.

Gurr, Ted R., and Keith Jaggers. 1995. Tracking democracy's third wave with the Polity III data. *Journal of Peace Research* 32 (4): 469–482.

Haggard, Stephen. 1990. *Pathways from the periphery*. New York: Oxford University Press.

Hamilton, Kirk, Giles Atkinson, and David Pearce. 2003. Genuine savings as an indicator of sustainability. CSERGE Working Paper GEC 97–03. http://www.uea.ac.uk/env/cserge/pub/wp/gec/gec_1997_03.pdf (accessed March 4, 2009).

Henisz, Witold J. 2000. The instititutional environment for economic growth. *Economics and Politics* 12 (1): 1–31.

Huntington, Samuel P. 1968. *Political order in changing societies*. New Haven, CT: Yale University Press.

Jensen, Nathan, and Leonard Wantchekon. 2004. Resource wealth and political regimes in Africa. *Comparative Political Studies* 37 (7): 816–841.

Keech, William R. 1995. *Economic politics: The costs of democracy*. Cambridge, UK: Cambridge University Press.

Krieckhaus, Jonathan. 2004. The regime debate revisited: A sensitivity analysis of democracy's economic effect. *British Journal of Political Science* 34:635–655.

Lafferty, William M., and James Meadowcroft, eds. 1996. *Democracy and the environment: Problems and prospects*. Cheltenham, UK: Edward Elgar.

Lake, David A., and Matthew A. Baum. 2001. The invisible hand of democracy: Political control and the provision of public services. *Comparative Political Studies* 34 (6): 587–621.

Lipset, Seymour Martin. 1959. Some social requisites of democracy: Economic development and political legitimacy. *American Political Science Review* 53 (1): 69–105.

Lipset, Seymour Martin. 1993. Reflections on capitalism, socialism and democracy. *Journal of Democracy* 4:43–55.

Li, Quan, and Rafael Reuveny. 2003. Economic globalization and democracy: An empirical analysis. *British Journal of Political Science* 33:29–54.

Loayza, Norman, Klaus Schmidt-Hebbel, and Luis Servén. 1999. What drives private savings across the world? *Review of Economics and Statistics* 82 (2): 165–181.

Loayza, Norman, Klaus Schmidt-Hebbel, and Luis Servén. 2000. Saving in developing countries: An overview. *The World Bank Economic Review* 14 (3): 393–414.

Marshall, Monty G., and Keith Jaggers. 2002. Polity IV Dataset. College Park, MD: Center for International Development and Conflict Management, University of Maryland. http://www.systemicpeace.org/polity/polity4.htm (accessed March 4, 2009).

Midlarsky, Manus I. 1995. Environmental influences on democracy: aridity, warfare, and a reversal of the causal arrow. *Journal of Conflict Resolution* 39 (2): 224–262.

Midlarsky, Manus I. 2001. Democracy and the environment. In *Environmental conflict*, ed. P. F. Diehl and N. P. Gleditsch, 155–178. Boulder, CO: Westview.

Millennium Ecosystem Assessment (MEA). 2003. *Ecosystems and human well-being: A framework for assessment*. Washington, DC: Island Press.

Milner, Helen. 1999. The political economy of international trade. *Annual Review of Political Science* 2:91–114.

Mueller, Dennis C., and Thomas Stratmann. 2003. The economic effects of democratic participation. *Journal of Public Economics* 87:2129–2155.

Murdoch, James C., Todd Sandler, and Keith Sargent. 1997. A tale of two collectives: Sulphur versus nitrogen oxides emission reduction in Europe. *Economica* 64 (254): 281–302.

Myers, Norman, and Julian L. Simon. 1994. *Scarcity or abundance? A debate on the environment*. London: W. W. Norton.

Neumayer, Eric. 2003. Are left-wing party strength and corporatism good for the environment? A panel analysis of 21 OECD countries, 1980–1998. *Environmental Economics* 45 (2): 203–220.

Olson, Mancur. 1993. Dictatorship, democracy, and development. *American Political Science Review* 87 (3): 567–575.

Payne, Rodger A. 1995. Freedom and the environment. *Journal of Democracy* 6 (3): 41–55.

Przeworski, Adam, Michael E. Alvarez, Antonio José Cheibub, and Fernando Limongi. 2000. *Democracy and development: Political institutions and well-*

being in the world, 1950–1990. Cambridge Studies in the Theory of Democracy. Cambridge, UK: Cambridge University Press.

Reuveny, Rafael, and Quan Li. 2004. Democracy and environmental degradation: A formal and empirical investigation. Paper presented at the International Studies Association Annual Meeting (ISA), Montreal, Canada, March 16–21.

Rodrik, Dani. 1996. *Why do more open countries have bigger governments?* Cambridge, MA: National Bureau of Economic Research.

Romer, Paul M. 1986. Increasing returns and long-run growth. *Journal of Political Economy* 94:1002–1037.

Romer, Paul M. 1993. Idea gaps and object gaps in economic development. *Journal of Monetary Economics* 32:543–573.

Ross, Michael. 2001. Does oil hinder democracy? *World Politics* 53:325–361.

Ross, Michael. 2004. How do natural resources influence civil war? Evidence from case studies. *International Organization* 58 (2): 35–67.

Sandholtz, W., and W. Koetzle. 2000. Accounting for corruption: Economic structure, democracy, and trade. *International Studies Quarterly* 44:31–50.

Shapiro, Ian, and Casiano Hacker-Cordón, eds. 2002. *Democracy's value.* New Haven, CT: Yale University Press.

Sirowy, Larry, and Alex Inkeles. 1991. The effects of democracy on economic growth: A review. In *On measuring democracy: Its consequences and concomitants*, ed. L. Sirowy and A. Inkeles, 125–156. New Brunswick, NJ: Transaction Publishers.

Stata. 2003. *Cross-sectional time-series: Reference manual release 8.* College Station, TX: Stata Corporation.

Thomas, Vinod, Mansoor Dailami, Ashok Dhareshwar, Daniel Kaufmann, Nalin Kishor, Ramón López, and Yan Wang. 2000. *The quality of growth.* New York: Oxford University Press, for the World Bank.

Vanhanen, Tatu. 2000. A new dataset for measuring democracy, 1810–1998. *Journal of Peace Research* 37 (2): 251–265.

Walker, Peter. 1999. Democracy and the environment: Congruencies and contradictions in southern Africa. *Political Geography* 18 (2): 257–284.

Wittman, Donald. 1995. The myth of democratic failure: Why political institutions are efficient. Chicago: University of Chicago Press.

World Bank. 1997. Expanding the measure of wealth: Indicators of environmentally sustainable development. Washington, DC: World Bank.

World Bank. 2002. World Development Indicators CD-ROM. Washington, DC: World Bank.

World Commission on Environment and Development (WCED). 1987. *Our common future.* Oxford: Oxford University Press.

14

Environmental Transborder Cooperation in Latin America: Challenges to the Westphalia Order

Alexander López

The Internationalization of Environmental and Resource Management

In Latin America, as in most parts of the world, environmental and resource management has traditionally been the preserve of national governments. Crucial environmental issues such as the use of rivers and watersheds remain largely within the regulatory ambit of states. However, nowadays it can be argued that the internationalization of environmental problems and its impacts on national structures is having a profound effect on how such resources are managed, and therefore on how cooperation is understood and operationalized. In Latin America this internationalization and the new framework of environmental cooperation in most cases is the product of four factors: first, there is a new understanding of the international effect of the process of environmental change; second, environmental problems have become more international because the internationalization of the Latin American economy has intensified pressures on national ecological systems; third, the existence of natural ecosystems shared by two or more states, such as a river basin, requires new frameworks for regional cooperation; and finally, the transborder externalities produced by the exploitation of such resources have contributed to the internationalization of problems, and consequently these externalities have challenged the traditional means of cooperation.

This internationalization of environmental and resource management has important implications for national environmental policies. Therefore, it is argued that domestic structures and international forces currently interact in such a way that they bring about important national policy changes, among them changes in the operationalization of interstate cooperation and in key concepts of the Westphalian order such as national sovereignty and security. Thus, in order to illustrate these arguments, two cases from Latin America are presented here: the Meso-american Biological Corridor and the 1969 La Plata Basin Treaty In addition, the two cases allow me to demonstrate how the more environmental matters are regulated by international norms of cooperation, the more permeable state boundaries become for transnational activities. According to one perspective, international environmental commitments such as the La Plata Basin Treaty and the Mesoamerican Biological Corridor are reshaping a crucial element of sovereignty, which is the idea of territoriality. In fact, if territory is a crucial element for state sovereignty, then transnational environmental problems and efforts to address them seem to be reshaping that crucial element. Both the Mesoamerican Biological Corridor and the La Plata Basin Treaty appear to support Keohane's (1995) thesis, which states that sovereignty, rather than connoting the exercise of supremacy within a given territory, provides the state with a legal grip on an aspect of a transnational process.

One important aspect that has influenced transborder cooperation is the globalization and internationalization of problems, which have been major factors in decreasing countries' autonomy and control over environmental issues. In addition, the increased globalization of environmental problems has made it even more important for nations to act collectively to address environmental problems.

Key Problems to Overcome in the Construction of Regional-Transborder Environmental Cooperation

The first issue to deal with is border problems. In Latin America, transborder environmental activities have been greatly influenced by border disputes in which natural resources have been involved. The complex processes by which some Latin American states were shaped and the long history of armed and political conflicts that produced their present political boundaries took no account of conservation and environmental management considerations. Paradoxically, natural resources frequently have been used by states to draw the lines that separate them. This typically has been the case with rivers, which historically have been used for demarcating frontiers.

For instance, in Central America the constitution of borders among countries has been a long process derived from conflicts among states over differences in the demarcation of their boundaries. This is a highly relevant fact for understanding the complexity involved in the establishment of institutions for transborder environmental cooperation. The

Sarstún, Lempa, and San Juan international river basins represent three cases in Central America where the creation of transboundary institutions have had to face the challenge of overcoming prevailing tensions. For instance, the Sarstún River is not officially recognized as frontier because of the territorial disagreement between Guatemala and Belize. In the Lempa River Basin, the war between Honduras and El Salvador in 1969 and the territorial tensions produced by the "Bolsones," areas in Honduras where Salvadoran people live, may eventually represent a challenge that must be overcome. Finally, in the case of the San Juan River, the rights and conditions for navigation are still in dispute between Costa Rica and Nicaragua (López 2007).

The second problem to be solved is the type of institution required to cope with environmental change presenting transnational threats. The starting point is that current structures in Latin America do not correspond to the new reality, because most of them are based on national considerations. The transborder issues make necessary the adoption of new regulatory frameworks that in most cases reduce the internal territorial power of the sovereign state, but at the same time guarantee for the state an important role in the management of any shared ecosystem at a regional level.

A third set of problems relates to the fact that the handling of transnational threats pushes the reconceptualization of the classical notions of national security, sovereignty, and territoriality. In fact, is assumed that transboundary environmental problems necessarily undermine state sovereignty; thus, while states may claim sovereignty over natural resources, they have come under mounting pressure to manage their resources according to international norms. The problem in Latin America is that states still feel a strong link with the notion of traditional sovereignty, territoriality, and national interests. However, the sovereignty concept is losing national territoriality as its most significant defining component.

Despite these factors the Latin American countries increasingly have recognized this environmental interdependency and have responded by developing a wide range of international environmental agreements such as the La Plata Basin Treaty and the Mesoamerican Biological Corridor.

The Governance of Regional Ecosystems in Latin America

A region in ecological terms normally includes several nation-states as defined by a common sea, watershed, forest, and so on. Therefore, nowadays it is accepted that the governance of these regional resources require the participation of all those who use it. In this chapter, the La Plata River Basin and the Mesoamerican Biological Corridor are presented as regional examples for discussion of the implications of transboundary environmental cooperation.

A key question in understanding the dynamic of international cooperation is: why do states cooperate over regional ecosystems? One of the most cited arguments explaining cooperation at the regional level is that if participants perceive that they have common interests and that the benefits—the payoffs—of joint action are greater than those of unilateral action, they are likely to cooperate, and then possibly form a regime. The Mesoamerican Biological Corridor exemplifies this; it has constituted itself as an international regime where its actions need to be implemented multilaterally, because ecosystems do not respect frontiers.

In addition, transborder environmental cooperation has to be understood as the interplay of national and international forces. However, one should be aware that the links between domestic and international levels are reciprocal, and do not operate in only one way. It is well known that the international system influences and to a certain extent shapes the domestic environment, especially in developing countries. However, in a significant number of cases the domestic structure exercises a powerful influence in how the state behaves in the international sphere. For example, national governments may represent their countries in international environmental negotiations, but they are unlikely to take positions as they please. Thus, ratification of international environmental agreements (IEAs) is not an assurance of their successful implementation, since industries and interest groups often delay and potentially avoid implementation of international obligations.

Domestic structures are likely to determine both the availability of channels to engage transnational actors in the political system and the requirement for winning coalitions to change policies. Domestic structures and international institutionalization are likely to interact in determining the potential for transborder cooperation. Thus, the more a given issue area, such as transboundary environmental cooperation, is regulated by international norms of cooperation, the more permeable state boundaries should become for transnational activities.

Brazil constitutes a good example of such a situation. Since the beginning of the 1990s, Brazil has changed its policy substantially toward the Amazon rainforest, partly as a response to international pressure (López 2002). Indeed, as pointed out by Hurrell (1992), the discrimination that

Brazil was facing for issues related to the Amazon rainforest was starting to have a negative impact on Brazil's broader foreign policy goals. Brazil's policy change also reflected new political demands for environmental protection expressed at the domestic level since the return of the country to democracy in 1984. With that return, the ecological movement established itself as a permanent political actor and environmental issues became a locus for the exercise of citizen rights. The new constitution of 1988 dedicates a chapter to environment, creating specific laws for public action in the case of environmental damage. It also declares the Amazon rainforest part of Brazil's national heritage.

Transborder Environmental Cooperation in Mesoamerica: The Case of the Mesoamerican Biological Corridor

Bioregional planning is a valuable new approach that helps integrate protected areas into the wider landscape (Bushell and Eagles 2007). Bioregional planning is associated with biological corridors, which is a tool that tries to connect two or more protected areas across the landscape, permitting the migration of animals and plants. Other components of this approach are core areas (protected areas), and the buffer and transition zones among the core areas.

The most notable example of bioregional planning with biological corridors is the Mesoamerican Biological Corridor, which has been described as the largest and most complex conservation and development project to date, encompassing all Central American countries and southern Mexico (Bushell and Eagles 2007; Miller, Chang and Johnson 2001).

In 1989, the Central American governments created the Central American Commission on Environment and Development, designed initially to lead the preparation of a unified regional presentation for the 1992 United Nations Conference on Environment and Development. "In August 1994 the Central American presidents, gathered at Guácimo in Costa Rica, issued a joint declaration calling for the creation of an "Alliance for Sustainable Development" as a "comprehensive Central American initiative that addresses political, economic, social, and environmental issues," which they hoped would become a model for other regions" (Conroy 1996).

On October 12, 1994, the region's presidents (and a representative of Belize's prime minister) met in Nicaragua to sign the fundamental document of the Alliance for Sustainable Development (ALIDES). Former

U.S. Vice President Al Gore witnessed the signing and promised wide-ranging U.S. support for the effort. In December 1994 the ALIDES became the focal point for a public agreement between the United States and the Central American governments. The agreement pledged the United States to partnership with Central America in the pursuit of sustainable development in the region.

What the Central American Countries Gain from Signing the ALIDES

The signing of the agreement has created a modest amount of international political space for the development of social and economic policy alternatives that may be other than those required by stabilization and adjustment packages, just as the peace agreements of 1987 created domestic political space for closing down the Contra camps in Honduras and Costa Rica, over the objections of the U.S. administration at that time. Thus, ALIDES has to be understood in light of transborder environmental problems, basically related to natural resources shared by several states and the negative externalities caused by their exploitation. Moreover, ALIDES is seen as providing potential bases for strengthening environmental protection in the whole region, with international support over the continued objections of the domestic business sector. This is particularly relevant in terms of the discussion of the role of the domestic structure.

One of the most important outcomes of ALIDES is the Mesoamerican Biological Corridor (see figure 14.1). The corridor was endorsed by all seven Central American presidents at a 1997 summit. As conceived, the Mesoamerican Biological Corridor will stretch from the southeast of Mexico along the Atlantic coast of Belize and Guatemala. It will continue down the Atlantic Coast of the isthmus and spread into the interiors of Honduras, Nicaragua, and El Salvador. The corridor will wind down the Atlantic coast of Panama and finish (for now) in the Choco region of Panama and Colombia. Despite its name, the Mesoamerican Biological Corridor is not just a conservation project.

An important aspect of the Mesoamerican Biological Corridor is that it is composed of several national parks, most of them located in border areas linking these country-level efforts together. In fact, the construction of the corridor means the integration of such areas in one transborder unit. As can be seen in figure 14.1, the most important conservation areas are transborder zones: Darien (Panamá-Colombia), La Amistad

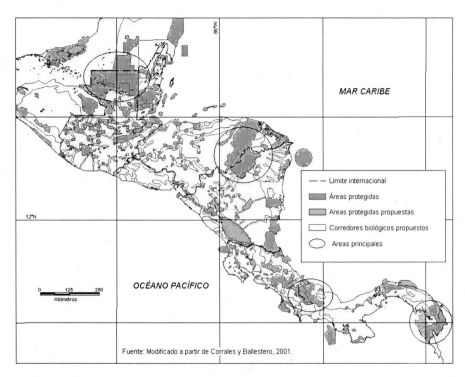

Figure 14.1
The Mesoamerica Biological Corridor: Main transborder areas

(Costa Rica Panamá), Corazón (Nicaragua-Honduras), and Selva Maya (México-Guatemala-Belize).

In this case the identifiable ecosystem cuts across the boundaries of several Central American states, and the issue is whether they are willing to engage in joint or compatible management. The answer already is positive; however, the most important remaining issue seems to be whether the agreed-upon management regime will limit its sovereignty.

ALIDES and the Mesoamerican Biological Corridor show the interplay between international forces and national environmental policies. In the initial stage, the institutional framework of ALIDES has been the main conditioning factor of success for this project, by creating an adequate space in which to strengthen the relationships of cooperation between national and international forces. Besides the national commitments to the corridor, there are also regional actors involved in its implementation.

In short, the corridor's implementation has produced specific benefits that have an impact on building cooperation among Mesoamerican countries. For example, it promoted harmonization of national environmental legal frameworks by serving as a platform unifying conservation goals and methods of both government and non-government initiatives; built capacity through training and exchanges for regional work; and promoted at political levels the importance of implementing integrated ecosystem approaches that go beyond national boundaries to protect endangered ecosystems (López and Jimènez 2006). The establishment of transboundary biological corridors is increasing the region's capacity to deal with the complexity of transboundary resource management.

The La Plata River Basin: Bridging Domestic and Regional Environmental Policymaking

Despite the potential for dispute in international basins, the record of acute conflict over international water resources is limited. On the contrary, in most cases the management of an international river basin can build cooperation and contribute to peace[1]. It is important to recognize, however, that an international river basin does not provide a good foundation for regional cooperation simply by virtue of its crossing national borders. Normally, greater interdependence among riparians and the generation of externalities increase the need for and possibility of international cooperation. For transboundary environmental cooperation to be effective, however, solid institutions should be developed. Institutions normally establish a set of rules of conduct that define practices and assign roles when grappling with collective problems. For the parties involved in the management of international river basins, this collective process implies sharing responsibility both for making decisions and implementing them, as well as a fair opportunity to either prevent conflicts or manage them. In this context, cooperation among the riparian states of the La Plata Basin constitutes a good example.

The La Plata River Basin comprises the Parana-Paraguay Rivers system and the Uruguay River system; it is shared by Argentina, Bolivia, Brazil, Paraguay, and Uruguay, and is the second-largest waterway in South America and the fifth largest in the world. The countries have been working together for the joint development and management of the basin since 1967, when discussions were held before the signing of the La Plata River Basin Treaty in 1969 (UNEP and GEF 2003).

Figure 14.2
The La Plata River Basin

As can be seen figure 14.2, the La Plata River Basin is an important economic artery in the region. Potential impacts arising in the La Plata Basin extend throughout the La Plata system from the Andes to the coastal zone, and these impacts affect many other developmental activities throughout the Mercosur and La Plata Systems, including impacts on the proposed Paraguay-Parana Waterway and the La Plata estuary. Transborder problems such as erosion are linked to land degradation that is connected to excessive soil losses from the slopes of the Andes, which lead to sedimentation and loss of beneficial uses downstream.

The La Plata River Basin provides water for domestic use to major cities such as Buenos Aires, Asunción, and São Paulo, and supports irrigation, transport, hydroelectric projects, industry/mining, and an effluent disposal site (Anton 1996). With such a variety of needs required of the basin, it is difficult to optimize the use of waters.

The La Plata River Basin is a very large, complex watershed complete with high population density, significant urban centers, climate variability, and many more challenging elements than a management institution is responsible for mitigating (López, Wolf, and Newton 2007). The Intergovernmental Coordinating Committee (CIC) has been very good at facilitating cooperation around riparian areas and initiating projects related to transportation (Wolf 1999). In the past few years, CIC has also been able to set criteria for standardized water-quality measurements, implement a flood warning system, and employ a geographic information system (GIS) with databases involving hydrological, legal, institutional, and project-related information (Calcagno et al. 2002) in order to facilitate data sharing among governments. While progress may be in small steps, this is how an institution builds a solid foundation to later confront bigger issues with firmer footing.

It is important to note that about 70 percent of the combined GNP of the five countries is produced within the La Plata River Basin, which is also inhabited by about 50 percent of their combined populations. Some of the main developments causing environmental impacts on the La Plata Basin have been the following: (1) development of many hydropower reservoirs in the upper Paraná river, in Brazil; (2) deforestation in the Paraná, Uruguay, and Paraguay Basin; (3) introduction of intensive agricultural practice after 1970; (4) and urban development, which changed the flood regimes.

The La Plata River Basin shows the important implications of regional transboundary natural resource agreements both for the national development of the countries involved and for the operationalization of the principles related to the Westphalia order (sovereignty, national security, territoriality, and so on). It should be remembered that the La Plata dams have modified rivers and environmental conditions both upstream and downstream. A good illustration of the regional transboundary dimension is the Bermejo River. This river is shared by Argentina and Bolivia, and is a regionally important part of the La Plata Basin. Erosion and sedimentation are serious issues: it has been estimated recently that the Bermejo Basin produces about 80 percent of the sediments in the La Plata River, which clearly makes the management of the basin a transboundary issue.

Assessing the La Plata River Basin Treaty introduces the discussion on the limitation of national sovereignty. It is interesting to note that the notion of sovereignty is not introduced in the treaty text. In fact, the word *sovereignty* is not mentioned at all. Instead, the notion of community of interests is stated and developed in the treaty. This could reflect the signatories understanding that sovereignty is less a territorially defined barrier than a bargaining resource for politics characterized by complex transnational networks (Keohane 1995).

In short, the La Plata River Basin Treaty seems to support Douglas Johnston's reports stating that international river law has developed away from the principle of unrestricted territorial sovereignty to the emerging principle of limited territorial sovereignty. In this case, ownership and control have been limited in order to foster trade and regional integration.

Conclusion: The Payoffs of Environmental Regional Cooperation

One could start by asking: what could the Latin American governments accomplish through cooperation at a regional level that they could not accomplish by acting unilaterally? At a general level it is clear that they can increase the governance of transboundary regional resources such as the La Plata River Basin and the Mesoamerican Biological Corridor. Without effective regional governance, these regional resources can generate a prisoner's dilemma paradox, in which individually actors' rational strategies lead to regional irrational outcomes.

Another conclusion relates to the following question: what are the main effects of transborder cooperation in Latin America? Taking into account that transborder cooperation implies a strong interaction between national and international forces, such linkages are making states richer in shared knowledge and more aware of the need for cooperation in environmental protection efforts. And through these linkages important economic resources can be transferred from the international to the domestic level, as the Mesoamerican Biological Corridor shows. These international-national linkages can influence the cost-benefit analyses by introducing significant gains among actors, altering their interests or perceptions, which is what has happened in Central America with the creation of the La Ruta Maya (the Mayan route), a regional tourism project that attempts to highlight attractions from state to state to maximize economic profits among participants. Furthermore, such links have also altered more fundamental elements of states through the creation of new institutions such as ALIDES and the Comité Intergubernamental Coordinador, which is the permanent institution of the La Plata Basin Treaty. And finally, these links represent a channel by which the Central American states can bring their demands and concerns to the international negotiating table. As the case of ALIDES has illustrated, Central

American countries have effectively introduced their concerns about socioeconomic development into broader environmental policy debates.

Transborder cooperation in Latin America also demonstrates the need to accommodate the new requirements for management and conservation of shared natural resources and border ecosystems within new frameworks. These new frameworks—as represented by the La Plata Basin Treaty and the Mesoamerican Biological Corridor—in most cases reduce the internal territorial power of the sovereign state, but at the same time guarantee for the state an important role in the management of a shared ecosystem at a regional level. This means that transborder environmental cooperation and state sovereignty do not necessarily stand in opposition to one another. As pointed out in the case of the La Plata Basin Treaty and the Mesoamerican Biological Corridor, the negotiation and implementation of these frameworks are largely in the hands of the South and Central American states.

In conclusion, and following the argumentation of this book, one should ask: what is the relationship of transboundary natural resources management in Latin America and human security? For instance, let us take the case of transboundary water resources; there it is clear that scarcity and/or pollution of transboundary freshwater resources impedes development, undercuts human health, and can potentially create some level of social unrest. The development of good institutional frameworks in transboundary river basins is urgently needed. As stated, these institutions can play a critical role in fostering cooperation among states and communities, thereby promoting development, peace, and human security.

Thus, in Latin America there is a profound relationship between water and human security. Despite its water wealth, there are millions of inhabitants without basic access to drinking water and sanitation services in Latin America. Its potential for hydropower is enormous, yet millions are without electricity (López, Wolf, and Newton 2007). The international river basins of Latin America contain abundant amounts of water, yet there are still many people who do not have safe drinking water or sanitation. For example, countries such as Argentina, Bolivia, Brazil, Peru, and Ecuador provide less than 50 percent of their rural populations with the infrastructure for basic sanitation services (WHO 2000 and WFP 2005). And without adequate access, people must live under stressed conditions, malnourishment becomes more prevalent, their economic development is slowed, and their overall living conditions are poor.

Notes

1. As Aaron Wolf (1998) points out, "The last 50 years have seen only 37 acute disputes (those involving violence); of those, 30 were between Israel and one or another of its neighbors, and the violence ended in 1970. Non-Mideast cases accounted for only five acute events, while, during the same period, 157 treaties were negotiated and signed."

References

Anton, D. 1996. *Ciudades sedientas: Agua y ambiente urbanos en América Latina* [Thirsty cities: Water and urban environments in Latin America]. Ottawa, Canada: International Development Research Centre.

Bushell, Robyn, and Paul F. J. Eagles, eds. 2007. *Tourism and protected areas, benefits beyond boundaries.* Wallingford, UK: CABI.

Conroy, Michael E. 1996. Sustaining peace in Central America: The challenges of the Central American Alliance for Sustainable Development. http://www .utexas.edu/courses/sustdevt/papers/conroy.html (accessed March 5, 2009).

Hurrell, Andrew. 1992. Brazil and the international politics of Amazonian deforestation. In *The international politics of the environment*, ed. Andrew Hurrell and Bendedicte Kingsbury, 398–429. Oxford: Clarendon Press.

Keohane, Robert. 1995. Hobbes's dilemma and institutional change in world politics: Sovereignty in international society. In *Whose World Order?*, ed. Hans-Henrik and George Sorensen, 165–186. Boulder, CO: Westview Press.

López, Alexander. 2002. Environmental change and social conflicts in the Brazilian Amazon: Exploring the links. Ph.D. dissertation. University of Oslo, Norway.

López, Alexander, and Alicia Jiménez. 2006. *Environmental conflict and cooperation: The Mesoamerican Biological Corridor as a mechanism for transborder environmental cooperation.* Report for the Division of Early Warning and Assessment. UNEP, Nairobi, Kenya.

López, Alexander, Aaron Wolf, and Joshua Newton. 2007. *Hydropolitical vulnerability and resilience along international waters: Latin America and the Caribbean.* UNEP. Division of Early Warning and Assessment. Nairobi, Kenya.

Miller, Kenton, Elsa Chang, and Nels Johnson. 2001. *Defining common ground for the Mesoamerican Biological Corridor.* Washington, DC: World Resources Institute.

United Nations Environment Programme (UNEP) and Global Environment Facility (GEF). 2003. *Concept document for sustainable water resources management in the La Plata River Basin.* Prepared by the Intergovernmental Coordinating

Committee of La Plata River Basin Countries (CIC) and the General Secretariat of the Organization of American States (GS/OAS). Washington, DC: Organization of American States.

World Food Programme (WFP). 2005. *Faces of hunger*. World Food Programme. http://www.wfp.org/country_brief/hunger_map/map/hungermap_popup/map _popup.html (accessed November 15, 2008).

World Health Organization (WHO). 2000. *Global water supply and sanitation 2000 report*. New York: WHO/UNICEF.

Wolf, Aaron. 1998. *Conflict and cooperation along international waterways*. Water Policy 1 (2): 51–65.

Wolf, Aaron. 1999. *La Plata Basin*. Transboundary Freshwater Dispute Database, Oregon State University Department of Geosciences. www.transboundary .orst.edu.

V

Conclusion

15

Charting the Next Generation of Global Environmental Change and Human Security Research

Jon Barnett, Richard A. Matthew, and Karen L. O'Brien

This volume is part of a broader literature that, since about 1994, has effectively established the domain of global environmental change and human security research. The authors gathered here have shown how environmental change can be a contributing factor to human insecurity in many places and to violent conflict in certain circumstances, and have argued that solutions lie in forging peaceful, ecologically sustainable, and just social-ecological systems.

In part II of the book the authors all emphasize that environmental change is a risk to human security, and none of the subsequent chapters disagree with this fundamental finding. However, as the chapters in part II show, and the examination of solutions in many of these chapters imply, environmental change never causes insecurity in isolation from other social factors, such as poverty and inadequate or discriminatory institutions. Indeed, the same is true for the chapters that explore the links between environmental change and violent conflict: none of the authors of these chapters in part III argue that environmental change in and of itself is a cause of violent conflict. Whereas it seems likely that in some cases environmental change is a primary trigger of a significant decline in human security, violent conflict rarely if ever is primarily triggered by environmental change.

Many of the chapters of this book agree, although some more explicitly than others, that democratic institutions reduce the risks environmental change poses to human security. However, there is less agreement about the effects of liberalized markets on environmental change and human security. In as much as all the authors agree that poverty is a powerful driver of human insecurity, and in as much as there is a broad association between liberalized markets and higher average incomes, then most authors would agree that market liberalization can be a pathway to decreasing human insecurity. The points of difference concern, on the one hand, the distributional effects of market liberalization and its contribution to inequities both within and among nations (see, e.g., chapter 8 by Karen L. O'Brien and Robin M. Leichenko), and, on the other hand, the environmental effects of increasing consumption of goods and services that far exceed levels required for the satisfaction of basic material and psychosocial needs. These remain the core dilemmas of sustainable development, and they are no less germane to the issue of environmental change and human security.

Another subtheme of this book, which is explicitly discussed in chapter 10 by Betsy Hartmann, but identified in many other chapters, is the way in which simple representations of the security issues arising from environmental change justify misguided and in some cases counterproductive policy responses. This is Hartmann's point about the dangers of mischaracterizing population growth as a danger to Northern security, and it is O'Brien and Leichenko's point when they refer to the lack of recognition that the security of people in wealthy countries may also be highly at risk from environmental change. Indeed, this concern about the framings and representations of environmental change and the implications for policy is central to the securitization critique discussed by Jon Barnett, Richard A. Matthew, and Karen L. O'Brien in chapter 1. This concern points to the need for grounded research that collects evidence about human insecurity that is free from the ideological biases and prejudices inherent in popular narratives about the poor and vulnerable. This concern calls for those engaged in security, development, and environmental change research and for policy communities to be more attentive to evidence, more self-aware of their biases and knowledge limitations, and more attuned to the potentials and risks of policy discourses influencing outcomes. Many of the chapters in this volume in various ways support the need for good social science informing careful and reflexive policy.

The chapters all share a concern for breaking down the divisions among human security, sustainable development, and global environmental change. Although some scholars work at the interface of two of these fields, and others combine insights from all three, for the most part they remain largely distinct research and policy areas. Many of the chapters, and in particular those in part IV, show that there is much that each research and policy community can learn from the other about ways to reduce the insecurities arising from environmental change. In terms of policy, there may indeed be very few new ideas required—much is known about what needs to be done—but there is great scope for many new insights into the barriers to policy implementation and ways to overcome them.

A substantial contribution of this volume is its more extensive treatment of areas that hitherto have been somewhat peripheral in the environment and security literature, and largely absent from mainstream debates about global environmental change. Analyses that emphasize the complex linkages among environmental change, equity, vulnerability, and livelihoods lay the foundations for future research. Indeed, we believe that further research on environmental change and human security should and is likely to examine the extent to which many other socially differentiating processes—such as constructions of age, ethnicity, and race—influence vulnerability; improve understanding of the highly dynamic spatial, temporal, and social processes that strengthen or undermine human security; and study the actual and potential ways that groups do and can peacefully respond to environmental change. We now outline what we consider to be seven key areas that require further investigation in order to enhance understanding of the causes of and solutions to insecurity arising from global environmental change.

Suggestions for Further Research

Whereas it is now well understood that class is as important a determinant of vulnerability as the physical processes that create risk (and indeed that where people live is often a product of class), other social causes of vulnerability to environmental change have yet to be seriously investigated. As Heather Goldsworthy explains in chapter 11, one key axis of social differentiation is gender—the set of socially constructed characteristics associated with masculinity and femininity that shape social practices (Seager 1993). Many social practices enabled by constructions of gender create differences in the vulnerability of men and women to environmental change. For example, women are more likely than men to be sole parents; to have lower incomes through lower wages and/or casual or part-time jobs; to have less access to education; be survivors of domestic violence; to have less secure access to land; have less secure access to credit; to have less representation in formal decision-making structures; and to be more dependent on natural resources for their livelihoods (Agarwal 1997; Enarson et al. 2003). Yet women are not powerless "victims": they are most often the key actors in local social networks, informal production systems, and child and maternal services; they are more likely than men to save money and invest in child health care and education; they are more likely than men to engage in sustainable resource management; and they are the primary agents of adaptive activities within households and local communities (Enarson et al. 2003; Roy and Venema 2002). Investigating the ways in which gender structures, and can mitigate, vulnerability is therefore an important and emerging research theme; in particular, it is important to consider how gender roles and identities are changing and what the implications are for vulnerability. Gender is likely to be a key theme of environmental change and human security research in the future.

A second key area for further research concerns the mediating role that *perceptions* play in the interface between environmental changes per se and social responses. Most of the environmental change and environmental security research thus far has assumed that there is a mechanistic cause-and-effect relationship between environmental changes and social responses. Yet people interpret the changes they observe, learn about changes from other sources such as the media and popular discourses, consider the risks these changes pose, consider the distributional effects of these changes within their social spheres, assess their motivations to act, and consider their capacity to adapt to these changes. All of these cognitive processes are critical in decision making about responses (Grothmann and Patt 2005). For example, in terms of environmental change, people tend to underestimate certain high-probability risks and do not act, yet may act to mitigate low-probability risks. Or they may choose not to act if they perceive their adaptive capacity is high, and may unnecessarily take adaptive actions if they perceive their adaptive capacity is low (Grothmann and Patt 2005).

Closely linked to perceptions is the role that values, beliefs, and world-views play in determining impacts and responses to environmental change. For example, traditional, modern, and post-modern values can lead to very different prioritized responses to climate change in terms of both mitigation and adaptation (see chapter 8 by O'Brien and Leichenko). One individual or group's adaptation may affect what others value, and potentially increase vulnerability. For example, in Rwanda the government's response to land scarcity and climate change effects is a nationwide process of agricultural consolidation and intensification in an effort to maximize agricultural outputs. But Rwandan culture places a high value on independence and status through individual land and cattle ownership. There is a great danger that cultural values will continue to inform the decisions of the wealthier portions of the population, while the impoverished are compelled to accept the consolidation efforts that, unfortunately, may also diminish their real and perceived social position.

In terms of violent conflicts (in which environmental change may be a factor), it has been argued that perceptions of an insecure future are important in the decision of actors to join armed groups (Stewart and Fitzgerald 2000; Ohlsson 2000). It has also been argued that perceptions of actual or potential "unfair" changes in the distribution of entitlements throughout a community may also increase the risk of armed groups forming (Goodhand 2003). Indeed, this issue of perception informing action is hardly new to security studies; for example, at the heart of the security dilemma is the problem of risk perception. It is also central to the critiques of environmental security, where it has been argued, rather like Betsy Hartmann does in chapter 10, that when the developed countries perceive the developing world to be a site of future wars fought over scarce resources, that perception most likely leads to security responses that increase the likelihood of war (Barnett 2001). So, investigating the ways in which perceptions of change, its outcomes, and capacities to respond interact is important and, we suggest, will become a major theme of environmental change and security research in the future.

A third key area for more research is the interface between environmental change and human health, as Bryan McDonald suggests in chapter 3. Most research thus far has focused on the ways in which environmental changes can be drivers of health problems—for example, through changes in disease vectors (Hales, Weinstein, and Woodward 1999), changes in food security (Parry et al. 1999), and increasing mortality and morbidity arising from climatic extremes (Bouma et al. 1997). Less well understood are the ways in which social drivers of changes in health shape vulnerability to environmental change. Processes of economic integration, for example, are creating a "nutrition transition" whereby imported high-fat and high-sugar foodstuffs are becoming cheaper so that consumption is increasing (Drewnowski and Popkin 1997). This in turn changes the disease burden in developing countries such that malnutrition decreases, but noncommunicable diseases increase. It is not clear if the net effect of such changes in the longer term may be increased vulnerability of people to environmental shocks resulting from high rates of obesity and cardiovascular diseases. Other large-scale health transformations are also important; for example, Alex de Waal and Alan Whiteside's (2003) "new variant famine" hypothesis suggests that HIV/AIDS may be a powerful new driver of vulnerability to environmental change. Finally, another subject worthy of further investigation is the ways in which public health programs, human development, and economic development interact (see Sen 1999) to influence collective capacities to adapt to environmental change.

A fourth theme of more recent and of further research in environmental change and human security is a shift to focus on *peaceful* responses to environmental change as opposed to violent outcomes (see chapter 14 by Alexander López in this volume, an example of this kind of research). This is partly a response to the methodological limitations of past research on environmental change and violent conflict, which sought to trace the causes of violent conflicts after they had occurred while ignoring altogether the countervailing forces for peace. Indeed, if the point of research on violent conflicts is to avoid them, it is ironic that research on environmental change and conflict has learned far more about the causes of violence than it has about the causes of peace, with some worrying outcomes for foreign policy. There has been little explicit examination of cases where environmental stresses are occurring, and where the risk of violent outcomes seems high according to various risk factors, yet where violence has not been the result (Hartmann 2001). Research of this kind can reveal much about the processes that cause or prevent conflict in places where theory would suggest it is most likely to arise, and is crucial to enhancing peaceful adaptation to environmental change. It is also likely to be essential to building peace in areas where the environment was in some way involved in the conflict. Research of this kind is beginning to emerge; for example, there has been some investigation into cooperation between states over shared resources, transboundary rivers and seas in particular (see Wolf 1999; Conca and Dabelko 2002). However, this explicit focus on peace has yet to examine smaller scales of cooperation, and the endeavor as a whole has yet to reach a stage of critical mass whereby clear findings can emerge (Matthew and Dabelko 2000). Nevertheless, it seems likely to be an important theme of future research on environmental change and human security.

A fifth emerging theme in environmental change and human security research concerns not the causes of violent conflict, but rather its *impacts* on human security and vulnerability to environmental change. Past research has shown that violent conflict is a significant cause of damage to natural capital (Seager 1993; Westing 1980), and more recently there have been some detailed investigations of the impacts of violent conflict on economic and social capital (Stewart and Fitzgerald 2000). However, the combined effects of these impacts of violent conflict on the vulnerability of people to environmental change have barely been considered. Yet, as suggested by Sen's (1992) account of the way violent conflict increases vulnerability to famine, and by a more recent if cursory examination of the ways in which violent conflict has reduced the adaptive capacity of people in East Timor (Barnett 2006), violence powerfully shapes vulnerability to environmental change. Given that globally there were over forty violent conflicts in 2002 (HIIK 2002), and thirty-five countries in some state of "post-conflict" recovery, it is important to understand the ways in which violence creates vulnerability to environmental change (and other shocks), and to devise processes that can mitigate this vulnerability.

There is also a need for greater consideration of the linkages among human rights, human security, and environmental change. As has recently been argued with respect to climate change, environmental change puts at risk many of the rights enshrined in international law (Humphries 2008; OXFAM 2008). Conversely, as implied in a number of chapters in this volume, people living in societies where human rights are upheld typically are less insecure than people whose rights are violated. It may also be that societies where human rights are upheld are more capable of reducing their consumption of goods and ecosystems services than those where rights are partly or largely not upheld. Finally, to the extent that it can be proved that environmental change does significantly impact on people's rights, and can be attributed to an actor, then it may be possible to use litigation to seek redress for environmental impacts. This would reinforce the growing recognition that people and institutions have legal as well as moral responsibilities to ensure that their actions do not lead to environmental changes that undermine the rights of others.

Finally, we need to be mindful in our critique to avoid misrepresenting others, as there is danger in speaking of vulnerability and insecurity without recognizing always the strengths and capabilities of those most at risk. Discourses of vulnerability tend to downplay the resilience of people and communities, to cast them as powerless, to further entrench the position of the weak in terms of the powerful, and to make more likely crude interventions in the name of humanitarianism (Campbell

1997). Identifying deficiencies suggests directing resources to solve problems that may not be tractable, whereas identifying strengths encourages committing resources to activities that have been demonstrably successful. Therefore, for both ethical and practical reasons, there is a need to shift from the present approach of emphasizing the causes of insecurity, to balancing this with identification of the strengths and capabilities of individuals and communities.

These seven key areas for further research are not so much "new" areas as they are logical extensions of the existing research on global environmental change and human security, as showcased in this volume. Further research along these lines, coupled with greater attention to the transfer of findings to the security, development, and sustainable development policy communities, and greater dialogue among these policy communities, can contribute to a reduction in the impacts of environmental change on human security.

References

Agarwal, B. 1997. Gender, environment, and poverty interlinks: Regional variations and temporal shifts in rural India, 1971–91. *World Development* 25 (1): 23–52.

Barnett, J. 2001. *The meaning of environmental security*. London: Zed Books.

Barnett, J. 2006. Climate change, insecurity and justice. In *Justice in adaptation to climate change*, ed. W. Adger, J. Paavola, M. Mace, and S. Huq, 115–129. Cambridge, MA: MIT Press.

Bouma, M., S. Kovats, S. Goubet, J. Cox, and A. Haines. 1997. Global assessment of El Nino's disaster burden. *Lancet* 350:1435–1438.

Campbell, J. 1997. Examining Pacific Island vulnerability to natural hazards. In *Proceedings, VIII Pacific science inter-congress*, ed. A. Planitz and J. Chung, 53–62. Suva: United Nations Department for Humanitarian Affairs, South Pacific Programme Office.

Conca, K., and G. Dabelko, eds. 2002. *Environmental peacemaking*. Baltimore: John Hopkins University Press.

de Waal, A., and A. Whiteside. 2003. New variant famine: AIDS and food crisis in Southern Africa. *Lancet* 362:1234–1237.

Drewnowski, A., and D. Popkin. 1997. The nutrition transition: New trends in the global diet. *Nutrition Reviews* 55 (2): 31–43.

Enarson, E., L. Meyreles, M. Gonzalez, B. Morrow, A. Mullings, and J. Soares. 2003. *Working with women at risk*. Miami: International Hurricane Centre, Florida International University.

Goodhand, J. 2003. Enduring disorder and persistent poverty: A review of linkages between war and chronic poverty. *World Development* 31 (3): 629–646.

Grothmann, T., and A. Patt. 2005. Adaptive capacity and human cognition: The process of individual adaptation to climate change. *Global Environmental Change* 15 (3): 199–213.

Hales, S., P. Weinstein, and A. Woodward. 1999. Ciguatera fish poisoning, El Nino, and sea surface temperature. *Ecosystem Health* 5:5–20.

Hartmann, B. 2001. Will the circle be unbroken? A critique of the project on environment, population, and security. In *Violent environments*, ed. N. Peluso and M. Watts, 39–62. Ithaca, NY: Cornell University Press.

Heidelberg Institute on International Conflict Research (HIIK). 2002. *Conflict barometer 2002*. Heildelberg: University of Heidelberg.

Humphries, S. 2008. *The human rights dimensions of climate change: A rough guide*. Geneva: International Council on Human Rights Policy.

Matthew, R., and G. Dabelko. 2000. Environment, population, and conflict: Suggesting a few steps forward. *Environmental Change and Security Project Report* 6:99–103.

Ohlsson, L. 2000. *Livelihood conflicts: Linking poverty and environment as causes of conflict*. Stockholm, Sweden: Environmental Policy Unit, Swedish International Development Cooperation Agency.

OXFAM. 2008. *Climate wrongs and human rights: Putting people at the heart of climate change policy*. OXFAM Briefing Paper 117. London: OXFAM.

Parry, M., C. Rosenzweig, A. Iglesias, G. Fischer, and M. Livermore. 1999. Climate change and world food security: A new assessment. *Global Environmental Change* 9 (1): 51–67.

Roy, M., and H. Venema. 2002. Reducing risk and vulnerability to climate change in India: The capabilities approach. *Gender and Development* 10 (2): 78–83.

Seager, J. 1993. *Earth follies*. New York: Routledge.

Sen, A. 1992. War and famines. In *Economics of arms reduction and the peace process*, ed. W. Isard and C. Anderson, 219–234. Amsterdam: North-Holland.

Sen, A. 1999. *Development as freedom*. New York: Anchor Books.

Stewart, F., and V. Fitzgerald, eds. 2000. *War and underdevelopment: Volume 1. The economic and social consequences of conflict*. Oxford: Oxford University Press.

Westing, A. 1980. *Warfare in a fragile world: Military impacts on the human environment*. London: Taylor and Francis.

Wolf, A. 1999. "Water wars" and water reality: Conflict and cooperation along international waterways. In *Environmental change, adaptation, and security*, ed. S. Lonergan, 251–265. Dordrecht: Kluwer Academic Publishers.

Contributors

W. Neil Adger is a Professor in the School of Environmental Sciences, University of East Anglia, Norwich, United Kingdom. He leads the research program on adaptation in the Tyndall Centre for Climate Change Research. He undertakes research on social vulnerability, on resilience and adaptation, and on justice and equity across scales. He was a Convening Lead Author for the Fourth Assessment Report of the Intergovernmental Panel on Climate Change in its assessment and evaluation of adaptation.

Jon Barnett is a Reader and Australian Research Council Fellow in the Department of Resource Management and Geography at the University of Melbourne. He is an interdisciplinary social scientist, with a Ph.D. from the Centre for Resource and Environmental Studies at Australia's National University. He is interested in environment and security, with an emphasis on development, particularly in relation to small island states. He has published research related to the environmental effects of free-market reforms, adaptation to climate change in the context of uncertainty, peace and development, justice, and sustainability. Internationally, Barnett's work is highly regarded in the field of international relations. His book on *The Meaning of Environmental Security* (London: Zed Books, 2001) was praised as pathbreaking. His articles have appeared in journals such as *World Development, Climatic Change, Energy Policy, Global Environmental Change, Climate Policy,* and *Environment, Development and Sustainability.* He has wide interests across development studies and security issues, coupled with sound regional knowledge of Asia and the Pacific.

Jennifer Bailey is Associate Professor of Political Science at the Norwegian University of Science and Technology. Her fields of interest are comparative and international politics (with an emphasis on environmental topics, including fisheries issues), U.S. politics, and qualitative methodology. Bailey is currently working on a project examining how varying forms of democratic institutions impact political culture in the United States and Norway. The study does this by investigating the ways U.S. and Norwegian advocacy and interest groups have framed the issue of commercial whaling over time. Other topics of current interest are U.S. civil society and political culture more broadly conceived. Bailey has also been a visiting scholar at the School of Public and International Policy at George Mason University and the Center for Advanced Studies in Oslo.

Victoria Basolo is an Associate Professor in the Department of Planning, Policy, and Design at the University of California, Irvine (UCI) and affiliated faculty for the Program in Demographic and Social Analysis. Her research interests include housing and economic development policy, intergovernmental relations, urban politics, public choice theory, institutional theory, disaster preparedness, and regionalism. Her work has been funded by the National Science Foundation, California Policy Research Center, the U.S. Department of Housing and Urban Development, the National Center for the Revitalization of Central Cities, as well as local governments and nonprofit organizations.

Hans-Georg Bohle is chair of development geography at the Geography Department of Bonn University. His academic work is directed on issues of vulnerability, risk and human security, with special emphasis on food, water, and health. His regional focus is on South Asia (India, Pakistan, Nepal, Bangladesh, Sri Lanka). He serves on the Steering Committee of GECHS (Global Environmental Change and Human Security) and on the International Scientific Advisory Board of GECAFS (Global Environmental Change and Food Systems). He is a member of the European Academy of Science and of the German Academy of Sciences Leopoldina. He is currently guest professor at the University of Basel/Switzerland and the 2006–2010 chairholder of the MunichRe Foundation Chair on Social Vulnerability at UNU/EHS in Bonn.

Mike Brklacich is a Professor and Chair of the Department of Geography and Environmental Studies, Carleton University, Ottawa, Canada. His research over the past twenty years has focused on human dimensions of global environmental change (GEC), with specific interests in vulnerability of human systems to multiple stressors, food security, and the capacity of human systems to adapt to GEC. He is also a lead author for Fourth Assessment by Intergovernmental Panel on Climatic Change Working Group II, and former Chair of the Scientific Advisory Committee to the Inter-American Institute for Global Change Research and the Global Environmental Chair and Human Security Project.

May Chazan is a Ph.D. candidate at Carleton University and research associate with the Health Economics and HIV/ AIDS Research Division at the University of KwaZulu-Natal in Durban. The majority of her research has focused on the vulnerabilities of women to the HIV/AIDS epidemic in South Africa. She has also sought to develop vulnerability concepts more broadly, looking at overlaps and disjunctures between how vulnerability is understood among scholars of HIV/AIDS and global environmental change.

Chris Cocklin is the Deputy Vice-Chancellor (Research and Innovation) at James Cook University in Queensland, Australia. His research interests are in the human dimensions of global environmental change, environmental governance, agriculture and rural systems, and corporate sustainability. He was formerly a member of the GECHS Scientific Steering Committee, and he was appointed Lead Author of the IPCC's Fourth Assessment Report.

Indra de Soysa is an Associate Professor of Political Science at the Norwegian University of Science and Technology in Trondheim. Born and raised in Sri Lanka, he received his undergraduate and graduate training in the United States. His postdoctorate experience provides GECHS with perspectives gained within academic research institutions as well as development agencies. He has published extensively on development, globalization, civil war, and resources and environmental conflict in journals such as *World Development, International Organization, Global Environmental Politics, Journal of Conflict Resolution,* and *Journal of Peace Research.*

Heather Goldsworthy is a doctoral candidate in Social Ecology, with a graduate emphasis in Feminist Studies, at the University of California at Irvine. She is a research associate with the Center for Unconventional Security Affairs and is a Dissertation Fellow with the University of California Office of the President. Goldsworthy's dissertation research examines microfinance, as a poverty alleviation strategy, and its empirical and theoretical relationship to sustainable environmental development.

Betsy Hartmann is the director of the Population and Development Program at Hampshire College in Amherst, Massachusetts. A long-standing activist in the international women's health movement, she writes and speaks frequently on international population, development, environment, and security issues in activist, academic, and policy venues. She is the author of *Reproductive Rights and Wrongs: The Global Politics of Population Control* (Boston: South End Press, 1995) and a political thriller about the "far right" called *The Truth about Fire* (New York: Carroll & Graf, 2002), and coauthor with James Boyce of *A Quiet Violence: View from a Bangladesh Village* (London: Zed Books; San Francisco: Food First; and Delhi, India: Oxford University Press India, 1983). She is a coeditor of the new anthology *Making Threats: Biofears and Environmental Anxieties* (Lanham, MD: Rowman and Littlefield, 2005).

Laura Little has bachelor of Laws and bachelor of Arts degrees from the University of Melbourne, Australia. She has worked in a variety of sustainability roles over several years, including international environment and human rights law and sustainability investment. She currently works as a consultant, providing advice to companies on managing sustainability issues.

Robin M. Leichenko is Associate Professor and Graduate Director in Geography at Rutgers University. Her research program emphasizes the connections between climate change and globalization, focusing on how these processes jointly affect vulnerable regions, households, and social groups. Her current research projects explore economic vulnerability and adaptation to extreme climate events in urban areas. Leichenko's new book, coauthored with Karen L. O'Brien, is titled *Environmental Change and Globalization: Double Exposures* (New York: Oxford University Press, 2008). The book draws upon prominent climate-related events—Hurricane Katrina, recurring droughts in India, and the melting of Arctic sea ice—to show how broader human security concerns including growing inequalities and vulnerabilities and unsustainable rates of development are integrally connected to larger processes of global change.

Alexander López is currently the director of the Institute for International Affairs of the Universidad Nacional de Costa Rica. He has worked and conducted extensive field work in the Brazilian Amazon focusing on environmental conflicts related to mining. In Mexico and Central America he has been working for many years on issues related to socioenvironmental conflict resolution and the management of transboundary river basins. His latest publication in English is *Hydropolitical Vulnerability and Resilience along International Waters: Latin America and the Caribbean* (Nairobi: UNEP Division of Early Warning and Assessment, 2007).

Richard A. Matthew is Director of the Center for Unconventional Security Affairs and Associate Professor of International and Environmental Politics in the Schools of Social Ecology and Social Science at the University of California at Irvine. He is also the Senior Fellow for Security at the International Institute for Sustainable Development (IISD); a member of the World Conservation Union's Commission on Environmental, Economic and Social Policy; and a member of the Homeland Security Advisory Council (Region 1). Recent books and coedited volumes include *Contested Grounds: Security and Conflict in the New Environmental Politics* (New York: SUNY Press, 1999); *Dichotomy of Power: Nation versus State in World Politics* (Lanham, MD: Lexington, 2002); *Conserving the Peace: Resources, Livelihoods, and Security* (Geneva: IISD, 2002); *Reframing the Agenda: The Impact of NGO and Middle Power Cooperation in International Security Policy* (Westport, CT: Praeger, 2003); and *Landmines and Human Security: International Relations and War's Hidden Legacy* (Albany: SUNY Press, 2004).

Bryan McDonald is the Assistant Director of the Center for Unconventional Security Affairs. He received a Ph.D. in Social Ecology from the University of California, Irvine, a master's degree in Political Science from Virginia Tech, and a bachelor's degree in English from Virginia Tech. His research explores the impacts of processes of global change on politics and security with a focus on human, environmental, and international security. Current research projects include threats and vulnerabilities of the emerging network of global food systems; the environmental dimensions of peace building and post-conflict reconstruction, and social and political impacts of the changing global security landscape. He is coeditor of *Global Environmental Change and Human Security* (Cambridge, MA: MIT Press, 2009) and *Landmines and Human Security: International Politics and War's Hidden Legacy* (Albany: SUNY Press, 2004).

Eric Neumayer is Professor in Environment and Development at the London School of Economics and Political Science. Before joining LSE, he was an academic assistant at the Centre for Law and Economics at the University of Saarbrücken, Germany. An economist by training, he is the author of *Weak versus Strong Sustainability: Exploring the Limits of Two Opposing Paradigms* (Cheltenham, UK: Edward Elgar, 1999; rev. ed., 2003), *Greening Trade and Investment: Environmental Protection without Protectionism* (London: Earthscan, 2001), and *The Pattern of Aid Giving: The Impact of Good Governance on Development Assistance* (London and New York: Routledge 2003), as well as numerous journal articles. Together with Giles Atkinson and Simon Dietz, he is the coeditor of the *Handbook of Sustainable Development* (Cheltenham, UK: Edward Elgar, 2007). His teaching focuses on neoclassical environmental and ecological economics.

Kwasi Nsiah-Gyabaah is the Principal of Sunyani Polytechnic in Ghana. His research focuses on the relationships among poverty, environmental degradation, and sustainable development in peri-urban areas of Ghana. His work with the EU ENRICH project on Expanding the Network on Environment and Security has broadened his research experience and allowed him to set his West African–based research within a global context. He was active in the development of the urbanization scoping team, which led to the establishment of urbanization as a core project of IHDP in March 2005.

Karen L. O'Brien is a Professor in the Department of Sociology and Human Geography at the University of Oslo, Norway, and chair of the Global Environmental Change and Human Security (GECHS) project of the International Human Dimensions Programme on Global Environmental Change (IHDP). Her research focuses on climate change vulnerability and adaptation, and on the role that values and worldviews play in responding to environmental change. She has recently published a book with Robin Leichenko on *Environmental Change and Globalization: Double Exposures* (New York: Oxford University Press, 2008).

Marvin S. Soroos is Professor Emeritus of Political Science at North Carolina State University (Raleigh, NC), where he taught courses on global problems and policies, with emphasis on environmental problems. He is the author of two books, *Beyond Sovereignty: The Challenge of Global Policy* (Columbia: University of South Carolina Press, 1986) and *The Endangered Atmosphere: Preserving a Global Commons* (Columbia: University of South Carolina Press, 1997) and numerous articles in the field of international environmental law and policy. He has been a visiting professor at Williams College and the American University in Bulgaria.

Bishnu Raj Upreti is South Asia Regional Coordinator of Swiss National Centre of Competence in Research (NCCR)-North-South, based in Kathmandu. He is actively engaged in resource and environmental conflict and environmental security related research and teaching. During his twenty-seven-year professional career, he has engaged in teaching and research at University of London and University of Surrey in the United Kingdom and at Kathmandu University and worked in different international organizations in the capacity of professional staff, resource person, and consultant. He has twelve books to his credit on conflict- related subjects and many articles and chapters in different national and international journals, magazines, and edited books. He has been widely quoted in national and international media about Nepal's armed conflict.

Index

Adaptive capacity, 38, 46, 84, 122, 165–166, 179, 185–186, 188, 241, 310
Africa, 196, 200, 201, 204–206, 239, 245, 249–253
Alliance for Sustainable Development (ALIDES), 295–297, 301
Anglo-Nepalese War, 137
Anthrax, 55, 58–59, 67–68
Armed groups, 125–128, 311
Assets, 39, 41, 42, 46, 49, 84–85

Bienville. *See* Le Moyne, Jean-Baptiste
Biodiversity loss, 16, 42, 66
Biological weapons, 59
Birendra, King, 141
Boserup, Ester, 197, 202
British East India Company. *See* Anglo-Nepalese War
Brundtland Report, 198, 237

Caste, 138, 151
Centers for Disease Control, U.S., 68
Central Intelligence Agency, 59, 199
Chlorofluorocarbons (CFCs)
emissions, 182, 183, 267–269, 278
Cholera, 67, 81
Civil wars, 127, 131, 140, 272, 275
Climate change, 65–66, 101, 122, 132, 138, 160–171, 225, 246
Clinton administration, 199
Cold War, 138, 180, 198, 199, 205, 207, 247

Colonialism
colonial policies, 87, 196, 199, 206
colonization, 122
decolonization, 150
legacies of, 242
Commission on Human Security, 9, 19, 54
Communist Party of Nepal-Maoist (CPN-M), 137–147
Conflict-resolution mechanisms, 127, 129

Degradation narrative, 197–198, 200–201
Democracy, 44, 130, 137, 138, 139, 142, 150, 189, 207
Demographics, 139, 150, 193–194, 203, 243, 271
Demographic shifts, 44, 78, 122, 167
Dengue fever, 65, 81
Department for International Development, UK, 253
Development, 184, 178–180, 241–244, 261–270. *See also* Sustainable development
Disaster, 82, 97, 106–107, 184, 187, 216, 221–232, 245
Diseases
and animals, 62–63
historical examples of, 58

East Timor, 121, 313
Ecofeminism, 216–217

Economic development, 169, 261–265, 281
Economic globalization, 44, 122
Education, 219–220, 231
Emissions, 6, 16, 132, 178, 182–184, 205
Environment, Development and Sustainable Peace Initiative (EDSP), 199–200
Environmental change, 123, 177–178, 187, 203, 307–314
Environmental conflict, 12, 13, 119–132, 196, 198, 206
Environmental degradation, 122, 196–197, 203
Environmental economics, 160
Environmental factors, 146–151
Environmental insecurity, definition of, 18
Environmental policy, 160, 164, 294, 298, 302
Environmental refugees, 197–198, 228
Environmental security, 120, 144–145, 195, 198–199, 206, 207, 227, 250–251, 310
Environmental stress relationships, 46, 79, 198, 227, 312
Environmental threat, 178, 186, 189–190
Equity, 46, 159–160, 157–171, 241
  definition of, 159–160
Ethnic conflict, 125, 197, 198, 240, 245, 246

Favelas (in Rio de Janeiro), 83
Feticide and infanticide, 219
Flood control, 99, 101, 108
Flooding, 100, 147
Food, 62, 65

Gates Foundation, 69
Gender, 138, 141, 151, 160, 168, 203–204, 309–310
Gender roles, 218–219, 220, 222
Global environmental change, 42–46, 67, 71, 81–82, 122, 157–158, 170–171, 177, 221, 308–314

global financial crisis and, 138
  interaction with urbanization, 78–83, 91–92
Global Environmental Change and Human Security (GECHS) project, 140, 194, 215, 240, 314
Global health threats, 55, 63, 71
Globalization, 120, 131, 168–169, 246. *See also* Economic globalization
  health, 60–62, 63
Governance, 139, 237, 293–295
Great Depression, 100
Green Revolution, 196
Greenhouse gas (GHG) emissions, 79, 157, 162–164, 168, 205
Gyanendra, King, 137, 139, 143

Hantavirus, 66
Haq, Mahbub ul, 240, 244, 251
Hazards, typology of, 36–37, 41, 79–80
Helsinki Protocol, 182–183
HIV/AIDS, 56, 180, 220, 245, 247, 312
Homer-Dixon, Thomas, 12, 198–199
Housing
  construction of, 86–87
  economics of, 85–86
  financing, 88–89
  government policy, 89–90
Human development, 162, 170
Human Development Index, 141, 145
Human development paradigm, 244
Human security
  definition of, 6–9, 37–39, 54, 79, 81, 120, 140, 170, 194–195, 208, 215, 237–241
  and equality, 168–171, 219
  and health, 71–72, 227, 311
  threats, 244–251
  disaster, 98, 108, 111, 222
  environmental, 121–122, 138, 181, 207, 221, 312–313
  violent conflict, 123, 125, 127–132, 143, 149–151, 207, 247, 249, 311

Human trafficking, 143
Hurricane Betsy, 100
Hurricane Gustav, 109, 110
Hurricane Katrina, 97–111, 168, 222, 225
Hurricane Mitch, 187

Indonesian tsunami (2004), 224
Industrialization, 119, 242
Inequality, 218–219
Infectious diseases, 55–68, 81, 83–84. *See also individual diseases by name*
Influenza A (H591), 62
Informal employment, 221, 222, 223, 228
Insecurity, definition of, 178
Intergovernmental Coordinating Committee (CIC), 300
International cooperation, 13, 68, 182, 184–185, 189, 190, 238, 251, 254, 255, 291–303, 312
International Health Regulations (IHR), 68
International Human Dimensions Programme (IHDP), 240
Internationalization, 291–292
International Monetary Fund, 130, 181

Kashmir earthquake, 226
Kathmandu, 137–150
Koshi Tappu Wetland, 148–150
Kyoto Protocol, 163–164, 183

Land acquisition, 87–88
Land degradation, 12, 27, 195–208, 215–217, 221, 225, 227–228, 231, 243
La Plata River Basin Treaty, 298–301
Latin America, 207, 291–303
Le Moyne, Jean-Baptiste, 98
Livelihood, security of, 35, 72, 119, 120, 124–131, 148, 150, 202–203, 219, 228, 240–248
Luke, Timothy, 63, 71
Lyme disease, 67

Malaria, 55, 58, 63, 69, 81
Malnutrition, 58, 60, 220
Malthusian, 11–12, 13, 25, 194–196, 199–207
Maoists, 139, 142–151
Market liberalization, 44, 169, 307–308. *See also* Trade liberalization, 122
Marxist, 242
McNamara, Robert, 252
Mesoamerican Biological Corridor, 295–298
Microfinance, 70, 228–231
Migration, 122, 131, 139, 142–148, 198, 201, 203
Millennium Development Goals (MDGs), 5, 21, 244, 250
Mississippi River, 98–101
Mississippi River Gulf Outlet project, 100
Montreal Protocol, 183, 189

National security, 5, 7, 123, 199, 249
Nepal, 137–151
   civil war, 137, 139, 143–146, 149
   demographics of, 144–146, 150
   history of, 98–99, 102, 141–142
   population of, 139–141, 144–150
   poverty in, 138, 141, 144–146, 149
New Orleans, 97–113
   demographics of, 101, 103–106
   Lower Ninth Ward, 97, 100, 106
   population of, 103–104
   St. Bernard Parish, 100, 108
Non-governmental organizations (NGOs), 69–70, 142–144, 151, 232

Peace-building endeavors, 126, 140
Planning and preparedness, 106–108, 110–111
Policy, 9–10, 89–92, 194–196, 254, 266, 281, 296, 308
Pollution, 82, 147, 167, 183, 227, 250, 263, 267–269, 272, 278

Population, 126, 131, 139, 188, 193–207
depopulation, 202
Population Action International, 193
Poverty, 78, 81–82, 85, 105, 121, 126–127, 197–198, 203, 205, 216, 221, 225, 228, 238–255, 307
Public health, 53–54, 56, 60–64, 67–68, 70, 72, 121, 312

Racial disparity, 105
Resource management, 291–292, 298
Rwanda, 12, 13, 201, 245, 310–311

Securitize, 9, 20
Security, definition of, 5–6
Segregation and Jim Crow laws, 102
Severe acute respiratory syndrome (SARS), 55, 57
Sexual violence, 223–224
Shah, Prithvi Narayan, 137, 141
Slums, definition of, 77, 82–83
Socioecological threats, 46
Socioeconomic conditions, 36, 41, 44, 79–80, 104–105, 138, 139, 150, 166, 239, 242, 249, 250, 252, 264, 302
Socioenvironmental conditions, 44, 46, 47, 122
Sociopolitical conditions, 39, 41, 206
State, the, 123, 129–130, 139, 182, 239
Sulfur emissions, 182–183
Sustainable development, 70, 170, 197–198, 229–231, 237–255, 308

Terai, 141, 145–147, 148
Threat, response to, 179, 180, 186, 189, 190
Transnational networks, 55, 60–62, 301
Transnational threats, 56, 293–294
Trade liberalization, 122

Unemployment, 104, 123, 127, 129, 145

UN International Conference on Population and Development (ICPD), 194
United Nations, 62, 69, 77, 81, 86, 140, 180, 249
Conference on Environment and Development (1992), 11, 254
UN–HABITAT, 86, 87
United Nations Development Programme (UNDP), 54, 184, 240
Human Development Report (1994), 8, 54, 195, 237, 243, 245
United Nations Environment Programme (UNEP), 181, 200
UNEP report on Africa (1999), 200
United Nations Expert Group Meeting, 82
Universal Declaration of Human Rights (1948), 237, 239
World Commission on Environment and Development, 237 (see also Brundtland Report)
United States, 99, 102, 111, 138, 144, 150, 163, 164, 168, 182, 187, 194, 225, 249, 296
Urbanization, 44, 62–64, 78–79, 92, 146, 193, 242, 247, 272–275

Violent conflict, 10, 123–132, 139–140, 307
Vulnerability, 36–41, 78, 84, 97, 110, 120–122, 165–166, 170–171, 218–219, 231, 239–240, 251
and access to housing, 85–86
capacity to reduce, 187
definition of, 178–179
differential, 158, 165, 168
and disaster, 97, 107, 111, 223–224
social, 78, 81, 82, 90–91, 309–310
Vulnerability assessment, 47–48, 79–80, 184–185

Water
availability of, 83, 187–188, 246
cooperation around, 13
Welfare-centric paradigm, 243

Westphalia, 291, 300
White, Gilbert, 36
Women, 126, 194, 203–204, 215–
  232, 241, 242–243, 251
 discrimination against girls, 219–220
 vulnerability differential for, 309–
  310 (*see also* Vulnerability)
World Bank, 68, 130, 196–197, 252,
  261, 269, 270, 281
World Health Organization, 56, 60,
  61, 68–69, 181
World War II, postwar, 100, 141, 150,
  196, 245, 252